Frederick Douglass

American Political Thought

Wilson Carey McWilliams and Lance Banning
Founding Editors

Peter C. Myers

Frederick Douglass
Race and the Rebirth
of American Liberalism

University Press of Kansas

Published by the University Press of Kansas (Lawrence, Kansas 66045), which was
organized by the Kansas Board of Regents and is operated and funded by
Emporia State University, Fort Hays State University, Kansas State University,
Pittsburg State University, the University of Kansas, and Wichita State University

Library of Congress Cataloging-in-Publication Data
Myers, Peter C., 1959-
  Frederick Douglass : race and the rebirth of American liberalism / Peter
C. Myers.
    p.   cm. — (American political thought)
Includes bibliographical references and index.
  ISBN 978-0-7006-1572-8 (cloth : alk. paper)
  1. Douglass, Frederick, 1818–1895—Political and social views.
  2. Liberalism—United States—History—19th century.
  3. Natural law—History—19th century.
  4. Constitutional history—United States.
  5. African Americans—Legal status, laws, etc.—History—19th century.
  I. Title.
  E449.D75M94 2008
  973.8'092—dc22   2007037117

British Library Cataloguing-in-Publication Data is available.

Printed in the United States of America

10 9 8 7 6 5 4 3 2 1

For Paige and Eydie,
For ever and ever

All eyes are opened, or opening, to the rights of man. The general spread of the light of science has already laid open to every view the palpable truth, that the mass of mankind has not been born with saddles on their backs, nor a favored few booted and spurred, ready to ride them legitimately, by the grace of God. These are grounds of hope for others.
Thomas Jefferson to Roger Weightman, June 24, 1826

Expansion is an essential quality of an idea.
Frederick Douglass, "We Are Not Yet Quite Free" (1869)

Contents

Preface and Acknowledgments   *xi*

Introduction   *1*

1 "Killed All the Day Long": The True Philosophy of Slavery   *20*

2 The Moral Government of the Universe: Natural Rights,
  Natural Law, and the Natural Demise of Slavery   *47*

3 "The Pound of Flesh, but Not One Drop of Blood":
  The Constitution against Slavery   *83*

4 "Let Us Alone": Race and the Constitution of Liberty   *110*

5 The Waves and the Sea: Race, America, and Humanity   *151*

Conclusion   *195*

Notes   *205*

Index   *251*

Preface and Acknowledgments

THIS BOOK IS A STUDY in American and African American political thought, informed by my broader interest in the principles and problems of liberal political philosophy. It is born of a political and philosophical concern for the fate of an idea (in the words of *Federalist* no. 1) in many respects the most interesting in the world. This idea, which Abraham Lincoln held to be "a standard maxim for free society," lies at the heart of political liberalism rightly conceived. It is epitomized by the self-evident truths to which the United States dedicated itself in the Declaration of Independence: that all men are created equal, that they are endowed by their Creator with certain unalienable rights, and that just governments are instituted to secure these rights for all. This fundamental, natural rights idea has been embattled from the beginning, hardly less in times of its seeming triumph than in times of peril. In America as in Europe, critics have attacked its proclaimed universality as a cloak for partial interests, rooted especially in socioeconomic class or ethnic identity. But in America, its most formidable challenges as well as its greatest triumphs have arisen from the perennially vexing matter of race. To assess the vitality of the natural rights idea in this country, it is necessary to assess the arguments of its greatest standard-bearers in the battles over race. So I come to the study of Frederick Douglass.

I am far from first on the scene. Recent decades have seen a great profusion of scholarship on Douglass. Among the many important insights one gathers in this increasingly well-tilled field, prominent is an appreciation of the extraordinary complexity of this man. Douglass presented himself variously as the traditional, bourgeois self-made man, literary descendant of Benjamin Franklin; the postmodern, self-fictionalizing self-made man (also Franklinian); the Jeffersonian individualist, partisan of minimal government; the Hamiltonian nationalist, partisan of energetic, unifying government; the romantic individualist, heroic rebel against tyranny and repressive convention; the parentless son, longing for home; the champion of minority rights; the radical majoritarian democrat; the bloody-minded millennialist, admirer of Nat Turner and friend of John Brown; the self-mastering lover of humankind, spiritual forebear of Martin Luther King, Jr.; the proudly American integrationist; the proudly black racial nationalist; the psychically divided mulatto; the apostle of self-help, grandfather of present-day black conservatives; the lifelong protester against racism, proponent of reparation and race preference, grandfather of present-day black liberals; and the list could continue. It is small wonder that highly able commentators find Douglass a "thoroughly human, complex, and contradictory" figure or trace his lasting popularity to the protean quality of his speech, adaptable "to the conveniences of any hour."[1]

This often-illuminating appreciation of Douglass's complexity can also obscure, if taken to excess. Though quite important, complexity or dividedness is not the most important quality of Douglass's mind. His thought has a unifying core, and to recover that core is to recover something vitally important about more than Douglass himself. So, at least, he would have advised us. In a nation as in an individual, he affirmed, the health of the soul is what matters above all else. This nation's Founders had made an admirable beginning in the formation of the American national soul. "No people ever entered upon the pathway of nations, with higher and grander ideas of justice, liberty and humanity than ourselves," Douglass told a New York audience on July 4, 1862. But the Founders and many later Americans had never owned their Declaration's principles in their full entailment. Alarming numbers in Douglass's day renounced them altogether. He therefore made it his great life's work to instruct his fellow Americans on the first principles of government, to bring the nation into consistency with itself and so to conceive a nobler liberalism than America had yet known. The purpose of the present work is to consider the meaning and soundness of that conception, represented in the natural rights arguments with which Douglass confronted the problem of race in America.

I happily acknowledge the personal and institutional debts I have incurred in the process of writing this book. Its defects are all mine, but they would be far more numerous were it not for all who helped me along the way. For their comments on portions of the manuscript and for illuminating conversations on Douglass and race issues, I thank Lucas Morel, Diana Schaub, Carl Dibble, and Michael Zuckert. The participants in an excellent Liberty Fund Colloquium on Douglass and other seminal African American thinkers, expertly led by Pam Jensen and Peter McNamara, contributed similarly instructive discussion. To Scott Yenor, I am in debt for his always stimulating conversation and for affording me several opportunities to test my Douglass ideas before seminar audiences. Two anonymous reviewers for the University Press of Kansas were exceptionally helpful in their careful, perceptive readings, fair-minded criticisms, and constructive suggestions. To the editor of that press, Fred Woodward, I am deeply grateful for his extraordinary patience, his abiding faith in the project, and his well-targeted reminders that political philosophy has a history, too. Among my departmental colleagues, Mike Fine, Jim Tubbs, and Rodd Freitag stand out for their friendship, support, authorial sympathy, and collegial coverage during my several leaves in the past few years. Crucial institutional support came from various sources. The University of Wisconsin—Eau Claire provided a faculty sabbatical grant for the 2002 spring semester and a Small Research Project Grant in the summer of 2007; the Earhart Foundation provided a fellowship research grant, effective in the fall of 2004; and the National Endowment for the Humanities provided a fellowship grant, effective in the summer and fall of 2005.

In the small world of book acknowledgments as in a far grander world, the last shall be first. Special mention goes to the one to whom I am indebted most, my long-suffering and much-beloved wife, Paige, who, hearing an earlier mention of her place on this page, responded, "What—for eye-rolling?" For her helpful reading, her loving patience and support, her timely eye-rolling, and most of all for reminding me throughout an agonizingly long writing process that there was a Great Day Coming, she has my bottomless gratitude and undying love. The same goes to our darling daughter, Eydie, two years old at the completion of this writing, whose unsinkable cheerfulness lifted me when I was low and who showed the makings of a fine editor in detecting in Daddy's book the fault she detects in many books: "Too many words!"

Introduction

The race-problem is a moral one. . . . Its solution will come especially from
the domain of principles.
   Alexander Crummell, "The Race Problem in America" (1888)

WE LIVE IN THE AFTERMATH of the revolution in racial justice that arose in
the 1950s and early 1960s—"America's third revolution," promising the
consummation of the partial victories achieved in the War of Independence and
the Civil War. Its renewed dedication to the spirit of 1776 and 1863 would "speed
the day," exulted Martin Luther King, Jr., "when 'every valley shall be exalted,
and every mountain and hill shall be made low: and the crooked shall be made
straight and the rough places plain.'"[1]

To King and those he joined in morally disciplined uprising, this third
revolution marked the culmination of a venerable tradition, the "Great Tradition" of black American protest, which had originated well before the birth of
the Republic.[2] The "dream" that he articulated in his most memorable speech
was the dream of the numerous great leaders and millions of freedom-loving
African Americans who preceded him. In that speech, delivered pointedly in
the foreground of the Lincoln Memorial in the Emancipation Proclamation's
centennial year, King epitomized the great tradition's inspiring sentiments.
"When the architects of our republic wrote the magnificent words of the Constitution and the Declaration of Independence," he instructed, "they were sign-
ing a promissory note to which every American was to fall heir. This note was
the promise, that all men, yes, black men as well as white men, would be guaranteed the unalienable rights of life, liberty, and the pursuit of happiness." To
its lasting shame, the nation had long defaulted on that promise. But for King
and the tradition that he continued, the point was to inspire hope, not to feed a
spirit of grievance. "I say to you, my friends, that even though we must face the
difficulties of today and tomorrow, I still have a dream. It is a dream deeply
rooted in the American dream that one day this nation will rise up and live out
the true meaning of its creed—we hold these truths to be self-evident, that all
men are created equal."[3]

As King affirmed, the traditional aspirations of black American protest are
"deeply rooted in the American dream." The hallmark of this mainstream tradition

is a seemingly irrepressible faith in America and in American principles, sustained by a still deeper faith in the moral ordering of the universe. "If there is to be peace on earth and goodwill toward men," King maintained, "we must finally believe in the ultimate morality of the universe."[4] The American principles that animate the mainstream black protest tradition are the principles of liberal political philosophy, beginning with the equality and dignity of all human persons as bearers of natural, inalienable rights. In the liberal faith of this tradition, the natural rights principles of the Declaration of Independence are eternally true and just, and notwithstanding their grievous violation over many decades of American practice, their ultimate fulfillment is not to be doubted. A fully integrated America, securing the blessings of liberty for all irrespective of color or ethnicity, is both desirable and achievable. In the long view, American history moves in a course similar to that described by the biblical prophet Jeremiah: an original dedication to righteousness; a subsequent betrayal; and a long, arduous, never simply linear ascent toward a final redemption.[5] For the mainstream black protest tradition, America remains through it all, in the words of historian Vincent Harding, a "strangely promised land."[6]

For many Americans, the experience of the past half century has largely vindicated King's and the great tradition's abiding faith in the American promise. The signs of progress are visible nearly everywhere in American life: in the sweeping changes in national civil rights laws and their enforcement; in the dramatic increases in African Americans' electoral participation and electoral power, reflected in the dramatically increased numbers of black elected officials and in the normalizing of blacks' service in the highest appointed positions in the executive and judicial branches; in the similarly dramatic increase in blacks' educational attainments, reflected in rates of secondary school graduation and college attendance; in the substantial growth of the black middle and upper classes; in the rapidly increasing numbers of black-white marriages (though the aggregate number remains small); and in the dramatic liberalizing of majority public opinion respecting racial equality, along with the virtually total eradication of public racial prejudice almost within the course of a single generation. With respect to race relations, for the optimistic many, in the post–civil rights era it is at last a new day in America.[7]

The bearers of such optimism, including most whites outside the academy, might be surprised to learn that after some of its greatest successes, this mainstream tradition now finds itself under powerful attack. Radical challenges to it are nothing new. In the nineteenth and twentieth centuries, black nationalists such as Martin Delany, Marcus Garvey, and Malcolm X attracted substantial followings by renouncing the liberal goal of integration into the American political and economic order, which they regarded as inherently oppressive to people of color. Comparable doubts have prevailed at times even in the minds of some of the mainstream tradition's greatest representatives. The tradition's preeminent scholar-activist, W. E. B. Du Bois, a founding father of the National Association for the Advancement of Colored People (NAACP) in 1909, became an apologist for the Stalinist Soviet Union in his later decades, and in the final year of his life, he became a citizen of the newly independent African state of Ghana, where he died in 1963. And although he never succumbed to such radical despair as had Du Bois, King declared late in his life that his famous "dream" had become a "nightmare," and he called for "a radical revolution of values" in America and in Western society at large.[8]

In recent decades, however, radical currents have gained such force among the generality of blacks as to threaten to displace the liberal mainstream of African American political thought. Based on extensive survey research, political scientist Michael Dawson has reported that a generation after what King extolled as the culminating revolution, "massive numbers of African-Americans, well over three-quarters of the black population, continue to believe in the fundamental unfairness of this society." An ideology of "disillusioned liberalism" has become "entrenched" among black Americans.[9]

To those subject to this disillusionment, other data and experiences tell a story sharply at variance from the optimists' account. Despite signs of progress, blacks as a class remain markedly disadvantaged relative to whites in numerous important respects: in poverty and unemployment levels; in the accumulation of wealth; in the persistence of segregation; in infant mortality rates and life expectancy; in educational attainments; and in the incidence of a variety of social pathologies, the most consequential of which concern family formation and a "crime gap" in which blacks commit crimes and are victimized by criminals at much higher rates than whites. Evidence of persisting racial prejudice fuels perceptions of pervasive antiblack discrimination in employment, housing, and finance and above all in the criminal justice system.[10] Associated with these problems in external relations is an internal crisis of morale. In an influential 1993 essay, prominent philosophy professor Cornel West framed the issue starkly. The "most basic issue now facing black America," West wrote, is "the nihilism"—the sense of "hopelessness, meaninglessness, and lovelessness"—"that increasingly pervades black communities."[11]

Introduction

The present disillusionment has a theoretical core. Among intellectual elites whose primary concern is race relations, a growing consensus holds that the twentieth-century civil rights movement has failed and that its failure exposes the inadequacy of the principles that guided it. Historian and political scientist Manning Marable expressed an increasingly common view in observing that after the murder of King, the liberal creed of individual rights, integration, and "color-blind" laws and institutions came to seem anachronistic and counterproductive. "A color-blind new racial domain" has emerged in the post–civil rights era, Marable has more recently contended, "constructed as a deadly triangle . . . of structural racism."[12] According to the ascendant critiques, the failings of the traditional civil rights creed inhere in its moral prescriptions and in the progressive understanding of U.S. history that it requires. In short, the natural rights principles of the Declaration have proved too partial in their conception of justice and too weak in their influence over most Americans to supply adequate direction for the movement to achieve racial justice in America.

At least with respect to African Americans, critics contend, the characterization of U.S. history as a triumphalist story of progressively expanding inclusion and liberation betrays a naive idealism at odds with the facts. Abraham Lincoln epitomized this sort of idealism when, speaking against the Supreme Court's *Dred Scott* ruling in 1857, he described the creed of the Declaration as "a standard maxim for free society, which should be familiar to all, and revered by all; constantly looked to, constantly labored for . . . and thereby constantly spreading and deepening its influence."[13] Likewise did Martin Luther King, as he invoked "those great wells of democracy which were dug deep by the founding fathers in their formulation of the Constitution and the Declaration of Independence."[14] In the contrary view of radical critics, most Americans from the founding generation onward have shown no deep or sustained interest in racial justice. With respect to race relations, the nation's history is best understood not as a gradual ascent to equal liberty but rather as a story of "cyclical failure," of recurrent promise and betrayal. In this critical counternarrative, the twentieth-century civil rights reforms represent a "second Reconstruction" whose gains, much like those of the first Reconstruction, were promptly stunted in an ensuing period of racial backlash. The turn toward political conservatism, post-1968 and especially post-1980, is thus interpreted as a national betrayal prefigured by the betrayal, beginning in the 1870s, of the original Reconstruction and by the original betrayal of the ideals of liberty and equality in the founding period. For law professor Derrick Bell, who established the influential Critical Race Theory school of legal thought, U.S. law reliably expresses no moral ideal but only the interests of its dominant racial faction, so that progress for African Americans tends to occur only at scattered, fleeting moments when their interests and those of the white majority converge.[15]

Foremost among America's racial betrayals and duplicities, critics charge, are those committed by its Founders. Reaffirming Chief Justice Roger Taney's opinion for the Court in *Dred Scott,* philosophy professor Charles W. Mills dismisses the Declaration's universalist pronouncement that "all men are created equal" as mere polemical boilerplate, never intended to include peoples of color within the protections of the new polity the rebels were fighting to establish. For all practical purposes, the great document's authors and adopters conceived of the bond of their nascent political society as a tacit "Racial Contract," restricting the possession of natural equality, freedom, and rights to white men. The new polity was to be a *"Herrenvolk* democracy"—democracy only for the "master race" or dominant group—founded on white racial supremacy rather than on any universal, humanitarian principle.[16] Important sympathizers of the mainstream protest tradition have been similarly harsh in their judgments of the Founders' thought and work. Distinguished historian John Hope Franklin, author of the standard overview of African American history, offered this comment: "Racial segregation, discrimination, and degradation . . . stem logically and directly from the legacy that the Founding Fathers bestowed upon contemporary America."[17] Focusing more specifically on the 1787 Constitution in a well-publicized bicentennial speech, Thurgood Marshall, the first African American U.S. Supreme Court justice and a genuine hero of the twentieth-century civil rights campaign, echoed the charge of the previous century's most radical abolitionists: "At the Constitutional Convention eloquent objections to the institution of slavery went unheeded, and its opponents eventually consented to a document which laid a foundation for the tragic events that were to follow."[18]

In the minds of radical critics, however, the ultimate problem with the nation's founding principles lies not in the Founders' and later generations' unwillingness to conform with them but rather in the inherent partiality of the principles themselves. Despite affirming the Declaration's universal, humanitarian spirit, W. E. B. Du Bois supplied an impetus for radical critiques of it by objecting to its "individualistic philosophy."[19] In part, Du Bois believed, the Declaration misrepresents actual human experience in its conception of human beings as generic individuals rather than as members of particular racial or ethnic groups. As it obscures the power of race and ethnicity as vital constituents of personal identity, according to this line of objection, so the Declaration's doctrine obscures its own grounding in racial or ethnic bias. Purporting to contain principles of justice proper to all humankind, it actually contains principles proper only to particular racial or ethnic groups. The practical implication, for critics of the mainstream civil rights creed, is to promote an understanding of integration into the majority society that would require of blacks a unilateral surrender of their racial identity, dignity, and group organizational power.[20]

Du Bois's objection to the Declaration also rested on grounds of political economy, out of which would grow his and others' more fully developed socialist or social democratic critiques. Tarring America in 1897 as a "mad money-getting plutocracy," he implied that the Declaration's classical-liberal rights doctrine, central to which are private, personal property rights, yielded ideas of laissez-faire government and individual responsibility that could only obstruct economic and social reform. Viewed in this light, the Declaration's rights doctrine generated an ethic of antisocial materialism.[21] Moreover, this political-economic critique entails a racial critique of its own, according to which the class-based injustice encouraged by the Declaration is perfected by racial injustice. The subordination of blacks disguises and thus reinforces the subordination of lower-class whites to white oligarchs; by diverting attention from the potentially deep antagonisms between upper- and lower-class whites, it makes democracy among whites possible. In this way, the argument of today's radical critics generalizes upon the claims of nineteenth-century apologists for slavery, taking the Old South as representative of the nation at large. For America as a whole, according to these critics, white supremacy functions just as it had for slavery's most forthright defenders, as an integral, stabilizing element—the "corner-stone," some of those defenders had said, most famously the Confederate vice president Alexander Stephens—of their society's republican order.[22] For radical critics, America's betrayals of the ideals of racial liberty and equality are betrayals *in* the nation's founding principles rather than betrayals *of* them.

The upshot of these arguments is that the watchword for African Americans, as for all those interested in racial justice, is not *integration* but *transformation.* The proper attitude, accordingly, is radical opposition, both to American practice and to the liberal, natural rights principles of the American founding, from which the civil rights protest tradition drew vital inspiration. As they await the "radical revolution of values" for which the increasingly frustrated King finally called, African Americans' alienation is epitomized in a remark by renowned novelist Toni Morrison, who declared in 1986, "At no moment of my life have I ever felt as though I were an American."[23]

Virtually all observers agree that the present condition of black alienation is fraught with peril, for African Americans in particular and for America as a whole. The challenge that it presents obviously calls for more than a theoretical response; in view of the hard theoretical core of that challenge, however, a theoretical response is indispensable. Just how compelling are the presently prevailing critiques? And what, if anything, can yet be said in favor of the old mainstream tradition of black activism and of the American creed that inspired it?

To answer such challenging questions, it makes sense to begin by examining the argument for the old mainstream tradition in its ablest theoretical articulations. My choice of particular subject matter rests on the premise that among its numerous eminent spokespersons, the nineteenth-century abolitionist and agitator for civil equality Frederick Douglass endures as that tradition's greatest representative, unequaled in his articulation of the first principles of natural rights liberalism in their application to racial justice in America. No less than the most disillusioned African American thinkers in his day or our own, Douglass was forced from the beginning to reflect on the unsettling question, "What country have I?" Early in his career, his answer sounded the depth of black anger and alienation: he had none.[24] But he grew quickly to affirm a vision of justice deeply rooted in American principles; and over the course of his long career, he produced the most powerful argument for the affirmation of those principles in the history of African American political thought. In the end, Douglass stands virtually unrivaled as the invincible adversary of black alienation, an exemplar and apostle of peculiarly American and African American forms of hopefulness.

Because Douglass made his autobiographies important vehicles for conveying his argument in political philosophy, it is necessary at the outset to provide a brief sketch of his singularly remarkable life story.[25] What follows is a summary of the biographical facts I judge essential for understanding the main principles of Douglass's political thought.

The boy who became Frederick Douglass entered the world, as he said later, "without an intelligible beginning."[26] Though he never knew for certain the year of his own birth, he was born into slavery on Maryland's Eastern Shore in February 1818 and given the improbable name Frederick Augustus Washington Bailey. His mother, Harriet, whom he barely knew, died before he reached the age of eight. The identity of his father has never been conclusively ascertained, but he was presumed to be a white slaveholder, most likely Frederick's first master, Aaron Anthony. His personal experience as a slave was varied and, on the whole, relatively mild. Most of his boyhood was spent in domestic service, first for Anthony and Anthony's employer, Edward Lloyd V, scion of Maryland's wealthiest and most prominent family, and later for the Auld brothers, Thomas (Anthony's son-in-law) and Hugh. In the Baltimore household of Hugh Auld occurred one of the great turning points of Frederick's life, when Hugh's young wife, Sophia, complying with Frederick's request, taught him the rudiments of literacy, which he perfected on his own after Hugh forbade further instruction. A dispute between Hugh and his brother returned Frederick to the Thomas Auld household and set the stage for a second great turning point.

To employ him more gainfully and perhaps also to discipline the increasingly angry young man, Auld rented Frederick, then turning sixteen years of age, to Edward Covey, a reputed "slave breaker," for a year of field labor. After six months of brutal abuse by Covey, Frederick reached his breaking point, and after his appeal to Auld for relief seemed to fall on deaf ears, he took the matter into his own hands. His successful physical resistance to the next attempted beating signified his psychological self-liberation and steeled his resolve to escape slavery altogether. After a failed attempt the following year, he succeeded in escaping on September 3, 1838. Aided by Anna Murray, a free Baltimore woman who would soon become his wife, he made his way via the Underground Railroad first to New York City and then to New Bedford, Massachusetts, where he settled and, at the suggestion of his initial host, assumed the surname that he would shortly thereafter make famous.

For three years in New Bedford, Douglass worked as a day laborer, developed his oratorical powers as a minister at the African Methodist Episcopal Church, and attended local abolitionist meetings. He became an avid reader of the *Liberator,* the influential abolitionist journal edited by the movement's militant leader, William Lloyd Garrison, whose attention he attracted at an 1841 antislavery convention in Nantucket—another turning point. Powerfully impressed by Douglass's impromptu speech there, Garrison solicited him to tell his story throughout the land as an itinerant lecturer for the Massachusetts Anti-Slavery Society. His reputation grew quickly in this employment, and with it arose doubts that a young man wielding such finely developed intellectual and oratorical powers could have spent most of his life in bondage. To prove the veracity of his story, Douglass wrote his first autobiography, *The Narrative of the Life of Frederick Douglass,* which quickly became a best seller. The further notoriety that he gained via the *Narrative* also brought further danger, as it clarified the young fugitive's identity to would-be slave catchers. In part to escape that danger, Douglass traveled to England shortly after his book's publication in 1845. There, his fame grew to international proportions as he labored for eighteen months spreading the antislavery message throughout the United Kingdom. There, too, was laid the foundation for his break from his erstwhile mentor, Garrison.

In late 1846, Douglass gained legal freedom in America when British admirers purchased his manumission from Hugh Auld. His British friends also urged him to launch his own antislavery newspaper, for which they would supply initial funding, upon his return to the United States in 1847. Later that year, he moved his family to Rochester, New York, and over Garrison's objections, he began publication of an abolitionist weekly, the *North Star*. As editor of his own paper, he grew in intellectual independence, within a few years breaking sharply from the Garrisonian orbit. In the course of the tumultuous 1850s, he became, in contrast to the Garrisonians, more patriotically American and more militant in his assessment of the need for violent force to bring an end to slavery. These and other changes in his thinking were represented in his second autobiography, *My Bondage and My Freedom,* published in 1855. As the decade neared its close, Douglass grew pessimistic as to the near-term prospects for abolition, but his pessimism proved momentary. After the attack on Fort Sumter in April 1861, he hurled himself into wartime punditry, laboring tirelessly to persuade President Abraham Lincoln and all who would listen that the Civil War's proper objective was abolition, not merely restoration, and that victory was best or only achievable by the enlistment of African American soldiers in the loyalist cause.

After the great war ended, Douglass rededicated himself to the cause of racial justice, laboring to preserve and expand the war's gains. He did so in part via his faithful service to the party of Lincoln. He campaigned energetically for the election of Republican candidates and was rewarded with federal appointments in the Hayes and Garfield-Arthur administrations. Ever a compelling speaker, he also became wealthy on the lecture circuit. Critics charged that his party relations and his newly acquired wealth combined, for a time, to blunt his criticism of federal failures to secure the freedpeople's rights against renewed assaults in the post-Reconstruction era. Nonetheless, his speeches from the early 1880s on displayed the same fiery militancy in opposition to persisting injustices, along with the undying hopefulness for a better American future, that had distinguished the best of his earlier oratory. In keeping with his professed devotion to humanitarian ideals, he was also a prominent advocate of woman suffrage. After returning from an afternoon at a woman's rights meeting, Douglass died at his Washington, D.C., home on February 20, 1895.

Living "in the day of moral giants,"[27] Douglass has long held a prominent place in the pantheon of American heroes. To his accomplished contemporary James McCune Smith, author of the introduction to *Bondage and Freedom*, he was even by the 1850s "a Representative American man," having raised himself "through every gradation of rank comprised in our national make-up."[28] In the reported judgment of Abraham Lincoln, the Great Emancipator himself, Douglass was possibly the most meritorious man in the United States. His numerous eulogists further attested his heroic proportions. To his occasional antagonist the Reverend Alexander Crummell, he was "a great genius" and "a great man." U.S. Supreme Court Justice John Marshall Harlan, heroic dissenter in his own right, declared that he had met no man of loftier character. Howard University law professor W. H. H. Hart lauded Douglass as "this incomparable champion of human rights . . . the central and colossal figure" of the American antislavery crusade, whose victory reached "immeasurably beyond anything ever attempted by mortal man."[29] Comparable assessments appear in the commentary of our own day.[30]

Among twentieth- and twenty-first-century scholars, Douglass's life and thought have attracted a great deal of attention, mainly from historians and professional students of literature but also from specialists in moral and political philosophy.[31] In this recent scholarship, a general admiration for its subject now coexists with a prominent spirit of critical diminution. In part, this critical spirit arises as a healthy corrective of a long-standing tendency toward hero worship and of a related tendency to allow Douglass to eclipse important colleagues and rivals among his African American contemporaries. Professor Wilson Jeremiah Moses rightly warns against thinking of Douglass as a "gigantic abnormality," towering above all other African American activists in the nineteenth century.[32] In the interest of restoring human proportions to their subject, Moses and others make a point of exposing what they view as significant tensions and inconsistencies in Douglass's thinking. For Professor David W. Blight, a generally admiring commentator, Douglass was a "thoroughly human, complex, and contradictory" figure, "forever balancing the duty of principle with the duty of hope."[33]

In part, too, the recently intensified critical spirit among Douglass scholars reflects the spirit of the day in post–civil rights era America, in which both the successes and the perceived failings of the mainstream civil rights tradition lend safety and urgency to criticism of its leading figures. In fact, the most important substantive criticisms of Douglass's political thought track closely with the main criticisms of the broader tradition. Like that tradition as a whole, critics charge, Douglass's thought suffered from excessive idealism, closely linked to his excessive faith in the receptiveness of America to racial reform. He "seemed to believe," according to Moses, "that truth and justice had irresistible metaphysical power in the providential course of history," and so he saw moralizing rhetoric rather than institutional organization as the key to reform. In the more sharply negative view of intellectual historian Waldo E. Martin, Jr., Douglass's "abiding faith in a moral universe" engendered in him an "overweening optimism" that "obscured the . . . ubiquitous influence of white supremacy" and so "proved illusory, sometimes delusory." For Martin, the "most telling limitation of Douglass's philosophy of social reform" was that "it generally neglected the crying need for fundamental structural changes." Douglass's steadfast hopefulness for reform in America, Vincent Harding has concluded, was grounded in little more than a "flight from the past."[34]

Likewise, Douglass's later critics have found in his thought the same vices of partiality that critics beginning with Du Bois saw in the natural rights principles of the Declaration. A recurrent charge in recent decades is that Douglass, seeking vainly to escape the reality of racial and ethnic division, betrayed an unconscious Eurocentrist bias by espousing as universal the norms of white civilization. Earliest and most notorious among these imputations is historian Peter F. Walker's suggestion that Douglass was animated by a "hopeless secret desire to be white." Less abrasively put but in a similar spirit are Martin's remarks concerning Douglass's Anglophilia and Europhilia, entailing a conception of assimilation in which Douglass urged blacks to become "like whites."[35] Still more common is the charge that Douglass's professions of universal natural rights were vitiated by a distinct socioeconomic class bias. Again prominent among the accusers is Martin, asserting that in "the thoroughgoing materialism of his bourgeois mentality," Douglass harbored a deep "procapitalist bias."[36] Charles W. Mills pushes these lines of critique to a harsh general conclusion: though Douglass is properly honored for his conviction and resolution—"he stood up for all of us"—the fact remains that on the fundamentals concerning race and rights in America, "everything Douglass said is wrong."[37]

This book presents a different view. To dissent from the main critical judgments does not require me to claim, contra Mills, that everything Douglass said was right. His political thought was indeed characterized by tensions and complexities, and he committed some significant misjudgments over the course of his long career. (Most notable among those are his radical-abolitionist reading of the Constitution, his demand for an overtly abolitionist war policy from the outset of the Civil War, and his initial opposition to the black exodus from the Deep South in the late 1870s.) Nonetheless, I argue here that Douglass's political thought *at its core* is both more coherent and more subtle and defensible in substance than his most challenging critics acknowledge. Above all, in contrast to the critics I have mentioned, I maintain that Douglass was right in finding in the natural rights principles of the Declaration of Independence a necessary and sufficient theoretical basis for addressing the nation's racial problems.

More specifically, I find that Douglass's remarkable hopefulness concerning the demise of slavery and white supremacy in America was not naively or obtusely idealist but was instead marked by a substantial moderation and realism. It was extended over the long term and grounded in a sober understanding of human nature and in evidence drawn from America's and other nations' historical experience. Likewise, although his natural rights argument did entail strongly moralized appeals for the cultivation of individual and collective virtue, his emphasis on the primacy of moral culture did not diminish his appreciation of the need for institutional reform. Nor did his individualism blind him to the social dimension of human nature. His commitment to the doctrine of natural individual rights did indeed comprehend a strong commitment to the natural right of private property, but this commitment supported, rather than weakened, his condemnation of economic exploitation. It did not function in his thought as a narrowly self-serving rationalization of middle- and upper-class success and thus blind him to the deprivations suffered by the poor, and it did not produce in him any dogmatic fealty to the principle of laissez-faire government. And finally, though Douglass viewed racial integration as both a moral imperative and the most likely long-term outcome, the universal, humanitarian vision yielded by his natural rights argument cohered with his realistic appreciation of the natural and historical power of racial and ethnic identities. He rejected any simplistic understanding of integration, especially any that required an uncritical affirmation of the Euro-American heritage or a racial self-effacement on the part of blacks.

The unifying core of Douglass's political thought, as I understand it, consists in his distinctive interpretation of the natural rights doctrine, applied particularly to race relations in the United States. His central claims can be simply summarized as follows: (1) the natural rights doctrine, as epitomized in the Declaration of Independence, is true as a set of moral prescriptions and sanctioned as a body of moral laws; (2) institutional systems of slavery and racial supremacy are unjust and ultimately weak; and (3) the national mission and the destiny of the United States are to become an exemplar of harmonious, integrated equality among the racial and ethnic varieties of humankind.

In this book, I examine these claims from the disciplinary perspective of political philosophy, considering Douglass's thought as an argument on first principles. To consider it as an argument, in a relatively strict sense, means to consider his thought as more than an expression of his personal psychology, polemical interest, or theological faith. Although I try to remain mindful of the shaping influences and practical motives out of which Douglass's arguments emerged, my primary interest lies in assessing their larger moral and political significance. Douglass claimed reasons for the positions he took, and he meant to use those reasons to persuade others, so far as possible. Further, in focusing on first principles, I intend to consider the core, not the whole, of Douglass's political thought. I attempt no comprehensive accounting of his positions on all the political issues that drew his attention; I examine mainly his arguments in the controversies in which he believed the first principles of political life and of the American Republic were most significantly implicated.

To take this approach is not necessarily to (mis)characterize Douglass as a disinterested observer of moral and political phenomena, motivated purely by his love of truth and wisdom. Nor is it to consider his thought ahistorically, abstracted from its originating contexts as if it were a pure revelation from eternity. To consider Douglass in his proper contexts means, first, to consider his thought in the various polemical arenas within which he and his fellow abolitionists, African American opinion leaders, radical Republicans, and other activists pursued their practical ends. It also means to consider his arguments in the light of the traditions of reformist rhetoric, especially those inspired by certain elements of American civil theology, from which he drew and to which he contributed.[38] But to complete the picture, it is necessary, too, to recognize the ways in which his thought engaged with traditions animated by broader rationalist ambitions in their reflections on natural justice and republican government, especially including early modern political philosophy and the political thought of America's founding.

Douglass was a man animated by extraordinarily powerful hatreds and loves, among which was a love of moral and political wisdom, fruitfully present in him even if often subordinate to other passions. Although he was primarily an activist and polemicist, he was a polemicist of a very high order. For over five decades, he undertook to educate himself, his fellow Americans, and all others within hearing on the pressing issues of his time, on the foundations of the American Republic, and on the primary issues of political life in general, convinced that they were all of a piece. Like Lincoln, Douglass seems to have been unusually subject to a law of philosophic gravity, drawing his mind irresistibly to foundational principles. The conflict to whose resolution he gave his life's work, as he told a Rochester audience shortly after the outbreak of formal war in 1861, far transcended merely sectional or national significance. It "sweeps the whole horizon of human rights, powers, duties and responsibilities," he declared. "The grand primal principles which form the basis of human society, are here."[39] Seeing with great clarity that the crisis of his time involved a mortal threat to the first principles of the American Republic and of free government, he reflected intensively on them. As he assumed editorial responsibility for the *North Star,* he felt compelled to perfect his arguments concerning the U.S. Constitution's relation to slavery by plumbing the depths of political philosophy—"to study, with some care, not only the just and proper rules of legal interpretation, but the origin, design, nature, rights, powers, and duties of civil government, and also the relations which human beings sustain to it."[40]

In his determination to illuminate the particular by the universal, Douglass exemplified the spirit grandly expressed by Du Bois, concluding a discussion of the proper objects of African Americans' education: "I sit with Shakespeare and he winces not. Across the color line I move arm in arm with Balzac and Dumas. . . . From out the caves of evening . . . I summon Aristotle and Aurelius and what soul I will, and they come all graciously with no scorn nor condescension. So, wed with Truth, I dwell above the Veil."[41] For African Americans, such education required escape from their own peculiarly forbidding "caves of evening." But for those with the virtue and fortune to resist, life in America issued an unusually urgent and transparent invitation to political philosophy.[42] Frederick Douglass, who sat with Shakespeare no less than did Du Bois, was moved as few if any other figures in the African American protest tradition have been moved to take up that philosophic invitation.

Douglass's great theme was rational hopefulness for the ultimate triumph of justice in U.S. race relations. He judged his hopefulness to be rationally grounded, in part by his observation of the dynamism inherent in human nature and powerfully represented in American history, African American history, and his own personal history. Yet the fundamental natural fact about human affairs was not their fluidity, in Douglass's understanding, but rather their *lawfulness*. He thought hopefulness was rational primarily due to his understanding of the moral laws of nature and their relation to American public life. In its account of the basic principles of natural human rights, Douglass's argument closely resembles the classic argument of John Locke, the great seventeenth-century English philosopher who inspired the authors of the Declaration. But Douglass went beyond Locke in his claim that the natural rights doctrine was not only true but also naturally sanctioned. Respect for natural human rights was commanded by genuine natural laws that he frequently described as "self-executing."

Here is an important, difficult, and underanalyzed element of Douglass's thought. The idea of a self-executing law of nature came to him primarily via the influence of the nineteenth-century Scottish phrenologist and natural-law theorist George Combe, whose widely read book, *The Constitution of Man*, "relieved my path of many shadows," Douglass recalled, when he read it sometime in the early 1840s.[43] In Combe's argument, Douglass saw a rational foundation for the idea that a moral design was visible in nature and human history. Conceiving of the moral laws of nature as self-executing or naturally sanctioned, he held that in the nature of human affairs, justice and other virtues tend to be rewarded whereas injustice and other vices tend to be punished. Human beings commonly, even chronically, fail to attend the immediate natural sanctions of the moral law; but over time, Douglass maintained, persistent virtue generally receives powerful reinforcement, and persistent violations of the moral law generally prove self-defeating.

What bears emphasis here is that in adapting Combe's natural-law argument to his special concerns, Douglass did not betray a naive or willful idealism. He did not affirm that racial progress was a simple historical inevitability. Nor did he expect that it would occur in a linear succession of events or that it would result directly from moral appeals for reform or from motives of unmixed moral purity. More painfully than most, he was mindful that the dynamism of nature and history brought reversals for ill as for good: "Revolutions may for a time seem to roll backwards."[44] The tenacity of the racial supremacist spirit was undeniable, and not even Douglass's optimism was impervious to any accumulation of setbacks, as his crisis of confidence on the eve of the Civil War illustrated. But on the whole, his argument was not decisively disturbed by the fact that racial progress has often been met with reactions and reversals or by the related fact that it has owed much to its intermittent convergence with whites' interests, as distinct from a reform of their moral sentiments. His admixture of realism in acknowledging these facts served instead to temper and so to sustain and fortify his rational hopefulness.

To vindicate the relevance of his natural-law argument to conditions in America, Douglass thought it sufficient to show that progress was real and that persistent, well-conceived efforts at moral reform and uplift were not futile. His claim of an effectively sanctioned natural law received impressive corroboration by his prediction of the demise of chattel slavery and was not refuted by the postwar reaction. Commemorating emancipation in an 1883 speech, Douglass regretted "to observe that even colored men are heard to deny that any improvement has taken place in their condition during the last twenty years." Among such men, a preoccupation with injustices yet to be overcome and heights yet to be reached, absent an appreciation of distances already traveled, engendered a disabling disillusionment. In the short course of twenty years, despite the powerful proslavery reaction in that period, substantial improvements in the condition of African Americans were undeniable. How others could deny that progress, Douglass commented, "I am utterly unable to see." Even in his 1889 speech "The Nation's Problem," one of the angriest of his postwar addresses—a speech in which he termed black citizenship a "delusion," decried the effectual return of slavery to the South, and approved black emigration from that region—he concluded on a note of empirically grounded optimism. Slavery was vanishing from the earth; increasing numbers of African Americans were gaining education; southerners' interests in material development would eventually awaken them to the appeals of justice and humanity; and the American people would prove themselves governed, at length, "not only by laws and selfish interests, but by large ideas of moral and material civilization."[45]

My discussion of Douglass's argument is organized thematically but also, as much as possible, according to the chronological development of his main concerns. In Chapter One, the argument begins where Douglass's argument began, with his descriptive analysis of slavery. As he reported in his second autobiography, he started his study of the institution very early in life: "I was just as aware of the unjust, unnatural and murderous character of slavery, when nine years old, as I am now."[46] His moral and political thought began from a perspective of opposition; the natures of right and law became visible to him through his intensive reflection on their negation. He certainly conceived his account polemically, to the end of "creating the hated enemy."[47] But he also designed it to reveal the essential truth about slavery as a form of rule. Against proslavery apologists' depictions of a system of paternal beneficence, he presented a carefully detailed rendering of slavery as an extreme, systematic despotism. Holding enduring interest for the student of political philosophy as well as the historian, Douglass's discussion of slavery, especially in *Bondage and Freedom,* is comparable in insight to the classic discussions of tyranny and despotism by Aristotle and Montesquieu, and it surpasses both in its terrible vividness.[48]

Chapter Two delves deeper into Douglass's oppositional perspective. Building upon his descriptive account, it develops his arguments first for slavery's natural wrongness, then for its natural weakness in conjunction with the right and virtue of resistance. Slavery is wrong because human beings possess natural rights, and human beings are rights-possessors by virtue of their natural endowment with moral rationality and with a strong desire for liberty. In Douglass's natural-justice argument, resistance to tyranny is at once a right, a duty, and a predictable effect. Slavery was not only wrong but also doomed, destined ultimately to fall victim to its own overreaching. A characteristic combination of arrogance and fear would move slaveholders to seek national dominion, offending a white majority as well as the black minority. But the fear that would move them to demand national hegemony would be aroused in large measure by slave rebellions. Eventual liberation would be the natural reward for acts of dutiful, virtuous resistance by slaves and others.

Moving beyond the spirit of opposition, Chapters Three and Four examine Douglass's understandings of civil government in general and of the U.S. constitutional order in particular. Chapter Three explores his argument on the highly charged question of the U.S. Constitution's relation to slavery. Initially accepting the Garrisonians' reading, Douglass soon reversed his position, aligning himself with political abolitionists in their argument for an antislavery Constitution. Characteristically adopting the most forwardly radical position in the controversy, Douglass argued, contrary to Garrisonians, slaveholders, and moderates such as Lincoln, that the Constitution licensed and in fact mandated national action to effect the immediate abolition of slavery everywhere in the United States. His constitutional vision thus involved an intransigent insistence on the recovery of the principles of 1776, along with a radicalization of the tradition of Hamiltonian nationalism.

Chapter Four explores Douglass's thoughts on the powers and duties of the federal and state governments in the matter of postslavery race relations. His thinking on these questions was provoked by the question, pervasive before and during the war, of what should be "done with the Negro" in the aftermath of emancipation. His repeated response, "*do nothing with us,*" is perhaps the most controversial and misunderstood of all his positions. It has been taken to support the charges that he lapsed, in the postwar decades, into callous endorsements of social Darwinism, laissez-faire capitalism, and a "bootstraps" theory of individual self-help for the freedpeople. But Douglass's notion of the moral imperative of self-reliance was more generous than such charges allow. In context, his "do nothing" doctrine carried specific affirmative as well as negative meanings. In its affirmative meanings, he broadly construed the basic governmental obligation to provide equal protection of person and property for all, and he cited the nation's enormous debt to its former slaves as he defended public policy proposals aimed at assisting the freedpeople and others in elevating their condition.

Douglass's constitutional thought, representing an attempt to unite American positive law with the universal law of nature, can also be viewed as an attempt to solidify American patriotism by uniting it with humanitarianism. In this respect, it belongs to his millennialist vision, in which historical, seemingly natural tensions between partial and universal identifications and duties would be finally resolved. That vision receives further discussion in Chapter Five, focusing on the social and cultural, rather than the legal, identity of the American nation. Expanding the national mission affirmed by the Founders, Douglass envisioned a perfected America as the great exemplar and herald of an epoch of democratic, humanitarian unity. Central to this vision was his approving prediction of the amalgamation of black, white, and other Americans into a single, "blended" nationality.[49]

Here above all, however, a significant realism tempered Douglass's enthusiasm. Amid his endorsement of radical interracial assimilation, Douglass maintained that fully equal citizenship for African Americans required both their fellow citizens' and, more fundamentally, their own recognition of their contributions to America. Likewise, in his broader vision of a "composite" American nationality, he insisted that proper assimilation could not involve the simple absorption of others by the Euro-American majority. His emphasis on the universality of natural human rights did not blind him to the natural partiality of all peoples. His cognizance of this partiality—of ethnic and racial groups' common need for completion through incorporation with other peoples, along with their respective powers to assist in others' completion—was the premise upon which his broadly inclusive American nationality was to be composed. In its realist dimension, Douglass's vision of our composite nationality approved a measure of group pride, achievement- and contribution-based, purchased by a reciprocal measure of group modesty. Group partiality would not be effaced but instead would be moderated, liberalized, and elevated. This idea of moderate, reciprocal assimilation shows Douglass at his most statesmanlike, providing instruction in the governance of deep tensions in American and human life, preserving and strengthening devotion to the universal by prudent concessions to partiality, and edifying our partial identities by the superintendence of universal principles.

In a concluding chapter, I offer some reflections on Douglass's enduring contributions to American liberalism, highlighting the forceful linkage of hopefulness and rationality in his statesmanlike defense of the universal principles on which free government depends. The principles of natural human rights, Douglass was convinced, represent both a permanent truth and the most practically powerful moral and political theory ever conceived. He found reason to love and identify with America, despite its grievous imperfections, primarily by virtue of its original and unforgettable dedication to those principles. And in his reasonable faith in their ultimate triumph in America, Douglass found an enormous reservoir of strength that he labored to share with others. Drawing upon that faith, he taught African Americans and other Americans to agitate for justice and to strive for excellence. He taught them through all their hardships to love their country and their future in it, and so, most urgently, he taught them to reject the spirit of alienation, which he saw as the greatest danger to any people's liberation and elevation. Over 100 years after Douglass's death, this teaching has lost none of its essential vitality.

"Killed All the Day Long":
The True Philosophy of Slavery

When the savages of Louisiana want fruit, they cut down the tree and
gather the fruit. There you have despotic government.
  Montesquieu, The Spirit of the Laws, bk. 5, chap. 13

FREDERICK DOUGLASS'S REFLECTIONS in political philosophy seem to have
begun in earnest one day, probably in 1826 or 1827, at the Baltimore household of Hugh and Sophia Auld. In response to the enslaved boy's forward request, Sophia had begun to teach young Freddy Bailey (as he was known at the
time) to read, and she proudly informed her husband of her pupil's rapid progress. She had not prepared herself for Auld's response. "Master Hugh was
amazed at the simplicity of his spouse," Douglass later recalled, and he
"promptly forbade the continuance of her instruction." To teach the boy to read,
Hugh warned, "'would forever unfit him for the duties of a slave.'" Meaning
only to reprove his wife, however, Hugh had apparently underestimated the
alert boy's comprehension. For even as Sophia had opened the door to literacy,
Hugh had unwittingly provided a lesson of nearly equal value—an "oracular exposition," even "a new and special revelation," as Douglass the adult author put
it. In scolding his young, northern-bred wife for her simplicity, Master Hugh
had allowed Frederick to glimpse "the true philosophy of slavery."[1]

To say that Douglass's reflections in political philosophy began there is to
say that his political thought began in a spirit of opposition. In his own telling,
his opposition to slavery preceded this Baltimore lesson: "I had already voted
against that on the home plantation of Col. Lloyd." What he learned from Hugh
Auld in this instance was specifically what to oppose in slavery and how to oppose it: "That which he most loved"—the slave's ignorance—"I most hated."[2]
From this crucial particular lesson, it is permissible to generalize. By learning

what slaveholders opposed or what slavery systematically negated, Douglass learned what to affirm. For him as for the founders of the classical liberal political philosophy that he adopted, the beginning of political wisdom lay in understanding the *summum malum*—the greatest evil or misery, that which is most to be avoided or resisted. The natures of law, right, and freedom became visible to him first by his experience of their radical negation. The natural starting point for our study of Douglass's first principles is therefore his understanding of slavery. Slavery is that to or from which all roads lead in Douglass's political thought.

Determined to expose the truth about American slavery from virtually the moment of his escape, Douglass presented in numerous speeches and writings a thorough analysis of its nature and ruling principles. His most elaborate analysis appears in his autobiographies, especially the second, published in 1855. In the July 2, 1855, letter that the book's original editor incorporated into its preface, Douglass proclaimed a distaste for merely personal narrative; he intended *Bondage and Freedom* to be read as an antislavery argument, not only as the particularly interesting story of one man. Just as he discussed slavery "in the light of *fundamental principles*" in his public letters and speeches, so he published his revised autobiography to vindicate "a just and benevolent principle . . . by revealing the true nature, character, and tendency of the slave system."[3] *Bondage and Freedom*, greatly expanding on his earlier *Narrative*, did much of the work of the systematic treatise on slavery that Douglass never wrote.

Douglass's choice to embed his analysis of slavery in his autobiographical story holds both personal and theoretical significance, as it reflects both his dissent from and his assent to a piece of advice from his initial mentors, the Garrisonian abolitionists. The latter greatly valued his story as a rebuttal to slaveholders' charges that they lacked any personal familiarity with the institution they denounced. But they seemed to distrust his capacity to interpret it. Early in his tenure as an orator in their employ, they had advised him to confine his efforts to narration: "Give us the facts," John Collins, general agent of the Garrisonian Massachusetts Anti-Slavery Society, had told him, and "we will take care of the philosophy." From the same quarters came subsequent, related suggestions that he was properly suited for platform oratory rather than for writing—for emotive expression, they seemed to imply, rather than for fully rational speech. Naturally bristling at such advice, Douglass quickly departed from it.[4] By writing a work of theoretical analysis, he asserted his personal and intellectual independence. And yet, by conveying that analysis through the medium of his story, he affirmed that, their condescension aside, the Garrisonians had been "not altogether wrong" in suggesting a narrative approach. In fact, Douglass repeatedly downplayed his theoretical design in *Bondage and Freedom,* telling readers that he confined its primary subject matter to "my experience, and not my arguments" and left it for others to "philosophize."[5]

What holds theoretical significance here is the measure of realism that Douglass displayed in his understanding of moral psychology. Such is the character of moral rationality that the appeal to audiences' understanding is best prepared by an appeal to their sentiments.[6] To be *seen* as an enormous crime, slavery had to be *felt* to be so, and it would be felt to be so only to the extent that audiences were moved to imagine themselves sharing the concrete experiences of its victims. Example is generally a stronger pedagogical tool than directly conveyed precept. Though frequently pleased to confront his audiences with unadorned assertions of antislavery principles, Douglass nonetheless agreed that moral philosophy operates more effectively as it is communicated less directly, through the medium of appeals to moral sentiment. Knowing that he needed to make something of a spectacle of himself, he presented his argument as his life, carefully fashioned and revised in the course of his several autobiographies.

The Nature of Slavery

Douglass's exposure of slavery's "true philosophy" comes into view, in its polemical context, as his rebuttal of the false philosophy propagated by slavery's defenders. As he was well aware, his account of slavery signified his entry into a furiously intensifying controversy over what had become the defining institution of the southern states.

The issue was awakened by the American Revolution, whose principles inspired a relatively uncontroversial wave of abolition in northern states from Massachusetts to Pennsylvania in the years following 1776. In the process of the Constitution's framing and ratification in the late 1780s, it provoked a more dangerous controversy, which was therefore carefully suppressed by a founding majority fearful for the survival of their fragile new union.[7] Even so, the Founders generally agreed that slavery was, in principle, an evil; for them, the issue concerned how far to tolerate that evil as a circumstantial necessity. But the controversy became irrepressible early in the nineteenth century, with the nation's great westward expansion following the Louisiana Purchase. The prospect of slavery's indefinite expansion was far more threatening to northern principles and interests than its accommodation in the original southern states had been;

conversely, the prospect of slavery's confinement to its original domain in an otherwise greatly expanding federal union was more threatening to perceived southern interests than the deferred antislavery sentiment of the founding majority had been.

With the stakes of the contest thus raised, the decades following 1820 saw the profound radicalization of both sides of the argument, precipitated by a crisis in the years 1819 and 1820 over Missouri's admission as a slave state. In the 1820s and early 1830s, a newly militant abolitionism arose, exemplified by the black writer David Walker's *Appeal to the Coloured Citizens of the World* (1829) and by William Lloyd Garrison's launching of what became the movement's leading newspaper, the *Liberator,* in 1831. In the same period, a no less militant proslavery argument moved to the forefront of southern thought, produced by a new generation of prominent southern intellectuals, lawyers, public officials, and clergy. The new proslavery militancy was heralded by a notorious 1837 speech of the eminent U.S. senator from South Carolina, John C. Calhoun. Provoked by a barrage of abolitionist petitions to the Congress, Calhoun took to the offensive: "The relation now existing in the slaveholding States between the two [races], is, instead of an evil, a good—a positive good."[8]

By Douglass's day, the wholehearted affirmation of slavery's absolute superiority as a social system had become predominant in southern thought. Summarized in its essentials, the radical proslavery argument that he was forced to confront began with a sentiment scarcely utterable in public to an earlier generation—an outright rejection of the principles of the Declaration of Independence. So said South Carolina governor (later U.S. senator) James Henry Hammond in an 1845 public letter to the English abolitionist Thomas Clarkson: "I repudiate, as ridiculously absurd, that much lauded but nowhere accredited dogma of Mr. Jefferson, that 'all men are born equal.' "[9] In very important respects, slavery's spokesmen contended, human beings were born and remained *unequal,* and that inequality constituted a primary condition of civilizational progress. "In all social systems," Hammond declared in a famous, belligerent defense of slavery on the floor of the U.S. Senate in 1858, "there must be a class to do the menial duties"; without it, "you would not have that other class which leads progress, civilization, and refinement. It constitutes the very mud-sill of society." Twenty years earlier, chancellor of South Carolina William Harper had made the point still more sharply: "Perhaps nothing can be more evident than that [slavery] is the *sole cause*" of civilization.[10] The idea was not that one class had to be sacrificed for the good of another or for society as a whole. Crucial to "positive-good" arguments was the claim that slavery was a benign form of so-cial inequality, genuinely good for *both* the master and servile classes. Moreover, their claim was that, of the various forms of slavery, the one prevalent in the American South was the most benign, due to its exclusive application to a race peculiarly suited for enslavement. To slavery's proponents, their universally held premise of Negro inferiority meant that American slavery was slavery in a uniquely humane and progressive form. In a regionally acclaimed early essay, the Virginian Thomas Roderick Dew, professor of law at the College of William and Mary, forwarded this representative assertion: "A merrier being does not exist on the face of the globe than the negro slave of the United States."[11]

The central issue can be framed in categories basic to political philosophy. The slaveholders' primary claim was that slavery was a species of *paternal* power. They indignantly denied what their opponents strongly affirmed—that slavery was the paradigmatic form of *despotic* power. Southern slaves were not at all be-ings devoid of rights, claimed slavery's spokesmen, but merely "permanent children."[12] Slavery as they conceived of it was paternal, mainly in its benevolent provision for the subsistence and comfort of a class of dependent laborers. Pur-suant to this idea, some even recoiled from using the term *slavery* in naming their institution. "Warranteeism, with the ethnical qualification" was the un-gainly coinage of Mississippian Henry Hughes, who insisted that in the U.S. South, "there are no slaves." As Hughes and others characterized it, the southern system was essentially a household-centered social security system, eliminating indigence and securing "warrantees'" (slaves') rights to "a comfortable dwelling . . . and a comfortable sufficiency of food, fuel, raiment, and of medical and other necessaries."[13] Southern slavery's benevolence was contrasted with the cruelty of the northern system of purportedly "free" labor, which to slavery's de-fenders was actually a malign, impersonal form of slavery that depended on the systematic exploitation of wage laborers.[14]

Douglass was thoroughly familiar with the claim of slavery's paternalism, and he would have none of it.[15] In late 1850—a year marked by the federal enact-ment of the revised Fugitive Slave Law, a law that itself sharply contradicted slavery's paternalist claims—he began a series of lectures on American slavery in his adopted hometown of Rochester, New York. In the first lecture, he pro-ceeded directly to the heart of the issue by presenting a concise definition of the master-slave relation: "A master is one . . . who claims and exercises a right of property in the person of a fellow man. . . . The law gives the master absolute power over the slave. . . . The slave is a human being, divested of all rights . . . a mere 'chattel' in the eye of the law."[16] In speeches later that decade, he described the essential implications in sharp, Lockean language. A deliberate assertion of "absolute and arbitrary power . . . by one man over the body and soul of another man," slavery stood altogether outside any normal or legitimate human relation. It constituted a "perpetual war . . . between the master and slave."[17] In stark opposition to his adversaries' evasions and obfuscations, Douglass contended that slavery was despotism, pure and simple.

More specifically, Douglass held that (1) slavery was sui generis, essentially incomparable to any other system of inegalitarian labor relations; (2) any benevolent acts or qualities associated with slavery were immaterial to the question of slavery's true, essentially despotic, character; and (3) the assertion of slavery's actual, characteristic benevolence was radically false. Each of these elements of his antislavery argument requires elaboration.

In Douglass's understanding, slavery was uniquely evil. Slaveholders had conflated the conditions of slaves and wage laborers for their own interested purposes, and some abolitionists had abetted them, linking abolitionism with socialism in a zeal for universal reform.[18] This, to Douglass, was both a tactical and a theoretical error. Sympathetic to victims of any manner of oppression, he acknowledged throughout the 1840s and 1850s, to British and American audiences, the genuine sufferings of the English poor and the Irish under English rule. Yet he saw in those conditions no analogy to slavery. Slavery was a "solitary horror." It was "the most abject, the most terrible bondage ever imposed on any portion of mankind."[19] The famous remark by Abraham Lincoln perfectly expressed Douglass's view: "If slavery is not wrong, nothing is wrong."[20] Slavery was no ordinary crime; it was the paradigmatic human evil. In John Wesley's memorable epitome, which Douglass often quoted, slavery was "the sum of all villainies."[21]

Douglass's insistence on slavery's unique, paradigmatic evil should not be passed over as a mere rhetorical intensifier. In the initial chapter of *Bondage and Freedom,* he disclosed the ruling principle of what he subsequently called slavery's "true philosophy." Its "grand aim . . . always and everywhere, is to reduce man to a level with the brute."[22] Despite their elaborate apologetics, slaveholders did not treat those they enslaved as mere children. Slavery's dehumanizing design was evident even in its structural definition: to subject any human beings to permanent, absolute, irresponsible human power meant to treat them as if they were mere brutes. Douglass granted that slaveholders may not have commonly believed their slaves to be actually subhuman; their own statements and their equivocal practices suggested otherwise. They enacted no laws to govern their irrational livestock, he remarked in his Independence Day oration of 1852, whereas they did enact laws to govern slaves. "What is this," he asked, "but the acknowledgment that the slave is a moral, intellectual, and responsible being?"[23] But slaveholders' equivocations did not mitigate their criminality. To the contrary, their deliberately brutal treatment of beings they knew to be human meant that a thoroughgoing mendacity and willfulness lay at the heart of slavery.

Herein lay the essence of slavery's unique, radical evil, along with the deepest meaning of Douglass's Lockean conception of slavery as a state of war. As Jefferson had charged in the original draft of the Declaration, slavery represented a cruel war not merely against the rights of particular individuals or classes but also against human nature—ultimately against the natural and divine orders of being. Douglass had this larger war in mind when he declared, shortly after the outbreak of the Civil War, that rebellion was of the essence of slaveholding.[24] Beneath the slaveholders' rebellion against positive constitutional laws were more profound rebellions against natural and divine laws. To redefine a class of human beings as something less than human was an act of the deepest lawlessness. In biblical terms, slavery signified a reenactment of the original human rebellion: a usurpation of the power to name good and evil. Its degradation of the slave implied an arbitrary refashioning of the distinction between human beings and brutes, and its elevation of the master implicitly effaced the distinction between human beings and God.[25]

It is important to bear in mind that Douglass's insistence on slavery's unique brutality did not depend on his observations of slavery's more palpable, day-to-day cruelties. As we will see shortly, he maintained that slavery was evil in its effects as well as intrinsically, and no one did more than Douglass to arouse a public abhorrence of its effects. Nonetheless, its intrinsic evil sufficed to close the case against it: "It was *slavery*—not its mere *incidents*—that I hated."[26] Had no slaveholder ever put the lash to his victim, slavery would have remained in its essential nature a system of unrestrained violence. In *Bondage and Freedom*, Douglass recounted how, after his horrible experience under Edward Covey, his condition was ameliorated in the service of William Freeland, "the best master I ever had, until I became my own master." But the point of his comment on Freeland's relative humanity was only to reaffirm his insistence on slavery's intrinsic evil. "The slaveholder, kind or cruel, is a slaveholder still—the every hour violator of the just and inalienable rights of man."[27] On this point, Douglass was in perfect agreement with the original American revolutionaries and with Locke: what confirmed the presence of tyranny was not the exercise nor even the possession of absolute and arbitrary power but only the manifest design to possess the power to brutalize with impunity.[28]

In Douglass's story, the most vivid and telling rendering of slavery's essential violence appears in his description of the "shocking" experience of his near sale upon the death of his first master, Aaron Anthony. The definitive evil and terror of slavery inhered simply in the fact that the slave was permanently liable to be sold.[29] That experience dramatized to Douglass the condition of radical exposure to arbitrary, irresponsible wills, capable at any moment of utterly transforming one's life circumstances, that defined a slave's existence.[30] In the theology to which he declared his early allegiance, all human beings were subject to a divine omnipotency whose design had to be presumed benevolent. Under slavery, that divine order was inverted, so that human beings were subjected to what was, in effect, a human omnipotency whose design could only be presumed malevolent.[31]

Slavery's Primary Effects

Douglass's arguments for the intrinsic evil of slavery were only the beginning of his analysis. As he told a Baltimore audience in 1864, slavery, like liberty, was "logical"; from its defining relation flowed "an unceasing stream of most revolting cruelties."[32] Because human nature is what it is, human beings in general will not freely accept absolute, perpetual subjection to their natural equals. Such subjection, violent in itself, can only be secured by violence both physical and spiritual. Slavery not only brutalized *formally,* by reclassifying some human beings as beneath the protection of laws, it also brutalized *effectively,* by endeavoring to transform them into brutes or domesticated animals, as the necessary means for perpetuating its treatment of them as such. Especially in this second sense, Douglass's insight into slavery's true philosophy accords with his mature analysis of slavery as a complex, logically organized *system* of injustice.[33] As his partially sympathetic discussion of Aaron Anthony illustrates, slavery's effective evils were not, in the end, traceable finally to any gross vices in slaveholders' individual characters. Rather, its brutality was a systemic imperative.[34]

In his carefully chosen illustrations of its brutalizing design at work, Douglass presented slavery as an extreme inversion of normal social and political life. Slavery was the epitome of barbarism, the antithesis of civilization.[35] Civilized society fostered the conditions of human virtue and happiness, whereas slavery systematically destroyed them. To realize its paradoxical claim to human property, slavery required "the complete destruction of all that dignifies and ennobles human character."[36] Asserting absolute power over body and soul, its physical cruelty was instrumental to its assault upon the qualities that elevate humankind above the lower animals. In Douglass's descriptions of the specific modes of this assault, we see more than devices for exciting shame and revulsion in his audiences; we gain a preliminary view of his understanding of the bases of human dignity. His account brings into view slavery's attempts to obliterate the human character of its primary victims as distinctively social, rational, spiritual, and moral beings.

Slavery's systematic assault on the slaves as social beings was a primary theme of Douglass's argument.[37] His own enslavement fresh in his mind, he observed in 1841 that its worst particular effect was its separation of friends and families.[38] In *Bondage and Freedom,* his first statement of slavery's dehumanizing design concerns its attempt to obliterate among slaves any idea of the sacredness of the family. "Slavery has no use for either fathers or families. . . . When they *do* exist, they are . . . antagonistic to that system."[39] Slavery needed to degrade, if not to dissolve, slaves' families for two main reasons: first, to eliminate a structure of authority that might challenge the masters' authority, and second, because the family was, then as now, foremost among civil associations in its power to provide the security, the moral guidance, and the senses of pride, responsibility, self-worth, and belonging vital for the development of self-governing human beings. For Douglass, the destruction of his family ties represented slavery's initiating brutality.

In his story, slavery's assault on his familial identity began even before birth and continued throughout his life. He allowed that he knew many things before he knew he was a slave, but he did not know some very important things that virtually all free children knew. He confessed, for instance, that "like other slaves, I cannot tell how old I am. This destitution was among my earliest troubles."[40] Likewise hidden was his paternity. In *Bondage and Freedom,* he reported with vague assurance that his "father was a white man, or nearly white." In *Life and Times,* he stated flatly, "Of my father I know nothing."[41] Of his mother, he knew but little, for "the practice of separating mothers from their children . . . was a marked feature of the cruelty and barbarity of the slave system."[42] From this enforced ignorance of his mother (who died during his boyhood), he suffered "a life-long, standing grief." His close association in his early years with his grandparents ended abruptly when he was removed from their Tuckahoe cabin at around the age of seven. His brothers and sisters, also present at the Lloyd plantation, were virtual strangers to him.[43] Slave children's estrangement from their families of origin would often be a foretaste of their estrangement as adults from their own children.

The significance of this fundamental fact of slavery was profound and varied. Its degradation of the family represented, first, a direct assault upon the individual slave's primary source of personal identity. Reflecting on his own deprivation in this respect, Douglass lamented that he "was left without an intelligible beginning in the world."[44] But the most telling symbol of the want of an intelligible beginning appears in a deprivation that Douglass himself did not suffer. In Maryland as elsewhere, it was "seldom that a slave . . . was honored with a surname."[45] This was more than a petty expression of disrespect. To refuse to recognize an adult slave by a surname was to refuse to apply to slaves any distinction between formal and informal modes of address. In keeping with slaveholders' professions of (a perpetuated and thus distorted) paternalism, such undifferentiated informality signified a reduction of adults to the status of children. It signified a denial of the slave's nature as a *progressive,* fully human being, capable of growing morally and mentally with age.[46] Douglass's main illustration of this principle involves Colonel Edward Lloyd's whipping of Old Barney, whom Douglass described as "a fine looking old man" who "wore a dignified aspect for a slave." As he recalled it, "the spectacle of an aged man—a husband and a father—humbly kneeling before a worm of the dust" was "one of the most heart-saddening and humiliating scenes I ever witnessed," revealing "slavery in its true color."[47]

In its deeper significance, Douglass's observation about surnames is closely related to his observations elsewhere concerning the distinctively human consciousness of temporal identity. So far as the surname constituted the main emblem of temporal identity, the effacement of slaves' surnames symbolized and reinforced slavery's perpetuity. Slaves were deprived of surnames as they were deprived of a past and a future.[48] To detach them from ancestors and descendants was to deprive them of any heritage to revere, honor, and bequeath. Denied these vital supports for the extension and moral development of an identity over time, the slave was to float adrift as a creature of mere present, momentary impulse, guided only by a master's command.[49] Essential to despotism was to *isolate,* temporally as well as socially.[50] To destroy its victims' personhood, slavery needed to isolate the individual self both from others and from its own identity extended over past and future. As we will see more fully in subsequent chapters, contrary to critics' charges, Douglass espoused no doctrine of antisocial individualism. He conceived of the radically isolated, "unencumbered" individual as the end product of slavery, not the model of freedom.[51]

The elimination of surnames among slaves obviously symbolized the effacement of familial identity as well as temporal identity. Fundamental to slavery's assault on the family was its destruction of marriage among slaves, the dehumanizing effects of which extended far beyond the realm of symbols. Douglass endeavored to make clear the moral perils that this policy held for slave adults as well as children (and not least, as we will see, for slaveholders themselves). His discussions of the subject seem to accord well with the moral sensibilities of mainstream, Victorian era audiences in America and Britain, and in composing them, he could hardly have been unaware of those sensibilities.[52] But to recognize their relation to Victorian mores is not to dismiss their vitality as a moral argument.

By eliminating marriage, Douglass argued, slavery robbed all its victims, men and women, "of every earthly incentive to a holy, chaste life." It reduced sex to a transient sensualism, left "no means for the honorable continuation of the race," and denied parental responsibility to the mothers as well as the fathers of slave children.[53] He drew attention to the particularly demoralizing effects of this policy on the respective sexes. Noting the special vulnerability of slave girls and women, he sounded a theme common among abolitionists: every slaveholder was "a legalised keeper of a brothel on his own plantation." The relegation of effectively fatherless children to the condition of their enslaved mothers "admit[ted] of the greatest license to brutal slaveholders" and their male relations and "[gave] to the pleasure of sin, the additional attraction of profit."[54] He found still larger significance in the demoralizing effects on males. By withholding recognition from slave husbands and legitimacy from slave children, slavery emptied the office of father of its moral responsibility. There, in particular, the "order of civilization [was] reversed."[55] Douglass held the principle of paternal responsibility to be indispensable to civilized society, and he seems to have regarded such responsibility as by nature distinctively fragile. In a later discussion, he suggested that the detachment of sex and procreation from the devotions and disciplines of marriage and childrearing was especially destructive to men, who tended to lapse into barbarism absent the civilizing influence of women and family life.[56]

But despite the depth of slavery's outrages upon manhood and womanhood, its worst crimes were perpetrated upon children. In his public "Letter to

My Old Master, Thomas Auld," written in 1848, Douglass declared, "A slave-holder never appears to me so completely an agent of hell, as when I think of and look upon my dear children. It is then that my feelings rise above my control." He indignantly contrasted his and his wife's authentic parenthood with the fraudulent paternalism of slaveholders. "These dear children are *ours*—not to work up into rice, sugar, and tobacco, but to watch over, regard, and protect, and to rear them up in the paths of wisdom and virtue."[57] In *Bondage and Freedom* and *Life and Times,* young Frederick, relieved by his mother's angry rebuke of the Lloyds' cook, the cruel Aunt Katy, learned that he *belonged* to someone, by nature rather than by arbitrary force: "I was not only a child, but *somebody's* child."[58] Children belong to adults who are not owners but parents, whose titles rest on natural affection and demonstrated care for their youngsters' well-being. In this aspect, slavery's assault on legitimate parenthood was an attempt to re-fashion children's original, formative idea of authority. Its displacement of legitimate parents by slave masters situated enslaved children in an arbitrary moral universe, denying them any knowledge or expectation of legitimate government. As Hugh Auld said in terminating Frederick's reading lessons, a slave had to "know nothing but the will of his master." Slaves were to be confined, from the earliest age, to the awareness that there was no authority save that of the slaveholder, and the essence of that authority was pure, irresponsible willfulness.[59]

Slavery's assault on the human sociality of its victims extended beyond its dismemberment of families, and its effects held structural as well as moral significance. Douglass granted that to a limited degree, slavery benefited from social ties that it could not altogether dissolve among slaves. Reflecting on his emotional state during his own escape, he opined that "thousands would escape from slavery who now remain there, but for the strong cords of affection that bind them to their families, relatives and friends."[60] But slavery's internal imperatives provided still stronger reasons to degrade such affections. Despotism must dissociate its victims both to deform their moral psychology and to render them powerless. It served his masters' vital interest to dissolve Douglass's family, to break up the Sabbath schools that he organized, and, more generally, to impair his capacity to trust and hence to combine with his fellows. Slavery needed to eliminate all mediating powers—there "must be no force between the slave and the slave-holder"—leaving only isolated, naturally weak individuals to confront the overwhelming organized force at the disposal of the masters.[61] For virtually all individuals, real power comes only through association with others. In his later autobiographies, Douglass emphasized the importance of association as a condition of resistance. Upon learning of the existence of abolitionists, he remarked, "I had a deep satisfaction in the thought . . . that *I was not alone* in ab-horring the cruelty and brutality of slavery." He made similarly clear that he could not have achieved his most important personal victories over slavery, his self-defense against Covey and his ultimate escape, without the assistance of fellow slaves and free blacks.[62]

Slavery's assaults upon the distinctive rational, spiritual, and moral qualities of humankind, in Douglass's telling, accorded closely with its assault on human sociality. As Hugh Auld first had taught him, the acquisition of knowledge and especially knowledge of the Bible rendered one unfit for slavery. By reason or rational faith, one came to know the higher law that confirmed slavery's injustice. Mindful that nature or the Creator designed human beings for purposes nobler than enslavement, the thoughtful slave became increasingly miserable and potentially rebellious. To secure itself comfortably, slavery required the degradation of slaves' minds and souls.[63] And the prohibition of slaves' literacy was the most obvious means to this end. Still further, Douglass observed that in important respects, slaves were deprived even of the power of speech—which, in conjunction with reason, was the most humanizing of mental powers. By various tactics of despotic surveillance, slaveholders aimed to engender a pervasive atmosphere of mistrust among slaves and thereby to prevent the exchanging of enlightening information and the formation of resistance schemes.[64]

In a more indirect mode, slavery's assault on rationality converged with its design to degrade slaves' moral character. Slavery ruled foremost by a constant excitement of the passion of fear. The field slave's daily motivation was "nothing, save the dread and terror of the slave-driver's lash," and for those slaves less regularly exposed to physical violence, there was the ever-present fear of being sold.[65] In slave holidays, the rule of fear was momentarily replaced by the no less debasing rule of the lower appetites. Those holidays reinforced the masters' despotic power, both by providing a "safety valve" for the dissipation of slaves' anger and also by deepening the slaves' brutalization. On such occasions, all self-directed work and rational enjoyment were discouraged. Slaves were encouraged to plunge "into exhausting depths of drunkenness and dissipation," degrading at once their desire and their capacity for freedom.[66]

Here appears one meaning of Douglass's observation in *Bondage and Freedom* that "the morality of *free* society can have no application to *slave* society."[67]

In context, that observation referred primarily to the perspective of the slave, the object of aggression in a state of war, for whom normally criminal acts such as stealing became blameless and even virtuous. But the observation held broader significance, too, as a corollary of Douglass's conception of slavery as the negation of civilization. To transform human beings into brutes also meant to transform human goods and excellences into their opposites. In the morally inverted world of slavery, feminine beauty became a terrible misfortune, as in the revolting story of Douglass's Aunt Esther, which we will consider in the next chapter; aging effected a loss of dignity and respect, as it had for Old Barney; sobriety and self-motivated industry were actively discouraged, as in the slave holidays; sloth and idleness brought reward (to the masters) whereas industry brought misery and degradation;[68] and education and enlightenment provoked external punishment even as they deepened slaves' internal misery.[69]

A Slaveholder's Challenge

In the foregoing short summary, American slavery in Douglass's account appears as a pure, unmixed despotism, enacting systematically dehumanizing policies in accordance with its defining principle. At this point, however, it is necessary to revisit the argument for the masters. Douglass's presentation of slavery as summarized thus far invited a basic objection, the full response to which shows his argument to be more powerful—more empirically scrupulous and analytically refined—than it has hitherto appeared.

Douglass was confronted with the general objection by a slaveholding correspondent from Mississippi, one W. G. Kendall, whose letter he published in the *North Star* in 1850. After reading that journal for a year (having subscribed to assess the argument of an antislavery acquaintance), Kendall wrote to protest Douglass's "*indiscriminate abuse*" of slaveholders." He complained that the former slave's account of slavery was "so highly colored, as not to be recognizable to the slave-holders." But Kendall offered no dogmatic defense of American slavery. He agreed with a southern acquaintance that slavery was "a great curse" to whites and claimed that he would prefer to see it replaced immediately by a system of "voluntary slavery" akin to indentured servitude. He conceded, too, that the treatment of slaves needed improvement, but he maintained that their condition could be properly ameliorated without abolition. He commended to Douglass the same acquaintance's further opinion that even in its existing practice, slavery was a "great blessing to the black race." Kendall thought slavery's cruelties were "unusual"; its systemic imperatives dictated the normally humane treatment of slaves. In his opinion, the primary error Douglass and other abolitionists made was to demonize slavery as a pure despotism. The effect of their inflammatory polemicism was to heighten the slaveholders' sense of insecurity and therefore to aggravate their cruelty toward the slaves: "You are doing harm to the black race," he warned, "and more firmly rivetting [*sic*] their chains." The abolitionists themselves were responsible for much of the misery they so violently deplored.[70]

The power of Kendall's challenge derived mostly from its relative moderation. The main purpose of his letter was to insist on slavery's complexity. Writing as an abstractly antislavery slaveholder, less proslavery than antiabolitionist, Kendall held that the truth about slavery was captured neither by abolitionists nor by "positive-good" extremists. The fundamental truth, as he saw it, was that slavery in its actual practice was neither purely despotic nor purely paternalist; it was a complex, composite regime incorporating both elements.

Nonetheless, Kendall saw abolitionism as the greater present danger, and his antiabolitionist argument was closely akin to arguments made by more ardent defenders of slavery. Even representatives of the "positive-good" position made superficially plausible claims to moderation. Acknowledging certain of slavery's evils, some of its most uncompromising advocates rested their case on the claim that slavery was only a normally imperfect human institution, no more marked by cruelties and abuses than other systems of dependency. Did incidents of spousal and child abuse, protested Governor Hammond, stamp marriage and the family as intrinsically despotic institutions?[71] Abolitionism, in this view, amounted to a destructively utopian demand for earthly perfection, whereas more sober and reasonable observers could simply assimilate slavery to other domestic relations, as a mixture of harshness and providential care. Slaveholders' power could then be judged legitimate so far as their severities were minimized and directed to the end of slaves' improvement. In fact, some proslavery advocates took the notion of slaves' civilization so far as to defend slavery as the surest, safest means of preparing for the slaves' emancipation, at some relatively distant future point.[72] The main obstacle to that happy outcome, as they saw it, was abolitionist agitation—"philanthropy in design, and misanthropy in deed."[73] This is what Kendall meant in charging that Douglass's "whole *policy*" was misconceived. In recent experience, slavery's partisans asked, thinking particularly of Haiti and the British West Indies, had immediate emancipation really elevated the condition of the former slaves? And was the strident advocacy of immediate abolition, with its unrelenting vituperation about despotism, at all likely to move slaveholders to be kinder or more receptive to the idea of emancipation? If the answers to these questions were negative, as Kendall and the others maintained, then did it not follow that a more moderate antislavery appeal, beginning with an acknowledgment of slavery's actual complexity, would better serve the near- and long-term interests of slaves and the nation as a whole?

Viewed in hindsight, Kendall's challenge gains credibility from historical scholarship in our own day, which can hardly be charged with any proslavery bias. Summarizing the results of his careful overview of that scholarship, Peter Kolchin concludes that slavery in the United States never really approached "the theoretical order the laws defined and critics decried." Contrary to Douglass's claims, U.S. slavery was relatively mild in comparison with other modes of slavery in the New World.[74] This observation remains far from the romanticized accounts of slavery's apologists; Kolchin notes that a "thin line . . . always separated paternalism from thuggery." Yet for Kolchin as for the scholars he summarizes, the key point is that slavery in practice was a mixed regime. Conceiving of the slave as both person and property, slaveholders strove "to protect their property interests and to create an order that conformed to their notions of morality and benevolence." As the nineteenth century progressed, "slavery became more restrictive at the same time that it became more protective."[75]

In response to Kendall, however, Douglass conceded not one inch. "Your fancied kindness, to what does it amount," he demanded angrily, "when set against the loss of liberty, the loss of progress . . . and the overwhelming degradation to which the slave is subjected. . . ? Perish all shows of kindness, when they are thought to conceal or to palliate the damning character of slavery."[76] Douglass seemed to claim a valid license for the selectiveness of which Kendall accused him. As slavery's cruelties far outweighed its kindnesses and in a polemical atmosphere in which any attribution of kindness to slavery would be misrepresented as a palliation, he was justified in polemically presenting only one side—the main side—of slavery. But his direct response to Kendall did not dispose of troubling questions concerning the fairness of his account of slavery.

Responding to a hyperbolic attack published in the *Liberator,* Douglass wrote to Garrison in 1860: "There is never any good reason for misrepresenting even an enemy."[77] But his own fidelity to this rule is questionable, particularly in light of an example in his autobiographies. In the *Narrative* and again in his 1848 "Letter to My Old Master," Douglass falsely alleged that Thomas Auld had left an aged, enfeebled Betsey Bailey, Douglass's grandmother, alone to die in the woods.[78] This charge was meant to negate the apologists' references to slaveholders' providential care for slaves who were too young, old, or feeble to work as evidence of the humanity of their system.[79] After learning of Auld's actual, far more humane treatment of Betsey, Douglass apologized in a second public letter—but subsequently reprinted the false charge in *Bondage and Freedom* and again in *Life and Times,* quoting at length and without further comment the precise language that he employed in the *Narrative.*[80] This example is representative of the manner in which Douglass treated Auld in the two antebellum autobiographies, summarizing him as a man "entirely destitute of every element of character capable of inspiring respect."[81] Various commentators, especially biographers Dickson Preston and William McFeely, have argued persuasively that Auld, Auld's first father-in-law, Aaron Anthony, and their families recognized young Frederick's exceptional natural gifts and showed uncommon solicitude for his well-being. They removed him from the Lloyd plantation to the far more humane setting of Hugh and Sophia Auld's Baltimore household; kept him there at a crucial moment in the settlement of Aaron Anthony's estate; protected the possibility of his ultimate freedom, when Thomas Auld refused to sell him to a still harsher enslavement in the Deep South and instead returned him to Baltimore, after his unsuccessful attempt to escape from the William Freeland farm; and even saved his life at least once, when Auld protected him against reprisals threatened by neighboring slaveholders, after the same unsuccessful escape attempt.[82]

That Douglass was or at some point became aware of these considerations is suggested by his unspecified reference in *Life and Times* to "all [Auld's] good deeds."[83] In his 1848 "Letter to My Old Master," he disclosed the likely reason for his reluctance to acknowledge them earlier. He intended "to *make use*" of Auld, he said, "as a weapon with which to assail the system of slavery . . . as a means of bringing this guilty nation, with yourself, to repentance."[84] Douglass would make of Auld a mere instrument in the service of a just cause, as Auld had used him for an unjust cause. The judgment of Preston and others seems well founded—that is, that Douglass's ruthless treatment of Auld, deliberately distorting his character and reducing a complex human being to a mere symbol, was a deplorable personal injustice.[85] Douglass seems to have subjected Sophia Auld, the woman he described as "almost a mother to me" in *Bondage and Freedom,* to a comparable injustice during his earlier speaking tour in the British Isles.[86] His treatment of the Aulds lends force to the question his slaveholding interlocutor Kendall had raised in regard to the reliability of his treatment of slaveholders and slavery in general.

Upon fuller consideration, however, Douglass's discussion of the significance of instances of humanity in slavery appears more careful and balanced and leaves his argument for slavery's essential despotism in a more defensible position than his immediate response to Kendall might suggest. Contrary to Kendall's charge, Douglass did not indiscriminately condemn slaveholders or slavery. Recalling a kindness done to him by Lucretia Auld (Thomas Auld's first wife, the daughter of Aaron Anthony), he was moved to a broader confession: "I love to recall any instances of kindness, any sunbeams of humane treatment, which found way to my soul through the iron grating of my house of bondage. Such beams seem all the brighter from the general darkness into which they penetrate, and the impression they make is vividly distinct and beautiful."[87] In fact, he frequently noticed instances of humanity in his experience with slavery,[88] and despite his claim of license to dismiss them, they were integral to his analysis. In his overall representation of it, slavery in practice was indeed a mixture of humanity with brutality or of paternalism with despotism. For Douglass, the decisive point was not that slavery always appeared as unmixed despotism but rather that slavery as a mixed regime was inherently nonviable. Slaveholders over time would necessarily prove unable to maintain "the double relation of master and father" in regard to their slaves.[89]

Douglass's more systematic response to the argument for slaveholders' paternal beneficence can be summarized as follows. First, although he noted numerous acts of humanity and some humane characters in his experience with slavery, he maintained that those did not represent the true nature of the regime. They proceeded generally from causes accidental to slavery rather than from systemic imperatives. Second, to the extent that occasional acts of beneficence did reflect a policy calculated to perpetuate the system of slavery, the policy would necessarily fail to establish the paternal character of slaveholders' rule. Slaveholders as a class could never be characterized by humanity because human beings as a natural rule are incapable of exercising irresponsible power benignly. Aaron Anthony "was not by nature worse than other men"; had he been brought up amid "the just restraints of free society," he might well have been a normally humane, morally respectable man. But since he had grown accustomed instead to the exercise of irresponsible power, whatever personal virtue he possessed and whatever interest in paternalist slavery he may have held were too weak to restrain him from committing "outrages, deep, dark, and nameless."[90]

The third point in Douglass's counterargument marks its culmination. Even if slaveholders' systemic policy were to maintain a mode of paternalism in their relations with slaves and even if they were for a time successful in conforming their behavior to such a policy, paternalism would inevitably fail to achieve slavery's defining objects. Sooner or later, slaveholders would feel compelled to abandon it. Douglass's discussion of his response to Freeland's relative justice and kindness is illuminating.

> Notwithstanding [my] improved condition . . . I was still restless and discontented. . . . When entombed at Covey's, shrouded in darkness and physical wretchedness, temporal well-being was the grand *desideratum;* but, temporal wants supplied, the spirit puts in its claims. Beat and cuff your slave, keep him hungry and spiritless, and he will follow the chain of his master like a dog; but, feed and clothe him well—work him moderately . . . and dreams of freedom intrude. Give him a *bad* master, and he aspires to a *good* master; give him a good master, and he wishes to become his *own* master. Such is human nature. You may hurl a man so low, beneath the level of his kind, that he loses all just ideas of his natural position; but elevate him a little, and the clear conception of rights rises to life and power, and leads him onward.[91]

A measure of humanity may or may not have been part of the slaveholders' general policy; Douglass left his discussion of this ambiguous. The point is that such a policy would have held negligible value. It would have intensified, not pacified, the slaves' resistance. Expressions of humanity *toward* slaves could only be received as reminders of the humanity *of* slaves. Hence, slavery's harshness could not be explained as a reaction to abolitionist incitements; its harshness inhered in the nature of the relation. Even if slavery were by design a mixture of despotic and paternal principles, the mixture was inherently unstable. A house divided against itself cannot stand; slavery, like Lincoln's Union, had to be all one thing or all the other.[92] Douglass's account of slavery was teleological: what slavery essentially *was* was revealed more truly by what it *needed to be*—by the systemic imperatives implicit in its defining relation—than by its self-contradictory practices. Irrespective of slaveholders' conscious design, the fact that no policy of paternal humanity could secure it meant that slavery could not be, in its stable essence, a mixed regime. In the final analysis, slavery had to obey the imperatives of despotism, pure and simple, or it would cease to be slavery.

The Formation of a Master Class

As Douglass explained in his comment on Freeland, the formation of true slaves, in fact as well as in form, required their systematic brutalization. Yet the brutalization of slaves was a necessary but not sufficient condition for slavery's lasting viability. To secure and perfect the exercise of irresponsible power, slavery required comprehensive control over the character formation and the internal and external relations of all within its orbit. Its deformative powers had to be applied not only to slaves but also to the members of the slaveholding class and their various agents and relations. In sum, slavery needed to pervade the entire moral culture of slave societies and even that of their neighbors.

Just as slavery had to deploy an array of denaturing measures to make some human beings into slaves, so it had to exercise corresponding powers to make other human beings into masters. "Nature," Douglass maintained, "fits nobody for such an office."[93] As we will see more fully in the next chapter, he did not deny that slavery had a natural foundation. Yet he insisted that in a complex, problematic way, human beings are by nature moral beings with genuine moral needs. We encounter great difficulty living with sustained violations of our moral sense, and the exercise of arbitrary power over a fellow person is plainly contrary to the moral sense. Deep down in the souls of slaveholders, too, resided an abolition conscience.[94] To protect their huge material and psychological investments in slavery, therefore, slaveholders were compelled to invest in it morally. Just as slavery needed to extinguish the natural love for liberty in the slave, so it needed somehow to evade, suppress, or corrupt the moral sense among the master class.

Slaveholders' most obvious evasive measure involved a practice of delegation.[95] To pacify their consciences, they removed themselves and to some degree averted their gaze from the execution, by others in their employ, of slavery's more revolting cruelties. Douglass presented the class of plantation overseers in general as a pitiably depraved lot, to whom fell the offices of administering and reciprocally absorbing much of slavery's primary brutality. His descriptions highlight the dehumanizing effect their occupation had on them. Aaron Anthony's overseer, a man named Plummer, appears as "a miserable drunkard . . . and a savage monster," a man "little better than a human brute"; Edward Lloyd's overseer, the mildly eponymous Sevier, is described as a "brute" who wore an expression of "unusual savageness"; the fiendish, calmly murderous Orson Gore is depicted as a menace to be shunned as a "rattlesnake"; and Edward Covey, a slave owner whom Douglass believed Thomas Auld employed as a slave breaker, is called a "snake," a "brute," a "heartless monster," and a "cowardly tyrant."[96] Douglass described the "debased and villainous" class of slave traders to similar effect. Imprisoned after his first escape attempt failed, he found himself set upon by a "swarm of imps, in human shape," circling about "as buzzards to eat carrion." Such creatures were "very offensive to the genteel southern christian public," whose members were apparently unstained, in their own minds, by the actions of their slave-trading agents.[97]

At best, however, the policy of evasion by delegation could be of only limited usefulness. Slaveholders could never entirely delegate to others or remove from their own view slavery's particular cruelties. In Douglass's observation, the masters themselves, when sufficiently provoked, committed even greater savageries than did their overseers. It was irresistibly natural for them to do so, as their power was far more irresponsible than that of their overseers.[98] In the end, they had no choice but to justify, to themselves and others, the inhumanities that they and their system commanded.

The imperative of self-justification required that slaveholders relocate slaves outside the class of rights-bearing beings. They could not do so by criminalizing them; the Lockean justification of slavery had no application to American slavery.[99] The only alternative was to ascribe to them natural inferiority. Douglass's moral psychology implies that the development of antiblack racism as a full-blown ideology resulted from the confrontation of the practice of slavery with the universalist natural rights principles to which America had dedicated itself.[100] But beyond establishing the premise of natural racial inequality, slaveholders still had to convince themselves that their treatment of slaves was consistent with the obligations of civilized beings to inferior classes. As they brutalized their slaves in fact, they needed to believe that they were doing them no essential violence, even that they were civilizing them as far as the slaves' supposedly lower nature permitted.

Contemplating these notions of natural racial inequality and of slavery's mutual beneficence, Douglass was impressed by the spectacular proportions of slaveholders' mendacity. He assailed slavery as "the most stupendous of all lies"; its perpetrators were "as great liars, as they [were] great tyrants."[101] Slaveholders first needed to be great tyrants over their own faculties, great liars to themselves as well as to others. To be a fully formed master, one with a good conscience, required a most impressive capacity for self-delusion. But as the human need, will, and capacity to think well of oneself are often overridingly powerful, the moral faculties frequently submit to such tyranny. "Conscience cannot stand much violence," he observed; its natural neediness controls its natural power.[102] The greater our injustices, the stronger is our inclination to declare our innocence. The abolition conscience that resided even in the souls of hardened slaveholders was often discernible only "deep down," and to the extent that it made its voice heard, it had the perverse effect of moving slavery's defenders to invest ever-greater energy in its palliation.

The slaveholders' task of self-justification and self-delusion was so naturally difficult and so vital to their perceived interest that it had to be made the object of a comprehensive societal effort. "Natural and harmonious relations easily repose in their own rectitude," Douglass observed shortly after the outbreak of the Civil War, whereas those "false and unnatural are conscious of their own weakness, and must seek strength from without." Hence, slavery, "like all other gross and powerful forms of wrong . . . has the ability and tendency to beget a character in the whole network of society surrounding it, favorable to its continuance."[103] To justify dependably their peculiar institution, slaveholders needed to establish slavery as a comprehensive cultural and political order, assuming unchallenged control over their society's predominant means of moral education.

Above all, that meant that the slave power needed to control the churches. Douglass was emphatic on this point in the 1840s and early 1850s, during and beyond his Garrisonian, moral-suasionist period. He argued that without the support of the churches, the "guardians of the public morality," slavery could have survived scarcely an hour.[104] The corruption of religion was predictable enough, in Douglass's reasoning, simply because people generally believe their Lord is like themselves. The churches stood "first among the influences which oppress us and prevent our improvement,"[105] especially in the South, where the "sham religion" propagated by the slaveholders "everywhere prevailed."[106] It seemed to have functioned quite effectively in enhancing the good conscience and the community standing of men such as Thomas Auld and Edward Covey. Slaveholders thought of their propagation of religion among slaves as attesting their paternal benevolence. As a boy, Douglass briefly had thought that religion among the masters would effect their moral improvement; he took great interest in Auld's religious conversion, hoping that the latter's newfound piety would move him ultimately to liberate his slaves.[107] He soon found that the slaveholders' religion had just the opposite effect.

Douglass contended that because their version of Christianity was an exercise in proslavery self-justification, slaveholders' professions of religion actually intensified their cruelty. "Of all slaveholders with whom I have ever met," he reported, "religious slaveholders are the worst."[108] On this point, his account of Edward Covey's behavior in the days leading to their Monday battle is especially remarkable. The preceding Friday and Saturday, Covey appeared as a merciless tyrant in his violent abuse of the sixteen-year-old Frederick. He then appeared as a seemingly transformed man—pious, civil, even sympathetic to Frederick—on Sunday as he prepared to go to church. On Monday, he reassumed his character as a violent despot. So extreme was Covey's oscillation from cruelty to piety and back that those two qualities in his soul must have been somehow symbiotic rather than mutually antagonistic. Thomas Auld, too, was "a much worse man after his conversion than before."[109] Douglass professed to leave it to others to explain these facts, but the explanation seems clear in the light of his own understanding of human nature and of the nature of slavery. The sanctification of slavery by the corruption of religion united the slaveholders' interest with their sense of duty. It removed a powerful source of moral restraint on— even as it added zeal to—their pursuit of their despotic interests.[110]

A similar design appeared in the slave power's attempt to color Americans' understanding of the other higher law prominent in public life, the law of nature. As we will see more extensively in the following chapter, this attempt involved, at a deep level, a corruption of natural science to buttress a denial of the full humanity of black Africans and their American descendants. And as we saw briefly in an earlier discussion, it involved, at a more directly moral and political level, an assault on the classic American statement of the natural law, the Declaration of Independence. Slavery had "seduced and bribed American orators," Douglass charged at an 1858 commemoration of the emancipation of the West Indies, "into the most shameless contraction, mutilation and falsification of the Revolutionary principles of American Freedom and Independence."[111] Proslavery theorists and their accommodators followed a variety of paths to that end. Some, such as Henry Hughes, held that the Declaration's principle of human equality in natural rights was both true and inclusive. Slavery, he argued, was consistent with the notion that slaves possessed inalienable rights; it was simply a form of virtual representation in which slaves' rights, like those of women and children, were protected by representatives they had no power to choose.[112] Others, such as Supreme Court Chief Justice Roger Taney, suggested that the Declaration's principle was true but not inclusive. In the infamous *Dred Scott* case, as Douglass observed, Taney propounded "the heartless dogma, that the rights declared in that instrument did not apply to any but white men"—"that 'all men' only means some men." Finally, still others, such as John C. Calhoun and his acolytes, rejected the Declaration's principle outright, contending that what it had called the self-evident truth of natural human freedom and equality was no more than a "self-evident lie."[113]

Because the moral sense receives instruction from lower, human laws as well as from higher, divine and natural laws, slavery further needed to control political governments as well as churches and schools. By the mid-nineteenth century, Douglass argued, it had accomplished this objective with astounding success. The slaveholding interest held "a complete monopoly of all that pertains to the government" of all the southern states, he observed in 1851 in the seventh of his slavery lectures in Rochester, despite the fact that those actually owning slaves composed a relatively small minority of the population in those states.[114] To the 1855 Convention of Colored Citizens of the State of New York, he contended that slavery's enormous concentration of wealth in human property, with the social and political privileges that attended it, "has made the South a unit on the Slavery question." Slavery functioned as the soul of the South, the unchallengeable source of "its laws, its morals, its social code, its interpretation of the Bible, its definition of the Declaration of Independence, its understanding of the Constitution of the United States."[115]

The task of forming slave masters suited to their peculiar office was still more complicated, however, than controlling local culture. To justify their institution and practices within their own states and region, slaveholders needed to control the external opinions to which residents of their states were exposed. Human beings are naturally social as well as moral beings; much as we cannot long endure condemnation by our own consciences, we cannot endure condemnation by others. "It is an attribute of man's nature to wish to stand approved in the eyes of his fellows," Douglass affirmed in June 1861, discussing the proper objectives of the Civil War: "It is impossible to overestimate the self-executing power of this unwritten, but all-pervading law." Slaveholders were quite sensitive to this natural concern. Their institution could not have endured, Douglass believed, had it been substantially harmful to slaveholders' reputations.[116]

Here, too, a policy of evasion served the slaveholders' interests. It was no accident that slavery appeared in its most openly cruel forms on plantations rather than in cities and in the Deep South rather than in the upper South. "Public opinion is, indeed, an unfailing restraint upon the cruelty and barbarity of masters, overseers, and slave-drivers," Douglass noted, "whenever and wherever it can reach them; but there are certain secluded and out-of-the-way places . . . where slavery . . . *can,* and *does,* develop all its malign and shocking characteristics." Slavery "dislikes a dense population, in which there is a majority of non-slaveholders." Such was the advantage, from the slaveholder's perspective, of the "secluded, dark" location of the Lloyd plantation, whose "whole public is made up of . . . three classes—SLAVEHOLDERS, SLAVES AND OVERSEERS."[117] Yet so long as they remained politically united with nonslaveholding states, slaveholders could enjoy physical or geographic seclusion only to a limited degree. To compensate, they sought moral and political seclusion. Unable to escape nonslaveholders' scrutiny altogether, the slave power sought at least to silence the abolitionists among them. Thriving only in darkness, slavery could not "bear the light of free discussion." Its "first purpose," Douglass maintained, was "the suppression of all antislavery discussion."[118] Along with the fear of slave insurrections, a concern to protect their moral sense against external assaults lay beneath slaveholders' several attacks on abolitionist publications and mailings in the South and on the right to petition the U.S. Congress.

Slavery's policy of suppressing dissent pointed to still more ambitious designs. For that policy to succeed beyond the South, the slave power needed to amass a constitutional majority powerful enough to disregard constitutional restrictions. The effective corollary of slaveholders' desire for seclusion was an inclination to expand slavery's domain dramatically. Seen in this light, slaveholders' endeavor to suppress antislavery agitation represented an element of a grander strategy whose ultimate end was to incorporate their erstwhile adversaries into one great, united slaveholding republic. In Douglass's account, the slave power's desire for self-preservation necessarily committed it to a policy of imperial expansion. Again pertinent is Lincoln's "house divided" principle: because it could not for long *be* a divided, mixed regime, it could not *live within* one. It could not secure itself in perpetuity as a mixture of paternal and despotic elements, and it could not avoid some measure of that destabilizing mixture as long as it was joined in constitutional union with states dedicated to freedom. Liberty and slavery were fundamentally antagonistic to one another,[119] and the most skillfully contrived system of constitutional federalism admitted no possibility of locally quarantining the two. The slave power's own internal logic impelled it to seek national, not only regional, sovereignty and even to expand its domain beyond the existing national boundaries. Douglass summarized this design in his 1855 convention speech:

The objects of the slaveholding party . . . are five in number. The first is the suppression of all anti-slavery discussion. The second, the extension of Slavery over all the Territories of the United States. . . . The third is, the nationalization of Slavery in every State of the Union. . . . The fourth is, the expatriation of every free citizen of color in the United States. . . . The fifth and grand object is, the absorption by the United States, of Mexico, southern California, Cuba, the Sandwich Islands, all the islands of the Caribbean Sea, and Nicaragua, bringing them into the Confederacy of our Union, and placing their black population, fourteen millions in number, under the ban of the slave power.[120]

Douglass's warnings about slavery's expansionism were grounded in fact no less than in conceptual understanding. By the 1850s, he maintained, slavery had actually achieved much of the expansionist, imperial design he ascribed to it. For over three-quarters of U.S. history since 1789, southerners had held the presidency. Up to the mid-1850s, it had controlled both major political parties.[121] Major national policies had repeatedly favored the slaveholding interest. "The purchase of Louisiana . . . the millions expended upon Florida, the annexation of Texas, the war with Mexico, were all measures commenced and carried forward to their consummation by that *mere fraction* of the American people, the Southern slaveholders."[122] With Congress's bipartisan enactment of the 1850 Fugitive Slave Law, the slave power secured the complicity of professedly free states and of the Union as a whole in the sordid business of slave hunting. To Douglass, the passage of that law meant that slavery had become a national institution, "to be maintained by all the powers of the United States Government."[123] With the *Dred Scott* ruling in 1857, the long, steady advance of the slave power seemed near its culmination. By conferring constitutional protection on the expansion of slavery into all U.S. territories, the high court majority had pledged the federal government "to support, defend and propagate the crying curse of human bondage."[124]

In sum, Douglass's original, intuitive opposition to slavery, first given direction by Hugh Auld's prohibition of his literacy, had moved him to inquire after its nature and justification. The fruit of that inquiry was the insight that slavery, contrary to its supporters' claims, was the very model of despotism. It was an antigovernment, a system of brutality impelled by its nature to do violence to the dignifying human qualities of all those within its domain and to the cause of civil government everywhere in its vicinity. But by learning what to oppose,

Douglass learned also what to affirm. His reflections on slavery's essential wrongness moved him to develop his ideas concerning the rights and duties of human nature. Moreover, by reflecting on slavery's wrongness, Douglass came to understand its weakness as well. His affirmative understanding of natural human rights and natural moral law—and his consequent prediction of slavery's impending demise—are the subjects of the next chapter.

The Moral Government of the Universe:
Natural Rights, Natural Law, and the
Natural Demise of Slavery

Thrice is he arm'd that hath his quarrel just.
  Shakespeare, The Second Part of King Henry the Sixth, *III.2.*

BY EVERY APPEARANCE, the 1850s marked the bleakest of decades for the anti-slavery cause in America. The decade began with the enactment of the most proslavery federal law in U.S. history, the new Fugitive Slave Law in 1850. Egregious in itself, that law heralded a series of federal actions that, to Douglass and other abolitionists, confirmed beyond doubt the slave power's national hegemony. Soon thereafter came the Kansas-Nebraska Act of 1854, which removed a federal prohibition on slavery's expansion into large portions of the Louisiana Territory. Next, in early 1857, came the most proslavery federal court ruling in U.S. history, *Dred Scott v. Sandford,* in which the Supreme Court conferred upon slaveholders a constitutional right to hold slaves in any territorial property of the United States. The culmination came in abolitionist militant John Brown's failed raid upon the federal arsenal at Harpers Ferry, Virginia, in late 1859. As many abolitionists (including Douglass) agreed, Brown's plan to seize federal arms to initiate a spreading slave rebellion was hopelessly ill conceived. But his attempt was indicative of the abolitionists' desperation, and despite their enthusiastic commentary on the meaning of his example, his failure and prompt execution must have intensified their growing fears that the abolitionist movement would end in failure.

In many cases, African Americans' responses to these developments were marked by alienation and despair. Thousands of nonslaves from northern states, placed by the Fugitive Slave Law in grave danger of kidnapping and enslavement, emigrated to Canada. Their hopes for liberation and elevation in the

United States exhausted, black opinion leaders conceived still more radical emigrationist sentiments and programs, and more than a few also left the country during this period.[1] "Reflecting on our condition," counseled the eminent black nationalist Martin Delany (initially Douglass's coeditor at the *North Star*) in 1852, blacks had to choose "emigration . . . in preference to any other policy that we may adopt."[2] Douglass, too, was affected by kindred sentiments. "The future of the anti-slavery cause is shrouded in doubt and gloom," he editorialized in August 1860. "The labors of a quarter of a century . . . seem to have reached a point of weary hopelessness."[3] His pessimism was still more marked a few months later as he rethought his long-standing antiemigration position. "The present condition of both countries, Hayti and the United States, is favorable to the revival of the feeling for emigration," he wrote in January 1861; in the United States, "it seems plain that the inducements offered to the colored man to remain here are few, feeble and very uncertain."[4]

As he reviewed the events of this grim decade, however, Douglass never succumbed to the pessimism that afflicted some of his peers. Throughout the trials of the antebellum decade, as in fact throughout his entire career, what typified his thought was not alienation or despair but instead a remarkably confident hopefulness.[5] After each seeming victory for the slave power, he reiterated his convictions that slavery's crimes could not long go unpunished and that slavery itself could not long survive. In his second lecture on American slavery, delivered shortly after the enactment of the Fugitive Slave Law, he warned the American people "that prouder and stronger governments than this have been shattered by the bolts of a just God."[6] Commenting on the passage of the Kansas-Nebraska Act, he decried the North's "contemptible pusillanimity" for collaborating in it, and yet he saw a silver lining in the repeal of the Missouri Compromise. "Woe! woe! woe to slavery!" he declared. "Her mightiest shield is broken."[7] His most heroic expression of optimism came in response to that "judicial incarnation of wolfishness," the *Dred Scott* ruling: "My hopes were never brighter than now. . . . I hold it to be morally certain that . . . slavery is doomed to cease out of this otherwise goodly land, and liberty is destined to become the settled law of this Republic."[8] He reaffirmed that sentiment shortly after Brown's arrest.[9] Even his warming toward emigration in early 1861 was no more than contingent, tactical, and momentary.

The present analysis of Douglass's invincible hopefulness begins with two basic premises. The first is that his optimism was real, reflecting his genuine conviction as to the future of slavery and freedom in America.[10] "Truth is mighty, and will prevail . . . is a *maxim*," he editorialized in 1855, "which we do not regard as a mere rhetorical flourish."[11] As David W. Blight has rightly observed, "Douglass believed what he preached."[12]

The second basic premise is that Douglass's conviction was grounded in rational argument. His core conviction about the universe's moral design does seem to have originated in a faith in divine Providence,[13] and as Blight has carefully documented, his arguments throughout the 1850s were suffused with biblical language, contributing significantly to various traditions in American political theology.[14] Nonetheless, Douglass labored mightily to affirm his faith as a rational faith, grounded in evidence that was visible to natural reason. In the basis as well as the substance of his moral principles, he followed the Declaration of Independence, which pointedly located the primary political truths not in positive revelation but instead in "the Laws of *Nature* and of *Nature's* God." In his second lecture on slavery in 1850, he invoked "the spirit of patriotism, in the name of the living God, *natural and revealed*."[15] Against the *Dred Scott* ruling, he declared that the "voices of nature, of conscience, of reason, and of revelation" alike proclaim the human right to liberty. Further, Douglass clarified his view of the order of priority between reason and positive revelation in early 1851, in his seventh lecture on slavery. He maintained that the moral teaching of the Bible was antislavery but then declared, "*Should* doctors of divinity ever convince me that the Bible sanctions American slavery . . . *then* will I give the Bible to the flames, and no more worship God in the name of Christ."[16]

The substance of Douglass's rational faith was contained in the proposition that the law of natural human rights was true in principle and sanctioned as law. Slavery and racial supremacy were naturally wrong, and in large measure *because* they were wrong, they were doomed to fail. What follows is an account of the reasoning whereby he supported these convictions.

The Truth of Natural Human Rights

Douglass united with proponents of the main alternative schools of antislavery opinion, from Garrisonian radicals to free-soil moderates, in affirming that the true principles of justice were summarized in "that glorious document which can never be referred to too often," the Declaration of Independence. "I love the Declaration of Independence," he told a Glasgow, Scotland, audience in 1846. "I believe it contains a true doctrine—that 'all men are born [*sic*] equal.'" The Declaration epitomized "the eternal laws of the moral universe," he later reiterated, as it represented "the basis of all social and political right." Its principles "would release every slave in the world." When they had at last begun to do so by early 1862, he told a Philadelphia audience that the terrible convulsion of civil war signified a reminder "that nations, not less than individuals, are subjects of the moral government of the universe."[17]

With the Garrisonians, Douglass followed the Declaration in affirming that the true principles of justice were self-evident to those of clear mind,[18] even that they were innately inscribed in the human heart.[19] From their accessibility to common sense, he inferred that present distortions and denunciations of those principles stemmed from causes deeper than mere errors in reasoning, and to remedy them required more than rational instruction. This consideration moved him at times to express indignant impatience with arguments on the moral fundamentals, as in his famous Fourth of July oration of 1852: "Would you have me argue that man is entitled to liberty? that he is the rightful owner of his own body? . . . Must I argue that a system thus marked with blood, and stained with pollution, is *wrong*? No! I will not."[20] To respond to slaveholders' claims by a patiently reasoned argument seemed to Douglass not only needless but, in important respects, likely counterproductive as well. To argue respectfully with the slave power was to risk conferring unmerited dignity on its claims, raising to the level of rational contest what were in truth merely apologetic effluvia of low passions and thus tacitly characterizing the conflict as one in which reasonable persons could disagree. But despite these strong misgivings and despite his belief in the self-evidence of the Declaration's truths, he did argue for the natural rights principles that it contained.

Douglass argued for those principles because he felt compelled to do so. The sophistic cleverness of slavery's defenders supplied the general impetus, but in particular what provoked him to develop and refine his natural rights arguments was the advent, in the antebellum decades, of a school of thought claiming the authority of natural science for propositions that directly challenged the Declaration's fundamental principles. Ethnology was the eighteenth- and nineteenth-century science respecting the division of humankind into races. In the 1840s arose the so-called American School of ethnology, originated by Samuel Morton and developed and popularized by George Glidden and Josiah Nott, whose book, *Types of Mankind* (1854), provided the compendious statement of this peculiar variety of science. The American School was distinguished fundamentally by its affirmation of the theory of polygenesis, or of the separate origins of various races of humankind. Not all who endorsed the polygenesis theory were proslavery apologists, but the theory's usefulness to their cause was obvious, as they linked the premise of diverse origins to claims of the permanent differences and natural hierarchy among the various races. Nott in particular actively promoted the theory for use by slavery's defenders. Douglass had little doubt as to the main cause of the theory's growing influence: "Ninety-nine out of every hundred of the advocates of a diverse origin of the human family in this country, are among those who hold it to be the privilege of the *Anglo-Saxon* to enslave and oppress the African."[21]

The proslavery ethnology elicited Douglass's most extended reflection on the foundation of human equality, "The Claims of the Negro Ethnologically Considered," an address delivered by invitation in 1854 to an academic audience at Ohio's Western Reserve College. Outlining the essentials of a thorough refutation of the racial supremacist ethnology, Douglass defended three fundamental "claims of the Negro" with respect to ethnological science: (1) that Africans and their descendants are full members of the human species; (2) that human beings most likely constitute a unitary racial "family," descended from a common origin; and (3) that even if human racial groups are descended from plural origins, they remain members of a single moral species and bearers of equal natural rights and duties.

The first claim, that of African humanity, was the one least in need of probative argument. Douglass defended it in response to the crudest of proslavery inferences from American School ethnology, which he found exemplified in an editorial from the *Richmond Examiner*. The editorial reassured its readers of slavery's justice, as Douglass paraphrased its claim, "BECAUSE (the Negro) IS NOT A MAN! In response, he could only "assert," not "argue," because he held it to be a simple fact that any minimally sensible human being recognizes fellow human beings. We "instinctively distinguish between men and brutes," and if need be, we can substantiate this natural recognition by a readily observable catalog of commonly shared and distinctively human qualities.[22]

Douglass was aware, however, that the proslavery ethnology did not rely on quite so crude an assertion of African subhumanity. Nott and Glidden explicitly declined to degrade any type of humankind to the level of brute creation, although their conception of gradations in racial capacities was to like effect, assimilating lower races of human beings to higher animals. Douglass dismissed as "scientific moonshine" their racial perversion of the great-chain-of-being argument. But he took more seriously their defense of polygenesis based on civilizational differences among the races. Scattered throughout their work were assertions of sub-Saharan Africans' inferiority in civilizational achievements and, by inference, in the natural capacity for improvement. In context, their observation of ancient Africans' enslavement appears to have been intended to support a characterization of the African race as naturally fit for slavery.[23] In Douglass's summation, a purported "inability to rise from degradation to civilization" held central importance among the "usual allegations against the oppressed."[24]

Against such allegations, Douglass could choose from among several possible responses. Most radically, he could have denied that the human mind is capable of a nonsubjective distinction between higher and lower levels of civilization or that the capacity for higher civilization represents a proper, qualifying criterion for a racial group's full membership in the human species. Less radically, he could have affirmed that criterion and then affirmed that Africans as a racial group had demonstrated their capacity for higher civilization by their actual achievement of it or conceded that Africans had not yet achieved a high level of civilization, due not to any natural incapacity but only to environmental causes.

For Douglass, to adopt either of the first two of these counterarguments was unthinkable. He was, as Wilson Jeremiah Moses has observed, a "civilizationist,"[25] holding a sharp distinction between civilization and barbarism as an essential element of his thinking. His counterargument was constructed upon the less radical propositions. He tentatively endorsed the third alternative, concerning Africans' historical achievement of high civilization, and he confidently affirmed the fourth, explaining any civilizational failings by Africans by reference to environmental causes. So he devoted much of his address to establishing a racial family relation between sub-Saharan Africans and the ancient Egyptians, the greatness of whose civilization was "not denied by anyone."[26] Whereas proslavery ethnologists labored "to separate the Negro race from every intelligent nation and tribe in Africa," Douglass drew upon various authorities to support the contrary conclusion "that the people of Africa are, probably, one people." This proposition of African racial unity meant only that African peoples represented various levels of civilizational achievement, "from the once highly civilized Egyptian to the barbarians on the banks of the Niger," and that they closely resembled the rest of humankind in that variety of achievement. African racial unity thus suggested a common origin not only of Africans but also of all human beings.[27]

Douglass acknowledged that in his arguments for monogenesis, *the wish* [might be] *father to the thought.*[28] Upon later reflection, he conceded more definitely this failing in his argument for African unity.[29] In the 1854 speech, he also expressed dissatisfaction with the strategy of leaving present-day blacks' claim of equal capacity for civilization to depend mainly on the achievements of an ancient people. A sounder approach, he argued, was to emphasize that the latter-day children of Africa demonstrated distinctively human adaptive and progressive qualities amid radically unfriendly circumstances; they clung tenaciously to the aspiration for higher civilization as they endured the "ten thousand horrors of slavery." That being so, it was reasonable to explain differentials in civilizational attainment between blacks and whites by reference to environmental causes rather than by imputed differentials in natural capacity. To the extent that slaveholders and their apologists ascribed to nature or to God the effects of their own oppressive institutions, "the very crimes of slavery become slavery's best defense."[30]

Douglass employed these arguments to show the strong likelihood of monogenesis, but his conclusion of human moral equality did not depend on the premise of a common biological origin. "A diverse origin does not disprove a common nature, nor does it disprove a united destiny," he reasoned. "The essential characteristics of humanity are everywhere the same." And prominent among the "essential characteristics" that Douglass identified are the moral qualities of human nature, as he made clear in establishing the "claim of the Negro" to full humanity. Irrespective of their origin or their variations in pigmentation and other superficial physical qualities, human beings constitute a unitary species by virtue of their likeness *in the morally decisive respects.*[31]

> Man is distinguished from all other animals, by the possession of certain definite faculties and powers, as well as by physical organization and proportions. He is the only two-handed animal on the earth—the only one that laughs, and nearly the only one that weeps. . . . His speech, his reason, his power to acquire and to retain knowledge . . . his hopes, his fears, his aspirations, his prophecies . . . his good and his bad, his innocence and his guilt, his joys and his sorrows proclaim [the Negro's] manhood in speech that all mankind practically and readily understand.[32]

Moreover, in this common moral nature, "human rights stand upon a common basis."[33]

In "Claims of the Negro," Douglass set forth the fundamentals of the argument concerning the basis of human rights that he employed consistently throughout his career, in his advocacy both of abolition and, later, of equal suffrage for formerly enslaved men and for all women. The fundamental claim of all those causes was the proposition "which entirely took possession of me, even in childhood," as he reiterated in 1864, and ultimately "filled the land with hostile armies": "Every man is the *original, natural, rightful,* and *absolute* owner of his own body . . . and can only part from *his* self ownership, by the commission of crime."[34] In keeping with the Lockean tradition of natural rights reasoning, Douglass held self-ownership to be at once the primary property right and the primary liberty right. But this fundamental claim of a right to oneself in turn required a foundation in our common nature. "I know I have a right to myself," Douglass told an English audience in 1846, "because God has given me powers and faculties."[35] For men and for women alike, he editorialized in 1870, our "natural powers are the foundation of our natural rights."[36]

This "faculties and powers" argument is more complex than it appears in Douglass's summary statements of it. Described in the language of later academic philosophy, his argument concerning the foundation of rights comprises deontological and consequentialist modes of moral reasoning: rights are properties of our intrinsic nature, and rights are the necessary means for our fulfillment of our indefeasible natural desires. This primary complexity is manifest in Douglass's uses of the terms *faculties* and *powers,* which are closely related but not interchangeable. Our faculties comprise various powers to engage in certain distinctively human activities. The more comprehensive term *powers* encompasses our faculties along with certain motive forces within us—the passions, desires, or sentiments that move us to exercise our faculties. Foremost among the faculties that qualify us as bearers of natural rights is rationality. It was telling that slavery found it imperative "to annihilate [slaves'] power of reason." Reiterating African Americans' humanity as the ground of their claim to equal citizenship, Douglass located the "foundation of all governments and all codes of laws . . . in the fact that man is a rational creature."[37] Correspondingly, conceiving of the powers that qualify us for rights as our natural, indefeasible desires or "wants," he affirmed that the desire for liberty "is the deepest and strongest of all the powers of the human soul."[38] Let us examine further both these elements of Douglass's rights argument.

In analyzing more particularly the dignifying, rights-conferring significance of the rational faculty, Douglass placed special emphasis on its character as the source of moral *responsibility.* Slavery's effort to destroy its victims' powers of reasoning signified its design "to blunt, deaden, and destroy the central principle of human responsibility."[39] Again presenting a core Lockean argument, Douglass held that the *right* of self-ownership depends on the *capacity* for self-ownership. A responsible, accountable being is an agent, a being capable of owning actions.[40] To be capable of owning actions first requires a personal identity extended through time, made possible by the mental powers of memory and foresight. Hence, the degradation of slaves' sense of temporal identity was also integral to slavery's design. In his repeated references to human beings as creatures of past and future as well as of the present,[41] Douglass referred to a quality essential to the rights-bearing nature. Second, to be an agent or an owner of actions requires the capacity for moral deliberation and choice. By virtue of the latter capacity, people are capable of governing their own lower passions, of freely and knowingly submitting to law, and of respecting the rights of other persons. With this capacity in mind, Douglass identified the "true basis of republican government" as "*moral intelligence* and the ability to discern right from wrong, good from evil, and the power to choose between them."[42]

A concern to highlight slaves' moral intelligence as a confirmation of their resilient, rights-bearing humanity is evident in a pair of refinements Douglass made in the retelling of his autobiography. In both the *Narrative* and *Bondage and Freedom,* he recalled his and his relatives' resort to "begging and stealing" to relieve the physical hunger that they suffered in the household of Thomas Auld. In the *Narrative,* he added only a brief comment: "The one [was] considered as legitimate as the other." But in *Bondage and Freedom,* he emphasized the moral deliberation that governed his action. His practice of taking food from his owner resulted from no "unreasoning instinct" but, to the contrary, from "a clear apprehension of the claims of morality. I weighed and considered the matter closely" and concluded "that the slave is fully justified in helping himself to the *gold and silver*" of a slaveholder because "the morality of *free* society can have no application to *slave* society."[43] To put the point more precisely, slaveholders' claims to property were nullified by the fact that those claims were based on their expropriation of others.

A similar refinement appears in his revised account of the battle with Edward Covey. In the *Narrative,* Douglass reported that he had resolved to resist only "at this moment"—the moment of Covey's attack. But in *Bondage and Freedom,* he claimed that he had come "to a firm resolve" the day before the battle, "during that Sunday's reflection." He added the further detail that he had conducted himself throughout the battle with impressive self-control, suggesting the strict governance of his passions according to rules yielded by his moral deliberations. Acknowledging that "the fighting madness had come upon me,"

Douglass did not acknowledge that such madness overcame him even temporarily. It "had come upon" him as Covey had, and he had successfully resisted and controlled both. In the battle against Covey, he had maintained a strictly defensive posture, "preventing him from injuring me, rather than trying to injure him." He had even responded politely to his assailant's question as to whether he meant to resist. In the subtle pedagogy of this account of the battle, Douglass conveyed the superiority of his moral rationality in two senses: reporting that he had governed the "fighting madness" as a combatant, he also made it serve his purposes as an author, as he disclosed its threatening, monitory presence. Slavery's friends and its adversaries could learn from the Covey episode that African Americans harbored "as much human nature" as any others in both reason and willful spirit, in the impressive scope and the reachable limits of their powers of rational self-control.[44]

But it was not enough for Douglass to argue for equal faculties. By the assertion that slaves were content in their condition, slavery's defenders implied that their fitness for slavery was based not only on incapacity but also on the absence of a *desire* for freedom. Douglass agreed that a claim of natural rights would be practically meaningless absent a natural desire to enforce it. But the claim that slaves lacked such a desire was to him indicative of the slaveholders' singular deludedness. The desire for liberty, he declared in his second lecture on slavery, "is the deepest and strongest of all the powers of the human soul."[45] He consistently affirmed the power of this desire, in his autobiographies as well as in his speeches and editorials. In *Bondage and Freedom,* he recalled that as a seven- or eight-year-old, he was "*even then,* most strongly impressed with the idea of being a freeman some day." That desire was "an inborn dream of my human nature." He showed its presence in slaves as a class in his discussions of their "sorrow songs" and of the custom of slave holidays, which served slaveholders as a necessary safety valve against the slaves' potentially explosive desire for liberty. Without those holidays, he believed, "the south would blaze with insurrections." In fact, albeit usually in indirect ways, slaves were "constantly in a state of rebellion, against the will and wishes of their masters."[46] Contrary to the slaveholders' claims, abolitionist agitation could not be blamed for slave resistance and rebellions; they resulted necessarily from slavery's violence to the liberty-loving human nature of its victims.

In Douglass's argument, both the desire and the capacity for liberty are essential elements of human beings' broader, progressive nature. To an English audience in 1846, he declared that "the improvement and expansion of our faculties" is "the great cause and mainspring of happiness in the human family." Likewise, in *Bondage and Freedom,* reflecting on his miserable futurelessness as a slave, Douglass observed that the soul's "life and happiness is unceasing progress."[47] The secure possession of natural rights is indispensable for the progressive employment of our natural faculties and powers in the pursuit of happiness, civilization, and virtue. At some level, Douglass insisted, everyone recognizes this truth. "There is not a man beneath the canopy of heaven that does not know that slavery is wrong *for him."* But as it is natural for us to claim our liberty, with our other fundamental rights, so it is naturally obligatory to respect that claim's simple corollary— "Grant it to your neighbors."[48]

The Right and Duty of Resistance

Slavery, in Douglass's reasoning, was essentially violent in its negation of the progressive, rights-bearing human nature of its victims. It constituted an ongoing state of war in the most fundamental way, and so it activated for slaves and their sympathizers a natural right of resistance. Here again, Douglass was in close accord with the liberal natural-law tradition and with the Declaration in particular. Drawing upon the great English jurist William Blackstone, he maintained that the "edicts of tyrants and oppressors are opposed to all law, and are no more to be obeyed as *law* than the murderous commands of the captain of a pirate ship."[49] A case in point was the Fugitive Slave Law, against which Douglass contended, "When government fails to protect the just rights of any individual man, either he or his friends may be held . . . innocent, in exercising any right for his preservation which society may exercise for its preservation."[50] Commenting on a Richmond newspaper account of the wounding of a rebellious slave, he echoed Thomas Jefferson as he remarked that the American revolutionary fathers "had not a thousandth part of the provocation to rebel, to kill and destroy their oppressors, that this poor Negro had."[51] Douglass reaffirmed the right of resistance with intensifying militancy throughout the 1850s, as in his 1857 declaration that the "slave's right to revolt is perfect."[52]

In his consideration of resistance in the light of natural moral law, Douglass went beyond the elementary claim that it was a natural right. He conceived of human rights as more than mere freedoms of choice or mere private properties, to exercise or decline to exercise according to one's personal will. The bearer of natural rights held compelling natural duties to practice the virtues necessary to secure and sustain those rights. Reflecting on his own career in an

1891 interview, he claimed, "Duty has been the moving power that has influenced all my actions during all the years of my life."[53] Generalizing on this principle as a young man, he held it "the duty of even the humblest to summon from the depths of his nature the most exalted sentiments of truth and justice, and to send them forth to battle."[54] Of greatest urgency was the duty to resist injustice, as the Declaration forcefully illustrated: when a people detects "a Design to reduce them under absolute Despotism, it is their right, it is their duty, to throw off such Government." Thus, Douglass meant to broaden and to deepen his fellow citizens' commitment to the general principle that the Declaration had already firmly established among them: "'RESISTANCE TO TYRANTS IS OBEDIENCE TO GOD.'" In the context of nineteenth-century America, resistance to slavery was a natural duty no less than a natural right.[55]

Often, Douglass presented this duty in extremely harsh terms. In each of his autobiographies, he recalled that, as a young man, he attempted to summon his fellow slaves' courage to escape by telling them that their very manhood was at stake: "If . . . they now failed to make the attempt, they would, in effect, brand themselves with cowardice, and might well . . . acknowledge themselves as fit only to be slaves."[56] Speaking in 1857 in commemoration of West Indies emancipation, he observed that the "general sentiment of mankind is, that a man who will not fight for himself, when he has the means of doing so, is not worth being fought for by others, and this sentiment is just."[57] In his final major speech, rising in outrage against a wave of racist lynchings, he again declared, "A people too spiritless to defend themselves are not worth defending." By an unforgiving law of nature, he warned a national convention of black men in 1883, "races that fail" to elevate and empower themselves are condemned to "die politically and socially, and are only fit to die."[58]

Coming from a man of Douglass's experience and sympathies, these statements may seem especially shocking. Did he really mean to say that by their passive vices, *some people deserve enslavement?* Taken literally, his argument would resemble the slaveholders' argument, inferring slaves' fitness for slavery from their seeming contentment, and as some commentators have noted, it would resemble, too, the reduction of right to power that is characteristic of Darwinian understandings of justice.[59] But there is good reason not to interpret his statements literally. His comments as to their intended rhetorical function suggest that they contain a substantial measure of provocative exaggeration. He contrived his youthful statements to his fellow slaves "to appeal to [their] pride" more than to their reason, whereas his remarks in the "West India Emancipation" speech were explicitly hortative: by his scolding reference to the "humiliating . . . indifference, the moral death which reigns over many of our people," he meant "to raise our aims and activities."[60] As he explained in a powerful editorial advocating fugitive slave resistance, he seemed to endorse the argument that submission justified subjection not because he believed it was a sound argument but rather because, despite its defects, the argument was commonly accepted in the public mind "and nothing short of resistance on the part of colored men, can wipe it out."[61] The hortative character of Douglass's condemnations of inactivity appears likewise in the fact that he affirmed its harsh consequences only hypothetically. He never named and surely expected never to discover an actual individual or class of human beings whose inaction justified their subjugation by others.

In his settled convictions, Douglass was no social Darwinian, nor did he affirm even abstractly any part of the proslavery argument. Yet his harsh admonitions, however provocatively exaggerated, were not purely rhetorical. He meant them also to convey a fundamental moral truth, for which he was primarily indebted to the Scottish thinker George Combe's widely read book, *The Constitution of Man* (1834). Although he read Combe's book critically and selectively, he evidently drew upon it for crucial elements of his understanding of the law of nature. The most important of these elements concerns the effectiveness of the natural moral law. In his frequent references to the "laws of eternal justice" as "self-executing" and as "imperative and inexorable,"[62] Douglass echoed Combe, who maintained that the laws of nature, physical and moral alike, are "universal, unbending, and invariable in their operation." This did not mean that those laws are perfectly immanent, so that all events in the physical and moral worlds are in perfect conformity with them. Rather, it meant that the natural laws are naturally *sanctioned:* although intelligent beings have the power to disregard or transgress them, obedience to each law is "attended with its own reward, and disobedience with its own punishment."[63] The interval between seed and harvest in the moral world may be unpredictably lengthy—"ages may intervene," Douglass allowed, years after the John Brown episode—but in the end, the just and the unjust will be seen as they are and will reap as they sow.[64]

For Combe, the sanctions attending violations of the laws invariably involve the punishment of the guilty, in "just proportion" to the offense. With respect to physical and moral laws alike, the attendant sanctions are such as to render great transgressions self-defeating if not literally self-destructive. A person who neglected the duty to respect the physical law of gravitation would likely fall to his death. To like effect, according to Combe, do the natural laws operate in the moral realm: "If the world be constituted on the principles of the supremacy of the moral sentiments and intellect, the method of one nation seeking riches and power, by conquering, devastating, or obstructing the prosperity of other states, had to be *essentially futile*," ultimately bringing about "the impoverishment and mortification of the people who pursue it."[65] Adapting Combe's principles to his own paramount concern, Douglass reasoned that the natural sanctions against so gross a transgression as slavery had to reach the utmost severity. His insistent predictions throughout the 1850s of slavery's impending demise were more than inspirational rhetoric in especially trying times. They proceeded from his understanding of the natural moral law, according to which slavery had to prove systemically self-destructive.

Douglass made the natural sanctions against slavery a prominent theme of his speeches and writings. Some of those sanctions were intrinsic to the lives of slaveholders, indicative of their terrible misconception of the nature of human happiness. In diagnosing slaveholders' natural unhappiness, Douglass applied an argument that was common among abolitionists. "There is more truth in the saying, that slavery is a greater evil to the master than to the slave, than many, who utter it, suppose," he observed. "The self-executing laws of eternal justice follow close on the heels of the evil-doer here, as well as elsewhere."[66] The slaveholder's claim to happiness reflected in part the notion that an essential element of human happiness was ease or luxury. But as a natural state of war, slavery could provide no real ease for the masters. Slavery signified war on several fronts, not the least of which was within the psyches of the slaveholders themselves. A primary case in point was Aaron Anthony. Douglass's old master was adequately endowed with a natural moral sense, capable at times of humanity and kindness; he "was not by nature worse than other men." Yet he was a "victim of the slave system," suffering a terrible moral disfigurement due to his participation in it. "Most evidently," Douglass observed, "he was a wretched man, at war with his own soul, and with all the world around him." In his almost sympathetic telling, within Anthony raged an irrepressible conflict between the moral sense's natural promptings and the systemic imperatives of slaveholding. By the end of his days, tormented to the point of insanity, Anthony served for Douglass as a symbol of slavery's deformative powers.[67]

Douglass developed this theme further in his discussion of the hidden vices and unhappiness afflicting the magnificent Lloyd family. By his description of the "pride and pomp" characteristic of slaveholding Maryland's first family, he represented slavery's deeper problem of moral excess. If the likes of Anthony and the Aulds had been insufficiently bred for the slaveholder's office, the Lloyds had been bred only too well for it. Surveying the scarcely imaginable luxury yielded by their immense wealth, Douglass provided a penetrating insight: "Here, appetite, not food, is the great *desideratum.*" To feast at the Lloyds' table, literally or metaphorically, required and engendered an enormous appetite. In starkly contrasting ways, slavery rendered both main classes of its victims creatures of appetite. It sharpened through deprivation the slaves' desires for physical necessities, even as it sharpened through superabundance the masters' appetites for dominion and luxury. In Douglass's estimation, the slaveholders' portion in this transaction brought them no real advantage. Thus, he diagnosed the perpetual, restless dissatisfaction inherent in the Lloyds' luxuriousness:

> The poor slave, on his hard, pine plank, but scantily covered with his thin blanket, sleeps more soundly than the feverish voluptuary who reclines upon his feather bed and downy pillow. Food, to the indolent lounger, is poison, not sustenance. Lurking beneath all their dishes, are invisible spirits of evil, ready to feed the self-deluded gormandizers with aches, pains, fierce temper, uncontrolled passions, dyspepsia, rheumatism, lumbago and gout; and of these the Lloyds got their full share. To the pampered love of ease, there is no resting place. What is pleasant to-day, is repulsive tomorrow; what is soft now, is hard at another time; what is sweet in the morning, is bitter in the evening. Neither to the wicked, nor to the idler, is there any solid peace: "*Troubled, like the restless sea.*"[68]

In a broad sense, these examples served Douglass as apt metaphors for the degrading, self-consuming quality of the slaveholding life. Slavery systematically retarded the civilizational development of its domain, as it degraded the slaveholders' faculty of practical reason. Members of the master class suffered an ultimately fatal inability to judge and pursue their true interest or happiness. In the members of that class, the "passions run wild. Like the fires of the prairie, once lighted, they are at the mercy of every wind, and must burn, till they have consumed all that is combustible within their remorseless grasp."[69] Over time, slaveholders would find themselves ever more tightly ensnared in an institution to which their faithful devotion could bring them only ruin, not happiness. In a general way, Douglass's predictions concerning slavery recall the classic assessments of tyranny and despotism by Aristotle and Montesquieu: each is, at bottom, a system of unrestrained, basely self-gratifying violence, and each, for that very reason, tends toward ultimate self-destruction.[70]

One must take care not to overstate the power of slavery's intrinsic sanctions in Douglass's account. The Lloyds prospered for generations, and most slaveholders, including most of those Douglass described, did not manifest the internal turmoil that he saw in Anthony and to a lesser extent in the Aulds. Whatever the masters' misgivings about slavery, no such sentiments sufficed to disable them in the performance of their peculiar office. Again consistent with Combe, Douglass held that the decisive natural sanctions against slavery's criminalities would come from external, not internal, agencies. For Combe, transgressors of the moral law of nature suffer especially the pain of becoming "objects of dislike and malevolence to other beings . . . who inflict on them the evils dictated by their own provoked propensities."[71] Douglass predicted slavery's self-destruction as a natural event in a moral universe governed by an analogue to Newtonian law: its innumerable injurious actions would naturally beget opposing reactions by many of those whom it offended. As we will see later in this chapter, Douglass saw powerful natural forces at the root of those reactions, yet he made clear that the decisive sanctions against slavery were the effects of human agency. With this consideration, we return to the duty of resistance borne by the oppressed.

In Douglass's understanding, the law of nature is stern and unforgiving to all its subjects, victims no less than transgressors. It assigns natural penalties both to criminal actions and to the *inaction* of those who fail to act virtuously in keeping with their natural duties. Subjection to injustice does not negate but rather intensifies the moral duties of those who are thus subjected. It is telling that he conceived of our rights-conferring qualities as *powers:* "Wisdom, virtue, and all great moral qualities command respect only as powers."[72] Human rights and dignity are grounded less in the dormant possession than in the efficacious exercise of our distinctive faculties and powers. Exhorting African Americans to virtuous activity in 1853, Douglass wrote: "Men are not valued in this country, or in any country, for what they *are;* they are valued for what they can *do. . . .* We must show that we can *do* as well as *be.*"[73] In context, he referred to a duty of free people to learn productive trades, but he applied the same principle to the still more compelling duty of all people to resist oppression where they are able to do so. A few years earlier, he had editorialized that "it is a doctrine held by many good men . . . that every oppressed people will gain their rights just as soon as they prove themselves worthy of them. . . . One of the first things necessary to prove the colored man worthy of equal freedom, is an earnest and persevering effort on his part to gain it."[74] Nature's sanctions against slavery would appear in their full force only if slaves and free African Americans performed their natural-law duties of effectual resistance and opposition.

Douglass affirmed at once the presumptive validity of all human beings' title to natural rights and the moral imperative for tyranny's victims actively to validate their title to those rights. This twofold affirmation marks a salutary tension but not a contradiction in his thinking. Defending emancipation in the West Indies and the United States against charges of its actual and potential ill effects, he insisted that liberty was not an experiment but rather the presumptive property of all human beings, unearned by any specific achievement.[75] Nonetheless, that principle was subject to a qualification of which it was important to remind the victims of injustice. The presumption of natural rights was rebuttable in particular cases, primarily by criminality but also, in principle, by extreme submissiveness. In the long run, natural rights could not exist as a common human possession absent their active, effortful affirmation by those denied their exercise. At some distant but conceivable point, wisely unspecified by Douglass, *unclaimed* rights would become *unpossessed* rights. Chronic failure to act in self-defense—failure so chronic as to stamp one's nature with it—would indeed effectively nullify those rights. Such an effect could not result from mere weakness.[76] The validation of rights does not require instant victory in the struggle to effectuate them, but it does require struggle. In Douglass's argument, the presumption favoring human rights signified a presumption that the bearers of rights would *act*, in keeping with their nature and as prudence dictates, to affirm their rights.

The Virtue of Resistance

Douglass went beyond exhorting his oppressed brethren to do their duty and defend their rights; he provided a thorough, complex instruction in the virtue of resistance. The focal point of that instruction is his now-legendary battle with the archtyrant Edward Covey. In his summary of its effect on him in *Bondage and Freedom,* he considered that battle the turning point in his life as a slave. "I was a changed being after that fight. I was *nothing* before; I WAS A MAN NOW. . . . I felt as I had never felt before. . . . I had reached the point, at which I was *not afraid to die.* This spirit made me a freeman in *fact,* while I remained a slave in *form.*"[77] In Douglass's account of the battle's significance appear all the essential elements of virtuous resistance as he conceived of it. Before considering further its particular elements, however, we must notice Douglass's concern to show this virtue's democratic availability.

Mindful that resistance to tyranny could be a general human duty only if it were a general human possibility, Douglass made clear that his signature act was not to be viewed as peculiar to himself and inimitable. He took care in his later autobiographies to present his inspiring act as only one, and not necessarily the greatest, among several similar acts committed by fellow slaves. He added to his later accounts the notable detail that he was nearly equaled in the display of personal courage by a "powerful woman"—Covey's slave Caroline, who directly refused the master's order to assist him and thereby, in the face of dire consequences, joined Frederick in "open rebellion." Later, recounting their failed attempt to escape from William Freeland's plantation, he described the heroic courage of his friend Henry Harris, who physically resisted, even at gunpoint, his captors' attempts to tie his hands. He made a point of comparing his friend's courage favorably to his own: "Henry put me to shame; he fought, and fought bravely."[78] Earlier, he prefigured his resistance by his laudatory reports of resistance to whippings by Colonel Lloyd's Nelly and by the unnamed slave of Rigby Hopkins.[79] Later, urging black men to enlist in the Union army in 1863, he promised similar subjective benefits to all who answered their nation's call: "You will stand more erect, walk more assured, feel more at ease, and be less liable to insult than you ever were before."[80]

In fact, Douglass thought of the virtue of resistance as a representative human virtue in a very profound sense. In an 1865 speech dedicating the Douglass Institute (established to promote intellectual advancement in Baltimore's African American community), he expanded upon the central theme of his autobiographies: "Man is distinguished from all other animals, but in nothing . . . more than in this, namely, *resistance,* active and constant resistance, to the forces of physical nature."[81] Douglass viewed the act that humanized him as representative of the action of humankind at large in its age-old struggle to liberate and elevate itself. More generally, he saw a kinship between resistance to particular human tyranny and resistance to the human species's natural subjection to impersonal necessity. Human history was comprehensible, in his view, as a grand slave revolt. He conceived of humankind as the distinctively resistant, revolutionary, and progressive species. Speaking soon after the publication of *Bondage and Freedom,* Douglass informed a Syracuse, New York, audience of the readiest category of punishable slave offenses: "Insolence, at the South, means presence of anything like manhood and consciousness of one's humanity." When he declared, "I was born insolent, and have always been insolent,"[82] he claimed for himself what he believed the species as a whole could claim for itself.

To Douglass, the humanizing power of virtuous resistance appeared most clearly in its most heroic element, the achievement of mastery over the most powerful fear. Summoning resistance to the Fugitive Slave Law, he exclaimed, "Oh! that we had a little more of the manly indifference to death, which characterized the Heroes of the American Revolution."[83] The right to life was "the most precious" and "most sacred of all rights," but it did not entail a categorical duty of personal self-preservation. Conceiving of human beings as persons extending though time, Douglass understood self-preservation as a natural right and duty to endeavor, even at risk to one's present safety, to create a stable *condition* of security for oneself. Likewise, he held that the objects of preserving oneself transcend mere security. "Life . . . is but a means to an end," he maintained, "and must be held in reason to be not superior to the purposes for which it was designed by the All-Wise Creator."[84] In its highest justification, the human right to life is a right to preserve a *properly human* life. Accordingly, in Douglass's understanding of the natural law, the natural right to life entails a natural duty, in certain circumstances, to risk one's mere life to secure a good life—a free, dignified, and civilized life, in keeping with human beings' distinctive natural gifts.

In Douglass's personal story, the act of resisting Covey was the crucial turning point in large part because in that act, he mastered his natural fear of death. By braving death, a mere man became a man in full, a virtuous man.[85] But what does this fearlessness more precisely signify, and how did the young slave achieve it? Douglass claimed that the answers were mysterious to him. But his subtle account suggests more definite explanations than he endorsed explicitly.

Douglass began his remarkable account of the climactic episode by declaring its purpose to be general and philosophical—to "help the reader to a better understanding of human nature, when subjected to the terrible extremities of slavery."[86] The trigger of his psychological transformation was subjection to slavery, not in itself but in its extremity. Coming close to the heart of the matter, scholars have suggested that the specific extremity of the young slave's experience was the fear of death or the spirit-deadening pain of the whippings.[87] But in the immediate aftermath of his worst beating, while suffering his greatest physical pain, young Frederick did not yet conclude that his only chance lay in resistance. To the contrary, he was virtually speechless and, though incapable of work, utterly compliant in spirit. And when, shortly thereafter, the pain abated and his "daring" returned, that daring manifested itself not in a resolve to resist forcefully but rather in the decision to flee and appeal to Thomas Auld. Nor did his fear of dying alone in the woods—of ending his short life as he had lived it, serving no higher purpose than to supply carrion for buzzards—mark his deepest extremity, for in the latter part of his journey, he had again "begun to hope." It was only upon reaching Auld that he came to the ultimate depth of his misery. "I had jumped from a sinking ship into the sea; I had fled from the tiger to something worse." Auld's (apparent) dismissal of Frederick's complaint delivered a "complete knock-down to all my hopes"; it had the effect of "fairly annihilating me."[88]

Here is the center of Douglass's transforming experience in the events leading to his momentous resistance. From this experience, he learned that the greatest misery for human beings, that which is most to be feared, is not imminent death or even violent death but instead hopeless subjection to radical arbitrariness.[89] What Douglass described as his *annihilation,* his experience of a living death worse than the prospect of natural death, occurred at the moment of sheer hopelessness when all his appeals had proved unavailing. Auld had "*prejudged*" the case against his young slave, presuming his guilt; he had refused to protect him even "as *his property.*"[90] These facts confirmed to Frederick, beyond any flicker of lingering hope, his subjection to an absolute, arbitrary power. The full meaning of that subjection appeared to him on his return to Covey, when, chased into the woods once more, he found himself alone in a terrible state of nature, "shut in with nature and nature's God, and absent from all human contrivances." He thought of praying for deliverance but could not do so. "All my outward relations," earthly or divine, "were against me," he wrote. In the extremity of slavery, his human nature had been not simply effaced but instead rendered intolerable, to the point that reason had seemed to counsel its own annihilation. "That day, in the woods, I would have exchanged my manhood for the brutehood of an ox."[91] Though only for a moment, slavery had consummated its despotic power over him: radically detached, isolated, exposed, powerless, hopeless, he longed only to become the beast to which slavery meant to reduce him.

Douglass claimed not to know "whence came the daring spirit" that animated his resistance nearly two days later. He employed a curious, almost passive construction in describing his state of mind as the battle with Covey began ("[the] fighting madness had come upon me"), as though his fighting spirit represented a mysterious infusion by some suprapersonal agency. As previously noted, he did not present himself as having lost his power of self-government during the fight: he maintained a strictly defensive posture throughout and even a lightly comedic decorum. By tracing his fighting spirit to an external, suprapersonal source, he conveyed a more specific message. The virtue of resistance did not represent a virtue peculiar to himself or to an elite few; again, Douglass's story was not meant to display the singularly "heroic achievements of a man."[92] Nor did it represent a national virtue, as most African American slaves could hardly claim any privileged acculturation akin to that of the American revolutionaries, bred in the proud tradition of English liberty. What they could claim, however, was their indestructible human nature, which Douglass had promised at the beginning of his account to help the reader better understand. The mysterious source of his fighting spirit seems to be human nature itself—the nature of the singularly resistant species—aroused in the young slave by his experience of extreme degradation in subjection to despotic power.

The human nature that the resistant Frederick exemplified represents a dialectical interplay between the distinctive and the common, the elevating sense of dignity and the leveling fear of death, among the human passions. At the moment he undertook it, his act of resistance was aversive at root, born of fear of the worst rather than of hope for the best. But his fear contained a self-overcoming quality: he had experienced the worst of the human condition and was no longer captive to the lesser fears that degrade and enslave human beings. In its affirmative aspect, his courageous resistance involved a conscious assertion of human elevation—of the superiority of a properly human condition to an utterly dehumanized, brutish condition. This is the meaning of his claim "I was *nothing* before; I WAS A MAN NOW." As submission to slavery meant moral death, so an overriding devotion to mere life meant self-denaturing to the point of self-nullification. What Douglass referred to as a natural human "want" or passion for liberty appears here as an assertive spirit of honor distinctive to humankind, scornful of identification with mere animality and supportive of venturesome resistance.[93]

Virtuous resistance as Douglass understood it required more than the death-defying spirit that he and other slaves displayed. As with virtue in general, virtuous resistance needed to be *effective*. The summation of the Covey episode bluntly states the point. Douglass's resistance transformed him, resurrected and dignified him, in the discovery that he possessed the *force* to effect significant changes in his condition. The condition of enslavement would be deepened and perpetuated by a debilitating fear for one's biological life and by an incapacity for taking effective, salutary action. "A man, without force, is without the essential dignity of humanity."[94] What did it mean for this virtue to be forceful or effective?

As he matured as a thinker and strategist in the 1840s and 1850s, Douglass became notably more militant in his reflections on the efficacy of virtuous resistance. He grew increasingly militant as he became convinced of the fecklessness of purely pacifist modes of resistance. As Leslie Friedman Goldstein has demonstrated, Douglass never followed William Lloyd Garrison in the latter's profession of the purely pacifist doctrine of Non-Resistance.[95] Nonetheless, during most of his Garrisonian period in the 1840s, Douglass did reject the use of violence as a means of moral reform, believing, with Garrison, that "moral suasion" would move slaveholders to emancipate their slaves. As late as his 1847 meeting with John Brown, Douglass maintained that "all that the American people needed . . . was light."[96] He rebuked the militant minister Henry Highland Garnet at the 1843 National Negro Convention, in response to Garnet's call for violent slave resistance. Within a few years, however, Douglass reversed his position. Though he was loath to credit his rival, the great and intensifying power of proslavery sentiment in the South, including an unyielding determination to maintain control of the federal government, convinced him that Garnet had been right after all.[97]

Douglass's renewed antislavery militancy reflected, at least in large measure, his realist understanding of the character and motivations of the slave power. A basic tenet of the realist view is that in the nature of political life, the contest of moral ideas is always entangled with and often dominated by the contest of practical interests. In the grip of overwhelmingly powerful economic, social, and political interests, along with similarly powerful psychological needs to justify themselves in their interests, slaveholders could only have been expected to defend their institution with the utmost tenacity. "One thing . . . is certain," Douglass observed in his speech on the *Dred Scott* ruling: "Slaveholders are in earnest, and mean to cling to their slaves as long as they can, and to the bitter end."[98] The Garrisonian strategy of peaceful moral suasion was hopeless. In fact, it had long prompted derision among the slaveholders themselves. To an incredulous James Henry Hammond in 1845, it could only have been contrived as a rhetorical cloak—"Consider: were ever any people civilized or savage persuaded by any argument, human or divine, to surrender voluntarily two thousand millions of dollars? . . . Away, then, with your pretended 'moral suasion.' . . . The abolitionists . . . aim first, to alarm us: that failing, to compel us by force to emancipate our slaves."[99] Hammond's candid acknowledgment of nonnegotiable interest corroborated Douglass's post-Garrisonian position. "Moral considerations have long been since been exhausted upon slaveholders," he concluded, defending John Brown a few weeks after the Harpers Ferry insurrection. "It is in vain to reason with them."[100]

Through the 1850s and beyond, Douglass glorified and even sanctified violent force, both in self-defense and to advance the abolitionist cause. In his second lecture on slavery in 1850, he betrayed an unmistakable relish in recalling Jefferson's fear of God's retributive justice, which might find its executors in "those sable arms," the country's erstwhile cultivators who could "yet become the instruments of terror, desolation, and death, throughout our borders."[101] In his 1853 novella, *The Heroic Slave*, he lionized Madison Washington, the leader of a successful rebellion aboard the slave ship *Creole* in 1841, tacitly counterposing him to the excessively spiritualized form of resistance represented by Harriet Beecher Stowe's initially beloved "Christian hero," Uncle Tom.[102] In *Bondage and Freedom*, Douglass described his enthusiastic reaction as an adolescent to the news of Nat Turner's rebellion in 1831 and "the alarm and terror which it occasioned." He had conceived his first hopes for the abolition cause when he "saw it supported by the Almighty, and armed with DEATH!"[103] Prompted by the 1854 killing in Boston of a man attempting to execute the Fugitive Slave Law, he penned a fiery editorial extending a lesson from the Covey battle: "Every slave-hunter who meets a bloody death in his infernal business, is an argument in favor of the manhood of our race." From 1851 forward, he sought to propagate an abolitionist reading of the Constitution, fully aware that any attempt to effectuate such a reading would provoke immediate civil war. He responded to the fall of Sumter and the onset of the Civil War with exultation: "For this consummation we have watched and wished with fear and trembling. God be praised! that it has come at last."[104]

The extremes to which Douglass was willing to carry his advocacy of violent resistance to slavery are evident in his judgments of instances involving violence against innocents. These cases went beyond his refusal to condemn any of the violence of Nat Turner or John Brown, both of whom caused the deaths of persons who were at worst indirectly associated with slaveholders' crimes. They involved violence committed by tyranny's innocent victims against *themselves* or against persons for whom they were custodially responsible. Douglass considered suicide contrary to the law of nature, in the normal human condition of freedom.[105] But here again, the morality of free society had no application to life under slavery. In an 1846 speech, he related approvingly the story of a fleeing slavewoman in the nation's capital, a modern Lucretia who saw no means to frustrate her slave masters' designs but to hurl herself off a bridge to her death.[106] A far more shocking extreme appears in his 1857 "West India Emancipation" speech, in which he related the horrible story of Margaret Garner (later fictionalized in Toni Morrison's profound novel *Beloved*). Garner was a fugitive slave in early 1856 who, facing recapture, stabbed one of her three small children to death and seriously wounded the other two—meaning, as she later testified, "to save them all from Slavery by death." Douglass saw in the story more than an excruciating illustration of the desperation to which slavery could drive its victims; its context in his speech was his general insistence upon resistance as an indispensable condition of reform. His comment indicates that not only did he refuse to condemn Garner's act but, to the contrary, he judged it a shining example of dignity-affirming resistance: "Every mother" who committed a like act "should be held and honored as a benefactress."[107]

These judgments are difficult to understand. In the abstract, Douglass's principles certainly warranted the judgment that death was to be preferred to slavery. Suicide was no more culpable than submission and might even have been morally superior to it, so far as it constituted an act of resistance. To take one's own life was a moral evil on the condition that it really was one's *own*. When it was not, suicide could be excusable as a desperate, fleeting reassertion of self-ownership, negating the slaveholder's usurpatious claim and returning oneself to the care of the ultimate proprietor. Yet Douglass's precise position was that death is to be preferred only to *perpetual* slavery.[108] A life that is not worth preserving is not simply a life without liberty but rather a life without any *hope* for liberty. The act of taking one's own life or the innocent life of one's dependent could be justified only on the premise of the utter hopelessness, then or ever, of escaping slavery. But his account of his own experience and character makes it clear that the perpetually hopeful and life-affirming Douglass could accept a conclusion of hopelessness only in the most extreme circumstances. He had rejected thoughts of suicide in the depth of his ordeal with Covey and apparently did not consider it after his failed escape from Freeland, when he faced the prospect of being sold into slavery in the Deep South.[109] Some measure of understandable sympathy might explain his approval of the suicides of adult, mature slaves, who might be presumed capable of making reasonable, though necessarily uncertain, judgments of the hopelessness of their circumstances. Even so, an irrevocable judgment of hopelessness concerning the life of a child seems altogether indefensible on the basis of his principles. Reflecting on his judgments in these cases, it is safest to say that they illustrate the power of Douglass's commitment to forceful resistance. Though he readily condemned his fellows for acts he deemed submissive, he apparently was resolutely unwilling to condemn any actual instance of slave resistance that came to his attention.

By his seeming glorification of righteous violence during this period, Douglass might seem to identify himself as a spiritual descendant or ancestor of the likes of Turner or Frantz Fanon.[110] As early as 1846, he offered an insightful self-analysis in a letter to his Garrisonian colleague Francis Jackson, in which he confessed somewhat ashamedly to a bloody-minded enthusiasm as he surveyed Scotland's hills and imagined the violent battles between liberty and slavery that had been waged on those hills in years past. That enthusiasm, moving him to "glory in the fight as well as in the victory" and to conceive of the fight often in bloody terms, was a permanent feature of Douglass's character.[111]

Yet, the heat of his rhetoric notwithstanding, Douglass's militancy did not signify an uncritical glorification of righteous violence. Although he expressed pride in drawing blood from the would-be slave breaker Covey, he nonetheless described his violence against him ambivalently, as "undignified" as well as dignifying. His subsequent attempts to provoke Covey were "not altogether creditable to my natural temper."[112] Though he did renounce Garrisonian moral suasion, Douglass never renounced the conviction that the defeat of slavery by "the arms of truth and love," as he characterized emancipation in the West Indies, represented "a happier result, a nobler warfare" than its defeat by physical force.[113] The rule of physical force was proper to barbarism, not to civilization.[114] Righteous violence was justified only by necessity, as the barbarism required to overcome barbarism. Vicious in their tendency to destroy rather than to build, the martial qualities could become virtues only so far as they were prudently deployed to defend or to prepare the construction of genuinely civilized society. Resistance had to be "wise as well as just." Violence was commendable not only by the subjective gratification and edification it might provide but also by a realistic assessment of its likely positive effects in the world.[115]

As he praised the gallant Henry Harris, the friend and fellow slave who "put [him] to shame" when he resisted capture at gunpoint, Douglass added a word to justify his own more cautious course: "I never see much use in fighting, unless there is a reasonable probability of whipping somebody." He knew that in holding violent force necessary to effective antislavery action, he had to show that slaves or African Americans were capable of marshaling sufficient force. We will see how this consideration complicated his militancy in the decade leading into the war as we consider more closely his prediction that by the law of nature, slavery was doomed to extinction.

Natural Law and the Demise of Slavery

In Douglass's understanding of the law of nature, the decisive sanctions against slavery would come by the reactions of those it offended. The efficient causes of its undoing would proceed in a chain of reactions that began with those of its most vengeful victims, the slaves themselves. His discussions of slave resistance were predictions as well as exhortations, designed to help lend conscious direction to motives already powerfully present among the enslaved.

Contrary to the slaveholders' self-delusions, Douglass presented slaves in general as a dangerously discontented lot. To fit them for slavery, masters had to demoralize and dehumanize them—"beat and cuff" them, render them "hungry and spiritless."[116] He sometimes suggested that such an outcome was available to slaveholders as a practical possibility, as in his confession that after a few months under Edward Covey, he "was broken in body, soul and spirit." But upon closer reading, even such passages as this indicate slavery's limited power. At the extremity of his condition, the slave yet retained the all-important power to *aspire*. Douglass considered taking Covey's life along with his own, and he was restrained from both acts by hope as well as by fear.[117] His depiction of human "elasticity" or resilience under a brutal enslavement attests his claims of an irrepressible human desire for liberty. At the beginning of the same episode, his amusing account of his failure to tame the natural force of Covey's oxen foretells the failure of Covey and slaveholders in general to suppress the spirit of liberty in Douglass and his fellows. Unlike oxen, human beings as a general rule could not be more than "half-broken."[118] Slavery's attempts to brutalize were attempts "to drive nature out with a pitchfork," in the Roman poet Horace's classic phrase, and they produced the natural result: *tamen usque recurret.*[119]

In the case of slaves, nature promised to return with a vengeance. For the wicked, there was no peace: Douglass's observation regarding the effects of the Lloyds' luxuriousness was still more apt with respect to slaveholders' brutality. Slavery's despotic imperatives placed masters, along with slaves, in a condition of perpetual insecurity. Compelled to oppress slaves without literally eliminating them,[120] masters inescapably exposed themselves to the danger of violent resistance. Slaveholders were the moral progeny of Macbeth, who "does murder sleep"; they felt compelled to sleep "often with pistols under their heads."[121] As noted earlier, Douglass closed his second lecture on slavery with a fearsome admonition: the American people should "*look to their ways,*" lest their country's cultivators become the "instruments"—slavery alone was the true agent—of its desolation.[122] The slaves' violence was sufficiently motivated by their rational, civilized desires for liberty and justice, as even some slaveholders acknowledged.[123] But the full magnitude of the perils to which slaveholders exposed themselves appears more clearly upon consideration of the more elementally natural passions that their abuses aroused. In his 1850 "Letter to the American Slaves," Douglass promised that "when the insurrection of the Southern slaves shall take place . . . the great majority of the colored men of the North . . . will be found by your side, with deep-stored and long-accumulated revenge in their hearts."[124]

The anger and vengeance to which Douglass referred were generated as much by the gross indignities as by the radical injustices to which slaveholders subjected their victims. Their most palpably outrageous crimes involved their treatment of the weaker members of the enslaved population—normally the women and children. We noted previously Douglass's personal confession that his "feelings rise above my control" in contemplating the evils that his own children could have suffered under slavery.[125] Similarly affecting were the sufferings of young slave women. The first physical atrocity recounted in *Bondage and Freedom* is the horrible beating of a female cousin of Frederick's by the brutish overseer Plummer. That anecdote functions as a lurid overture to the story of Aaron Anthony's violent degradation of his beautiful young slave Esther, who had excited her master's jealousy by falling in love with a young male slave. Sleeping unobserved in an adjoining closet, young Frederick awoke in the early hours one morning to her shrieks and Anthony's accompanying curses and then to the sight of Anthony sadistically whipping the helplessly bound, partially naked Esther. Douglass reported that such scenes "are common in every slaveholding community in which I have lived. They are incidental to the relation of master and slave."[126]

Esther's story powerfully illustrated the unruly lusts that slavery fostered in slaveholders, the latter's propensity to prey especially upon the weak, and the special degradation and misery that slavery inflicted upon women.[127] Most pertinent at present, however, is a further aspect of the story's significance that Douglass touched on lightly: the indirect assault on manhood that such crimes represented and the violent anger that they naturally aroused in enslaved men. A few seemingly slight modifications in his second telling of the story indicate Douglass's concern to convey these latter meanings. In the *Narrative*, he described his immediate reaction exclusively in terms of fear: "I was . . . terrified and horror-stricken." But in *Bondage and Freedom*, he added a suggestion of his violent outrage, likely intensified by his awareness of his own weakness: "Child though I was—the outrage kindled in me a feeling far from peaceful; but I was hushed, terrified, stunned, and could do nothing."[128] With still greater subtlety, Douglass invited his readers also to consider the far greater volatility of this sentiment in the hearts of grown men as compared to those of boys. Though he offered no overt discussion of the sexual dimensions of black manhood,[129] he did not render the subject altogether invisible. Enshrouded in silence, Esther's young suitor remained a provocative presence in Douglass's account. In the *Narrative,* he was identified as Ned Roberts, "Lloyd's Ned," whereas in *Bondage and Freedom,* he became "Edward," who "loved and courted" Esther and "might have been her husband."[130] Effectively emasculated—deprived of manhood's most significant offices and reduced to impotence in the face of the torturing of his beloved—Edward incarnated the silent sexual rage that enslaved males in their physical primes must have harbored as a result of the enforced concubinage of slavery.

The intensity of these considerations is heightened by an additional aspect of the story's significance, immediately disclosed in the *Narrative* and dramatically withheld, for a moment, in *Bondage and Freedom.* Esther was "Aunt Esther—for she was my own aunt," the sister of Frederick's mother, Harriet.[131] Douglass's aunt was subjected to shocking, sexually motivated violence by the same man who claimed the title of slave master over his mother and over himself. The questions instantly arise as to whether Douglass's mother—once again, a woman Frederick barely knew—was also a victim of Anthony's sadistic passion and whether Frederick himself was conceived in an act of sexual violence by his master.[132] In their more personal meanings, such questions certainly concerned him deeply.[133] But in a more general sense, the answer to the second question is self-evident: because slavery was by nature a state of war, Douglass could *only* have been conceived in an act of sexual violence, by his own master or by some other member of the master class. Contrary to the claims of some present-day commentators, Douglass did not engage audiences in voyeurism by telling this revolting story.[134] Rather, he meant it to solicit anger, not repressed prurient interests, in support of abolition. He appealed to readers to consider the formative effects on the thousands of slaves who lived with the knowledge that they were sired by slavemaster-fathers who raped their mothers at will or on the millions who lived with the knowledge that their enslaved mothers were constantly exposed to such assaults. The anger born of sexual indignity entailed also the anger born of filial devotion. Slavery naturally ignited in large numbers of slaves, as in Douglass, a profound, self-transcending rage, fueling a violent longing for a revolution in the social order, whatever its cost in bloodshed.

Seeking prudent direction for this natural anger, Douglass considered several specific modes in which the resistance that slavery provoked might become an efficient cause of its undoing. The most obvious and least likely involved a mass uprising in which slaves either directly overpowered their erstwhile masters or destroyed the viability of the slave system by some combination of violent revolt and mass flight. During the years closely preceding the outbreak of war, Douglass did allow his hopes to turn toward successful slave insurrections.[135] But those expressions of hope seem to have been mainly attempts to ward off despair, conceived in his growing fear that abolitionists' efforts to persuade the nation's nonslaveholding majority had proved futile. In the main, Douglass doubted that slaves by themselves could muster the organized power necessary to destroy the institution. It was primarily due to those doubts that he had come to oppose the Garrisonian strategy of disunion. Such a policy made no sense as an abolition measure, for it assumed "what is plainly absurd . . . that a population of slaves, without arms, without means of concert, and without leisure, is more than a match for double its number, educated, accustomed to rule, and in every way prepared for warfare."[136]

Douglass held stronger hopes that slave rebellions could succeed indirectly, perhaps by their effects on the moral sentiments of slaveholders. In an 1852 review of a collection of Garrison's writings and speeches, he explained that he rejected the principle of nonresistance, "without at all . . . losing faith in moral force."[137] Moral reform must always be a mix of persuasion and compulsion, in Douglass's realist understanding, so that moral suasion need not exclude the use or threat of violence as a permissible means. A dead slave hunter, he said in urging disobedience of the Fugitive Slave Law, could serve as an *argument.* Commenting on John Brown's raid on the Harpers Ferry arsenal, he observed that rebellious slaves could "reach the slaveholder's conscience through his fear of personal danger."[138] As Bernard R. Boxill has explained, the idea was essentially Hobbesian: the fear of physical harm would tame the masters' domineering pride and prepare their ultimate assent to the idea of human equality.[139] To this end, slaves did not need to risk a contest of arms with the aggregated forces of the slave power; the atmosphere of terror created by scattered acts of violent rebellion could effect the desired change. "Virginia was never nearer emancipation," Douglass contended in his 1857 "West India Emancipation" speech, "than when General Turner kindled the fires of insurrection at Southampton."[140]

It is tempting to find suggestions of this strategy in Douglass's reports on the effectiveness of resistance in his autobiography. In the Covey episode, he reported that he had chosen to fight when he could no longer tolerate the tyrant's treatment of him "like a *brute,*" thus indicating a purpose to achieve a kind of moral suasion in the latter's recognition of his human dignity. His report of the results of the battle might seem to confirm his success: from the day of the battle forward, Douglass reported, "I was never fairly whipped," by Covey or by anyone else.[141] Earlier in *Bondage and Freedom,* he prepared the climactic account by describing a similar instance involving Edward Lloyd's slave Nelly, a female counterpart to Douglass ("a bright mulatto . . . a vigorous and spirited woman," who "felt herself superior, in some respects, to the slaves around her"). Nelly "nobly resisted" a whipping by the overseer Sevier. She failed to deter a frightful whipping in the particular instance, but "her invincible spirit" remained "undaunted," and Douglass doubted that Sevier ever whipped her again. A further example reinforced the point: "'You can shoot me but you can't whip me,' said a slave to Rigby Hopkins; and the result was that he was neither whipped nor shot."[142]

The obvious moral of these stories affirms the slaves' power to compel some level of respect on the part of slaveholders by their acts of physical resistance. Viewed more closely, however, the same evidence also indicates the limits of their power to effect the masters' genuine moral suasion. In the main instance, there is no reason to doubt Covey's fear of the emboldened Frederick after the incident, but there are strong reasons to doubt that his subsequent forbearance signified any recognition of the young slave's full humanity. The first is a matter of simple logic: a wariness of offending a being that one regards as a powerful beast would not disturb the belief that the being is, in fact, a beast. A stronger reason for doubt is Douglass's own admission that he could not satisfactorily explain Covey's failure to respond punitively. He refrained from attributing Covey's forbearance to any glimmer of humanitarian respect;[143] and it was for good reason that he remained skeptical about the explanation that he proffered as most probable. The difficulties in Douglass's own and related explanations, along with other hints that he supplied (at times despite himself), lend credence to the explanation suggested by Dickson Preston and Wilson Jeremiah Moses that Covey's forbearance was ordered by Thomas Auld.[144] It seems that, for one reason or another, the nearly broken slave's appeal, which the master apparently rejected after a spasm of initial sympathy, did succeed in moving Auld after all.

More important, Douglass provided compelling reasons to doubt that physical resistance by slaves could generally succeed in effecting slaveholders' moral conversion. First, we have considered his insight into the powerful resistance that slaveholders' consciences would naturally mount against moral conversion. Second, his observation of the self-inflating power of exercising physical force carries a corollary concerning subjection to it. As the successful use of force tends to expand one's subjective sense of dignity, so the subjection to it tends to degrade and to humiliate—an especially intolerable effect to those holding the self-image of a master class. According to Douglass's understanding of human psychology, the masters' more likely immediate response to acts of slave resistance was not an awakening of moral enlightenment but instead a furiously indignant counteroffensive against those whom their interest, conscience, and subjective dignity combined to designate their natural inferiors. This psychological inference was confirmed by events; Douglass eagerly reprinted in his newspapers accounts of the alarmist rage and intensified tyranny with which slaveholding communities typically responded to the rumor as well as to the fact of slave rebellion.[145] As we will see in Chapter Five, the same psychological insight yielded his accurate warnings of the hostility with which defeated, ex-slaveholding communities would react to postwar attempts at racial integration.

That the moral reformation of slaveholders and their allies was beyond reach as a proximate objective did not mean that resistance was futile. It meant only that slaves and African Americans needed powerful allies of their own. A third mode in which their resistance might bear fruit, in Douglass's consideration, involved the moral suasion of nonslaveholding citizens, especially the majority in the northern states. In the opening scene of *The Heroic Slave,* he had the character Listwell, a northern white traveler in Virginia, overhear Madison Washington's initial expression of determination to free himself, whereupon Listwell resolved, "From this hour I am an abolitionist." Slavery's defenders were wise to come north, Douglass remarked in 1859, "for here its fate is to be decided."[146]

The crucial objective for well-conceived resistance and agitation was to arouse in northern whites a sentiment of moral sympathy for slaves and African Americans. Douglass's strategy for accomplishing this was again multidimensional. Most generally, it involved an appeal to universal human sentiments of respect and admiration. Concluding his account of the Covey battle, he observed, "Human nature is so constituted, that it cannot *honor* a helpless man, although it can *pity* him; and even this it cannot do long, if the signs of power do not arise."[147] Conversely, human beings naturally honor the self-reliant, especially those who are forceful in the defense of their own rights. Also in 1855,

Douglass contended that the slave power's depredations had stirred "among the colored people . . . a spirit of manly resistance well calculated to surround them with a bulwark of sympathy and respect hitherto unknown."[148]

For Douglass, the predisposition to honor and identify with those spirited in resisting oppression was both a broadly human and a distinctively American quality. Sympathy for the slave could then be cultivated by patriotic as well as humanitarian appeals. Reaffirming his hope in 1860, he remarked that the "American people admire courage displayed in defense of liberty, and will catch the flame of sympathy from the sparks of its heroic fire."[149] This national admiration for courage in the defense of liberty was the bequest of the American Revolution; and Douglass took every opportunity to establish the abolition cause as the Revolution's legitimate offspring. He honored the undeservedly obscure Madison Washington, whose principles "are the principles of 1776," as heir to Virginia's greatest heroes in more than his name. This later Washington was "a man who loved liberty as well as did Patrick Henry—who deserved it as much as Thomas Jefferson,—and who fought for it with a valor as high, and arms as strong, and against odds as great, as he who led all the armies of the American colonies through the great war for freedom and independence." Extolling "the fathers of this republic" in his famous Fourth of July oration in 1852, Douglass told his predominantly white Rochester audience that those fathers "were statesmen, patriots, and heroes, and for the good they did, and the principles they contended for, I will unite with you to honor their memory."[150]

Often, Douglass indirectly sought to stimulate other Americans' sympathetic identification with the African American cause by shaming those who failed to honor their own principles in the controversy over slavery. In the same Fourth of July oration, he invited his audience to cherish the memory of the fathers as a means of highlighting the failings of the sons. As the children of Jacob boasted of Abraham their father even though they had long before lost their father's faith and spirit, so Douglass's American contemporaries continued to claim, amid their deepening involvement in the crime of slavery, "'We have Washington to *our father'*"—the same Washington who "could not die till he had broken the chains of his slaves."[151] As the 1850s drew to a close, Douglass expressed increasing alarm at the absence of liberal militancy among his fellow northerners. In the northern reaction to the Harpers Ferry episode, he saw the prevalence of a meanly bourgeois moral calculus, bereft of devotion to any cause nobler than one's own comfortable self-preservation. "Are heroism and insanity synonyms in our American dictionary? Heaven help us!"[152] As events soon thereafter proved, Douglass's fears of the northerners' spiritlessness were overstated. But his denunciations of the latter, like his occasional praise for slaveholders' daring and his grudging admiration for southern unity and resolution in the war, were designed to provoke the true heirs of the American Revolution to recover the spirit and principles of their forebears.[153] Typical was the stiffening admonition he issued to a Rochester audience shortly after the commencement of war:

> The people of the North have long borne a bad reputation at the
> South. They have borne the reputation of being mean spirited and
> cowardly. All the bravery and manliness have been monopolized by
> the South. . . . We of the North may have learning, industry, and
> wealth without end . . . but so long as we are considered as destitute of
> manly courage . . . we shall be the victims of insult and outrage. . . .
> Now, instead of looking upon the present war as an unmitigated evil,
> you and I, and all of us, ought to welcome it as a glorious opportunity
> for imparting wholesome lessons to the southern soul-drivers.[154]

The prudence with which Douglass designed those appeals appears most substantially in his realist appreciation of the normal limits of active human sympathy. For most human beings, he observed, belligerence in defense of one's own rights coexists all too naturally with tolerance of threats to the rights of others. Herein lay a powerful source of the antiabolitionist mentality among northerners.[155] In the present case, had not union with the slaveholding South brought the North some very great goods, beginning with national security? Was it wise to imperil these to secure the rights of a people most northerners, too, regarded as unassimilably alien? To move the northern majority to embrace the slaves' cause as their own, Douglass knew that appeals to a sense of patriotic honor required reinforcement by more compellingly personal appeals. Slavery had to be opposed as an ever more brazen affront not only to the rights of slaves and African Americans, not only to the nation's moral ideals, but also to the dignity and rights of the northern white majority.

As was shown in the preceding chapter, events had made it increasingly easy for Douglass to make this case. A series of aggressive demands and practical victories beginning in the 1830s marked the slave power as a menace to more than the relatively insular class of African Americans, existing at some safe remove from northern whites. The slave power directly and palpably assaulted these whites as well, endangering their own rights in their own states and in all federal territories. So Douglass contended in 1855, in his militantly hopeful editorial

"The Doom of the Black Power": "[The] question is one in which white men, as well as black men, are immediately interested. . . . Slavery invades the rights of man, irrespective of color and condition."[156] He pressed the point in his still more militant and hopeful speech on the *Dred Scott* ruling. "Step by step we have seen the slave power advancing . . . growing more and more haughty, imperious, and exacting. The white man's liberty has been marked out for the same grave with the black man's. The ballot box is desecrated, God's law set at nought, armed legislators stalk the halls of Congress, freedom of speech is beaten down in the Senate."[157] An important dimension of the Fugitive Slave Law was its assertion by slaveholders of a property also in northerners' labor, compelling them to serve as slave hunters, to the end of deepening their complicity in slavery.[158] Even more significant were the slave power's persistent encroachments on the freedom of speech. "One end of the slave's chain had to be fastened to a padlock in the lips of Northern freemen, else the slave will himself become free. Now, gentlemen," Douglass inquired of his Chicago audience in the "Kansas-Nebraska" speech, "are you ready for this?"[159]

Douglass thought the answer was clear enough. In "The Doom of the Black Power" as in the *Dred Scott* speech, he anticipated slavery's impending fate. "A few more pro-Slavery demonstrations, a few more presses thrown into the river, a few more northern ministers driven from the South and West, a few more recaptures of Fugitives, near Bunker Hill and Plymouth Rock . . . and all will be well. We have no fears of ultimate success."[160]

Viewed in its totality, Douglass's confidence in slavery's impending demise was steadfast and abiding. Throughout the 1850s, he predicted that the despotic system would sooner or later come to ruin due to its own intrinsic flaws, which he conceived of in terms of both excess and deficiency. Slavery's fatal excess lay in its impressive success in forming a master class thoroughly possessed by the idea of mastery, with all its attending arrogance and love of dominion. Its essential deficiencies lay, first, in its general failure to form a class of people reliably suited for enslavement; second, in its inability to convince the nation of its moral rightness; and third, in the insecurity that the master class experienced due to those other deficiencies. Moved by its love of dominion to respond aggressively to its pervasive insecurity, the slave power would ultimately self-destruct because of its inability to circumscribe its own despotism. Confounding self-aggrandizement with self-defense, slaveholders would labor compulsively to the ultimate end of reconstituting the United States as a transcontinental slaveholding empire. In pursuance of this mad design, Douglass reasoned, the slave power would attempt in the end to extend its dominion over a population too power-ful for it to dominate. By 1855, he believed, its ultimate fate was clearly in view. The "Slave Power . . . has overreached itself." Added to its prior offenses, the "Fugitive Slave and Nebraska Bills . . . have sealed the doom of the Black Power."[161]

A few points merit repeated emphasis in closing. Douglass's insistent predic-tions of slavery's self-destruction stand as the most impressive expression of his characteristic rational hopefulness. These predictions were not merely rhetorical, and they rested most solidly not on a faith in divine Providence but rather on his rational understanding of the law of nature. He held the natural law whereby human beings possess inalienable rights to be true and efficacious, so that slav-ery, the most egregious violation of that law, would ultimately call upon itself crushing natural penalties. "Whence came the abolition of slavery?" Douglass asked in an 1869 commemoration of British and American emancipations, and his compressed postmortem analysis accorded with his long-standing argument. "To me the result is no miracle. . . . I contemplate the termination of slavery sim-ply as a natural and logical event. . . . A natural and prolific breeder of pride, self-ishness, and love of power, it perished at the hands of its own progeny."[162]

In Douglass's natural-law argument, the most important of slavery's patri-cidal progeny were its angry victims. The penalty for slaveholders' extreme love of dominion would be imposed on the condition that those whom slavery of-fended would rise in determined opposition, and the rising of sufficient opposi-tion depended first on the agency of slaves and other African Americans. Human nature had to rise in them as it had risen in Douglass against Covey, showing both its rational and its spirited qualities. To this extent, Douglass shared with Garrison a strategic calculation: persistent reminders of slaveholders' exposure to dangerous opposition would remind them also of their dependence on national support and so lend urgency to their demand that their cause be made the entire nation's property. Douglass's argument built upon the fear that Jefferson expressed in a famous 1820 letter occasioned by the Missouri agitation. "We have the wolf by the ears," the great Virginian had writ-ten, "and we can neither hold him, nor safely let him go."[163] Fearful of holding that wolf, slaveholders would demand the transfer of its custody to a nation in-creasingly ill disposed to accepting it. They would do so, that is, provided that slaves and their allies showed something of the nature of wolves. Absent slaves' forceful resistance, there could have been no viable abolitionism because human nature could hold no deep sympathy for the spiritless. And absent any forceful abolitionism, a crucial provocation for the slave power's fatal overreaching would have been absent, too. So it fell first upon African Americans to shoulder the burden of the revolutionary fathers' motto: "RESISTANCE TO TYRANTS IS OBEDIENCE TO GOD."

To raise the proper spirit of resistance, Douglass appealed to sentiments at once "manly," befitting human beings in general, and particularly American. There is something of further significance in this. Douglass's rational hopefulness for slavery's demise depended on the efficacy of natural causes, but it did so in a complex way. The demise of the evil institution, natural in a broad sense, would come as a result of voluntary action in conformity with the natural duty of resistance. But human beings are never purely and simply creatures of human nature or natural law. At best, our voluntary actions are reflective of nature as mediated by our particular moral-political cultures and positive laws. Surely, slavery's natural demise would be measurably hastened in a country that had explicitly dedicated itself to the principles of natural law. Among the crucial elements of Douglass's rational hopefulness were his convictions that the American heritage of rights and law were in fundamental accord with the laws of God and nature and that a majority of American people could be brought to see this with progressively increasing clarity. In a country that originated in a revolutionary declaration of the natural rights of humankind, it was fitting and prudent to appeal for national sympathy by draping the slave's cause in the familiar banner of the patriots of 1776.

A final point is no less crucial. In his prudent concern to Americanize the slave's cause, Douglass drew more from the American Revolution than a license for righteous violence. The Founding Fathers were lawgivers more than lawbreakers; their greatness consisted less in their zeal to destroy a system of injustice than in their sober determination "to establish justice." To carry their legacy forward effectively, Douglass recognized that the zeal to abolish had to be tempered by an appreciation of what was to be conserved. As the people of the North were "a law-abiding people," perhaps even to a fault, it was above all necessary to persuade them that the U.S. Constitution was, as Douglass maintained, a "glorious liberty document."[164] In the next chapter, we consider his attempts to do so.

3

"The Pound of Flesh, but Not One Drop of Blood": The Constitution against Slavery

No one can know what the written law is, until he knows what it ought to be.
Lysander Spooner, Unconstitutionality of Slavery

A S HE MATURED, Douglass became convinced that to secure their claims to liberty, his oppressed people needed to make those claims not only as abstractly human bearers of natural liberty but also as concretely American bearers of civil, constitutional liberty. Like their white compatriots, they, too, needed to claim "Washington to our father": they needed to affirm both their allegiance to the revolutionary nation for which Washington had fought and their protection by the fundamental law over whose establishment he had presided. The abolitionist revolution would succeed the original American Revolution in its radicalism and in its moderation. It would assert the right to abolish slavery in "any way," by any necessary means,[1] and as it did so, it would display a disciplined respect for law. Zealous revolutionary that he was, the mature Douglass was ever wary of the danger of carrying the revolutionary zeal to gratuitous extremes.[2]

Other prominent abolitionists were not. "Let us glory in the name of revolutionists," declared the Garrisonian American Anti-Slavery Society in an 1844 statement, envisioning a revolution far more profound than the one whereby the nation had won its political independence.[3] That society's commitment to radical revolution was evident from the beginning, as it adopted Garrison's words for its founding "Declaration of Sentiments" in 1833: "We have met together for the achievement of an enterprise, without which, that of our fathers is incomplete; and which, for its magnitude, solemnity, and probable results upon the destiny of the world, as far transcends theirs, as moral truth does physical force."[4]

Among some Garrisonians, the zeal for revolution appeared in the radically antinomian spirit of Non-Resistance, in which longings for liberation and perfection conjoined in a willingness to submit to God's government only and thus in a rejection of all human government as illegitimate.[5] The Garrisonian Henry C. Wright took this principle so far as to declare, in 1842, that if he could emancipate every slave in the country by casting a single vote, he would refuse to cast that vote.[6] But the more significant expression of the Garrisonians' extremism was their denial of the legitimacy of the U.S. government in particular, mandated by their reading of the U.S. Constitution as fundamentally proslavery. As early as 1832, Garrison had denounced the Constitution as "the most bloody and heaven-daring arrangement ever made by men for the continuance and protection of a system of the most atrocious villany [*sic*] ever exhibited on earth. . . . Such a compact was, in the nature of things and according to the law of God, null and void from the beginning."[7] This opposition grew even more intense over the years, culminating in Garrison's public burning of a copy of the Constitution at a July 4 meeting of the Massachusetts Anti-Slavery Society in 1854. From this rejection of the Constitution followed the signature position of Garrisonian abolitionism. "Henceforth," Garrison declared in 1845, "the watchword of every uncompromising abolitionist, of every friend of God and liberty, must be . . . 'NO UNION WITH SLAVEHOLDERS!' "[8]

In Douglass's mature thinking, this sort of extremism in the pursuance of liberation was a pernicious vice. The antipolitical utopianism and virulent anti-Americanism that Garrison propagated supplied the most powerful reasons for Douglass's break from his former mentors, which was complete by mid-1851. The group's "worst fault," he observed in an 1855 survey of abolitionist factions, was its promiscuous call for revolution. Non-Resistants foolishly made the elimination of all human ills a prerequisite for eliminating any of them, and Garrisonian abolitionists foolishly alienated themselves altogether from the republic they meant (or should have meant) to reform. By presenting themselves as enemies of law and of America, Garrisonians lent credence to a common view of abolitionists as irresponsible fanatics, and they thus obstructed the vital effort to broaden the class of sympathetic antislavery northerners. The same concern moved Douglass to oppose John Brown's plan to initiate a general slave rebellion by attacking the U.S. arsenal at Harpers Ferry.[9] As Brown would in his own distinctive way, Garrisonian disunionists interposed "the huge work of the abolition of the Government, as an indispensable condition to emancipation." And in the unlikely event that they succeeded in that work, the result would be to abandon the slaves to their fate, leaving them dependent on themselves to overcome the organized force of the slaveholding South. By calling for disunion,

Garrisonians meant to rid the nation and the nonslaveholding states of their legal responsibility for protecting slavery, but the more significant practical effect of their disunion policy would be to absolve those states and the nation of any responsibility for ending it. Douglass saw no moral purity in this position but only a plain abrogation of moral duty.[10] To marshal sufficient forces to defeat slavery, the legitimacy of government in general and of the U.S. government in particular had to be defended, not undermined.

On the broader issue, Douglass had little trouble dispatching the doctrine of Non-Resistance. His most concentrated defense of coercive government appears in his 1851 editorial "Is Civil Government Right?" composed in response to Wright's argument in a letter to the political abolitionist Gerrit Smith, Douglass's friend and patron. Despite our generally prevalent tendencies toward good, Douglass observed, human beings are by nature "constantly liable to do evil." Whatever the imperfections of life under government, "society possessing it, is a paradise to pandemonium, compared with society without it." Rejecting any distinction between legitimate and illegitimate government, Non-Resistants unwittingly aided the cause of tyranny. "Kings and despots flourish in such a soil," Douglass maintained, as that which Garrison, Wright, and the like were zealously preparing.[11] As the Declaration of Independence rightly prescribed, governments are instituted among men to secure the naturally insecure rights of the governed, and to achieve that end, those governments must always employ a mixture of persuasion and compulsion. Although unjust laws may be forcefully opposed, such opposition must be narrowly tailored to preserve the fundamental respect for law without which justice can never be effectuated.

As the natural moral law required the support of human positive law, so the efficacy of natural law in America required the support of American law. But for Douglass no less than for the Garrisonians, the prudential imperative to secure northern allies in no way overrode the duty to oppose unjust law. "If, indeed, the Constitution be for slavery," he allowed, then "reason, humanity, religion, and morality alike" enjoin support for "revolution, at whatever cost and at whatever peril."[12] In fact, the task of defending the Constitution was considerably more challenging than the defense of government in the abstract. Abolitionists had been divided since the 1830s on the question of the Constitution's relation to slavery. Against the proslavery reading upon which Garrisonians insisted, relative moderates such as Salmon Chase, James Birney, Joshua Giddings, William Jay, Charles Sumner, and John Quincy Adams and then radicals such as Alvin Stewart, Gerrit Smith, William Goodell, and Lysander Spooner argued for the antislavery Constitution and political abolitionism.[13] With the advent of the political-abolitionist Liberty Party, which split off from Garrisonian abolitionism in 1840, and the growing influence of political abolitionism throughout the 1840s and 1850s, Garrisonians intensified their opposition to the Constitution. That opposition was not simply reducible to antinomian enthusiasm. Perhaps the most formidable statements of the Garrisonian reading issued from the pen of Wendell Phillips, who was a graduate of Harvard Law School, a student of the great justice Joseph Story, and not a subscriber to the doctrine of Non-Resistance. From Phillips's work, we can derive a representative summary of the argument against which Douglass and others primarily had to contend in order to defend their claim that the Constitution, properly understood, was "a glorious liberty document."

The Garrisonian Constitution

Phillips published *The Constitution, a Pro-slavery Compact* in 1844 through the American Anti-Slavery Society. He did so, he indicated in the book's introduction, to defend the Garrisonian disunionist position against a "new theory," contrived "to serve the purposes of a party . . . that the Constitution does not tolerate slavery." The dispute over constitutional interpretation between Garrisonians and the Liberty Party's political abolitionists focused on the following five clauses, specified by Phillips in his introduction:

1. Article I, section 2: "Representatives and direct taxes shall be apportioned among the several States . . . according to their respective numbers, which shall be determined by adding to the whole number of free persons . . . three-fifths of all other persons";
2. Article I, section 8: "Congress shall have power . . . to suppress insurrections";
3. Article I, section 9: "The migration or importation of such persons as any of the States now existing, shall think proper to admit, shall not be prohibited by the Congress, prior to the year one thousand eight hundred and eight";
4. Article IV, section 2: "No person, held to service or labor in one state, under the laws thereof, escaping into another, shall, in consequence of any law of regulation therein, be discharged from such service or labor; but shall be delivered up on claim of the party to whom such service or labor may be due";
5. Article IV, section 4: "The United States shall guarantee to every State in this Union a republican form of government; and shall protect each of them against invasion; and, on application of the legislature, or of the executive . . . against domestic violence."[14]

Phillips allowed that the wording of these clauses was ambiguous in some respects. To ascertain their meanings and that of the Constitution as a whole with respect to slavery, he employed a theory of legal interpretation whereby the Constitution was to be read in the light of the original intention and under-standing of its framers, ratifiers, and subscribers. The bulk of his book, there-fore, was a compilation of historical evidence concerning the document's origi-nal design and the commonly accepted understanding of its meaning. He drew most heavily upon James Madison's *Notes of Debates in the Federal Convention of 1787*, first published in 1840, along with records of several state ratifying conven-tions and of debates in the First Congress of the United States. This evidence was further corroborated by the opinions and actions of succeeding generations. Defending this interpretive approach, Phillips challenged its critics: if the origi-nal understanding of the framers and ratifiers, along with "the unanimous, con-current, unbroken practice of every department of the Government . . . and the acquiescence of the whole people for fifty years do not prove which is the true construction, then how and where can such a question ever be settled?"[15]

Reading the text in the light of the pertinent historical evidence, Phillips be-lieved it was unquestionable that the Constitution embodied a deliberate, damning compromise with slavery. The purpose and effect of Article I, section 2, clause 3, commonly known as the three-fifths clause, were to provide "for the safety, perpetuity and augmentation of the slaveholding power" by allowing it additional representation in the House of Representatives and the Electoral Col-lege based on its claims to human property. The migration or importation clause of Article I, section 9 meant that for twenty years after ratification, "the citizens of the United States were to be encouraged and protected in the prose-cution of that infernal traffic," the African slave trade. The mandate in Article IV, section 2 requiring all states to return any escaped "person held to service or labor" was, in plainer language, a mandate to return fugitive slaves to their mas-ters, and the effect of this clause was to make "slavery a national institution, a national crime, and all the people who are not enslaved, the body-guard over those whose liberties have been cloven down." In Article I, section 8 and Article IV, section 4, the Congress's anti-insurrection power and the guarantee to the states of federal assistance against domestic violence "were adopted with special reference to the slave population, for the purpose of keeping them in their chains by the combined military force of the country." These clauses' "solemn guarantee of security to the slave system" Phillips declared, "caps the climax of national barbarity."[16]

To Phillips and other Garrisonians, the Constitution's clear accommodations of slavery could not be excused as prudent concessions by the Founders to the imperative of union in the face of pressing threats to national security. Rather, they had been framed and adopted in a spirit of pure venality. Singling out the agreement whereby northern delegates accepted the slave trade's extension in Article I, section 9 in exchange for an unrestricted national commerce power to protect northern industry, Phillips charged that "our fathers bartered honesty for gain and became partners with tyrants that they might share in the profits of their tyranny." All in all, he concluded, the evidence was overwhelming. The Constitution represented not the fulfillment but the betrayal of the Declaration of Independence; it was just what "our fathers intended to make it, and what, too, their descendants, this nation, say they did make it . . . a 'covenant with death and an agreement with hell.'"[17]

Douglass's Change of Opinion

Douglass endorsed the Garrisonian reading of the Constitution through the 1840s, though his confidence in it started to waver shortly after he began publishing the *North Star* in late 1847. "But for the responsibility of conducting a public journal, and the necessity imposed upon me of meeting opposite views from abolitionists in this state," he explained in *Bondage and Freedom,* "I should in all probability have remained as firm in my disunion views as any other disciple of William Lloyd Garrison."[18] Yet upon familiarizing himself with the arguments of leading political abolitionists, he came to find their antislavery reading of the Constitution compelling. When Douglass announced his change of opinion at the annual meeting of the American Anti-Slavery Society in May 1851, Garrison reacted with a mixture of incredulity and moral assault: "There is roguery somewhere!" The implication was that Douglass's revised opinion had been purchased by Gerrit Smith's financial support for Douglass's paper. Douglass persuasively denied the charge, which exposed an intolerant self-righteousness and also, perhaps, a measure of racial condescension in the man for whom he continued to express "a veneration only inferior . . . to that which we owe to our conscience and to our God."[19] But to credit Douglass's change of opinion to his independent reflection is not to deny either his intellectual debts in the field or the practical advantages to be accrued from the antislavery reading, both of which he readily acknowledged.

Commentators have commonly supposed that considerations of practical utility were more powerful than those of intrinsic persuasiveness in shaping Douglass's post-Garrisonian constitutional arguments.[20] It is beyond doubt that in reconsidering his opinion, Douglass was acutely aware that the issue held "vast importance" for the abolitionist cause. The conviction that the Constitution was an antislavery document yielded an abolitionism that was restorationist rather than revolutionary, loyalist rather than disunionist—one capable of deploying the broadest arsenal of weapons in the war against slavery. To spread the word concerning the antislavery Constitution was vital to his effort to build an effective political antislavery coalition, the "great Abolition Party of the land."[21] But all parties to the dispute over the Constitution saw practical utility in their readings, and to discover the utility in any of them is not to discredit its claim to interpretive respect. Douglass's revised opinion, unlike his original one, was based on extensive study of "the whole subject," comprehending the text and history of the Constitution and the fundamentals of political philosophy— "the origin, design, nature, rights, powers, and duties of civil government, and also the relations which human beings sustain to it."[22] For Douglass, the true meaning of the U.S. Constitution, as of constitutions in general, was fully intelligible only in light of the first principles of political life. To meet the challenge posed by Garrisonians' and slaveholders' readings, Douglass, along with other political abolitionists, drew upon a venerable tradition of natural-law jurisprudence in fashioning their novel constitutional arguments.[23]

The Rules of Legal Interpretation

Douglass specifically credited his change of mind regarding the Constitution's substantive meaning to his "careful study of the writings of Lysander Spooner, of Gerrit Smith, and of William Goodell."[24] His debt to them, above all to Spooner, began with his invocation of the "well established rules of legal interpretation" that supplied the grounding for their revisionist reading. For Douglass and Spooner, those rules were "as old as law," and they rose "out of the very elements of law."[25] Proper interpretation began with an understanding of the essential nature and purpose of law: "Law is not merely an arbitrary enactment with regard to justice, reason, or humanity"; it "is in its nature opposed to wrong."[26] Invoking the weightiest authority in the Anglo-American legal tradition, Douglass affirmed with Blackstone that law "is the supreme power of the state, commanding what is right and forbidding what is wrong."[27] The primacy of natural justice was the foundation and pervading inspiration of the rules of legal interpretation. But for both Douglass and Spooner, the interpretive rules yielded by this premise assumed stricter and looser forms, varying by the degree of independent authority they accorded to positive, or man-made, laws.

In its strictest application, the natural-law or natural justice interpretive principle entailed a perfect, unconditional subordination of positive law to natural law. Positive law could exist as law, could bind or oblige those subject to it, only so far as it conformed with the law of nature. As Douglass stated, "[Laws] against fundamental morality are not binding upon anybody." On this point, the authority of Blackstone accorded with the classical natural rights theory and with the "instinctive and spontaneous convictions of mankind."[28] On this radically antipositivist principle, where matters of fundamental justice were involved, neither the author's intention nor even the positive text itself could be decisive for the meaning of constitutional law. The specific controversy over the U.S. Constitution would appear to be baseless, as the document's justice would become a mere tautology: the Constitution did not enact or protect any injustice because no constitution *could* do so, irrespective of whatever express or implicit provisions it might contain.[29] The status of slavery in the Constitution would have been determined not by any particular consideration of the clauses in dispute but only by the judgment of moral philosophy as to its fundamental justice or injustice.

Neither Douglass nor Spooner insisted on this strict, uncompromising application of natural-justice jurisprudence. The interpretive principles upon which Douglass based his main arguments permitted a recognition of positive law as genuine, binding law—even, in some cases, when it stood contrary to the requirements of justice. The nature of law did not by definition *exclude* all injustice, but it remained "*opposed* to all such wickedness," making it "difficult to accomplish such objects under the forms of law." Legally authorized villainy had to be understood as anomalous; "the rules of legal interpretation hem it in on every side."[30] Those rules enjoined a presumption of the law's "innocence" or, in other words, of its conformity with natural justice and so of its protection of human liberty. The effect was to place a heavy burden of precision on those who would enact injustice into law. A law that would authorize an unjust power had to receive the strictest construction, begrudging to it at most a "pound of flesh" but "not one drop of blood." Where a text was worded ambiguously, in any contest between just and unjust meanings, the construction favoring justice had to prevail.[31] Again following Spooner, Douglass invoked the authority of the U.S.

Supreme Court, citing its statement in an early case unrelated to slavery, *U.S. v. Fisher:* "Where rights are infringed, where fundamental principles are overthrown . . . the legislative intention must be expressed with *irresistible clearness,* to induce a design to effect such objects." As Spooner put it, fundamentally unjust laws had to "perish for uncertainty."[32]

Just as this natural-law jurisprudence entailed certain presumptions respecting what the Constitution said or did not say, so, too, it carried implications respecting how to determine what it actually said and even what it actually was. Partisans of a proslavery interpretation betrayed an eagerness to enlarge the Constitution. They incorporated into it various extratextual sources, the most important of which contained evidence of the framers' intentions as expressed in their original deliberations. But the requirement of irresistible clarity rendered all such extratextual incorporations presumptively inadmissible, and Douglass came to view the Garrisonians' enlarging of the Constitution as a great error. In his most developed exposition of the abolitionist Constitution, presented in an 1860 speech in Glasgow, Scotland, in response to a speech by the leading British Garrisonian, George Thompson, he began by insisting on a properly compact conception of the Constitution. The decisive question, he maintained, "[is not] whether slaveholders took part in framing the Constitution; it is not whether those slaveholders, in their hearts, intended to secure certain advantages in that instrument for slavery; it is not whether the American Government has been wielded during seventy-two years in favour of the propagation and permanence of slavery; it is not whether a pro-slavery interpretation has been put upon the Constitution by the American Courts."[33] Even in its more permissive application, Douglass's natural justice interpretive rule greatly depreciated the framers' intentions as an independent source of constitutional authority.

In Douglass and Spooner's argument, what mattered for interpretive purposes was what the ratifiers adopted, not what the framers intended, because only the ratifiers, as representatives of the people of the United States, possessed formal lawmaking authority. The ratifiers conceivably could have adopted the framers' intent as their own, provided that the latter were commonly, publicly understood. But the secrecy of the framers' deliberations meant that their intentions, beyond what was conveyed by their text itself, were largely unknown to the ratifiers. To the extent that they represented only the framers' private or "secret" intentions, the Madison notes shed no light on the ratifiers' understanding of the document they adopted. Likewise, given the fragmentary and contradictory nature of the available evidence, the framers' communications to ratifying conventions could never authorize the reading of a given provision as serving an unjust purpose. We are entitled to conclude that the ratifiers adopted the framers' intentions "so far only, as we find those intentions plainly stated in the Constitution." Douglass summarized his understanding of the proper source of constitutional meaning in exaggeratedly simple, clarifying terms: the Constitution consisted in "only the paper itself, with its own plainly-written purposes."[34]

Douglass was well aware that the Constitution's text did not always yield a single, plain meaning. Two rules were paramount for the interpretation of ambiguous provisions. First, the Constitution's meaning and spirit were to be understood primarily by reference to its objects: one had to "look to the ends for which a law is made, and . . . construe its details in harmony with the ends sought." In keeping with the authoritative commentary of Justice Story, this rule required more specifically that one should be guided by the Preamble, which, as a summary of the Constitution's objects, was to be regarded as "indicative of the import of what is to follow."[35] Second, one had to interpret the Constitution, wherever possible, as an internally consistent whole: "One part of an instrument must not be allowed to contradict another unless the language be so explicit as to make the contradiction inevitable." A radical defect of the Garrisonian argument, Douglass contended, was that it rendered a constitution "full of contradictions."[36]

These interpretive presumptions in favor of internal consistency and the objects declared in the Preamble did not foreclose the possibility of anomalous provisions, representing exceptions to the principles and objects to which the Constitution was dedicated. But they did greatly reduce the likelihood of such provisions. Once again, Douglass's interpretive principle required that any anomalous, unjust provision be formulated with irresistible clarity, excluding any plausible attribution of a meaning consistent with justice. Here, it is also worth noting that in such cases, Douglass's principle allowed consideration of evidence beyond the bare text. Constructions based upon extratextual evidence of the ratifiers' understanding (perhaps as influenced by the framers) would be admissible to *reveal*, though not to *resolve*, constitutional ambiguity, where the effect would favor justice. Such evidence could render doubtful the reading of a given provision as serving an unjust purpose. Further, the rule of irresistible clarity for injustice was closely related to "another very important rule of legal interpretation," which disallowed any "'*unnecessary exception*'" to "'the prevailing provisions and principles of a law [that] are favorable to justice, and general in their nature and terms.'"[37] This rule would govern circumstances in which two clear, normally just objects of a law conflicted with one another, so that one temporarily had to give way, admitting a necessary exception to its enforcement.

For Douglass's purposes, the practical import of these rules of interpretation was clear. In the language of a later day, his jurisprudence was unabashedly "results-oriented." Although he may seem to have contrived its rules specifically to render an antislavery Constitution, for Douglass that result proceeded from no interpretive contrivance but rather from the essential nature of law: "neutral principles" of interpretation properly conceived could not require neutrality between justice and injustice. However that may be, by Douglass's interpretive rules, the presumption of an antislavery Constitution was virtually insuperable. For a constitution to be judged proslavery under them, its endorsement of slavery would need to be even stronger than that contained in Justice Taney's infamous *Dred Scott* formulation: it would need to affirm slavery "distinctly and expressly"[38] and also *unambiguously*. At least with respect to the issues surrounding slavery, to adopt Douglass's rules would mean to render detailed textual interpretation nearly supererogatory. Even so, his understanding of the rules of interpretation supplied only the blueprint, not the completed edifice, of his constitutional construction.

The Antislavery Constitution: The Presumption for Liberty

For Douglass, the postfounding triumph of the proslavery, Calhounian-Garrisonian reading of the Constitution represented "a great moral revolution"—in truth, a great counterrevolution, reversing the meaning of the founding. The *Dred Scott* ruling, its culmination, was a "huge judicial lie."[39] Yet, however plainly the Constitution's true meaning may have appeared to him, amid the complexity and confusion of prevailing argumentation, Douglass found it necessary to present varying arguments in support of his position. Simplified for convenience, they can be organized along two main lines. The first represents a more or less straightforward application of his natural justice rules of legal interpretation. In the second—the more complex, interesting, and powerful of the two—Douglass endeavored to show that his antislavery conclusions could withstand basic concessions to his adversaries' legal positivism. A summary of the first can mark a dialectical path to the second.

For Douglass's natural justice jurisprudence, the initiating question was the least difficult. That slavery constituted a gross violation of natural justice was beyond doubt. In its strictest application, his jurisprudence therefore implied that the U.S. Constitution was either antislavery or it possessed no authority as law. The latter, of course, was the conclusion reached by the Garrisonians. Rejecting any presumption in favor of liberty or justice in the interpretation of positive laws, Garrisonians went so far as to maintain that the identification of even a single unjust provision sufficed to nullify the whole of the Constitution.[40] Douglass argued entirely to the contrary, based on his presumption in favor of liberty. By a literalist reading of the "plain text," he not only affirmed the antislavery Constitution but also categorically denied "the presentation of a single pro-slavery clause in it."[41] He focused on two telling pieces of evidence: (1) the fact that the antebellum Constitution contained no explicit mention of slavery or servitude, and (2) the manifestly just, antislavery design of the Constitution's Preamble.

Douglass found great significance in the Constitution's omission of any explicit reference to slavery or servitude. To complicate Garrisonian readings of the historical evidence, he cited the testimony of Madison, who disclosed that "the convention would not consent that the idea of property in men should be admitted into the Constitution." But on the strict textualist principle, the decisive fact appeared in the Constitution's language. Making no express reference to slavery or servitude and referring to the inhabitants of the United States, without qualification by race or status in labor relations, as "the people," the Constitution could not be held to sanction slavery.[42] At the very least, its language in disputed passages introduced an element of ambiguity, which sufficed to establish the antislavery reading. To support this conclusion, Douglass surveyed the specific provisions commonly held to refer indirectly to slavery. He argued that the three-fifths clause in Article I, section 2 "might fairly apply to aliens—persons living in the country, but not naturalized." He conceded only for the sake of argument that Article I, section 9 referred to the "African slave trade"; the Constitution itself "[did] not warrant any such conclusion." In the troublesome provision in Article IV, section 2, the "persons held to service" could only signify indentured servants, not persons enslaved.[43]

As applied to the objects set forth in its Preamble, Douglass's plain-text reading implied that the Constitution not only withheld support for slavery but was, in fact, decidedly antagonistic to it. In his view, the antislavery position of the Preamble was clear in every clause. With justice and liberty intermingled among its expressly declared objects, the Preamble's principles were closely akin to those of the Declaration of Independence,[44] and neither could be held, despite the claims of Garrisonians and of the Taney Court, to sanction a regime of race-based inequality under the law. With their inclusive, unqualified references to "all men" and to "the People of the United States" and the "general welfare," the Declaration and the Preamble demanded and promised the securing of justice and the blessings of liberty for all Americans equally, irrespective of race or color.[45] The grave danger that slavery posed to "a more perfect Union" had long been evident. The Preamble's references to "domestic tranquillity," "the common defense," and "the general welfare" implied a national power and duty to eradicate slavery as the greatest threat to each. In this way, Douglass contended that even if one began from a positivist premise, conceiving of the Constitution as an instrument only of human, positive law, the conclusion of a natural-justice constitutionalism was inescapable. By virtue of the Preamble's linkage to the ideas of the Declaration, the positive law in this case *was* the natural law.

Furthermore, Douglass argued, the Constitution's proliberty position extended well beyond its statement of general purposes. The nation's supreme positive law guaranteed specific rights incompatible with slavery and delegated to the national government specific powers to act against slavery anywhere in the United States. Conceiving inclusively of U.S. citizenship under the Constitution, he inferred from various constitutional guarantees and prohibitions that the rights of U.S. citizens were incompatible with slavery. He cited the guarantee, in peacetime, of the writ of habeas corpus; the guarantee that no person shall be deprived of the rights of life, liberty, or property without due process of law;[46] the guarantee of a republican form of government to every state in the Union; and the prohibition of the enactment of any bill of attainder. It was squarely within "the power of the [U.S.] Supreme Court," as well as any lower federal court, "to abolish Slavery by a righteous decision" adjudicating any of these clauses. Likewise, the U.S. Congress held the specific powers to abolish the interstate slave trade, just as it had abolished the importation of slaves in 1808; to establish federal courts in slaveholding states and to appoint antislavery judges to them; to organize slaves as a militia; and to suppress insurrections, including their causes, among which slavery was certainly prominent. All in all, "Congress has power to abolish Slavery in the States, such Slavery being illegal, and unconstitutional."[47]

The militancy of Douglass's strictly textualist reading of the Constitution should be clear. For Douglass and Spooner, in contrast to more moderate political abolitionists, it was not enough to say that the Constitution was merely *antislavery* in its general spirit; rather, the Constitution was *abolitionist* in the precise sense. Slavery was worse than a constitutional anomaly—it was specifically *un-constitutional*. The Constitution conferred the duty as well as the power to abolish slavery everywhere in the nation. The federal government was "constitutionally bound to abolish Slavery in the States," pursuant to the supremacy clause in Article VI, section 2; abolition was a condition of the Constitution's standing as the supreme law of the land.[48] In this respect, Douglass's position represented a still more radical counterpart to Garrisonian immediatism. Rather than withdrawing political allegiance as a means of pressuring slaveholders to abolish slavery, as the Garrisonians did, Douglass demanded abolition by direct constitutional action, immediately upon the election of a government representing an antislavery majority. Anticipating a Republican victory in 1860, he believed that the moment was close at hand: "If 350,000 slaveholders have . . . been able to make slavery the vital and animating spirit of the American Confederacy for the last 72 years, now let the freemen of the North . . . resolve to blot out for ever the foul and haggard crime."[49]

At this point, a Garrisonian rejoinder is in order. As Douglass and Spooner characterized it, the Garrisonian argument entailed a reading of the Constitution as the product of a "bait-and-switch" scheme perpetrated by unscrupulous framers, who presented to the public a document cleansed of all references to slavery even as they intended it to aid in slavery's defense.[50] But the historical record, presented in abundance in Phillips's book, left no room for reasonable doubt: the Constitution's tacit recognition of slavery was publicly acknowledged, defended and deplored by various framers, and it was commonly understood by ratifiers. There had been no secret understanding whereby framers had defrauded ratifiers. The nation in 1787 and 1788 had entered into a constitutional bargain with slavery "willingly and with open eyes," wrote Phillips.[51] This fact enabled Garrisonians to object to the strict textualist position on moral as well as interpretive grounds. The original constitutional compromises were framed and adopted "in *good faith*." To affirm that the text mandated an abolitionist reading, contrary to the understanding of the framers and ratifiers, was "to advocate fraud and violence toward one of the contracting parties, *whose cooperation was secured only by an express agreement and understanding between them both, in regard to the clauses alluded to*."[52] Although a commitment by compact to abet injustice might be facially void, Garrisonians argued, in no case could a positive compact license action contrary to its originally agreed-upon meaning. Douglass and Spooner's natural-justice reading of the Constitution was itself an incitement to violate the natural law of keeping compacts.

Of all the objections leveled against constitutional abolitionism, Douglass found this one the most difficult to overcome. In a January 1851 letter to Gerrit Smith, written as his conversion to Smith's position was nearly complete, he declared himself "sick and tired of arguing on the slaveholders' side" of the constitutional debate, but he remained troubled by this question: "Is it good morality to take advantage of a legal flaw and put a meaning upon a legal instrument the very opposite of what we have good reason to believe was the intention of the men who framed it?"[53] Spooner's natural justice jurisprudence in its strict application yielded a simple answer: if the framers' intentions were criminal, good morality required that they be disregarded. But as he reflected upon this challenging objection, Douglass was evidently dissatisfied with any simple response. Moreover, the persisting influence of the opinion of the framers' proslavery intentions, which reached its extremity in the *Dred Scott* ruling, compelled him to address the objection on its own grounds. In his fuller statements affirming the antislavery constitution, he suggested a more complex line of argument, grounded in an alternative reading of the historical evidence of the framers' and ratifiers' understanding.

The Antislavery Constitution: The Design of Deferred Abolition

In developing this second line of argument, Douglass was willing to concede the interpretive relevance of evidence, beyond the text itself, regarding the framers' intentions. A companion concession directly followed—that various constitutional provisions did refer to slavery. He insisted that such concessions did not disturb his conclusion. The slavery provisions made no necessary, permanent exception to the instrument's general object of justice.

In his 1860 Glasgow speech on the Constitution and slavery, Douglass presented his most elaborate analysis of the four main provisions commonly cited in support of slavery. Considering, first, the three-fifths clause in Article I, section 2, he rejected the common reading, originated by dissenting antislavery founders, that the clause gave a political advantage to slaveholding states by increasing their congressional representation.[54] Supposing that "other persons" in that clause indeed signified those enslaved, Douglass observed that the three-fifths provision marked the lone instance in which the Constitution denied to states full congressional representation of any class of its inhabitants. The clause therefore represented "a downright disability laid upon the slaveholding states; one which deprives those states of two-fifths of their natural basis of representation." If the

Constitution supplied some political incentive for states to increase their slave populations, it supplied greater political incentives for slave states to liberate their slaves and thus to increase their representation by the further two-fifths.[55]

Douglass interpreted provisions in Article I, sections 8 and 9 in a like manner. Turning initially to what is commonly considered the slave trade clause (Article I, section 9), he contended, first, that even if that clause originally protected the slave trade, the protection had long since expired and thus had become a dead letter. More important, however, he found an antislavery design in the fact that the protection was merely temporary.[56] Concerning the insurrections clause in Article I, section 8, his argument was simpler. By a reasonable, broad construction, the power to suppress insurrections comprehended a necessary and proper power conclusively to suppress slave insurrections by abolishing their root cause, slavery itself. In fact, Douglass maintained from 1851 on, there was "no part of the Constitution from which slaveholders [had] more to apprehend" than from this clause.[57] If the Constitution recognized slavery's existence, it did not legitimate it. It recognized slavery even as it guaranteed individual and state rights incompatible with slavery and provided national powers to abolish it.

Having conceded that Article I, sections 2 and 9 might refer to slavery, however, Douglass refused to make any such concession regarding what seemed the most damning provision of all, commonly known as the fugitive slave clause in Article IV, section 2. Following Spooner, he persistently held that the clause referred only to "indentured apprentices and others" who were bound, "under contract duly made, to serve and labour." In the 1860 speech as in previous arguments concerning this clause, he based his claim on historical evidence as well as on the text itself. He was well aware of the historical evidence that Garrisonians adduced to support the contrary reading, drawn mainly from the 1787 Constitutional Convention and from Madison's explication of the clause at the Virginia ratifying convention. It was true, Douglass acknowledged, that the clause originated in an attempt by South Carolina delegates Charles Cotesworth Pinckney, Charles Pinckney, and Pierce Butler to insert a provision requiring that "fugitive slaves . . . be delivered up like criminals"; it was true, as well, that Madison had told Virginia's ratifiers that the clause would better secure their property in slaves. But it was also true that this attempt to gain explicit recognition of slavery in the Constitution was "promptly and indignantly rejected" in keeping with the Convention's view, as expressed and endorsed by Madison just a few days prior to the South Carolinians' proposal, that it was wrong to admit into the Constitution the idea that there could be property in men. At the very least, these ambiguities could be taken to show that neither the text itself nor the pertinent historical evidence yielded the "irresistible clarity" required to establish a proslavery provision.[58]

In making this argument, Douglass did not address the counterargument that the historical evidence concerning the framing of Article IV, section 2, clause 3 actually did demonstrate with sufficient clarity that the provision in question was meant to acknowledge slavery's local legality. The general principle of slavery's merely local legality was affirmed by more moderate proponents of the antislavery Constitution, including Supreme Court justices Benjamin R. Curtis and John McLean, the authors of vigorous dissents in the *Dred Scott* case.[59] With respect to the particular constitutional provision, the text did ultimately include a clause acceptable to Butler and the Pinckneys. In rejecting the South Carolinians' initial proposal, the convention seemed to reject only the national endorsement of slavery's moral legitimacy that its explicit recognition in the Constitution might have implied. So understood, that rejection was consistent with the reading of Article IV, section 2, clause 3 as a concession to slavery's local existence. These considerations might seem to support the charge that Douglass's refusal to concede a reference to slavery in that clause reflected his polemical and personal interests rather than a fair reading of the evidence. Impelled by his interest to advance the antislavery cause in the most efficacious manner possible, Douglass espoused a hard-line, abolitionist reading of the Constitution and also served personally as a leading agent of the Underground Railroad[60]—neither of which positions permitted him, on this objection, to concede even a limited accommodation of slaveholders' desire for a constitutional guarantee with respect to their recovery of fugitive slaves.

To vindicate on legal grounds his work for the Underground Railroad and his advocacy of resistance to the Fugitive Slave Law, Douglass needed more than his well-founded argument that the latter was unconstitutional irrespective of the meaning of Article IV, section 2, clause 3, as a violation of various criminal-procedure guarantees.[61] He also needed a more persuasive reading of that clause, one that acknowledged its relation to slavery and yet somehow showed that it imposed upon states no constitutional obligation to "deliver up" fugitives and thus to compel private actors such as Douglass to do so. Of course, no such reading was available to him. Still, the difficulties in his reading of the fugitive slave clause were not fatal to his larger argument. Although his work for the Underground Railroad did not permit him to concede the Constitution's accommodation of slavery on the issue of fugitives, such a concession would not have discredited his aggressively abolitionist reading of the Constitution as a whole. To see how he could have defended this position, it is necessary to reconstruct his second line of argument further, beginning with his revised reading of the Founders' original understanding.

Underlying Douglass's modified argument concerning the meaning of the Constitution's text was his modified understanding of the framers' intentions. In January 1851, he continued to affirm that the Garrisonians were "doubtless right" about the framers' proslavery intentions. But six months later, he reached the opposite conclusion.[62] He was well aware, as noted, that a few delegates at the Philadelphia convention spoke in defense of slavery. He was also aware of the softness of some Founders' opposition to slavery. He lamented the comfort that slaveholders could derive from the fact that some of the greatest Founders were also slaveholders; especially Washington's and Jefferson's "anti-slavery declarations are less potent for good than their pro-slavery examples have been made for evil."[63] Nonetheless, as even the ardently proslavery Georgian Alexander Stephens (soon to become vice president of the Confederate States of America) conceded, the emergence of a powerful proslavery partisanship postdated the founding: "All the public men of the South were once against [slavery]." The general truth was that the Garrisonians were wrong, as Justice Taney was still more grievously wrong, about the founding generation's opinions with respect to slavery: "The intentions of the framers of the Constitution were good, not bad."[64]

No less important than the Founders' general opposition to slavery, however, were the specific character and intensity of that opposition. Although most Founders shared with the succeeding generation's radical abolitionists a principled disapproval of slavery, they did not share the latter's insistence upon immediate abolition. But according to Douglass, that was because they saw no need for it. They regarded slavery as "an expiring and doomed system, destined to speedily disappear from the country." In the eyes of many Founders, to press for immediate, national abolition would have been dangerously imprudent, imperiling a fragile Union to achieve an end that, they supposed, would likely be achieved in any event in the reasonably near future. Fearful of a radical solution and hopeful for a moderate one, most of the Founders favored a policy of deferred and gradual emancipation.[65] More specifically, they believed that by licensing (and creating a powerful public expectation of) a federal prohibition on the importation of slaves into the United States after 1807, they had supplied the essential constitutional impetus for slavery's eventual abolition.[66] Of course, in Douglass's hindsight, the Founders' optimism concerning slavery's transience

"The Pound of Flesh, but Not One Drop of Blood"

appeared as a "stupendous error."[67] In fact, he believed them culpable, together with the succeeding generation, for missing repeated opportunities "to seal the doom of the slave system," first at the close of the War of Independence (when "slavery was young and small" and "the nation might easily have abolished it"), next at the framing of the Constitution, and finally in the dispute over the terms of Missouri's statehood in 1819.[68] But the relevant point concerned the intentions, not the effects, of their constitutional policy. Summarizing the argument in 1863, he fashioned a revealing metaphor: "If in its origin slavery had any relation to the government, it was only as the scaffolding to the magnificent structure, to be removed as soon as the building was completed."[69]

The full meaning of Douglass's scaffolding metaphor, which epitomized his second line of constitutional-abolitionist argument, deserves closer attention than it has yet received. Admirers of the metaphor have properly focused on its implication that the Constitution's accommodations of slavery were accidental, not essential, to its core meaning.[70] But difficult questions remain concerning specifically *when, how,* and *by whom* the building was to be judged completed and the scaffolding of slavery removed. On its face, Douglass's reading of the framers' intentions stands in uncertain relation to the conclusions in both his main lines of constitutional argument. In each, he concluded (1) that slavery had never been and could never be legal under the U.S. Constitution, and (2) that the Constitution required slavery's immediate national abolition, to be effectuated as soon as an abolitionist legislative majority was instated. But his reading of the framers' intentions seems to imply that the Constitution required no more than slavery's deferred abolition and therefore that it embodied some recognition, however limited and temporary, of slavery's legality. By this scaffolding argument, Douglass might seem to have endorsed in its essentials the moderate position taken by Lincoln and the Republicans. Admirers of this argument seem to approve especially its seeming assimilation of Douglass to Lincoln and the Founders. In his "Slaveholders' Rebellion" speech on July 4, 1862, arguing against the Missouri Compromise, Douglass praised as "wise" the Founders' policy, which, somewhat vaguely described, "was to confine slavery to its original limits, and thus leave the system to die out under the gradual operation of the principles of the Constitution and the spirit of the age."[71] Yet he consistently rejected as insufficiently radical the "nonextensionist" policy of the Free-Soil and Republican parties in the 1850s, even when he advocated voting for those parties' candidates.[72] The following seems the most reasonable construction of Douglass's argument.

Notwithstanding his Lincolnesque reference to slavery as constitutional scaffolding, Douglass never retracted his insistence that slavery never had been and never could be legalized. A brief expression of relative moderation by Spooner can help reconcile these two points. Around the time of the framing of the Constitution, according to Spooner,

> there very probably may have been a general belief among the people, that slavery would for a while live on, *in sufferance;* that the government, until the nation should have become attached to the constitution, and cemented and consolidated by the habit of union, would be too weak [to achieve abolition]. But to suppose that the nation at large did not look upon the constitution as destined to destroy slavery whenever its principles should be carried into full effect, is obviously to suppose an intellectual impossibility.[73]

This observation received little more than momentary attention from Spooner, but it played a more significant role in Douglass's argument. Construed on this premise, his scaffolding principle was perfectly consistent with the proposition that the Constitution in no way conferred legitimacy upon slavery or recognized its lawfulness, in the strict sense, anywhere. It embodied instead a policy of "sufferance"—of temporary, grudging tolerance—for an institution that its principles and many of its provisions plainly identified as evil. In light of the rules of legal interpretation summarized previously, the Constitution's concessions to slavery could appear as temporarily necessary exceptions to its dedication to universal liberty. The exceptions could be judged necessary in circumstances in which the Preamble's objects of securing the blessings of liberty to all and of forming a more perfect union temporarily conflicted with one another. The temporary tolerance of slavery was to function as scaffolding in aiding the construction of a union strong enough, in time, to contend with slavery directly. The founding period and the early years of the Republic would then represent a peculiar legal situation in which the Constitution's antislavery principles and powers were legally authoritative and yet, by common understanding, temporarily suspended in their practical operation.

Still, one may question how Douglass could have advocated slavery's immediate national abolition in view of his acknowledgment that the Founders supported, at best, a policy of deferred abolition. Although he would not concede the point, the optimism that forecast slavery's impending demise seems also to have justified, to the minds of many framers, a trust in the states to see the wisdom of abolition within the foreseeable future. So the difficult question persisted, raised by virtually all other parties to the controversy: how could the general government directly effect slavery's immediate, national abolition without brazenly violating the original understanding whereby slaveholding and antislavery states agreed to unite under law?

After a certain point, Douglass's argument in response becomes a matter of conjecture. But the basis of a defensible conjecture appears in his lengthy speech on the *Dred Scott* decision, wherein he contended (with some overstatement) that "all" the founders "looked for the gradual *but certain* abolition of slavery, and shaped the Constitution with a view to this grand result."[74] In brief, Douglass's inference seems to have been that his demand for immediate national abolition did not contradict the Founders' original support for deferred abolition. The latter policy might have *formerly* imposed a binding limit on national power, in the founding era and perhaps for a generation or so thereafter, but it was no longer binding on Douglass's generation. The premises of the Garrisonians' and slaveholders' argument could be turned against their authors. Their proslavery conclusion rested largely on the claim that a constitutional accommodation of slavery was a sine qua non of union for the southernmost original states. Because at least Georgia and the Carolinas would not have ratified a constitution lacking some such accommodation, it was illegitimate to read the Constitution later as permitting or mandating departures from that original understanding. But by the same token, the prevalence of antislavery opinion among most Founders requires that a corresponding condition be attached to at least some northern states' ratifications. Just as delegates from the Deep South would not have ratified a constitution that required or permitted immediate abolition, so, too, delegates from several northern states could not be supposed to have ratified a constitution that protected slavery in perpetuity. They could only be supposed to have ratified a constitution that honored their expectation that at some point, the odious scaffolding would be removed from their great edifice of liberty.

So understood, Douglass's scaffolding argument did not depend on any nineteenth-century conception of a "living Constitution." The claim was not that the Constitution's meaning had somehow changed over the decades from accommodative to prohibitive of slavery; it was, instead, that the Constitution was from the beginning antislavery and changed only from a *contingently* to an *actively* antislavery instrument. The original Constitution incorporated a tacit contingency principle, such that slavery was to be tolerated only temporarily, provisionally, and instrumentally—tolerated only so far as the policy of tolerance served to strengthen and to complete the constitutional union and only so long as the utility of that policy (and slavery itself) was understood to have a definite, proximate terminus. States were then entrusted with the power of abolition in the faith that they would exercise that power in due course. On Douglass's scaffolding logic, when the Union became sufficiently complete to elect abolition—or, less optimistically, when it became strong enough to withstand the upheaval of abolition—then the original constitutional imperative of tolerance would no longer be operative. The framers' decision in 1787 to defer slavery's abolition by entrusting it, for a time, to individual states would then be consistent with a constitutional mandate, at some point in the following century, to abolish it by national action.[75]

It must be emphasized that Douglass presented this argument only in fragmentary form, leaving it and the evidence on which it depended enshrouded in a troubling degree of indeterminacy. He neither did nor could specify, based on evidence in the Constitution's text or history, the period of time within which federal deference to the states on slavery was to be observed or the mechanism by which initially dormant federal abolition powers were to be activated. A further objection then arises, to the effect that indeterminacy of such magnitude mandated a strong presumption in favor of continuing the Founders' policy of tolerance. Douglass's proposal of a radical departure from that policy would seem justifiable, according to this objection, only in extreme circumstances—only when it had become clear, beyond reasonable doubt, that continued tolerance could no longer strengthen the Union or buy time for those seeking slavery's peaceful abolition but instead could only strengthen the forces dedicated to slavery's perpetuation.

Yet even this powerful reservation could not by itself overcome Douglass's argument for constitutional abolition. If an original "federal consensus" on slavery ever existed,[76] it must have included the conviction that slavery was unjust and impermanent in the American constitutional order. Such a consensus would have dissolved the moment the original understanding of slavery as a deviant institution in the course of its reasonably expeditious extinction was demoted to the status of a partisan opinion, opposed by an insurgent partisan opinion of slavery as a positive good worthy of expansion and perpetuation. In Douglass's judgment, precisely that dissolution had occurred. At some point subsequent to the founding—perhaps as early as 1793 with the invention of the cotton gin, perhaps in 1819 with the Missouri controversy, but certainly by the 1850s[77]—the slaveholding interest had renounced the original understanding and replaced it with an affirmation of slavery's permanent and even honored presence within the U.S. constitutional order. By terminating any reasonably conceivable original consensus on slavery, the slave power had also terminated any obligation on the part of northern states or the federal government to acquiesce in slavery's continuation. In this manner, Douglass could coherently argue that the Founders temporarily tolerated the existence of slavery in 1787 and that a national majority by the 1850s possessed a constitutional right and duty to effect its abolition as soon as possible.

A final, more pragmatic objection brings us to the heart of Douglass's antebellum argument. Garrisonians contended that the aggressive federal abolitionist action that constitutional radicals demanded would provoke immediate civil war.[78] Douglass did not deny the likely result; he simply judged it unobjectionable. He did, however, deny that such federal action could be properly viewed as a provocation. Slavery was by nature a war of masters against slaves and against the national law of liberty that bound them both; for the federal government to act directly against slavery would have signified only its decision to contest actively a war that was already long under way. Still, one might sharpen the objection. The generalized civil war that would have followed federal abolitionist action would have brought a dramatic escalation not only in violence but also in the present danger to the survival of the constitutional union. To insist on immediate political abolition was, then, to contemplate a national peril easily comparable in gravity to the situation in 1787. If Douglass could concede (at times) that the toleration of slavery had been reasonably regarded as a necessary exception to the Constitution's dedication to liberty in 1787, why could he not follow moderate Republicans such as Lincoln in judging such a concession reasonable in the 1850s and beyond? Even granted his claim that the federal government possessed the constitutional power to abolish slavery, why could he not agree that it remained for the time being unwise to exercise that power?

The answer, for Douglass, lay in the alteration in the slave power over time. In 1787, the Founders confronted slaveholding powers that seemed, even to many slaveholding statesmen themselves, clearly in decline. Amid such circumstances, they could reasonably regard immediate abolition as presenting a needless danger to their nascent Union. By the 1850s, although the Union itself had gained great strength, the slave power had metastasized into a formidable tyranny, animated by a combination of massive material interest, arrogance, and paranoia, by whose lights the distinction between legitimate self-defense and aggressive expansion no longer held meaning. The implication was that the

Founders' containment policy could no longer be justified by the Founders' principles or by the Constitution's Preamble. The old policy had failed: successive attempts at compromise had left slavery stronger, not weaker,[79] so that by the 1850s at the latest, no compromise held any hope of restoring it to "the course of its ultimate extinction."[80] Douglass's conclusion can be clarified by language drawn from twentieth-century international politics. With respect to slavery, the distinction between containment and appeasement had collapsed. American slavery constituted an evil empire; it was a system of giant wrongs harboring aggressive designs, and the proper response to it was neither to appease it nor to contain it but simply to defeat it.[81] For the antebellum generation, the Founders' principles entailed a policy they themselves had not foreseen: to form a more perfect union and to secure the blessings of liberty both required direct national action against slavery. In the novel circumstances of Douglass's day, moral principle, prudence, and constitutional law converged in mandating an aggressive, conclusive antislavery policy.

Constitutional Abolition and Rational Hopefulness

In the enthusiastic judgment of biographer Philip S. Foner, Douglass's prophetically early understandings of the prudence and necessity as well as the justice of waging an abolitionist war "stamp him as one of the greatest minds of his time, a master strategist and tactician, and a people's leader of superb statesmanship." For Foner and others, the implication is that Douglass was superior in prudence not only to the Garrisonians but also and especially to the more revered, yet more conservative and reactive Lincoln.[82] But in Douglass's own understanding, his claim to prudence or wisdom in statesmanship depended in significant part on the soundness of his reading of the law. Indispensable to his hopefulness were his convictions that the American people as a whole could be returned to their original constitutional faith and that the Constitution in which they had vested the authority of the supreme positive law was itself informed by the antislavery principles of the law of nature.

Critics in our own time, no less than those in the antebellum period, challenge the reading of the Constitution on which Douglass rested his hopes. For law professor Robert M. Cover, author of a thorough study of antislavery jurisprudence in the Anglo-American tradition, Douglass and other radical political abolitionists were "constitutional utopians," reading into the existing document their ideal visions of a law that guaranteed liberty for all. Likewise for William

Wiecek, author of a thorough history of antislavery constitutionalism in the United States, the radicals' arguments were "flawed and disingenuous." Philosophy professor Charles W. Mills holds Douglass's constitutional arguments to be so transparently wrong that they excuse the suspicion (which Mills rejects) that Douglass contrived them in an act of polemical "masking."[83] The thrust of this line of criticism is to characterize Douglass's constitutional abolitionism as a further mode of heroic opposition, vindicated in the end only by the force of arms. As a gigantic violation of the natural law, slavery activated a natural right and duty of opposition by any proper means—including, it would seem, the polemical reinterpretation of constitutional law. Viewed in this light, Douglass carried the spirit of his friend John Brown into the field of constitutional law, summoning allies by appropriating the Constitution as his own abolitionist arsenal.

To give such critics their due, one must acknowledge the difficulties in Douglass's reading of the original constitutional consensus. Neither the Constitution's text nor its history supported his inference that the framers contemplated the delegation of a plenary national abolitionist power in any circumstance short of actual civil war. One can hardly doubt what Douglass himself came close to acknowledging—that his abolitionist reading of the Constitution was colored by his sense of urgency in opposing the monstrous evil of slavery. Without wholly endorsing the opinion that he treated constitutional law as merely another form of arms, one can fairly say that in the field of constitutional interpretation, Douglass argued more as a lawyer than as a judge.

At the same time, if such criticisms succeed in exposing flaws in Douglass's constitutional arguments, they do not thereby vindicate Garrisonian or neo-Garrisonian perspectives. The portion of justice in those criticisms tends instead to support the positions taken by Republican or political-antislavery moderates, and the support it lends the latter positions permits an appreciation of a substantial measure of wisdom in Douglass's constitutionalism. The antislavery sentiment of most Founders, even if abstractly held, was beyond doubt, and the wisdom that Douglass and constitutional radicals shared with moderates extended beyond their affirmation of the Constitution's antislavery spirit. The slave power's reaction to Lincoln's purportedly moderate, legalist containment policy confirmed Lincoln's view that that policy was far more radical than Douglass and other radical abolitionists had expected.[84] But as Foner emphasized, that fact supplied important vindication for Douglass, too. That the slaveholding South mainly viewed Lincoln's mere election, on a nonaggressive platform, as itself an intolerable provocation confirmed Douglass's view of the slave power as intransigently committed to slavery's perpetuation and expansion and therefore as rebellious to the core, posing by its very nature a mortal danger to lawful government everywhere in the United States and beyond. The war came, as Douglass expected, because it naturally had to come; the conflict between liberty and slavery truly was irrepressible.[85] And in the natural course of the war, national action against slavery became a constitutional as well as a moral imperative. Douglass's insistence on an abolitionist war from the outset, though not as distinctive to the radicals as he believed at the time, was nonetheless prophetic.[86]

In his second argument, constructed upon his reading of the external historical evidence of the Founders' understanding, Douglass implied that the Constitution delegated to the federal government contingent abolition powers that were activated by the slave power's postfounding commitment to the perpetuation and nationalization of slavery. That a majority of the Founders would have rejected this understanding of the conditions that activated a federal abolition power is overwhelmingly likely. To hold that the change in slaveholding states' commitment to their institution sufficed to activate such a power was unwarranted on constitutional grounds and perhaps also dangerously premature on prudential grounds. But the difficulties in Douglass's understanding of its particular activating conditions do not discredit his general contention that the Constitution provided a contingent federal abolition power. If the circumstances post-1793 or post-1819 marked a novel constitutional situation, according to Douglass, the onset of formal war in April 1861 meant the emergence of a still more radically novel situation, one that could effectually unify the positions of constitutional radicals and moderates. The event of an actual attack on the constitutional union meant the activation of at least one contingently delegated federal power upon which radicals and moderates agreed. Near the end of that fateful April, Douglass welcomed the opportunity to plant his argument for constitutional abolition on the comparatively solid ground suggested by "that great statesman, John Quincy Adams" and soon to be occupied by the newly inaugurated Lincoln. The former president "once told the Chivalry to their faces," Douglass informed his Rochester audience, "that the power to set the slaves at liberty was clearly implied in the war-making power."[87]

With the arguments elaborated in this chapter, despite their serious flaws, Douglass contributed vital elements of constitutional statesmanship both to the abolitionist movement and to the Union cause in the Civil War. His and other political abolitionists' rejection of the proslavery Constitution bolstered loyalist efforts by refusing to concede the ground of legality to the rebel cause. At the same time, by his rebuke of Garrisonian calls for disunion, Douglass rejected the superficially appealing, ultimately self-destructive posture of alienation from law and country by which, as we shall see, racial reformers were recurrently tempted. In the field of constitutional law in relation to slavery, the case for Douglass's rational hopefulness was strong. Contrary to radical proslavery and abolitionist critics, he and the political abolitionists insisted on interpreting the Constitution in light of the objects declared in its Preamble—a position that was squarely in the mainstream of U.S. constitutional interpretation—and their arguments for an interpretive bias toward liberty and natural justice made a historic, revitalizing contribution to a great tradition of natural-law jurisprudence. On the decisive issue, despite its originally compromised character, the Constitution, when put to the ultimate test, did provide sufficient resources for lawful abolition.

In the final analysis, it is therefore best to understand Douglass's arguments as instances of constitutional teleology rather than of constitutional utopianism. Though prone to interpretive excess, Douglass read the Constitution not simply as he *wished* it to be nor even as it *needed* to be to conform with the principles of natural justice but rather as it truly *was* in its essential, completed form, with its disfiguring provisional scaffolding finally removed in fulfillment of its original design.

With this conclusion, however, the case for Douglass's rational hopefulness—for the justice of the Constitution and the efficacy of natural law in America, applied to race relations—remains far from complete. An abolitionist Constitution was not yet a properly egalitarian Constitution, for a condition of nonslavery or natural liberty was not yet one of equal and full citizenship. Douglass's arguments for the rationality of hopefulness as he turned his attention to the construction of a new republic including new African American citizens provide the subject matter of the next two chapters.

4

"Let Us Alone":
Race and the Constitution of Liberty

It will be equally forgotten that the vigor of government is essential to the
spirit of liberty.
  Alexander Hamilton, Federalist *no. 1*

IN *LIFE AND TIMES*, first published in 1881, Douglass reflected on the momentous events of 1865, which had seemed at the moment to conclude "the
deepest desire and the great labor of my life." He recalled experiencing a
strangely human sadness: "I felt that I had reached the end of the noblest and
best part of my life; my school was broken up, my church disbanded, and the beloved congregation dispersed, never to come together again."[1] The forces of
union and liberty had finally prevailed in the war; the Thirteenth Amendment
had been ratified; there was talk of disbanding the American Anti-Slavery Society; and the indefatigable Garrison would soon discontinue publication of the
Liberator.[2] The grand, self-transcending passion of his entire life to that point
now seemed fulfilled, and Douglass confronted his own mortality as he contemplated the fading of the revolutionary pathos that had sustained, ennobled, and
defined him.

But his sadness could be only momentary. Douglass knew very well that the
achievement of formal emancipation did not mean the coming of a new millennium in America. The events of 1865 marked not the end but only the end of the
beginning of the abolitionist revolution, which awaited its consummation in the
establishment of liberty for all. For the friends of universal freedom and racial
equality, much remained in doubt, and the doubts centered on a question that
had long bedeviled their cause. "Everybody has asked the question," Douglass
observed at the beginning of that year, "and they learned to ask it early of the abolitionists, 'What shall we do with the Negro [once emancipated]?' "[3]

Douglass saw in that question "the one grand cause of the tremendous war now upon us, and likely to continue upon us, until the country is united upon some wise policy concerning it."[4] From the founding period onward, fears concerning the consequences of emancipation had done much to sustain slavery. Again representative is the foreboding of Thomas Jefferson, who had believed it unsafe for slaveholders to release their slaves. More committed defenders of slavery had pointed to the experiences of Haiti and the West Indies to make the point that slavery was preferable to the conditions likely to emerge after its abolition.[5] Such obstructive fears were not peculiar to the slaveholding South. In a January 1862 editorial, Douglass detected beneath the fears attending the post-emancipation question a "slavery-engendered prejudice, which every-where pervades the country." At times, those fears even appeared "with a show of sincere solicitude for the welfare of the slaves themselves." Many northerners who disapproved of slavery in principle still saw no future for a large class of freed-people in America. They might not desire to work, in which case they would "become vagrants, paupers and criminals, overrunning all our alms houses, jails and prisons." Or they would desire to work but "their former masters would not employ them." After emancipation, "they would all come to the North," where they would conflict with white laborers over jobs: "A fierce war of races would be the inevitable consequence, and the black race would . . . be exterminated."[6]

To be controlled by such fears, Douglass continued, would be to reduce liberty from a mandate of the natural moral law to a mere experiment. It would mean that the audacious nation to which James Madison once credited "a revolution which has no parallel in the annals of human society," even as it emerged from an unparalleled war fought to defend that revolution's achievement, showed itself still timid and reluctant to own its revolutionary heritage in its full entailment.[7] But despite his great confidence in the natural law of liberty, Douglass acknowledged that the question facing the nation was not an easy one. Anticipating the aftermath of war in 1862, he foresaw the "tremendous undertaking" of reconstruction. "When slavery the grim and guilty motive for this horrid war shall have been abolished . . . when sullen, silent, and gloomy but subdued hate shall settle upon the Southern mind, then will come the time for the exercise of the highest of all human faculties. A profounder wisdom, a holier zeal, than belongs to the prosecution of war, will be required."[8] This "profounder wisdom," transcending that of the revolutionary destroyer of an unjust order, was the wisdom proper to the genuine founder of a new order. In this chapter, we will consider Douglass's contributions to that wisdom in his reflections on the nature and conditions of freedom and progress in the postemancipation United States.

"Do Nothing!"

A problem appears at the outset. Emphasizing the depth of wisdom required, Douglass nonetheless offered what may seem a perplexingly simple answer to the central postemancipation question. In an impromptu speech to the annual meeting of the Massachusetts Anti-Slavery Society in 1865, he came again to that troublesome question, "What shall we do with the Negro?" and he repeated his oft-stated reply: "Do nothing with us! Your doing with us has already played the mischief with us. Do nothing with us! If . . . the Negro cannot stand on his own legs, let him fall. . . . All I ask is, give him a chance to stand on his own legs! Let him alone!"[9]

This response is among the most widely assailed of Douglass's positions. Given the extreme vulnerability of the freedpeople's condition, the insistent "do nothing" rhetoric in which Douglass clothed his appeals for formal rights could seem grossly misconceived, along with the theme of self-reliance or of "self-made men," of which he made himself a primary champion. Did not such rhetoric place an unjust and unrealistic burden on those lately enslaved to elevate themselves—did it not tacitly "blame the victims," as we say—while excusing from responsibility the nation that profited from their enslavement? And how could it cohere with his various calls for public responsibility toward the freedpeople? In recent decades, critics have contended that Douglass could supply no satisfactory answers to such questions; the "do nothing" doctrine betrayed an intellectual inconsistency and a serious moral failing on his part. For William S. McFeely, Douglass displayed a callousness toward the destitute southern farmworkers "with whom he had once shared a field." In presenting a "pull-up-your-socks sermon" at a time of great peril for African Americans (in 1877) and in objecting to the "exodus" of southern blacks who migrated to the North and West beginning in the late 1870s, McFeely charges, Douglass affirmed "the reasoning of the white Redeemers."[10] From a different perspective, Wilson Jeremiah Moses agrees that Douglass's rhetoric reflected an element of Jeffersonian, laissez-faire individualism that fatally compromised his vision of Reconstruction.[11]

These objections rest on oversimplifications of Douglass's meaning. Douglass acknowledged the seeming contradiction between his demands for vigorous federal protection of the rights of freedpeople and other people of color and his equally forceful demands that postemancipation America "do nothing with us" or "let us alone." But he denied any such inconsistency in fact,[12] and if we allow for a measure of rhetorical inflation, he stood on solid ground in doing so. A fairer representation of his position may be summarized as follows. Douglass's self-reliance rhetoric was necessary to his argument for both principled and prudential reasons, but his simpler formulations must not be taken in abstraction from their accompanying qualifications. In fact, Douglass did not issue his "do nothing" demand in terms committing him to a dogmatic individualism or laissez-faire ideology. Restated in its proper refinement, his demand "let [the Negro] alone" meant "give him fair play and let him alone, but *be sure you give him fair play.*"[13] To an audience of Boston abolitionists in early 1862, he explained the general meaning of this notion by reference to a principle of nonexceptionalism. His demand for nothing but fair play from the American people meant that the ruling majority should "do nothing with us, by us, or for us *as a particular class.* . . . The broadest and bitterest of the black man's misfortunes is the fact that he is everywhere regarded and treated as an *exception* to the principles and maxims which apply to other men."[14]

The idea of fair play carried specific moral and constitutional implications in Douglass's argument. Consistent with reasonable understandings of self-reliance and constitutionally limited government, his idea encompassed a broad array of affirmative as well as negative duties of government, involving not only protective but also remedial and developmental powers. In his final presentation of his "Self-Made Men" speech, he reiterated in 1893, "I meant all that I said and a good deal more than some understand by fair play."[15] But before we consider its specific applications concerning governmental powers and duties, it is necessary to understand the principled and prudential reasons for Douglass's "do nothing" demand. Central to this reasoning was his understanding of the indispensable virtues of self-reliance.

Self-Made Men

Douglass's "do nothing" rhetoric of the 1860s and 1870s represents one aspect of his career-long championing of the virtues of self-reliance or self-making. The principle is prominent in his autobiographies, ordered as a succession of declarations of independence from various paternal authorities ranging from the falsely paternalist slave masters to Garrison to the Founding Fathers and perhaps even to "Father Abraham" Lincoln.[16] In the late 1850s, he composed

"Self-Made Men," which would become his signature, most popular speech, as he delivered variations of it approximately fifty times from 1859 to 1893. He summarized his great theme as he concluded the 1881 edition of *Life and Times:* "I have taught that the 'fault is not in our stars, but in ourselves, that we are underlings,' that 'who would be free, themselves must strike the blow.'"[17] The virtues of self-making or self-reliance also play prominent roles in the more direct counsels that Douglass addressed to the various classes with which he identified.[18]

The primacy of self-reliance is viewed by some as an Emersonian element of Douglass's moral thought and by others as a restatement of the classically American theme originally sounded by the representative man of revolutionary America, Benjamin Franklin.[19] But its deepest roots were in the principle of self-ownership that Douglass held to be fundamental to his natural rights arguments. In the argument of John Locke, the preeminent philosopher of natural rights liberalism, human rights are conceived of as properties, and one originates a property through the application of one's labor. Human beings are self-owners so far as they are self-*makers*—the makers and owners of actions and thus responsible agents capable of identity over time, of law, and of happiness.[20] For Douglass, the principle of self-making could not be reduced to an expression of American mythology or of middle-class, bourgeois prejudice. He placed it at the center of his moral thought because he understood it to be inseparable from the natural rights principles without which his opposition to slavery and his affirmation of free, democratic government were unintelligible.

Moreover, in this instance, too, Douglass's natural-rights argument was also a natural-law argument. He held self-making to be at once the basis of natural rights, a right itself, and a duty. On the state-of-nature premise of his classical liberalism, natural human rights are naturally threatened, and that fact entails a natural duty of self-defense. We saw in Chapter Two that one of the aims of slavery was to reduce its victims to creatures of the present moment. Freedom requires one's temporal extension; it is necessarily forward-looking. The duty of self-defense also entails a duty to combat prospective aggressions and thus to provide against weaknesses that invite predatory assaults. "Ignorance and moral degradation made us the easy victims of slavery in the first place," Douglass reminded an 1885 audience, and they effected an equally dangerous exposure in the postemancipation years.[21] Given slavery's design as the negation of human nature, the full overcoming of slavery required a strong affirmation of moral human nature. Especially among those struggling for liberation, the natural law commanded a strong affirmation of moral agency and a strong repudiation of any dependence on others that might provide support to slavery.

Douglass took pains to diminish the harshness of this rule by stressing its universality. It was certainly true that postwar African Americans faced extraordinary disadvantages. But in the more distanced perspective that he recommended, the intensifying injustice that they confronted in the post-Reconstruction years was best viewed as the effect of a natural "law of society," not essentially dissimilar to adversities that other peoples had confronted and overcome.[22] Anglo-Saxons, Jews, and many other peoples had been forced to overcome the scorn and opposition of temporarily more powerful others, and he himself had had to rise from a low beginning in the "singularly unpromising" district of Tuckahoe. All these were mere episodes, Douglass argued, in the story of the human species as a whole, which had elevated itself from its own distinctively disadvantaged beginning. He provided his most vivid summation of this central theme of the human story in one of his last major speeches, at the 1894 dedication of the Colored Industrial School at Manassas, Virginia. "Of all the creatures that live and move and have their being on this green earth, man at his birth is the most helpless and the most in need of instruction. . . . Yet this little helpless weakling . . . is the lord of creation . . . the discoverer of unknown islands, capes and continents, and the founder of great empires and capable of limitless civilization."[23] In Douglass's didactic history, human beings stand out as the distinctively progressive, revolutionary, self-made—and therefore the distinctively rights-bearing—species.

Douglass's exhortations to self-help were not only lofty invocations of a natural duty; they also represented his prudent responses to concrete situational imperatives. First, his harsher, seemingly Darwinian formulations ("let him fall!") are best understood as rhetorically inflated, made necessary in context by the same fears that generated the postemancipation question in the first place. In the face of widely held opinions that Africans and their descendants were unfit for and even imperiled by freedom—opinions gaining renewed vitality with the advent of racial-Darwinist theories after the war[24]—the danger was great that any significant concession of a need for assistance or any failure to call for the cultivation of virtue among the freedpeople would be misconstrued as evidence of African Americans' inferiority. Given the prevalence of such opinion, Douglass's "do nothing" demand was likely meant as a defiant rebuke to slavery's persisting sympathizers and as a calling of the bluff of those who made a mere show of solicitude for the freedpeople's welfare.

Rhetorical exaggerations aside, however, Douglass had reason to believe that it was genuinely necessary, especially in the early postemancipation years, to exhort audiences of free or newly freed people of color to develop the virtues required for material independence. This was, in part, due to his long-held sensitivity to the poverty endemic among them and the fundamental dangers that it posed to their freedom. "Poverty is our greatest calamity," he told a large Nashville, Tennessee, audience of African American farmers and mechanics in 1873. "It draws down upon us the very condition which makes us a helpless, hopeless, dependent, and dispirited people, the target for the contempt and scorn of all around us."[25] Persistent poverty deformed one's human character as a distinctively progressive being and planted in others an opinion of one's incomplete humanity. It therefore signified persistent exposure to tyranny. And conversely, when they could boast of a "class of men noted for enterprise, industry, economy and success," Douglass assured an African American audience in Elmira, New York, a few years later, "we shall no longer have any trouble in the matter of civil and political rights."[26]

To overcome their impoverishment, Douglass offered intentionally simplified advice, as to his Nashville audience in 1873: "Work for [money] and save it when you get it. . . . We can work, and the grateful earth yields as readily and as bountifully to the touch of black industry as of white. We can work, and by this means we can retrieve all our losses."[27] Perhaps he was excessively hopeful in offering such advice. Urging the freedpeople to cultivate the virtues they needed to make good on their new opportunities, he may have presumed too confidently that those opportunities were, in fact, available, trusting too much in the Republican Party's hold on national power and in its resolve to enforce African Americans' newly affirmed constitutional rights. His return to fierce oppositional rhetoric in the 1880s may indicate his own assent to this criticism in hindsight. But if there was an excess of hopefulness in his exhortations to virtue, there was also a substantial element of realism. Douglass's special appeals to industrious self-help on the part of the freedpeople must also be understood as a commentary on the lingering effects of slavery's systematic despotism. Despite his occasional denials,[28] he feared that a degradation of the work ethic among African Americans was among slavery's most damaging legacies.

Speaking to a mostly African American Baltimore audience in November 1864 (shortly after Maryland's enactment of emancipation), Douglass issued "to my colored friends" a special reminder: "You must not think that freedom means absence from work."[29] That he had some cause to worry about such an attitude is indicated by a fact of postwar life in the South that was at once threatening and gratifying to the old master class. There can be "no doubt," according to the eminent historian Leon F. Litwack, that the former slaves' "productivity declined under freedom. . . . What most planters suspected and many freedmen readily conceded was a general and deliberate slowdown."[30] Their aversion to regular labor was understandable, largely reflecting a desire to experience their newly gained freedom as something palpably different from their daily grind in slavery. But for Douglass, that aversion likely also reflected the disdain for labor that pervaded the slaveholding South, beginning with the master class. Among slavery's great transgressions of the natural moral law was its severing of the natural linkage of prosperity to virtue, by rewarding sloth and robbing labor of its proper rewards. "There are not, under the whole heavens," he had observed in *Bondage and Freedom,* "a set of men who cultivate such an intense dread of labor as do the slaveholders." In the slaveholders' ethos, laboring was a low, degrading, purely necessary activity, suitable mainly for slaves, whereas freedom, dignity, and happiness were identified with ease and luxury. And in his habituated "modes of labor" as in other respects, Douglass believed, "the Negro . . . is pre-eminently a Southern man."[31]

In recommending the virtues of industrious self-reliance to his Nashville audience, Douglass drew attention to the novelty of his argument in a manner that exposed an additional corrupting legacy of slavery. "This may sound to you like a new gospel," he told them. "You have been accustomed to hear that money is the root of all evil; that it is hard for the rich to enter the kingdom of Heaven; that this world is of no account. . . . In answer to all which I say: that no people can ever make any social or mental improvement whose exertions are thus limited."[32] As Douglass himself had renounced "the slave's religious creed" of nonresistance to vindicate his dignity against Edward Covey,[33] so many of his fellow African Americans had to renounce their otherworldly creed in favor of a more activist and progressive Christianity. Contrary to what "we have so long heard in our pulpits," he told a predominantly black Rochester audience in 1885, "so far from being a sin to accumulate property, it is the plain duty of every man to lay up something for the future. . . . I am for making the best of both worlds and making the best of this world first, because it comes first."[34] Douglass found it necessary to commend a version of what would later be known as the "gospel of wealth" as an element of the Christian doctrine of self-making that he advanced against the enervating creed propagated by slavery's sympathizers. "Christianity . . . teaches that a man shall provide for his own house."[35]

Douglass's appeals for industrious self-reliance may also have targeted a further possible effect of slavery's despotism. Slavery not only taught all within its orbit that labor was an indignity, it also engendered in many of its victims a powerful psychology of opposition. The hallmarks of that psychology were a deep-seated mistrust of all authority and, among slavery's most spirited opponents, a habituated passion for righteous opposition as a soul-enlarging, intoxicating pleasure. Douglass's own sadness at the end of the Civil War attested the powerful gratifications of this psychology and the difficulty of letting go of it when the time for opposition had passed. For those driven by this quixotic passion, the call to forswear the heroic in favor of the "bourgeois" virtues entailed a task of extraordinary psychological difficulty.

Douglass did not make this concern a prominent theme of his postwar advice to his fellow African Americans. But its concrete significance appears forcefully in his reluctant observations concerning Haitian elites' disastrous failure to make their own transition from revolutionary preoccupations to the virtues proper to domestic, civil life. The "revolutionary spirit of Haiti," he contended in an 1893 address, "is her curse, her crime, her greatest calamity and the explanation of the limited condition of her civilization." The persistence of this spirit among ambitious elites was manifested in their passion for martial adventurism and their destabilizing preoccupation with political victory. The result was to reduce public life in the young black republic to a succession of military coups or eruptions of civil war. The Haitian women were superior in moral character to the Haitian men, Douglass pointedly observed, due largely to the fact that the latter spent much of their lives as soldiers. The women were, for the most part, responsible for the "industry, wealth, and prosperity of the country," whereas the ambitious (male) elites and the men who followed them were "too proud to work and not disposed to go into commerce."[36] The remedy was to highlight the heroic quality of productive labor, as Douglass did in Nashville as he spoke to his audience of black farmers about their vocation. The life of a farmer, he enthused, "is a constant battle." Destructive insects "spring out of the ground like armed warriors," compelling the besieged cultivator to "fight or die." The farmer "must make war upon the enemy," displaying not only industry but also "wisdom, courage, and vigilance."[37] The reader might think that with such remarks Douglass verged on self-parody, but whatever their excesses, they convey the serious point that the oppositional virtues could and ultimately had to be domesticated by their incorporation into the productive-acquisitive virtues.

In sum, in Douglass's analysis, a disdain among the freedpeople for regular labor was easily understandable, and, in fact, it contained a substantial measure of justice given their well-founded doubts as to whether they would be fairly compensated. Nonetheless, to call upon them to cultivate the virtues of industrious self-reliance entailed no lack of sympathy for their condition. To the contrary, it reflected a respect for their humanity and a clear-sighted awareness that to refrain from the cultivation of such virtues would be disastrous in the long term. Douglass's sympathetic appreciation of the difficulties in the freedpeople's condition in the postwar decades did not negate the permanent truth that he expressed in "Self-Made Men": elevation is achievable only though "patient, enduring, honest, unremitting and indefatigable work." For individuals, classes, and the species as a whole, "we may explain success mainly by one word and that word is WORK! WORK!! WORK!!! WORK!!!!"[38]

From Douglass's perspective, it was a pernicious error to hold that the cultivation of virtue had to await the establishment of full justice for the freedpeople. There was no contradiction between the exhortations to "agitate!" and to "work!" To the contrary, it was morally imperative to call simultaneously upon the freedpeople to exercise their proper measure of self-reliance and upon the American government to make good on its promises. In demanding nothing but fair play, Douglass insisted on the duties of both parties. A helpful summary of his understanding of the negative and affirmative public obligations toward African Americans in the postemancipation period can be distilled from his May 1863 discussion of various answers then "floating about in the public mind, to the question what shall be done with the Negro." He saw five main possibilities: (1) the reinstitution of formal, racial slavery; (2) the expatriation of African Americans; (3) the replacement of formal slavery by the neoslavery of a racial caste system; (4) the waging of an outright war of extermination by U.S. whites against blacks; and (5) the extension to African Americans of full and equal citizenship.[39] In general terms, fair play meant the rejection of possibilities (1) through (4) and the adoption of possibility (5). More specific analyses follow, first of the negative and then of the affirmative meanings of fair play as Douglass conceived of it.

Against Colonization

Of the various conceivable reactions, two seemed to Douglass especially threatening by virtue of the broad and long-standing influence that their supporting

Chapter Four

arguments had held over the public mind. The first of those was the policy of expatriation, or "colonization," and the second, closely related, was the perpetuation of a racial caste system.

The colonization issue was second only to abolition in the order of Douglass's priorities as an advocate.[40] It was necessarily a high priority through his abolitionist days. The linkage of emancipation to expatriation had long served as a seductive diversion for antislavery moderates and therefore as an obstruction to the cause of abolition. The issue was central to the differences between the "old school" abolitionism of the post-Revolution period and the later, militant abolitionism that emerged with the publication of David Walker's *Appeal* in 1829 and gained force through the efforts of Garrison and others dating from the early 1830s.[41] For leaders of the founding generation as well as those to come, opposition to slavery did not entail endorsement of a racially integrated America. Proponents of colonization as a condition of abolition included some of the most illustrious of the Founders, beginning with Thomas Jefferson and James Madison. Madison as U.S. president provided crucial early support for the American Colonization Society, organized in 1816 to promote the resettling of free African Americans to a colony in West Africa, and he served as that society's president from 1833 until his death in 1836. The idea received further support from some of the most eminent statesmen of the postfounding generations, including Senators Henry Clay and Daniel Webster and, for most of his career, Abraham Lincoln. Douglass remarked in 1849 that "almost every respectable man [in the United States] belongs to [the Colonization Society], either by direct membership or by affinity."[42]

To its antislavery supporters, colonization appeared necessary as a condition of abolition in view of the impossibility, in any foreseeable future, of racial equality in the United States. "Deep rooted prejudices entertained by the whites," along with manifold other difficulties, ruled out any hope for equal citizenship, wrote Jefferson in an infamous section of his *Notes on the State of Virginia,* and others less captive to such prejudices agreed.[43] Moreover, on a narrow reading of the Declaration of Independence, it was possible for antislavery colonizationists to argue that their obligations to those enslaved did not extend beyond emancipation, expatriation, and temporary provisional assistance. The proper remedy for slavery's injustice, in this view, involved only the restoration of the slaves' natural liberty, along with some assistance that they might secure the conditions of civil liberty. The foundational truths that all human beings are created equal and endowed with natural and inalienable rights did not imply that members of all human subgroups, irrespective of their particular histories and cultural formations, could live with one another to mutual advantage in a political society.[44]

From his early Garrisonian period to the end of his days, Douglass vigorously rejected the notion that expatriation had to follow emancipation. "*We are here* . . . and must remain [here] for ever."[45] He was first moved to devote serious attention to the issue in 1849, as the congressional debate over the disposition of the southwestern territories newly acquired in the Mexican War, along with a gradual emancipation plan proposed by Henry Clay, gave it renewed public prominence. Douglass argued, first, that colonization was impracticable; second, that it was immoral; and third, that because it was impracticable, it was doubly immoral in its effects.

In an editorial published late that year, "The Destiny of Colored Americans," Douglass summarized the reasons for concluding that colonization was impracticable. "We are rapidly filling up the number of four millions; and all the gold of California combined would be insufficient to defray the expenses attending our colonization. We are, as laborers, too essential to the interests of our white fellow-countrymen, to make a very grand effort to drive us from this country among probable events." The all-white or at least nonblack America fancied by colonizationists was an imaginary republic. Further, even if colonization were practicable, Douglass argued, it would be actively unjust in that it could only be accomplished by a massive policy of forcible expulsion. "We are of opinion that the *free* colored people generally mean to live in America. . . . Our minds are made up to live here if we can, or die here if we must." He wrote this before the enactment of the Fugitive Slave Law, but the emigration of many free blacks in reaction to that law did not alter the fact that the great majority were committed to remaining in the United States, as a matter of justice as well as of national and social sympathy.[46]

Expanding on the case against colonization on grounds of justice, Douglass held that the proper remedy for slavery went well beyond the restoration of natural liberty. African Americans had compelling claims to American citizenship, beginning with the fact that for all but a very few, America was the land of their birth. Descendants of a peculiar class of involuntary immigrants, they could not be treated as if they were a population of illegal aliens. Justice could hardly permit their expulsion from their native land by those who had compelled them to make that land their home. A still stronger claim was grounded in the principle of distributive justice. African Americans had made vitally important contributions to the nation's well-being, and they deserved a share in its civic honors and offices in return. "He who fights the battles of America may claim America as his country," Douglass declared as he called his brethren to arms in the Civil War. As he noted in an earlier speech, the claim was not merely prospective: "Some of our number have fought and bled for this country" in previous wars. But their most substantial contribution was that of their largely uncompensated productive labor, so obvious as to require mention only amid the hostility that surrounded them. "What class of people," he demanded, "can show a better title to the land on which they live than the colored people of the South? They have . . . produced whatever has made it a goodly land to dwell in, and it would be a shame and a crime little inferior in enormity to Slavery itself if these natural owners of the Southern and Gulf States should be driven away from their country." By virtue of their huge material contribution, not only the South but America as a whole "belonged to them" in their proper measure.[47]

Douglass argued that the colonization idea was doubly immoral in its practical effects. Continued public consideration of colonization as a live possibility tended to perpetuate the vicious assumption on which it was grounded, namely, the impossibility of civil and political equality between white and black Americans. During the slavery period, the effect of adopting that premise was to make emancipation contingent on an impossible resolution of the problem of race relations in the United States and so to support the continuance of slavery. And after the sudden and violent emancipation effected in the Civil War, the persistence of that premise would have the effect of conditioning a majority of Americans to accept what Douglass judged the worst of all possible outcomes—colonization's closest practicable alternative, the domestic quarantining of African Americans as a degraded caste.[48] The most urgent of the concrete negative imperatives in Douglass's postemancipation demand were thus closely linked: "do nothing" with us meant, most importantly, do not attempt to colonize us and, failing that, do not proscribe us as a class of inferiors.

Against Racial Caste

Throughout his life as a free man, Douglass vigorously opposed the practice, in custom and law, of separating people and assigning them differential rights based on color or race. To the point of personal physical resistance, he fought such segregation in a wide variety of venues (churches and schools, public accommodations such as restaurants, hotels, and theaters, public conveyances such as trains and ships), and he exhorted other African Americans to similar opposition.[49] All black-white segregation was designed to insult and degrade African Americans as an inferior caste—a species of moral lepers, as he put it in an 1859 article. In this way, it bore a close family relationship to slavery itself, with both formal slavery and segregation generating and sustaining themselves by the same "wicked, unnatural, and blasphemous prejudice."[50]

Douglass held that the spirit of racial caste was evil in its predictable effects as well as in its design. To sustain a proper spirit of opposition to it, he commended an attitude of self-reliant imperviousness. In *Life and Times*, he reported his answer to a friend's query as to how he felt when he encountered personal insult due to his color: "I feel as if an ass had kicked, but had hit nobody." Booker T. Washington admiringly recounted a similar story. "Frederick Douglass was on one occasion compelled to ride for several hours in a portion of a freight car. A friend went into the freight car to console him," reported Washington, "and said to him that he hated to see a man of his intelligence in so humiliating a position. 'I am ashamed that they have thus degraded you.' But Douglass, straightening himself up in his seat, looked the friend in the face and said, 'They cannot degrade Frederick Douglass.'"[51] Even so, Douglass did not discount the moral damage that institutionalized race prejudice inflicted. As we saw in his analysis of slaveholders' moral psychology, he took it as a general truth that few if any human beings are so self-reliant as to be indifferent to the opinions those in their surrounding society hold of them. However useful it might have been for them, it was unrealistic to expect African Americans in general to be impervious to others' prejudices: "If from the cradle through life the outside world brands a class as unfit for this or that work, the character of the class will come to resemble and conform to the character described."[52]

The ill effects of a perpetuated racial caste system would be objective as well as subjective, Douglass warned, and would defy efforts to contain them within a single class. To consign African Americans to the status of a degraded caste would be to "make pestilence and pauperism, ignorance and crime, a part of American Institutions. . . . The dreadful contagion of their vices and crimes would fly like cholera and small pox through all classes. Woe, woe! to this land, when it strips five millions of its people of all motives for cultivating an upright character. . . . Do anything else with us, but plunge us not into this hopeless pit." It was for these reasons that as he surveyed the possible postemancipation outcomes in 1863, Douglass judged the entrenchment of a racial caste system "about the worst" of them—worse even than the reinstitution of formal slavery or the annihilation of African Americans in a final race war.[53] The latter prospect at least afforded the possibility of ennobling resistance, along with the eternal relief from enslavement that death would bring. We recall that Douglass regarded subjection to permanent enslavement without hope for liberation as the worst of all human miseries. In judging consignment to a degraded racial caste to be worse even than formal reenslavement, he implied that such a caste system would represent slavery perfected: little less confining and degrading than before and, due to cosmetic refinements that assimilated it to conditions prevailing also in northern states, supported by a broader and deeper national consensus.

Its potentially broad acceptance made a racial caste system not only the worst of postwar outcomes but also an imminently real danger. "Law and the sword can and will in the end abolish slavery," Douglass editorialized in January 1863, but they could not so soon abolish "the malignant slaveholding sentiment which has kept the slave system alive in this country during two centuries. . . . The slave having ceased to be the abject slave of a single master, his enemies will endeavor to make him the slave of [white] society at large." The work of elevating the freedpeople to equal citizenship would meet "a harder resistance" even than that which abolition had to overcome.[54] Speaking to the annual meeting of the American Anti-Slavery Society in 1869, Douglass emphasized the actual power of that resistance, by then sufficiently evident, as he justified the society's continued existence. "In the nature of the case, there can be no such thing as the immediate, unconditional, complete abolition of slavery, any where in the world. It would be to contradict human nature, and all the social forces of which we have any knowledge, to assume such a possibility."[55] That the spirit of slavery would survive emancipation and the conclusion of formal war was wholly in accord with our natural moral psychology as he understood it.

The malign forces of human nature to which Douglass alluded were certainly visible, though not universally active, in the postwar South. Despite the hope that Lincoln expressed in his finely wrought second inaugural address, neither the war's outcome nor the hugeness of the losses it inflicted stirred a proper contrition in most of the vanquished Confederates. Burdened with so enormous a transgression, the conscience in its natural need for self-justification would resist any such impulse. "We may easily forgive those who injure us," Douglass acutely observed in 1881, writing on the persistence of color prejudice, "but it is hard to forgive those whom we injure."[56] Humiliated in military defeat by forces they had held in disdain, faced with the collapse of the way of life upon which they had based their very identity, many southern whites in the postwar years experienced a profound need for self-justification. They found it in abundance, as before, supplied by their representative authorities in religion and science. Their religion taught them that God had permanently divided his human creatures into hierarchically ranked racial classes; that consigned to the bottom of that hierarchy was the unfortunate black race, whose members were perpetually stained as descendants of the accursed Ham; that a regime of civil or social equality among members of the radically polarized black and white races would constitute a gross violation of God's law; and, after the surrender at Appomattox, that the South's defeat had to be received as God's test of his chosen, a necessary preparation for redemption in the restoration of the divinely ordained regime of white supremacy. Their science taught them likewise that the racial hierarchy they favored was grounded in the natural order of being: their defense of white supremacy was a natural-law imperative, necessary to prevent the biological degradation that racial miscegenation (the inevitable result of civil and social equality) would produce.[57]

To Douglass and his fellow radical Republicans, the defeated Confederacy's will to self-redemption showed itself almost immediately after the end of formal war, for in 1865 and 1866, legislatures of numerous southern states enacted laws known as Black Codes that imposed a variety of civil and political disabilities on African Americans. At least in some states, the material purpose of those laws was to preserve the essentials of the labor relations that prevailed under slavery, so that, by carefully defined employment and vagrancy laws, African Americans in general were compelled to remain in those states and to work for white employers in agricultural or household occupations. The larger social and moral purpose of the codes was to reaffirm a conception of blacks as beings of an inferior order, lacking the complete array of rights proper to fully human beings and unfit to associate as equals with members of the white race. Alongside the labor restrictions, typical laws circumscribed African Americans' rights to testify in court and prohibited them from attending public services or riding in public conveyances reserved for whites and, above all, from bearing firearms. Reviewing the particulars in his compendious *Black Reconstruction in America, 1860–1880*, W. E. B. Du Bois called them "an astonishing affront to emancipation."[58] For Douglass, too, their kinship to slavery was unmistakable. In the severe restrictions imposed by the former master class on freedpeople's opportunities for saving, accumulation, and geographic and economic mobility, he contended in an 1869 speech, "there is clearly seen the purpose to crush our spirits, to cripple our enterprise and doom us to a condition of destitution and degradation."[59]

The Black Codes provoked outrage among northerners, particularly among the Republicans who controlled the U.S. Congress. Their response was the prompt enactment of the Civil Rights Act of 1866 and then, to remove any doubt as to that law's constitutionality, the adoption of the Fourteenth Amendment. Douglass cheered these developments, of course, but with prudent reservation. The Reconstruction Amendments were intended to secure freedom for all, irrespective of race, and so were fully consonant with the spirit of the Declaration of Independence; Douglass comforted his "Democratic friends" in an 1870 speech with the thought that Thomas Jefferson authored the Fourteenth.[60] Yet it was imperative to bear in mind that those amendments contained only parchment guarantees. From his political-abolitionist perspective, as he told an 1872 Republican audience, the "trouble never was in the Constitution, but in the administration of the Constitution. All experience shows that laws are of little value in the hands of those unfriendly to their objects." Everything depended on their interpretation and enforcement, and a substantial portion of the country viewed the postwar amendments as illegitimate. Without proper congressional enforcement in particular, the latest constitutional protections would be no more effective than the originals had been.[61]

Douglass's insistence on legislative enforcement as "the very essence" of those amendments, especially in the face of persisting, virulent notions of black exceptionalism, points to the more affirmative significance of his demand that the nation ensure fair play for African Americans after emancipation. In an 1862 iteration of his "do nothing" doctrine, he maintained that "the great majority of human duties are of [a] negative character." The rights of individual persons imposed upon others, for the most part, a relatively narrow range of duties to refrain from obstructing the exercise of those rights.[62] But this principle of negative, minimized obligation did not apply in the same way to governments as it did to individuals. Even as he endorsed the maxim that "that government is best which governs least" in an 1871 editorial on African American political participation, Douglass made clear that government's primary duty was not simply to *forbear* violating individuals' rights but to *protect* them—"to secure these rights," as the Declaration stated.[63] Moreover, he made clear elsewhere that government's primarily protective duty could be interpreted quite broadly and yet be consistent with the bedrock principle of personal responsibility. In his understanding, the principle of limited, protective government did not contradict but rather encompassed the principle that he had affirmed in his earlier essay on civil government—that a legitimate purpose of government was to facilitate "the very highest development of human perfection."[64]

Political Rights

The context of Douglass's January 1865 speech to the Massachusetts Anti-Slavery Society, "What the Black Man Wants," was that convention's discussion of General Nathaniel Banks's proposal to implement, as a measure for Louisiana's reconstruction, an "apprenticeship" system regulating freedpeople's employment. Douglass joined the convention's denunciation of that proposal, but he did not focus on the specific issue of labor or employment rights. Instead, he went straight to what he considered the heart of the matter. "I have had but one idea for the last three years to present to the American people. . . . I am for the 'immediate, unconditional, and universal' enfranchisement of the black man, in every State of the Union," he declared. The civil rights that were or would be affirmed in the Thirteenth and Fourteenth Amendments held vast potential importance, but the right of suffrage was "all-important." The securing of this one indispensable right would effectively guarantee all the other legal conditions of emancipation.[65] Douglass therefore greeted the ratification of the Fifteenth Amendment with barely restrained exuberance: "Henceforth we live in a new world. . . . We have ourselves, we have a country, and we have a future in common with other men. . . . Never was revolution more complete." His delight permitted only a muted note of caution—it "seems almost too good to be true."[66]

Douglass argued that suffrage was immediately necessary for a variety of reasons. First and foremost were considerations of simple natural justice. "We want [the right to vote] because it is our *right*," grounded in the possession of common human rationality. To be contented despite the deprivation of this right would be to insult one's human nature.[67] The fundamental liberal principle of human self-ownership rendered illegitimate any scheme of virtual representation for normally rational adults: "No man can be said to represent another, who has not been chosen by that other to represent him."[68] This argument applied as well to women as to men and so committed Douglass to his longtime advocacy of woman suffrage. No less compelling than the claim of natural desert, however, was an imperative of prudence, which also applied equally to men and women (though more urgently, in Douglass's judgment, to black men than to white women). Without the vote, African Americans would remain America's stepchildren, disinherited and dependent for their security and happiness on the white voting majority. The suffrage right was the indispensable guardian of every other right, "the keystone to the arch of human liberty." Civil government's fundamental obligation to protect its subjects' rights included a duty to provide for them the means to their *self-*protection. "If the elective franchise is not extended to the negro," Douglass told a woman's rights convention in 1868, "he dies—he is exterminated."[69] Along with other rights such as the rights to jury trial and jury service, the voting right belonged to a class of civil, democratic rights that were necessary, effectuating conditions of natural, inalienable rights.

Further, more relative arguments buttressed Douglass's case. The right to vote and be voted for was not only a natural right but also a democratic right. In the context of a democratic order in particular, in which "universal suffrage is the rule," to withhold the voting right from blacks as a class was to violate the central principle of fair play as Douglass conceived of it. It was "to make us an *exception,* to brand us with the stigma of inferiority, and to invite to our heads the missiles of those about us."[70] This claim of right went hand in hand with an appeal to the nation's interest. African Americans' suffrage rights would not only integrate a hitherto despised class into American society, they would also contribute crucially to the broader reintegration of the American constitutional union. In Douglass's hopeful vision, African Americans' stature in the nation's constitutional order would be dramatically elevated by their crucial part in its reconstruction. The health of a republican government, more than of any other form, depended on the friendship of those whom it governed. In the vanquished rebel states, the large populations of freedpeople were the Union's only real friends, alone capable of forming a "natural counterpoise" to the hatred of the Union that would naturally smolder among many whites.[71] More strongly stated, Douglass's idea was that newly enfranchised African Americans in the South would assume an honored position as the indispensable American loyalists, serving more than any others to bind the former rebel states to the Union that those states had lately attempted to destroy.

Despite its obvious radicalism, this argument bore also a significant aspect of conservatism. Douglass suggested that by its revolutionary transformation of slaves to full citizens, enfranchisement would establish them not only as the cement of a reconstructed Union but also as the ironic preservers of the constitutional tradition of states' rights. The "right of each State to control its own local affairs," he observed in his 1866 essay "Reconstruction," was "an idea . . . more deeply rooted in the minds of men of all sections of the country than perhaps any one other political idea"—more deeply rooted in Douglass's day than the idea of natural human rights upon which an earlier generation of Americans had based its revolutionary claims. Happily, in his initial suggestion, "to render the government consistent with itself," no revolution in state-federal relations was needed. To "render the rights of the States compatible with the sacred rights of human nature," what was needed was only to enfranchise the freedpeople and thus to establish safely loyalist local control over the recently rebellious states.[72] The radical measure of enfranchising multitudes long enslaved would then preempt the greater radicalism of overturning the traditional, Madisonian constitutional order that reserved to states the primary responsibility for securing individuals' rights.

Douglass's argument for universal suffrage as the crucial means for reconciling individuals' rights with states' rights carried a further, unstated implication that underlines its significance for African American dignity. The obvious objection was that suffrage for the freedpeople would hardly bind the restored Union in friendship; instead, it would significantly intensify the rage of the vanquished southerners. That objection invited the obvious rejoinder that to leave erstwhile Confederates in control of their states would effectively reward disloyalty, nullify the Union victory, and desecrate the graves of the masses who fell to achieve it.[73] To effectuate and preserve the war's gains would require, for a time, the suppression of southern rage by a vigorous exercise of governmental power. At least in 1866, Douglass judged the federal government incapable of performing such a task, absent its investment with powers that even he described as "despotic."[74] A much superior alternative—both more just and potentially more effective—was to assign primary responsibility to those who held the most direct interest in completing the Union victory. In Reconstruction as in abolition, "[he] who would be free, must himself strike the blow." Suggesting that the freedpeople's power in Reconstruction governments would be power to aid their (pro-Union, Republican) friends, Douglass also implied that it would be power to harm their enemies. Suffrage would dignify by conferring, along with moral recognition and civic education, a share in the government's monopoly of legitimate violence. It would establish the freedpeople as *"a power on earth,"* capable of disciplining the Edward Coveys and Orson Gores of the postslavery generation.[75]

As indicated previously, Douglass argued that suffrage for African Americans was not only a *necessary* condition, it was *the sufficient* constitutional condition of their liberation. To explore the grounds for this latter claim is to see the profound democratic radicalism in Douglass's idea of liberal, constitutional government. Beyond being radical for his day in supporting universal suffrage, irrespective of color, ethnicity, or sex, Douglass was radical for any period of U.S. history in supporting unchecked, majority-rule democracy.

Douglass made clear his principled democratic convictions as early as 1851, in an essay on civil government that he wrote as a rebuttal of Garrisonian Non-Resistance. Declaring his trust in the preponderant goodness in human nature, he allowed that if that trust were unfounded, "it would, indeed, be dangerous for men to enter into a compact, by which power should be wielded by the mass." In part for this reason, his idea of popular government extended significantly beyond the principle of popular consent affirmed by Locke and the Declaration of Independence. Douglass maintained that not mere consent but active political power properly belonged to "the people, who are supposed to know their rights and to understand their interests."[76] In the antebellum years especially, he repeatedly ridiculed "republican slavery" in America, contrasting it with the climate of liberty in monarchical England and even with the impending emancipation in despotic Russia. But the fact that American republicanism was a "sham" discredited America, not republicanism. An inveterate enemy of all established inequality, Douglass stood as an unwavering partisan of republican government. He labored for its realization and perfection, not its replacement. Arguing for woman suffrage in 1868, he declared, "Let government rest squarely and universally down upon the whole people."[77]

Douglass's partisanship for popular government appears in its full significance in his positions relative to two pivotal controversies in the postwar years. The first was the dispute over the proper terms of Reconstruction between the Republican congressional majority and President Andrew Johnson, a Democrat from Tennessee. Sympathizing strongly with Radical Republicans in Congress and incensed by Johnson's vetoes of several of their Reconstruction measures, Douglass weighed in with an extraordinary speech, "Sources of Danger to the Republic," delivered numerous times in the winter of 1866–1867. He began with an amusing but revealing introduction—"I am here tonight as a democrat, a genuine democrat dyed in the wool"—and then advanced an argument that might have made Alexander Hamilton and James Madison turn over in their graves. He contended that an adequate response to Johnson's obstructions required more than an attempt to persuade the public to support the Republican program or to remove Johnson from office in the next election. Judging the core of the problem to be not only partisan but constitutional, he called for the abolition of the independent chief executive and of major elements of the constitutional system of checks and balances. He proposed the elimination of the presidential veto, calling it "alien to every idea of republican government"; the abolition of the president's power to pardon and eligibility for re-election; the curtailment of the office's patronage powers; and the abolition of the office of vice president, seeing in it an institutionalized incentive to conspire against the president.[78] In one version of the speech, he wondered whether the United States would be better off with no president at all.[79]

One must take care not to overstate the significance of these proposals. Douglass issued them in a state of intense anger and alarm, provoked by what he regarded as Johnson's effort to undo the great and costly gains of the war. He made no sustained campaign to secure their enactment, and in most particulars, he did not repeat them beyond this brief season. To this extent, his biographer Benjamin Quarles seems justified in viewing them as a momentary loss of balance on Douglass's part.[80]

Nonetheless, Douglass's attack on the independent executive was grounded in a principle that informed his thinking before, as we have seen, and also after the Johnson years.[81] A genuine republic was "a genuine *democratic* republic."[82] This principle reappeared in his argument for woman suffrage in 1868, after the Republican Ulysses S. Grant had won that year's presidential election. It also reappeared in 1883, in Douglass's speech in response to the U.S. Supreme Court's ruling in the *Civil Rights Cases*. In that ruling, which will be discussed further in the next section, the Court held unconstitutional the 1875 Civil Rights Act, a federal law prohibiting racial discrimination in various public accommodations. Douglass acknowledged flaws in the law's letter and enforcement, but he nonetheless judged it "a noble moral standard, uplifted for the education of the American people." The Court's invalidation of it struck him as a "moral cyclone" comparable in importance to the *Dred Scott* ruling. In his response, he showed greater caution than he had exhibited seventeen years earlier against President Johnson.[83] Yet although he directly proposed no constitutional reform of the Court's structure or powers, he strongly implied the need for it with a suggestion grounded in the same principle that informed his "Sources of Danger" speech. Even more than the president had been in the late 1860s, Douglass contended, the Supreme Court in the subsequent decades had showed itself to be "the autocratic point in our National Government. No monarch in Europe has a power more absolute" than that wielded by the Court. What "His Holiness, the Pope, is to the Roman Catholic Church, the Supreme Court is to the American

State."[84] Such a characterization plainly implies the illegitimacy of the judicial review power in any truly republican constitutional order.

In his "Sources of Danger" speech, Douglass characterized the defect in the Founders' Constitution as symptomatic of a still deeper defect in the constitution of human nature. "Such is the constitution of the human mind, that there can be no such thing as immediate emancipation, either from slavery or from monarchy."[85] As he, his fellow abolitionists, and Lincoln, too, had argued all along, the issue in the war against slavery was essentially the same as the issue in the American Revolution.[86] The Founders were born under a monarchy and remained under its influence even as they waged war against it. "They gave us a Constitution made in the shadow of slavery and of monarchy," Douglass commented, "and . . . it partakes in some of its features of both those unfavorable influences." In contrast to *The Federalist*, Douglass held that the American Republic was not a pure republic but instead a mixed constitutional form and that its main defects were traceable to its admixture of nonrepublican elements. Its "first source of weakness" was its incorporation of the spirit of "Monarchical man-worship" and the various forms of nondemocratic power in which it issued.[87] Whether explicitly, as in 1866 and 1867, or only implicitly, as in 1883, Douglass's argument entailed a call for basic changes in the U.S. government's constitutional structure. The American Revolution could not be complete until all of the Constitution's countermajoritarian features were expunged.

Structurally, democratic-republican government entailed, first, the primacy of the legislative power relative to the other powers of government. The Congress, Douglass argued against Johnson, comprises the true "representatives of the republic." To that extent, he remained in agreement with the original framers. He also agreed that Congress's dependence on the people provides the primary check against abusive legislation, but he rejected Publius's insistence on the need for further, "auxiliary precautions." Legislative primacy meant that the other, properly subordinate branches should not function as checks upon congressional power. "We are great on checks," he observed sarcastically.[88] In the *Civil Rights Cases* speech, he made a most puzzling claim: "All men who have given any thought to . . . the structure, and practical operation of our Government, must have recognized the importance of absolute harmony between its various departments of powers and duties. They must have seen clearly the mischievous tendency and danger to the body politic of any antagonisms between its various branches."[89] In striking contrast to the famous argument for governmental checks and balances in *Federalist* no. 51, Douglass held that harmony, not competitive ambition or defensiveness, should characterize the three branches' interrelations. An energetic executive and an activist judiciary were compatible with a republican constitution only as long as that energy and activism operated to enforce national laws against disobedient states and private parties, not to overrule the will of the national legislature.

In its grander institutional significance, the Civil War as Douglass understood it signified a constitutional restoration that pointed toward a reformation. It signified the restoration of the original Constitution in both its actual (nationalist and abolitionist) and its purified (majoritarian-democratic) designs. In this respect, Douglass was to the Civil War what Thomas Paine was to the original American Revolution. Each found in an epochal war a mandate for his countrymen to align their political constitution with the radically democratic principles of natural human rights and the millennial meaning of the age. The comparison highlights the important fact that Douglass understood his ideas on constitutional reform as the fulfillment of founding principles, not a departure from them. His radically democratic vision reflected his desire not to remove all restraints on governmental power but rather to clarify and to strengthen the only reliable source of good government and the only reliable protection against arbitrary government. In his early essay on civil government, he maintained that the "very fact that a government is instituted by all, and rests upon all for support and direction, is the strongest guarantee that can be given that it will be wielded justly and impartially." Further, democratic government promised the greatest degree of competence in the exercise of political power. "A majority . . . may be presumed, as a general rule, to take a wiser and more comprehensive view . . . than the minority." For woman suffrage, he argued (again in 1868), "when you want good government go to the mass."[90]

At first sight, this may seem a very odd argument for a man of Douglass's experience to make. Given that congressional government was likely to represent the majority best, did not the experience of Douglass and his fellow African Americans provide crushing evidence of the danger of majority tyranny? Was Douglass forgetting so soon the wrongs that U.S. Congresses had been responsible for, including the Fugitive Slave Law, the Kansas-Nebraska Act, and numerous other instances of unjust legislation in the slavery period? In view of all that, would it not have been more reasonable for him to affirm, not to reject, the Madisonian argument for republican constitutional complexity?

The thrust of such questions suggests that Douglass's millennialist propensities got the better of him in his constitutional thought or that his simplified democratic constitutionalism rested on a utopian hope for overcoming what Madison held to be our natural, permanent propensity toward faction. Yet, however it might appear, Douglass's trust in simple, majoritarian democracy was not based on a millennial or utopian faith. To the contrary, it was based mainly on his deliberate, realist assessments of the protections and advantages inherent in the majoritarian principle and of the imperfections of the Madisonian model.

Douglass was well aware of the standard liberal-constitutionalist concern that an electoral majority might itself be tyrannical. In the "Sources of Danger" speech, he squarely addressed the objection: "We have recently been told that majorities can be as destructive and more arbitrary than individual despots. . . . If this be so . . . I think that we ought to part with Republican government at once." He did not deny that majorities can be and had been arbitrary; he simply asked, "Arbitrary to whom?" Congressional abuses such as the Fugitive Slave Law actually supported his argument. The majorities in those instances violated the rights of unrepresented classes, and Douglass's claim was that majorities are arbitrary *only* to those classes. The true protection against governmental arbitrariness was simply a "consistent republic in which there shall be no unrepresented classes," one that effectively enforced the principle of universal suffrage. Absent such representation, the constitutional system of checks and balances had not succeeded in securing equal rights for all, and with such representation, no additional checks would be needed.[91] To those who maintain that minority rights in the United States depend on Madisonian checks, especially on federal judicial protection, a defender of Douglass's constitutionalism would reply that the fully democratic government he envisioned would have produced civil rights measures that were stronger than those Congress actually enacted and that were much more likely to be sustained by supportive federal courts, which would have been composed of judges and justices appointed by genuinely representative elected officials.

Without directly addressing *The Federalist*, Douglass's argument implies the superiority of the famous *Federalist* no. 10 (on the formation of national majorities) to the also famous *Federalist* no. 51 (on checks and balances) as a theory of republican constitutionalism. From his perspective, Madison had started down the right path in no. 10, paying attention to the cultural and demographic formation of majorities and placing his primary trust in national rather than state majorities. Madison attributed the relative trustworthiness of national majorities to their moderation, in turn derived from their diversity and fluidity or dynamism. To govern the extended republic of the United States would require the continual composing and recomposing of majorities out of numerous, diverse groups animated by potentially factious interests, opinions, and sentiments. Faced with such electoral demographics, parties and candidates could not long ignore the interests of any substantial group of voters, certainly not one so numerous as the population of African Americans. It was a variant of Madisonian realism, not utopianism, that Douglass expressed for the Colored National Convention of 1864 when he argued that once African Americans had the vote, politicians' interests would quickly overcome their prejudices. Like newly arrived immigrants, the freedpeople and their racial brethren would be "courted by the leaders of all parties," and the laws they would share in making would no longer tolerate violence against them.[92]

But even though Douglass shared Madison's trust in the relative virtue of national majorities, he did not conceive of that virtue primarily in terms of moderation. Madison's argument in no. 10 rested on an expectation that in America's extended, commercial republic, only relatively loosely united, hence moderate, governing coalitions would be likely to form. The problem was that in their very diffuseness, such majorities were vulnerable to capture by a firmly united, intensely committed minority faction. This point had been fully appreciated by the eminent proslavery constitutionalist John C. Calhoun. For Calhoun and those who carried forth his legacy, the forging of an unbreakable unity among southern electorates—a solid South—was needed to defend their region's peculiar customs against a northern majority only loosely united by interests and moral sentiments opposed to their own.[93] For Douglass, the most glaring vice in the Madisonian system of institutionalized checks was that it magnified the power of factious minorities such as that represented by Calhoun. The "auxiliary precautions" that Madison defended in no. 51 had operated, in practice, to weaken, not to strengthen, the protection of individual rights. Perhaps those constitutional checks served the cause of justice in protecting innocent property holders in the eighteenth century, as Madison himself intended, or in vindicating the claims of (mostly disfranchised) African American citizens in the 1950s and 1960s. But in Douglass's experience, their benefits were largely hypothetical and their costs only too real. Throughout the nineteenth century and for much of the twentieth century, they proved primarily useful to perpetrators of injustice, first the slaveholding minority and then the unreconstructed white supremacists of the 1870s and beyond.

In this vital dimension of his constitutional thought, Douglass was anti-Madisonian because he was anti-Calhounian—inversely Calhounian. For both sides, in contrast to Madison, the proper constitutional security inhered in unity, not diversity. Patriotism and constitutional fidelity had come to require intense partisanship. Alarmed by the diffuseness of northern sentiment in the face of the determined faction to the South, Douglass labored to give the slave-holders and the racial supremacists who survived them what they most feared— an equally intense and disciplined anti-Calhounian party to the north, a "nu-merical majority" united in the desire to destroy slavery and the regime of racial supremacy that supported and succeeded it. In its near-term practical context, beneath Douglass's principled conception of universal suffrage as the vital guar-dian of rights lay a call for temporary authoritarian rule by a humanitarian ma-jority, whereby slavery's spirit would be finally destroyed and white suprema-cists would be forced to be free.[94]

To Madison, Douglass's calls for the weakening of constitutional checks as protections for minorities would likely have seemed descended from the claims of "theoretic politicians, who . . . have erroneously supposed that by reducing mankind to a perfect equality in their political rights, they would at the same time be perfectly equalized and assimilated in . . . their opinions, and their pas-sions."[95] As this remark suggests, the ultimate issue in this dispute concerns the moral pedagogy of the laws.

National majorities were certainly not incorruptible, in Douglass's under-standing, though he, like Madison, believed them less easily corrupted than mi-norities or state majorities. But the American national majority had been cor-rupted by a regime of racial proscription. Douglass's expectation was that a regime of universal suffrage and representation, unprecedented in American history, would generate a culture of humanitarian nationalism that rendered safe and even desirable the rule of majorities subject only to electoral checks. His preoccupation with the one essential right of suffrage was based in significant part on this expectation. Speaking to the American Anti-Slavery Society in 1869, he rehearsed a Reconstruction debate over black suffrage between Democrats and "Abolitionists" in which the former charged and the latter denied that such suffrage would lead to racial amalgamation. He responded simply: "It will lead just there. Don't be afraid."[96] By conferring authoritative public recognition of rights-bearing humanity, laws such as the Civil Rights Act or a universal suffrage law would edify the nation's moral sentiments. As suggested earlier, universal suffrage in particular would have a powerful indirect agency in fostering interra-cial unity and sympathy, as office-seekers and party loyalists would be moved by electoral interest to make common cause with voters across race and color lines.

A final element of the moral pedagogy of Douglass's majoritarian democracy concerns its special effect on African Americans' morale. To be denied the vote in a democracy was not only to be stigmatized as an exception but also to be relegated to the status of a plaintiff, with one's rights and interests dependent on appeals for countermajoritarian actions by executive or judicial officials. Douglass's strong abhorrence of this condition must have contributed to his disrespect for the system of constitutional checks. Whatever their potential advantages, such checks also carry the danger that they would habituate those who relied on them to the practice of oppositional, minoritarian politics, which he disdained as a source of demeaning, dispiriting dependency similar in principle to the condition of those excluded altogether from political society. From the 1850s on, Douglass affirmed that a truly reliable and dignifying security for individual rights could only be found in active republican citizenship—in regular participation in electoral contests, endeavoring to assemble a majority coalition capable of governing on its own initiative and responsibility. Fundamental to his constitutionalism in the prewar and postwar periods alike was his urgent insistence on the active self—on self-liberation, self-elevation, and self-government.

Civil Rights

Douglass's idea of the sufficiency of the voting right of course carried the presumption that those empowered with the vote would use it to secure by law all the properties inhering in full citizenship, including the full complement of civil rights. This, too, was essential to the fair play upon which he insisted, especially for those newly freed. "The true object for which governments are ordained among men," he reminded his audience in an 1888 commemoration of emancipation in the District of Columbia, "is to protect the weak against the encroachments of the strong, to hold its strong arm of justice over all the civil relations of its citizens." Government's core purpose was to secure "the humblest" in the "full possession of his rights of person and of property."[97] It was government's moral duty to protect the weak against *all* the strong, private parties and states alike, and so to adopt the broadest reasonable construction of the civil rights under its protection.

With the adoption of the Reconstruction Amendments, this moral duty had become more clearly inscribed than ever before in U.S. constitutional law. What had been highly controversial inferences by constitutional abolitionists in the antebellum years now appeared as explicit constitutional prohibitions

138

Chapter Four

and delegations of federal power against slavery and racial supremacy. Once again interpreting ambiguous constitutional provisions with a bias toward liberty and natural justice, Douglass found broad national protective powers in the Thirteenth Amendment. In his reading, the prohibitions of that amendment already comprehended the prohibitions and guarantees in its two successor amendments. A kind of slavery persisted in various practices in landownership and labor relations employed by the postwar master class;[98] wherever blacks were deprived of the right to vote or to testify in a court of law; and more generally, wherever the word *white* appeared in legislation.[99] The nonslavery guaranteed by the Thirteenth Amendment was then effectively indistinguishable from full, equal citizenship. But the adoption of the Fourteenth Amendment should have removed all ambiguity. With respect to civil rights proper, the key provisions lay in that amendment's privileges or immunities, due process, and equal protection clauses, all of which were encapsulated in its guarantee of citizenship to every person born in the United States and subject to its jurisdiction.

In the postwar period as in the antebellum period, however, Douglass's understanding of American governments' concrete moral and constitutional obligations appeared mainly in his discussions of their derelictions. Two practical developments held decisive importance for the nineteenth-century fate of the Reconstruction Amendments. The more dramatic of the two was the Compromise of 1877, a political agreement fashioned to resolve the disputed presidential election of 1876. To gain the presidency, the Republican Rutherford Hayes required the assent of southern Democrats in Congress, and the price for that assent was the removal of federal troops remaining in the states of the old Confederacy. This marked the end of the Reconstruction era and, with it, the end of any serious federal attempt to secure African Americans' constitutional rights in those states. Critics from the beginning have regarded the compromise as a Republican betrayal of African Americans. Douglass, by then a loyal Republican and a newly appointed official in the Hayes administration, seems to have been initially silent on the Hayes policy, which was directly contrary to his longstanding objection to any compromise with the proslavery South. But within a few months and for years thereafter, he publicly denounced it and its effects.[100]

The second decisive development came in a series of Supreme Court rulings, beginning during the Grant presidency and continuing for decades thereafter, in which the Court repeatedly affirmed the narrowest of interpretations of the rights guaranteed and the enforcement powers delegated by the Fourteenth Amendment. The first of these rulings came in 1873, with the Court's first adjudication of a claim made under that amendment. The *Slaughterhouse Cases* (as this set of consolidated cases is commonly known) did not directly concern the rights of freedpeople, but the Court's ruling held great indirect significance for them. Rejecting the claim by a group of New Orleans butchers that a state-conferred monopoly violated their constitutional right to pursue a lawful occupation, the Court held that such a right was not a property of U.S. citizenship under the Fourteenth Amendment. To reach this conclusion, the Court severely diminished the concept of national citizenship and the rights pertaining to it, implying that virtually all civil rights remained under the exclusive protection of the states. Douglass commented only briefly and privately on the ruling, but he made clear his sweeping objection to it in an 1874 letter to Gerrit Smith. Now renouncing altogether the relatively conservative, states'-rights position that he had provisionally taken in his arguments for voting rights in the immediate aftermath of the war, he objected to the notion that *any* rights should be placed under the exclusive power of the states. The Court's "impractical doctrine of two citizenships," he argued to Smith, effectively meant "no citizenship. The one destroys the other. . . . The true doctrine is one nation, one country, one citizenship and one law for all the people."[101]

For the zealously humanitarian Douglass, the central principle of progress was unification, of nations as well as of humankind. In his hopeful interpretation, the Civil War victory, as codified in the Reconstruction Amendments, heralded the perfection of national union in the composition of Americans as a single, homogeneous people. Exposing as "anachronisms and superstitions" the disintegrative, sectionalist, or states'-rights constitutionalism championed by Calhoun and his acolytes,[102] the Union's victory also signaled America's ultimate overcoming of the spirit of racial or ethnic caste. But the Supreme Court saw matters very differently. In *U.S. v. Cruikshank* (1875) and *U.S. v. Harris* (1883),[103] the Court heard cases arising from acts of horrific violence against African Americans, and its judgments severely limited Congress's enforcement powers under the Fourteenth Amendment. It invalidated major sections of the Enforcement Act of 1870 and the Force Act of 1871, which made it a federal crime to interfere with another in the exercise of a constitutional right or to deprive any person of the equal protection of the laws. Following the logic of its *Slaughterhouse* ruling, the Court held that the rights guaranteed in the Bill of Rights were enforceable only against the federal government, not state governments, and that the protections of the Fourteenth Amendment applied only against the actions of state governments, not against acts by private parties. In *U.S. v. Reese* (1875), the Court imposed a similarly narrow construction on the Fifteenth

Amendment. The effect of these rulings was once again to leave all meaningful civil and political rights under the virtually exclusive control of the states.

Although Douglass apparently made no public comments on these specific rulings, his considered judgment of the Court's reading and his understanding of the true meaning of the Fourteenth Amendment appear in his 1883 speech on the *Civil Rights Cases,* which he regarded as the Supreme Court's most important and damaging postwar ruling on constitutional civil rights issues. Here again, the Court had advanced the causes of "slavery, caste, and oppression" and left African Americans "as a class, grievously wounded . . . in the house of our friends."[104] In this latest ruling, the Court invalidated the 1875 Civil Rights Act, which prohibited privately owned public conveyances, inns and hotels, and places of public amusement from discriminating by race, color, or previous condition of servitude. Prefacing his comments on the ruling, Douglass claimed to speak only as a "layman," with standing only to denounce the ruling for its injustice. But as always when he addressed constitutional issues, his argument was characterized by an interweaving of moral and legal reasoning. The Court majority, he protested, had effected "a sudden and causeless reversal of all the great rules of legal interpretation by which this Court was governed in other days." It had "construed the Constitution in defiant disregard of what was the object and intention of the adoption of the Fourteenth Amendment."[105] And in the ruling's practical effects, it had licensed the humiliation of American blacks and diminished the American nation: "It presents the United States before the world as a Nation utterly destitute of power to protect the rights of its own citizens upon its own soil."[106]

These charges required more substantiation than Douglass provided on this or any other occasion. But he supposed at the outset of his speech that Justice John Marshall Harlan, whom he admired greatly, "must have had weighty reasons" for issuing the lone dissent in the case, and, in fact, his summary objections correspond closely with most of the essentials of Harlan's opinion.[107] A brief elaboration of those objections in the light of Harlan's dissent, with which Douglass must have been partially familiar, can clarify the latter's specific objections to the Court's ruling and his understanding of the Fourteenth Amendment.

The core of the majority's ruling with respect to the Fourteenth Amendment consists of two propositions: (1) that the enforcement power delegated to Congress in section 5 is limited to the correction of state actions that violate rights guaranteed in section 1, and (2) that racial discrimination by proprietors of the types of public accommodations specified in the statute does not qualify as a state action and therefore does not authorize any corrective legislation by Congress under the Fourteenth Amendment. The restrictive reading of Congress's enforcement power as merely corrective was the main target of Douglass's charge that the Court had departed both from its own previously stated rules of interpretation and from the correct rules. He first complained that during the slavery era, the Court had construed the Constitution according to its supposed intention (to accommodate slavery) in disregard of its plain language (deliberately noncognizant of slavery). But in the *Civil Rights Cases* ruling, "the plain intention of the law had been strangled by the letter of the law."[108] More important, the Court's narrow reading of congressional power contravened both the natural-law mandate to interpret positive laws so as to favor the ends of liberty and justice and the positive-law rule of interpreting specific provisions in light of the general objects of the Constitution.[109]

Against the majority's confinement of constitutional wrongs to direct state actions, Douglass opposed a characteristically pragmatic reading of the framers' intentions, in keeping with his notion of governmental fair play. "What does it matter to a colored citizen that a State may not insult and outrage him, if a citizen of a State may? The effect upon him is the same, and it was just this effect that the framers of the Fourteenth Amendment plainly intended by that article to prevent."[110] Harlan agreed, citing constitutional text and several Supreme Court precedents in support of the conclusions that the pervading purpose of all the Reconstruction Amendments had been simply *to secure the civil rights of the freedpeople*—against all assault, not against only those assailants acting in some official state capacity—and that their delegation of enforcement powers to the Congress was sufficient for that purpose. The majority erred both in restricting Congress's enforcement power to the mere correction of state wrongs and in conceiving too narrowly of the class of state actions (or inactions) that could qualify as wrongs.

Against the claim that Congress's enforcement power under the Fourteenth Amendment was merely corrective, Harlan expounded the notion of national citizenship that Douglass often invoked. The broad conferral of citizenship status in section 1 comprehended all rights that were attributes of U.S. and state citizenship. According to Harlan, the power granted Congress to enforce *all* the amendment's provisions therefore included a power to secure, by primary and direct legislation, all rights inherent in both levels of citizenship, including a right of U.S. citizens to be protected against racial discrimination in civil rights.[111] Against the majority's improperly narrow conception of state wrongs,

Harlan held further that by common-law tradition and Supreme Court precedent, public accommodations such as common carriers and inns did exercise "a quasi public employment" and so bore a responsibility to serve the whole public in facilitating the exercise of the right of locomotion or travel, a right considered fundamental to civil, personal liberty.[112] A state's licensing of the abridgment of rights or its failure to enforce this common law for the benefit of all would violate the privileges and immunities guarantee and deny the equal protection of the laws. Douglass tacitly invoked the latter argument in explaining the limits of the right of association. Landlords or innkeepers "keep a public table, advertise to accommodate the public, and have no arbitrary right over the table. The table really belongs . . . equally to those who pay for it."[113]

In sum, Douglass's reading of the Fourteenth Amendment extends the main themes of his prewar constitutionalism. Contrary to the opinion prevalent among moderate Republicans, he saw in the amendment's design more than the corrective federalism that Madison had originally espoused.[114] For Douglass, the Fourteenth Amendment confirmed the radical nationalism that was inherent in the original Constitution and vindicated by the Civil War. It is therefore a mistake to locate him in a Jeffersonian tradition of laissez-faire government. Implicitly affirming with Harlan the nationalist tradition of Alexander Hamilton, Justice Marshall, and Justice Story, Douglass insisted that the U.S. government held constitutional powers adequate to all exigencies of the national union.[115] Again with Harlan, he saw in the Reconstruction Amendments an expansion upon that tradition, in their recognition of race relations as an urgent national problem. Douglass held that natural law and constitutional law alike endowed Congress with a plenary power to secure civil rights for all. Congress had the power and duty to prevent not only direct violence, whatever the source, against person and property but also the invitation to such violence that attended officially sanctioned segregation, in which the design or effect of such segregation was arbitrarily to "insult and outrage" a discrete class of citizens.[116]

The exercise of that power was a minimum condition of governmental legitimacy. As he surveyed the results of Republican officeholders' growing fecklessness, in conjunction with the Supreme Court's obstructions, Douglass was forced to conclude that toward the black American, "every attribute of a just government is contradicted." In relation to the national government, he was "a deserted, a defrauded, a swindled, and an outcast man. . . . The government professes to give him citizenship and silently permits him to be divested of every attribute of citizenship. It demands allegiance, but denies protection." So protested

Douglass in his District of Columbia emancipation speech in 1888.[117] So long as such conditions persisted, it would be necessary to maintain the pressure of agitation ("Agitate! Agitate! Agitate!") that he renewed in the 1880s and 1890s and that he made his epitaph in an 1895 interview to a Howard University student.[118]

Reparation and Development

Even the expansive notion of fair play as elaborated to this point was incomplete, in Douglass's view, in its exclusive focus on formal civil and political rights. The formal right to acquire property, for instance, was of little use to one lacking any real means to acquire it and any real knowledge of how to manage it. Speaking in 1875, as the end of Reconstruction drew near, he insisted that something more was needed as he firmly rejected the notion that the nation had done enough for the freedpeople. "The world has never seen any people turned loose to such destitution as were the four million slaves of the South. . . . They were free, without roofs to cover them, or bread to eat, or land to cultivate, and as a consequence died in such numbers as to awaken the hope of their enemies that they would soon disappear."[119]

In the principles of moral right as well as in his nationalist constitutionalism, Douglass found warrant for the federal government to exercise broad powers to repair past injustices and to assist individuals in the development of their own powers to protect themselves against prospective injustices. The true object of government, he declared in his 1888 emancipation speech, was not only to secure formal rights but also "to see that all have an equal chance in the race of life."[120] His general position on the question of reparations is evident in his approving quotations of the "brave good words" of Lincoln's second inaugural address: "If God wills that [the war] continue until all the wealth piled by the bondsman's two hundred and fifty years of unrequited toil shall be sunk and until every drop of blood drawn by the lash shall be paid by another drawn by the sword, as was said three thousand years ago, so still it must be said: 'The judgements of the Lord are true and righteous altogether.' "[121] The nation's debt to African Americans was literally inexpiable, as Douglass maintained in one of his final great speeches, delivered in 1894.

> People who live now, and talk of doing too much for the Negro . . . forget that for these terrible wrongs there is, in truth, no redress and no adequate compensation. The enslaved and battered millions have come, suffered, died and gone with all their moral and physical

wounds into Eternity. To them no recompense can be made. If the American people could put a school house in every valley; a church on every hill top in the South and supply them with a teacher and preacher respectively and welcome the descendants of the former slaves to all the moral and intellectual benefits of the one and other . . . such a sacrifice would not compensate their children for the terrible wrong done to their fathers and mothers.[122]

Douglass employed this argument for national reparations in support of several specific proposals to ameliorate the condition of the freedpeople and of African Americans in general. The most important of those concerned land-ownership and education. The freedpeople had an urgent need and a strong expectation, fueled by federal promises, for landownership. They held capital only in their own labor and confronted a conspiracy among southern landowners and employers to refrain from selling land to them or compensating them for their labor in a manner that would permit any accumulation of money.[123] To secure "fair play in the acquisition of land," Douglass proposed as a Reconstruction measure the creation of a federal corporation empowered to purchase tracts of land and then resell or lease them on favorable terms to freedpeople.[124] Further, in keeping with his lifelong belief (first instilled by Hugh Auld) in the liberating power of education, Douglass ardently supported a federally funded system of public education, along with laws making school attendance compulsory for all American children. In support of the (perennially rejected) Blair education bill pending in Congress, he wrote in 1890 that the measure would be "at least a recognition of a great national duty towards a people to whom an immeasurable debt is due. It will tell that people and all others that the nation has the disposition if not entire ability to do the Negro right and justice."[125]

Douglass was untroubled by questions of constitutional license for the extraordinary assertions of federal power that he proposed. Insisting on broad federal protective powers in his District of Columbia emancipation speech in 1888, he observed, "Whenever an administration has had the will to do anything, it has generally found constitutional power to do it."[126] This remark was an expression not of cynicism but rather of his conviction that the Constitution supplied powers fully adequate to the nation's needs. In his view, Congress possessed plenary powers to enact progressive as well as protective legislation. For the exercise of federal power in public education, he found sufficient authority in the Preamble, probably in conjunction with the general welfare clause of Article I, section 1. He referred to three of the Preamble's objects as he argued for the Blair bill. The bill would do justice to African Americans, redeeming part of the nation's immeasurable debt to them; it would "promote the general welfare of diffusing knowledge and enlightenment, in the darkest corners of the Republic"; and it was further justified by the fact that "Liberty had become [explicitly] the base line of the Republic and the fundamental law of the land."[127] Such arguments would equally well justify the other remedial and constructive measures Douglass proposed, as they would justify virtually any exercise of national power for which a progressive justification could be conceived.

According to Douglass's argument, just as these appeals for national assistance were consistent with constitutional government, so, too, were they consistent with appeals for self-reliance among their beneficiaries. This means both that Douglass's concept of self-reliance or self-making was broad enough to accommodate a measure of dependence on others and that his appeals for national assistance, broad as they were, were nonetheless limited in keeping with his classical liberal principles.

In his ideas concerning specific measures to remedy the injustices suffered by the freedpeople, Douglass's relative moderation is notable. With respect to land reform, he agreed with fellow Radical Republicans on the urgency of the need. The freedpeople "are in a deplorable condition," he wrote only a few years after the war ended; "the great mass are struggling against wind and tide, and very many must go under unless they have aid." To supply the essential aid, Pennsylvania congressman Thaddeus Stevens, leader of the Radical Republicans in the House of Representatives, proposed a "plan for confiscation" in 1867, whereby lands belonging to the former Confederate states and their soldiers would be deemed forfeited and then distributed in parcels of forty acres as homesteads to the freedpeople. Douglass, together with most other Republicans, was reluctant to go so far. In a short manuscript (circa 1869) that he described as only "a rough outline," he instead proposed the chartering of a "national land and loan company," empowered to purchase "large tracts of land, which are to be sold in any state" and then to sell or lease them to the freedpeople.[128] Douglass's discussion of his proposal did not clarify the precise grounds of his disagreement with Stevens, and it is possible that the relative moderation of the proposal was merely a reflection of what was politically possible.[129] It is likely, however, as Martin and Blight have suggested, that his moderation in this regard reflects more importantly his classical-liberal respect for the property right, a basic natural right and an indispensable practical guarantor of the property in one*self* that African Americans for so many years had longed to secure.

Moreover, it is evident that he was motivated, here as elsewhere, by a concern to promote a condition and spirit of independence among the freedpeople. The source of their plight, he observed, was the design of "the old slave owners . . . to keep them poor and dependent." A major virtue of his proposed remedy was to provide a fair opportunity for them to "go to work and make themselves homes." Although Douglass certainly believed that those enslaved had already earned a title to some substantial portion of the South's wealth, he may have preferred his proposal to that of Stevens on the grounds that it was more fully consistent with the principle of self-reliance and also held forth the promise of greater societal recognition of the freedpeople's virtue in providing for themselves.[130]

While acknowledging that "benevolence with justice is harmonious and beautiful,"[131] Douglass remained acutely wary of the dangers that benevolent missions could pose to the development and exercise of virtue. Suspicious since his slavery days of whites' professions of paternal care, he remained sensitive in the postemancipation period to the self-indulgence of "sharply-pious" liberal reformers. But the primary danger lay in fostering a condition of dependence. Reflecting in *Life and Times* on the distinctively vulnerable condition of the freedpeople, he reiterated a basic principle of moral realism: "No man can be truly free whose liberty is dependent on the thought, feeling, and action of others."[132] In his warnings of the social and psychological effects of excessive dependence, Douglass again echoed Thomas Jefferson, who famously observed, "Dependance [*sic*] begets subservience and venality, suffocates the germ of virtue, and prepares fit tools for the designs of ambition."[133] This was true even if those whites upon whom freedpeople were dependent were figures no more malevolent than teachers from freedmen's aid societies. Douglass voiced a concern he shared with other, closer representatives of the freedpeople when, at an Independence Day celebration in 1875, he addressed an audience of black Washingtonians and issued an indignant call for their own renewed "declaration of independence": "To ask for help in [the condition of slaves] involved no disgrace. But all is changed now. . . . [The] suppliant, outstretched hand of beggary does not become an American freeman, and does not become us as a class, and we will not consent to be any longer represented in that position."[134]

At the same time, Douglass was fully aware that no one is purely independent. Near the outset of his trademark speech, he acknowledged that its title represented "something like a solecism. . . . Properly speaking, there are in the world no such men as self-made men. That term implies an individual independence of the past and present which can never exist." His concept of the self-made man was a pedagogically exaggerated representation of the humanizing power of agency, in particular the power to overcome adversity. It was a representation that was useful at all times but imperative amid circumstances such as those facing nineteenth-century African Americans. Real-life examples of greatness, he explained, assure us "of the latent powers and resources of simple and unaided manhood" and enable us "to take hold of the roughest and flintiest hardships incident to the battle of life, with a lighter heart, with higher hopes and a larger courage." Nonetheless, the exemplary individuals he singled out were only "in a *peculiar* sense, indebted to themselves for themselves." Their self-making virtue was consistent with the "brotherhood and inter-dependence of mankind."[135] In his emphasis on exemplary self-making, Douglass was calling African Americans to display exceptional virtue by elevating themselves from an exceptionally disadvantaged condition. But he was not calling them to do so alone. The independence proper to equals in society consisted in *inter*dependence or in mutual, reciprocal dependence. The condition against which he warned was not simply dependence but exceptional dependence, exceeding the debts that individual persons bear to one another by virtue of our natural sociality.[136]

In its fully refined meaning, Douglass's self-reliance and nothing-but-fair-play rhetoric was not a plea for the nation to do nothing at all or nothing specifically for the freedpeople or for African Americans. It was a plea to do nothing *invidious,* nothing that stigmatized them by designating them as exceptions to the natural-law rules that governed free, rights-bearing persons. For Douglass, properly limited, "do nothing" government meant a vigorously active government that confined its activity to measures that impartially protected and promoted its citizens' rights. It meant a government that acted instrumentally, not providentially, with respect to the rights and happiness of its citizens. Such a government promoted citizens' dignified independence by securing them from injustice, assisting them in the development of their natural faculties, and endeavoring to create conditions of broadly available opportunities for the fruitful exercise of their natural rights. Douglass's calls for self-reliant individualism and his calls for fair play involving substantial, primarily federal, governmental assistance to the freedpeople are, in this way, mutually consistent, with both grounded in a coherent understanding of the natural basis of rights and the conditions of their efficacy.

Rational Hopefulness in Postemancipation America

Douglass's postemancipation thought was essentially continuous with his thought in the abolitionist period, animated by a fundamentally liberal political philosophy. What was needed to secure the conditions of real freedom for African Americans after emancipation was a program of liberal reforms centering on the protection of formal civil and political rights (foremost among them the right to vote), including the provision of fair opportunities for acquiring property and education. The liberal, universal principles of the Declaration of Independence were adequate to the purpose, and the U.S. Constitution conformed with the Declaration, now more clearly than ever before. To realize the needed reforms, the Constitution had only to be properly enforced. Its amendment to form a more purely democratic national government would assist in this enforcement, Douglass believed, but it sufficed for the present that the supreme law of the land required the protection of formal civil and political rights and permitted further measures to assist the freedpeople in their self-elevation.

Continuing, as ever, to affirm that "the moral government of the universe is on our side," Douglass maintained his hopefulness in the decades after emancipation no less ardently than in the antebellum years. His hopefulness was not unqualified, and it did not rest on a blindness to present conditions. After 1880, he was increasingly direct in denouncing the "deplorable condition" in which the freedpeople remained confined over two decades after emancipation. "Peace with the old master class," he observed in 1883, "has been war to the Negro." By 1894, many of the war's essential gains were gravely imperiled, as he charged in perhaps the angriest of all his postwar speeches. Soon to be disfranchised again, southern blacks already lived mostly in a state of peonage similar to slavery, terrorized by mobs that regularly committed violence against them with impunity.[137] Yet his hopefulness perdured. "Nothing has occurred within these twenty years," he concluded in another 1883 retrospective on emancipation, "which has dimmed my hopes." Similarly undaunted in 1894, he found "many encouraging signs in the moral skies. . . . There is no time in our history that I would prefer to the present."[138]

Douglass claimed solid grounds for his faith in the eventual triumph of justice in America. That faith rested on no forgetting of history, on his part—in fact, quite the contrary. Recent history had shown that momentous change could emerge suddenly out of the bleakest conditions: in just six years, *Dred Scott* had given way to the Emancipation Proclamation.[139] Even the interruptions and reversals of the post-Reconstruction period could be viewed as signs of African American progress. "The Negro in ignorance and in rags meets no resistance," Douglass reminded the audience at the dedication of the Colored Industrial School at Manassas in 1894. "It is only when he acquires education, property, popularity and influence . . . that he invites repression." Postemancipation progress in education was undeniable, and further progress was sure to follow. Twenty years was "but a moment in the life of a nation." Postwar whites' hostility or weariness toward demands for justice would pass, and the demands themselves would never cease until they were satisfied. That, too, was a lesson of American history: repeated attempts to settle the slavery controversy by evasive compromise had only intensified it. The simple human nature of black Americans ensured that wave after wave of agitation would batter America's political shores as long as the injustice persisted, and the same human nature in white Americans ensured that they could not forever contravene the moral spirit of their own laws and of the revolutionary civilization that they represented. "The American people have their prejudices," Douglass observed, but "all their tendency is to progress, enlightenment and to the universal."[140] By the higher law and the human law alike, the regime of racial supremacy in the United States was proscribed and doomed just as surely as formal slavery had been.

Here again, it must be emphasized that realism was no less essential than idealism to Douglass's argument. It was eminently rational to hope, but necessary to hope soberly. The law of nature was not instantly self-enforcing; "ages may intervene" between seed and harvest in the moral world.[141] It was also a law of nature, Douglass believed, "that nothing valuable shall be obtained without labor and agony," and he knew that racial supremacy in America was a considerably more powerful adversary than formal slavery. Given the degradations inflicted by slavery, the deep-rooted bigotry that it had produced and fed upon, and the intense humiliation of military defeat with which emancipation was associated in the minds of southern whites, there could be no immediate emancipation in full, nor anything close to it.[142] In its more considered, sober expressions, Douglass's hopefulness applied to the longer-term prospect of life in America. As he contemplated the fading of Reconstruction's promise, he had to acknowledge that generations might pass before liberty and justice for all would be fully achieved. "Great bodies move slowly," he counseled a gathering of black Republicans in 1880.[143] It had taken nearly ninety years for the Declaration's principles to bear fruit in emancipation, and after formal emancipation, it was wise to prepare for a comparably lengthy struggle for full freedom.

But to look ahead to another extended struggle for a distant reward also meant to confront the danger that Douglass's vision of universal justice in America would come to appear as nothing more than a cruel delusion to many African Americans. The extended effort that his vision likely demanded of them was inconceivable absent their profound, abiding devotion to America. To explicate and solidify the proper grounds of African Americans' devotion to their country required more than theoretical appeals to the soundness of America's creedal identity or its constitutional guarantees. It required an emphasis on America's actual and potential greatness as a nation and on the dignifying share that African Americans could claim in it. In the next chapter, we will consider Douglass's fuller understanding of the terms whereby African Americans could fully embrace their American national identity.

The Waves and the Sea:
Race, America, and Humanity

Whatever else the true American is, he is also somehow black.
   Ralph Ellison, Going to the Territory

AS LATE AS 1894, Douglass again felt compelled to dispose of the nettlesome idea of colonization: "We are here and are here to stay. It is well for us and well for the American people to rest upon this as final." But in arguing against colonization this time, he was not only arguing against white extremists' hopes for blacks' expulsion. "The bad thing about it is, that it has, of late, owing to persecution, begun to be advocated by coloured men of acknowledged ability and learning."[1] Whites' acceptance of blacks as fellow citizens was one problem; the depth of blacks' desire for that status was another. Given the effort required to achieve acceptance and the uncertain prospect of success, it was plausible to argue that blacks' hopes and labors were better invested elsewhere. Of the wisdom of their permanent presence in America, many African Americans, too, required further persuasion.

In this chapter, we will consider Douglass's arguments against emigration and for America. He argued that schemes of emigration were hopelessly impracticable and, in their effect on African Americans' morale, pernicious. He also argued that they were unnecessary because antiblack prejudice in the United States, however virulent for the time being, was remediable. But beyond the question posed by emigration advocates lay the question made famous in the succeeding generation by W. E. B. Du Bois in *The Souls of Black Folk:* how was it possible "to be both a Negro and an American," to reconcile two identities that for many of their bearers had seemed at war with one another?[2] To complete his case against emigration and for the continued struggle for integration, Douglass needed to explain the meaning of the American identity he recommended—to what degree and on what terms he urged African Americans to affirm their Americanness. His arguments against emigration led to his fuller reflections on the meaning of America and, still more generally, on the claims of race in relation to those of humanity.

Against Emigration

In 1894, when he said that emigrationist advocacy by African American leaders had begun "of late," Douglass must have meant that it had begun anew. Naturally enough, emigrationist sentiment among African Americans tended to rise during periods when their prospects for equal rights in the United States looked especially bleak. One such period comprised the years following the end of Reconstruction in 1877, and another was the decade of the 1850s. In response to developments that seemed to secure slavery in perpetuity, such as the enactment of the Fugitive Slave Law and the *Dred Scott* ruling, prominent African Americans argued publicly for emigration. Douglass's former *North Star* coeditor, Martin Delany, made an extended case for it in his first book, *The Condition, Elevation, Emigration and Destiny of the Colored People of the United States* (1852). Delany played a major role, too, in organizing the National Emigration Convention that met in Cleveland in 1854. New York–born and Cambridge-educated Rev. Alexander Crummell spent the 1850s and 1860s engaged in missionary work in Africa, returning briefly to the United States during the Civil War to promote emigration to Liberia. Crummell's lifelong friend Henry Highland Garnet, also a New York–born black nationalist minister, founded the African Civilization Society (ACS) in 1858 to promote African American resettlement to West Africa.[3] With these men and others, Douglass carried on a sometimes heated controversy over the issue throughout the decade of the 1850s.

Proper consideration of Douglass's antiemigration argument begins with a distinction. To black emigrationists, an unbiased consideration of their proposal required its dissociation from colonization proposals. For our present purposes, the term *emigration* refers to a genuine migratory initiative undertaken by African Americans, whereas *colonization* refers to a policy akin to deportation, urged if not imposed upon them by white Americans. Expressing qualified support for the idea of emigration, Garnet declared, "I am *not* a Colonizationist. . . . I have hated the sentiments of the American Colonization Society from my childhood."[4] To the preeminent emigrationist Delany, that society loomed large among "the most arrant enemies of the colored man."[5] As we have seen,

Douglass emphatically agreed with his emigrationist adversaries on the narrow question of colonization: the American Colonization Society was an "arch-enemy" whose purpose was to expurgate the idea of a free African American from the American mind.[6] But to emigrationists, the malign motives of many colonizationists did not discredit the policy of African American emigration, organized and directed by African Americans themselves.

In brief summary, the case for emigration was as follows. First and foremost, emigrationists contended that emigration was necessary due to the persistent power of race prejudice in the United States. Left to their own resources, blacks in America would always remain a weak and despised "nation within a nation," perpetually subject to injustice at the hands of the white majority.[7] Second, emigration was to be affirmed as a heroic enterprise and thus as a powerful means of eliciting virtue. Delany advertised his proposal in terms akin to Douglass's description of his battle with Covey: African American emigration would call forth "bold, adventurous deeds of daring—contending against every odds—regardless of every consequence." For Crummell, emigration would activate "the noblest faculties and the highest ambition."[8] Such an enterprise could not be consistently opposed by a onetime fugitive slave such as Douglass or by any admirer of the American colonists, whose own flights from oppression marked the beginnings of grand new personal and national careers.[9] Third, emigration represented a practicable means of engendering respect for African populations worldwide. The serious proposal involved not a mass relocation of African Americans but instead a migration of sufficient numbers to found or revitalize an independent black nation that eventually would be capable of commanding respect among the world's sovereign powers.[10]

Douglass's response to these arguments might seem a peculiar mixture of moderation and extremism. He granted that in some sense, the disagreement involved a question of tactics.[11] Although he objected strenuously to emigration proposals, his objection could not be categorical. Migration or locomotion was a fundamental natural right. He had "no objection whatever" to "natural, self-moved, spontaneous emigration. . . . Man is emphatically a migratory animal."[12] Nor did he object categorically to "artificial" migrations, organized as a matter of policy. In response to the Kansas-Nebraska Act, he himself had conceived one such policy, proposing that "a large and well-disciplined body of free Colored People from the Northern States" should emigrate to Kansas and settle there.[13] The pertinent distinction was between progressive and regressive emigration. Personal or group emigration was to be judged progressive so far as it was well designed to advance the cause of freedom. As his own case demanded, Douglass readily affirmed that tactical retreat was justified to the end of attaining freedom or for self-preservation or in preparation for a future advance. Such concessions were in line with his general insistence that the opponents of injustice should maintain the most advanced positions possible for as long as possible, conceding ground only as a last resort.

Douglass considered organized African American emigration to be regressive in part because he considered it unrealistic and diversionary. Its lack of realism stemmed from more than the expense and logistical difficulty of a mass migration. To dispel the dream of salvation by means of a black sovereignty, he maintained, first, that pretensions to rulership by an African American colonial elite in Africa or anywhere else would be no more legitimate than the corresponding pretensions by European colonizers. "Altogether too much is made of similarity of color"; the lesson of history was "that colonists generally take up an anti-native position." Second, he contended that even if a black nation led by African American émigrés were successfully established, such a nation would probably not materially enhance the well-being of black Americans. "We have an African nation right under our *national* nose," he observed, referring to Haiti. But Haitian sovereignty had done nothing to reform white opinion or to enhance black security in the United States, and there was no reason to believe that a much more distant nation would marshal, in any foreseeable future, the power and will required to challenge America's white supremacist regime.[14]

In general, Douglass opposed strategies of indirection: "We instinctively shrink from any movement which involves a substitution of a doubtful and indirect issue, for one which is direct and certain. . . . The African Civilization Society proposes to plant its guns too far from the battlements of slavery for us."[15] The main theater of anti–white supremacy operations could only be America. The indirectness of the emigrationists' approach marked it a diversionary exercise, ineffective for good and, in its very inefficacy, productive of much evil for African Americans.

Douglass's tactical objections do not, however, explain the importance he ascribed to the issue or the polemical harshness of his attack. Their different motivations notwithstanding, he viewed black emigrationists as no less dangerous in practice—in fact, much more so—than white colonizationists. To the post-Garrisonian Douglass, the vices of emigrationism were, in principle, identical to those of his former colleagues' disunionism. In his 1851 call for such able leaders as Garnet and Crummell (then abroad) to "come home" that they might be "seen hand to hand with the enemy" (with the accompanying complaint that "we have lost some of our strong men"), his implication was clear.[16] Emigration's "doctrines and measures were those of doubt and retreat." Their proponents' response to the injustice suffered by African Americans was to "turn their backs upon the contest, and flee from the country."[17] The enemies of blacks' elevation could only rejoice at the call for a national emigrationist convention. Even to talk of emigration was to afford "aid and comfort . . . to Slavery and prejudice."[18] In Douglass's estimation, organized emigration or its advocacy constituted a dereliction of duty approaching the magnitude of treason.

One might sympathize with Douglass's emigrationist adversaries for thinking that his treatment of them was abstractly ideological and needlessly harsh and divisive. Himself hardly free of the schismatic temper that he regretted in Garrison, Douglass by implication hurled accusations of treasonous collaboration at men who hated racial domination just as zealously as he did.[19] He did so, despite his respect for their personal merits, in the belief that the disagreement reached a fundamental, urgently consequential moral principle. At the heart of the controversy were the implications of emigration and its advocacy for African Americans' morale and virtue. What emigrationists commended as heroically self-liberating and self-elevating Douglass regarded as disastrously demoralizing. To renounce one's native country and one's home could be virtuous when necessitated by extreme, otherwise insuperable adversity, but the "*habit* of roaming from place to place . . . is never a good one."[20] The danger lay not in opportunistic migratory acts but rather in the fostering of a migratory state of character, a perpetual attraction by the lure of immediate, radical change. By exaggerating the virtue of adaptability especially among blacks, as Delany had,[21] or by denigrating the "home-feeling" as an obstructive vice, as Crummell had, emigrationists promoted emigration needlessly and thereby fostered such a disposition. Beset by an unwarranted and debilitating pessimism with respect to the achievement of black elevation by direct means in the United States, they propagated profoundly destructive qualities of precipitancy and escapism. "Here, then, do we make the issue with Emigrationists. They are confounded with that despondency and despair which preclude the possibility of their working for their elevation here."[22]

Rather than the despairing escapism that he believed emigrationists unwittingly engendered, Douglass urged his fellow African Americans to cultivate more "staying qualities," grounded in the vitally important sentiment of attachment to home. In an editorial critique of Garnet's African Civilization Society, he observed, "Permanent location is a mighty element of civilization. . . . There is a powerful motive for the cultivation of an honorable character, in the fact that we have a country, a neighborhood, a home."[23] The inestimable worth of that sentiment, with its close relation to hopefulness, was a recurring theme in Douglass's thought.[24] He provided a concentrated statement of it in one of his last great speeches. "Every man who thinks at all, must know that home is the fountain head, the inspiration, the foundation and main support, not only of all social virtue but of all motives to human progress, and that no people can prosper, or amount to much, unless they have a home, or the hope of a home. A man who has not such an object . . . is a nobody and will never be anything else."[25]

Douglass's argument provoked a particularly important challenge from Crummell, who contended that it was both internally inconsistent and wrong-headed in its implicit conservatism. According to Crummell, Douglass's "exaggeration of the 'home-feeling'" as a source of virtue was "exceedingly opposite to Anglo-Saxon influences" whose emulation Douglass often recommended.[26] In Douglass's varied observations, African Americans were at once "a remarkably home-loving" people and a people needing more "staying qualities," with both those characteristics traceable to their experience under slavery.[27] As Crummell observed, Douglass's commendations of the home-feeling or the virtue of constancy for African Americans seemed to contradict his laudatory descriptions of the progressive virtues of Anglo-Americans in particular and human nature in general. An admirer of Tocqueville's *Democracy in America,* Douglass sounded one of its prominent themes in "Self-Made Men," describing "the restless activity and ever-changing relations of American society."[28] In that speech and elsewhere, he characterized humankind as the distinctively revolutionary species, distinctive above all in its powers of migration, adaptation, innovation, self-making, and self-remaking. Crummell, too, saw Anglo-Americans' dynamism as integral to their progressive achievements, and in apparent contrast to Douglass, he maintained that African Americans would benefit greatly from more of that spirit. A great hindrance to their progress, warned the emigrationist minister, was "the stolid inhabitiveness of our race. As a people, we cling with an almost deadly fixity to locality."[29]

Crummell's charge was perceptive, but in Douglass's understanding, the tensions in his own arguments did not amount to self-contradictions. When he called for a stronger home-feeling among African Americans, he understood that feeling partly as a corrective to vices engendered by slavery, which he believed would be magnified by the spread of the emigrationist idea. Slavery naturally engendered among slaves a spirit of escapism, a tendency to equate freedom with the mobility systematically denied them. Douglass saw manifestations of that spirit in the early postemancipation years, as in his admonition to an audience of African Americans in Louisville, Kentucky, in 1873: "The trouble of many of us now is that as soon as we get money we want to travel."[30] It was perfectly natural that enslaved people would come to feel a constant desire to escape their present circumstances and that newly emancipated people would want to confirm their liberty by making sometimes immoderate use of the elementary freedom of locomotion.[31] Douglass did not contradict himself in warning of the harmful effects of such desires even as he affirmed the general importance of the migratory, innovative virtues. It was both possible and sensible for him to commend the virtues that generate upward mobility while condemning the dissipation of energy in aimless escapism.

This consideration carries a deeper significance. At bottom, Douglass viewed his controversy with emigrationists as a controversy over the moral and psychological conditions of freedom and slavery. At this level, his idea of home comprehended much more than the locus of physical shelter, legal protection, and familiar association. To have a home, in Douglass's teleological understanding, meant to have all the vital requisites of a fully developed, rights-bearing self, capable of extensive enterprise and progressive civilization. It meant being a socially and temporally extended self with a rooted identity, a stable structure of affections and duties, a relation to past and future, a heritage to honor, and a legacy to build. Comprising attachments to local causes larger than one's momentary gratifications, it supplied a vital condition for the development of grander devotions. Home, for Douglass, was the radiant center of concrete motivations for the various forms of agency whereby human beings construct the ever-improving edifice of civilization: "The men who made Rome worth going to see were the men who staid [sic] there."[32] In this way, what might initially appear as a self-contradiction is better understood as Douglass's appreciation of the need to harmonize two divergent human sentiments. Progress requires conservatism along with dynamism. As a plant rises above the earth only by its rootedness in the earth, so the free, rights-bearing self requires and develops a stable, concrete identity as a condition of its further progressive development.

The converse was no less important. As home represented an indispensable condition of civilization and civilized personhood, so homelessness or alienation represented their antithesis. Here is the nerve of Douglass's opposition to emigrationism. "To have a home," he continued in his 1894 speech, "the Negro must have a country, and he is an enemy to the moral progress of the Negro, whether he knows it or not, who calls upon him to break up his home in this country, for an uncertain home in Africa."[33] As white colonizationists had claimed to support abolition even as they made it contingent on a practical impossibility, so black emigrationists propagated a utopian vision of African Americans' true home, the effect of which would be to render them perpetually homeless.[34] This Douglass feared above all else. A perpetuated sentiment of homelessness or alienation was simply incompatible with the spirit of faithful struggle required for African Americans to ameliorate their condition. Emigrationism presented no realistic opportunity for the exercise of moral agency, no realistic means for showing themselves to be the "*power*[*s*] *on earth*" that their human dignity required.[35] Instead, it offered a diversionary hopefulness that would inevitably settle into an angry or resigned hopelessness. The "worst thing, perhaps," about emigrationism was that it tended "to throw over the Negro a mantle of despair."[36]

The worst thing about emigrationism, in other words, was its tendency to engender a psychological condition closely similar in principle to the spirit of hopeless, futureless alienation that Douglass identified as the depth of his degradation while enslaved. Envisioning its adherents as deprived of a meaningful social and political identity, Douglass assimilated them to the radically expropriated, disintegrated self to which slavery aimed to reduce its main victims. His ferocious opposition to emigration derived ultimately from the same concern that moved him to insist on physical resistance, come what might, to the worst of slavery. He emphasized this concern in protesting the worst of his country's assaults against his people. As he thought of "the accursed Fugitive Slave Bill," he told an 1851 Rochester audience, it was "impossible not to feel that we are in an enemy's land." By the *Dred Scott* ruling, he lamented in 1860, free blacks were made "aliens and enemies in the land of their birth." In the wake of the *Civil Rights Cases* ruling, he warned, "Our legislators, our Presidents, and our judges should have a care, lest, by forcing these people, outside of law, they destroy that love of country which is needful to the Nation's defence in the day of trouble."[37] To foster in African Americans a sense of radical alienation would be self-destructive for America, and for African Americans to submit to that sense would be morally suicidal.

Douglass warned, in relatively concrete terms, of the destructive effects on personality wrought by a chronic sentiment of alienation. In his estimation, the likely damages to the capacity for constructive, progressive agency fell into two main classes. He worried more often about *enervation,* a resigned refusal to undertake any significant mundane action. To the belief that one has no proper worldly home, such resignation would be one plausibly rational response. So Douglass feared that emigrationists would foster a climate of opinion in which many African Americans would see only futility in any extended efforts to educate themselves, improve their labor power, save their earnings and accumulate wealth, develop familial and communal associations, and the like.[38] In one form, such enervation might reflect the self's disintegration into a condition of crude egoism, concerned for little beyond present, sensual pleasures and pains. In another, it might reflect the self's diversion, so that its agency would find expression only in works of the imagination. Douglass complained of emigrationism's tendency to enthrall the imagination with "Utopian and impossible enterprises abroad," diverting it from "practical advantages and duties here."[39] In the latter form, the effect was similar to that of the otherworldly Christianity that he disdained as a proslavery religion. It taught its faithful to think of themselves as mere transients, hovering in a condition of suspended animation, longing for deliverance in the next life and inattentive to improvement in the present life.[40]

Alternatively, the damaging effect of the sentiment of homelessness might appear in the replacement of constructive agency with actively destructive vices. Douglass's reflection on the dangers yielded insights similar to those of Thomas Jefferson and the great eighteenth-century Swiss philosopher Jean-Jacques Rousseau: chronic dependence on an alien power tends to generate not only servility but also anger.[41] As the sad example of Haiti illustrated, the longing "for some mighty revolution in our affairs" could generate a violent factiousness, inconsistent with civil peace or progress. The effect of that spirit in America would be generally destructive, as we saw in Douglass's warning of the terrible effects of abolishing slavery without guaranteeing equal rights.[42] After the *Civil Rights Cases* ruling confirmed that the nation would adopt that worst course, he reiterated the warning in a spirit of measured anger, reminding his fellow citizens of the efficacy of the natural law. As "sure as there is a moral government of the universe, so sure will the harvest of evil come." Out of the perpetuated degradation of caste would emerge a "black Ireland"—an American counterpart to the chronically aggrieved, unproductive, and disproportionately criminal (under)class that Douglass saw as the natural issue of England's injustice: "Weeds do not more naturally spring out of a manure pile than crime out of enforced destitution. Out of the misery of Ireland comes murder, assassination, fire and sword."[43] In America, the consequences would be no less dire.

Revisiting the emigrationists' objection, one might regard as overwrought Douglass's attack on them as unwitting propagators of moral nihilism. In some circumstances, he likely misapplied his insistence on the home-feeling, notably in his objection to the post-Reconstruction exodus, as he himself later acknowledged. But the serious issue concerned his insistence on the United States as the proper home for African Americans. That insistence depended on his judgment that emigration was unnecessary; reform in America could be achieved more satisfactorily than could the establishment of a home in Africa or elsewhere. If his hopeful expectations of America were well founded, then his view of emigration as a self-destructive surrender would be vindicated. Conversely, if his emigrationist adversaries were right in believing America to be incorrigible in its racial bigotry, then they also would have been right to view Douglass's insistence on an American home and identity as a self-destructive mulishness. The difficulty of this question, viewed from a nineteenth-century perspective, is undeniable. By his own admission, Douglass at times had to walk by faith, not only by sight.[44] But in his settled understanding, his appeal to African Americans to invest their hopes in America was grounded in rationally compelling evidence and argument.

For America

The case for identifying with America rested fundamentally on the contention that race prejudice in the United States, powerful as it was, was ultimately weak and would be overcome. Antiblack prejudice, Douglass maintained in an 1850 editorial, was "the greatest of all obstacles in the way of the anti-slavery cause." It was also the greatest obstacle to African Americans' elevation after emancipation.[45] The overcoming of that prejudice was the grand object for those who sought to put slavery, in form and spirit, to permanent rest. Douglass was convinced that that object was achievable, but he was not naive about the difficulties it would involve.

On the question of the source of American color prejudice, as on other important questions, Douglass's argument was multilayered, with relatively simpler, more polemical arguments overlying more complex analyses. To begin with the simplest binary alternatives, his most emphatically affirmed position was that such prejudices were merely conventional, not natural attributes of the minds of whites. They indicated a pathological rather than a normal mental state. It made no sense to claim nature's sanction for a sentiment that had been promulgated only after the beginning of the African slave trade and that remained unheard of wherever colored persons had not been enslaved.[46] In a wartime editorial, Douglass got to the heart of the matter as he angrily denounced Lincoln for endorsing colonization: "Negro hatred and prejudice of color are . . . merely the offshoots of that root of all crimes and evils—slavery."[47] Race prejudice was the peculiar emission of the peculiar institution.

As we saw in Chapter Two, Douglass suggested that slavery generated color prejudice out of a need to rationalize its injustice. Having originated in naked material interest, along with an opportunism that preyed upon its victims' weakness, the system of forced labor imposed upon imported laborers by the English and various European settlers in the Americas could be race-specific without immediately generating a virulent ideology of racism. After it hardened into formal slavery and especially after the moral upheaval initiated by the American Revolution, that system found itself exposed to moral challenges that dictated the construction of explicitly racial defenses. Paradoxically, it was the slaveholders' very status as moral (hence, naturally self-justifying) beings that explained the tenacity with which they defended their institution and the stubborn persistence of their bigotry after its forced abolition. No confession to so gigantic a moral transgression as slavery could come easily, during or after its commission. It was on this reasoning that Douglass assigned causal primacy to both slavery and race prejudice, holding slavery to be the deep cause of racial bigotry and yet also holding the elimination of racial bigotry, not formal abolition, as the grand antislavery desideratum.[48] The color prejudice widespread among northern and nonslaveholding whites had to be likewise understood, in this argument, as a by-product of the deeper prejudices held by slavery's direct practitioners.[49]

If the source of American color prejudice was convention, not nature, that prejudice was nonetheless powerful. Yet in his considered understanding, Douglass allowed that the cause of Americans' antiblack prejudice was not limited to slavery. Contemplating its presence in the American Anti-Slavery Society, Douglass traced it to an "Anglo-Saxon pride of race."[50] Something in the broader character or experience of Anglo-Saxon peoples was also a source of corruption. But Douglass's most general explanation of the causes of race prejudice extended well beyond any Anglo-Saxon peculiarity. In fact, he believed some degree of prejudice respecting race or ethnicity was virtually universal. In an 1869 discussion of Americans' hostility to Chinese immigrants, he observed, "Repugnance to the presence and influence of foreigners is an ancient feeling among men." In a later speech he went further, maintaining that "the world was never yet without prejudice" of one form or another.[51] The near universality of this phenomenon suggested that prejudice respecting color or ethnicity was, in some sense, natural to humankind, not simply conventional in this or that group. Douglass seemed to locate the natural basis of such sentiments in the universal passion of pride: "A man must be low indeed when he does not want some one below him." The claim "that the feeling itself is entirely natural" seemed to him one of the two strongest justifications for a regime of racial supremacy.[52]

Mindful of its conventional and natural bases, Douglass well understood that the elimination of race prejudice would not come easily to America. His white compatriots found it "almost as hard to get rid of [race hatred] as to get rid of their skins," he complained to Garrison in 1846. A few months prior to the outbreak of war, he predicted that the bigotry that attended slavery would endure long after legal abolition, perhaps for "several generations."[53] His persistent hopefulness notwithstanding, Douglass recognized that a disastrous victory by the spirit of slavery remained a real possibility. America represented the focal point of progressive humankind's deepest fears as well as its highest hopes. It might yet emerge as the world's great exemplar of racial supremacy rather than of humanitarian republicanism.

Nonetheless, Douglass consistently maintained that emigrationists and colonizationists decisively overestimated the staying power of American racial bigotry. With respect to the claim that such bigotry had a natural basis, he responded that it is not natural in the strong sense needed for it to be a permanent or a morally legitimate human sentiment. He summarized this response in his 1881 essay "The Color Line." Although race prejudice in some form may have been present among all peoples, antiblack prejudice in particular was not universal; it was not present among all Caucasian peoples; it was not present among white American children; it was present to a diminished degree at the higher levels of American society; and in those who did harbor it, it was corrigible.[54] Further, in Douglass's teleological understanding, the *fully* natural was distinct from the *merely* natural: whereas some natural qualities were morally essential to humans, constituents of their moral perfection, others were morally retrograde.[55] The work of properly civilized persons was to ensure that the former prevailed over the latter. Whether it would signify a victory of the natural over the conventional or of the higher over the lower nature, race prejudice could yet be overcome.

By a confluence of powerful natural and historical causes, Douglass believed, the forces of higher human nature and natural law were gaining ascendancy in the nineteenth century, both in America and throughout the Western world. Though he renounced his youthful Garrisonian faith in the power of plainly stated moral truth to compel assent, he affirmed throughout his maturity that truth was mighty and would ultimately prevail.[56] And the triumph of the truths of human equality and rights seemed to him no distant projection. In the spirit of Jefferson, Paine, and (with a different emphasis) Tocqueville, Douglass spoke as a self-conscious representative of the age of revolution, deeply impressed by the progressive changes sweeping the world in morals and politics as well as in science. From the vantage of its penultimate decade, he viewed his own century as unequaled "for its vast and wonderful contribution to the moral and material progress of mankind." His belief in the propitiousness of the times for moral reform never left him. In his 1883 commemoration of emancipation in the District of Columbia, echoing his 1848 reflections on that year's political revolutions, he exulted: "The ideas of a common humanity against privileged classes, of common rights against special privileges, are now rocking the world."[57] Nor could the impending triumph of those ideas be dismissed as a passing fancy of disgruntled peoples or oppositional elites; he believed the equal rights revolution was ultimately irreversible.[58]

As he considered the dominant spirit of the age, Douglass found a special cause for confidence in the onset of what today's partisans celebrate and deplore as "globalization." Like Alexander Hamilton, he espoused a moralized materialism. He believed that material-scientific and moral progress occurred in tandem, and here was a crucial point of convergence. Placing his own stamp on the notion of modernity's universalizing, homogenizing tendencies, Douglass found in aspects of the modern technological revolution a solid, empirical basis for his moral hopefulness. The world-shrinking, barrier-dissolving inventions of modern communications technology, largely called into existence by commercial aspiration, were making possible truly globalized commercial relations. Douglass believed that their effect inexorably would be to dispel prejudice. Once again, despotism requires isolation, of its victims from each other and of itself from opponents' moral reprobation. The great virtue of modern commerce would be to render such isolation ultimately impossible by ensuring the worldwide propagation of morally irresistible ideas. The mind cannot long resist exposure to enlightening ideas, and in the modern age, neither slavery nor racial supremacy could long shield itself from such exposure.[59]

Centrally important in Douglass's notion of progressive modernity was the rising American nation. The moral significance of its founding ideas, its practical significance as a great power among nations, and the stark opposition between the contending principles in its slavery controversy led Douglass to think of his country in grandiose, even apocalyptic terms. As early as 1848, he declared, "The grand conflict of the angel Liberty with the monster Slavery, has at last come." The age-old conflict of civilization versus barbarism or of liberty versus despotism seemed to him to be culminating in his own time and place. This is the larger meaning of his 1856 remark, intended to arouse fellow African Americans to antislavery action and again echoing expressions by prominent American Founders: "Generations unborn will envy us the felicity of having been born at a time when such noble work could be accomplished, when the foundations can be laid deep and strong for the future liberation of the race."[60] As late as 1885, sobered by events in the intervening years, Douglass saw in the Civil War and emancipation a significance unparalleled in modern history.[61]

This point deserves emphasis. America, for Douglass no less than for Lincoln, was "a new nation," the world's first nation explicitly dedicated to the true principles of human equality, rights, and self-government. It was the nation destined by its principles and circumstances to effectuate the unity and dignity of humankind and thus to overcome racial, ethnic, and sectarian bigotries.[62] As numerous events in Douglass's lifetime had seemed to make clear, America was destined to emerge as the world's preeminently powerful nation, wielding moral and cultural influence commensurate with its material supremacy. A victory for the forces of liberty in the American Civil War could therefore appear as a victory for all humankind, as the nation that emerged from it could become the most powerful example and force for liberty that the world had ever seen.[63] The wave of abolition then sweeping the Western world was unprecedented in human history, and the greatest of all emancipations was that in the United States. The Civil War heralded the completion of the American Revolution and the culmination of enlightened modernity.[64] For Douglass, as for Jefferson, the authors of *The Federalist,* and Lincoln, America represented, if not the last, yet the best hope of earth.

Douglass's moral thought was thoroughly imbued with Enlightenment rationalism. The highest of human virtues was the rational virtue of discovery,[65] and the ultimate condition of liberation from prejudice, as of human liberty in general, was enlightenment into "the essential nature of things."[66] Nonetheless, his expectation that color prejudice in the United States would be overcome did not depend on a utopian faith in human enlightenment.[67] The realism in his argument is nicely illustrated by a pair of autobiographical anecdotes, presented specifically to contest the proposition "that there is . . . an invincible repugnance in the breast of the white race toward dark-colored people." In these two incidents, Douglass was a passenger on Massachusetts trains, initially shunned by white passengers as a despicable "negro" and then instantly transformed in the eyes of those same whites into a respectable and even sought-after traveling companion by friendly attentions from prominent public figures who had recognized him. The lesson of these episodes, according to Douglass's brief comment, was that race prejudice was a matter of mutable "pride and fashion."[68] But this did not mean that the sudden visibility of Douglass's full humanity signified a triumph of enlightened reason over fashionable prejudice. Even after Douglass's transformation in their eyes, his fellow passengers remained bearers of prejudice. The lesson of these stories was that in its campaign against color prejudice, moral reason could prevail by an alliance with relatively sounder forms of prejudice.

One implication of Douglass's understanding of the home-feeling is that most morally healthy human beings, like unhealthy ones, are creatures of prejudice. They are creatures of particular identifications and affections, motivated to virtuous action by preferences for their own over others that are at best only partially grounded in reason. Douglass's stories show how such sentiments could work for, not only against, African Americans. Like other Americans and human beings in general, his fellow passengers harbored benign as well as malign prejudices. Their benign prejudice consisted in the authority they vested in the "great men" who recognized Douglass, one the present and one a future governor of Massachusetts. The prejudice whereby they trusted in the "excellency" of these two men negated the prejudice whereby they had disdained Douglass. More generally, white Americans (or, to begin with, many northern whites) could be made receptive to the truth of black humanity by the association of that truth with those in whom whites invested high authority. Douglass's estimation of this lesson's potential power appears more clearly when his anecdotes are considered in relation to his practice of associating the African American cause with authorities far more elevated than any Massachusetts governor. If the sympathetic notice of a state's highest elected official could humanize him to his bigoted fellow passengers, Douglass seems to have reasoned, then all the more powerful should be the endorsement of the African American cause by the architects of America's revolution and founding, along with the martyred savior of the republic they created.

In sum, to the charge that he harbored a naive faith in the self-enforcing power of moral truth, Douglass's fuller response reflects the realist, anti-Garrisonian dimension of his thought. Patriotism was not the highest human virtue, but it was a powerful natural sentiment and often a genuine virtue. American patriotism was often a prejudice, but it was a relatively just prejudice, containing the necessary elements of a remedy for Americans' unjust prejudices. It was to this prejudice that Douglass appealed in his powerful Fourth of July oration; in his defense of the Constitution; in his postwar efforts to deepen the nation's reverence for Lincoln; and in presenting himself as a representative American, by his adaptation of the "Self-Made Men" story. Essential to his strategy to overcome American color prejudice was his effort to forge and to force his fellow Americans to confront an indissoluble identification between that which they revered—the founding, the fundamental law, and the symbols of the nation's civil religion—and the racial group they reviled. The rebels' example notwithstanding, his calculation was that for a sufficient number of Americans, reverence ran deeper than racial aversion, so that the association would work, over time, to elevate African Americans rather than to lower America in their minds.

At least by the judgment of a large majority of African Americans, Douglass won his argument with the emigrationists. But it was not enough for him to demonstrate the abstract moral necessity of having a home in one's country, nor even to demonstrate that the majority of Americans could be brought to welcome the idea of African American fellow citizens. What remained was for Douglass to explain the specific manner and extent of African Americans' proper identification with their country, as well as the specific meaning of the America with which they would identify.

Assimilation and Race Pride

Douglass never believed what Du Bois would believe—that to be an African American was to harbor "two warring ideals in one dark body." Yet questions akin to those that possessed Du Bois were alive in his own thought. On what terms were African Americans to identify themselves as Americans? Were they to consider their racial identity as alienable or inalienable, accidental or essential to their identities as citizens and human beings?[69] Du Bois also conveniently encapsulated Douglass's answer. Douglass stood for racial assimilation "*through* [African American] self-assertion."[70] Du Bois's trenchant observation is especially useful in suggesting the complexity of Douglass's conception of African American identity. Douglass has been widely and, in general, rightly understood as approving an assimilationist model of racial integration in the United States. But in his more particular reflections, his assimilationist teleology was compatible with and even required the persistence of race consciousness over an extended period. Still more significantly, the self-assertion upon which Du Bois conditioned Douglass's assimilationism meant mainly racial, not individual, self-assertion. Douglass endorsed a provisionally persisting race consciousness not only as a measure necessary for self-defense but also, in part, as a means of genuine self-affirmation. We will begin our consideration of the relevant complexities by reviewing Douglass's arguments in favor of full assimilation or amalgamation as the natural, desirable completion of racial integration in the United States.

Douglass suggested two mutually complementary lines of argument for racial assimilation in America. The first proceeded from a foundation in natural science. In Chapter Three, we examined his ethnological argument, in which he maintained that the preponderant evidence supported the conclusion of a monogenetic human origin and that any lingering uncertainty in that conclusion did not disturb the more important conclusion of humankind's biological and moral unity. At bottom, the common notion of a plurality of human races rested upon an error: "I know no race . . . but the human race."[71] The decisive evidence for biological human unity appeared in the ability of members of different subclasses to procreate with one another.[72] Douglass acknowledged the limits of that argument: the biological possibility of miscegenation across (what are commonly termed) racial lines did not establish the necessity, likelihood, or desirability of interracial amalgamation, in America or anywhere else. He nonetheless denied that the cultural differences associated with racial differences imposed any truly durable barriers to amalgamation. He was confident that what the experience under slavery had already suggested would be still more conclusively confirmed after emancipation—the natural forces impelling amalgamation would prove stronger than the artificial enforcements of separation. "Contemplation of the forces of nature is enlarging," he remarked, recalling his voyage overseas in 1886. A moment of such contemplation on the deck of the great ship *City of Rome* suggested to him a useful simile: the various types of mankind "differ like the waves, but are one like the sea."[73]

Douglass's simile suggests that he expected the particular "types of mankind," including racial groups, to have finite life spans as distinctive subclasses. Humankind would persist in a natural condition of dynamic flux, dividing and redividing into various subclasses, with each destined ultimately to lose its distinctiveness and reblend into the human "sea" from which it arose. "Races and varieties of the human family appear and disappear," he observed shortly after the Civil War, "but humanity remains and will remain forever." He expected not only the progressive elimination of civil and legal classifications based on race or ethnicity but also, much more radically, the cultural and biological amalgamation of historically distinct groups. In the American context, his "strongest conviction as to the future of the Negro therefore is . . . that he will be absorbed, assimilated, and will only appear finally . . . in the features of a blended race."[74] Although the full amalgamation that he described might come "only in the fullness of time," the process was already under way. Americans were already "a composite race" and not only by virtue of the ongoing amalgamation of various white ethnicities.[75] Even between whites and blacks, "an intermediate race . . . is constantly increasing." That the generation of a mixed-race population numbering roughly one million could occur amid slavery's barriers gave cause to expect, Douglass reasoned hopefully, that that class would be greatly magnified as black Americans shed slavery's degradations and joined the mainstream of American education and prosperity.[76]

In the 1866 essay in which he predicted ultimate amalgamation, Douglass disclaimed any advocacy of intermarriage. He spoke only as a "prophet," not a "propagandist." His disclaimer was understandable in a context in which exigencies of legal and political reform required deference to the distinction between civil and social equality. But it was also entirely incredible, even coming nearly twenty years before his own controversial second marriage (to Helen Pitts, his white clerical assistant in the District of Columbia recorder's office, in 1884). For Douglass, interracial amalgamation was natural in the fullest degree—both empirically predictable and morally desirable. Here again, the moral law of nature and the biological law were complementary and ultimately convergent.

In Douglass's understanding, differences of race and color were to be seen morally as mere accidents. Central to Christianity was the idea that "of one blood God has made all nations to dwell on all the Christian earth."[77] By the light of natural reason or moral philosophy, race and color differences likewise had to be judged morally meaningless. They played no part in the constitution of moral personhood, nor, in their strict conception as biologically heritable qualities, did they proceed from the exercise of moral personhood. They provided no justification for any claim of racially differential rights or for any sentiment of racial pride or shame. Douglass readily acknowledged that racial subgroups constructed differing cultures that might justify different levels of pride in their cultural or civilizational achievements. What he sometimes called the Anglo-Saxon "race" could well take pride in its productive industry and inventiveness and also in the liberal principles of its constitutional-law tradition. But the proper source of such pride inhered in the *exercise* of faculties that human beings commonly possess rather than in any racially distinctive *possession* of those faculties, so that its justification could never extend to claims to rulership by one racial group over another.[78] Such claims could be justified only by a radical, permanent disparity in the possession of the faculties that constitute moral personhood.

In view of the ultimate moral insignificance of racial difference, Douglass argued that such matters as the choice of one's marital partner and even the choice of the country in which to make one's home properly belonged primarily to the sphere of personal, private rights. Amid a general statement discrediting southern whites' visions of the parade of horribles that would attend full civil and political equality, he declared in 1890 that the question of intermarriage held "no vital concern to anybody. . . . Individual interests, personal preferences, public sentiment, may be safely left to regulate the relation of the races in respect of intermarriage."[79] He treated the question of immigration as analogous, seeing no reason why considerations of race, ethnicity, or even national origin should constrain the exercise of personal rights of migration and association. In his important 1869 speech "Our Composite Nationality," reflecting on the specific issue of Chinese immigration to America, he endorsed, on grounds of both right and wisdom, a policy so radically libertarian as to call into question the very legitimacy of national, political boundaries. "If the white race may exclude all other races from this continent, it may rightfully do the same in respect to all other lands . . . and thus have all the world to itself. . . . I hold that a liberal and brotherly welcome to all who are likely to come to the United States is the only wise policy which this nation can adopt."[80]

Although he insisted that these issues concerned the exercise of private rights, they held important public significance for Douglass. Race mixing, by the composition of multiracial nations and by intermarriage, was an important public good. Concretely exemplifying the triumph over arbitrary prejudice, it would advance the cause of popular enlightenment and expand the sphere of civic friendship that gives health to a democratic republic. Voluntary racial amalgamation in America would be all the more impressive, involving "opposite extremes of ethnological classification" divided by a long history of one-sided injustice.[81] Douglass saw in this America's great moral mission and national destiny: "Our geographical position . . . our fundamental principles of government, world-embracing in their scope and character, our vast national resources, requiring all manner of labor to develop them, and our already existing composite population, all conspire to one grand end . . . to make us the [most] perfect national illustration of the unity and dignity of the human family that the world has ever seen."[82] The Civil War was once again a great turning point, pointing toward the end of Americans' deep historical divisions by race and national origin as well as by state and section. When Douglass displayed some pride in presenting himself as a product of a racially mixed parentage—"a very sensible modification of black," he told an 1872 Raleigh, North Carolina, audience[83]—he was implicitly presenting himself as a prototype of the future American, even of the modern man of the future.

The writer Charles Chesnutt, an early Douglass biographer and a sensitive analyst of the complexities of racial amalgamation, speculated ironically in a 1900 essay on the ease with which racial blending in America could be achieved. Suppose, he suggested, that there were laws that favored black-white intermarriage as strongly as actual turn-of-the-century laws opposed it, so that each black or colored person were compelled by promiscegenation laws to marry a white. The result would be that in three generations, the entire U.S. population would be composed of "octaroons, or persons only one-eighth Negro, who would probably call themselves white."[84] Chesnutt's fanciful suggestion pointed to the absurdity of both sorts of laws and indirectly indicated the doubtful prospects of thorough racial amalgamation in any near term. Douglass harbored similarly realistic expectations. Perhaps his more enthusiastic claims of the impermanence of races were meant to rebut the contrary thesis by the racist ethnologists Nott and Glidden.[85] However that might be, alongside Douglass's extrapolations of a racially blended America, one must consider his qualification that such an amalgamation would be achieved "only in the fullness of time." For the foreseeable future, he observed in 1893, "the Negro, like the Jew, can never part with his identity and race."[86] This realism concerning its near-term prospects identifies his second line of argument for racial assimilation.

In his example as well as in his advocacy, Douglass himself affirmed a strong spirit of racial identity throughout his career. Even amid a strong condemnation of race pride in 1889, he declared, "there is no other man in the United States prouder than myself of any great achievement, mental or mechanical, of which any colored man or woman is the author."[87] In *Bondage and Freedom,* he took special pride in his mother's reputed literacy, ascribing his own love of letters "*not* to my admitted Anglo-Saxon paternity, but to the native genius of my sable, unprotected, and uncultivated *mother.*"[88] He pointedly drew attention to the unmixed African ancestry of the likes of Garnet, Samuel R. Ward, the inventor and architect William Dietz, and Toussaint L'Ouverture as he praised them for their intellectual and moral virtues. Similarly praising the accomplishments of Benjamin Banneker, he regretted that Banneker was not entirely black, in view of the opportunity that "the slightest infusion of Teutonic blood" left for bigots to discredit any black or African claim to virtue.[89] Above other great civilizations of antiquity, he took a special interest in ancient Egypt, which he regarded at least for a time as an ancient black civilization. Above other modern revolutions in inspirational potential stood the Haitian revolution, which gave birth to the world's first black republic.[90]

Although he adamantly opposed racial segregation, Douglass endeavored for most of his career to promote a spirit of enlightened racial partiality among his fellow African Americans. To this end, he issued frequent calls for racial unity and supported various "complexional" or race-specific institutions and associations. He deplored division among blacks, believing it to be socially and politically debilitating.[91] He promoted and participated in the Negro convention movement in part to lend institutional weight and momentum to the imperative of unity. In "An Address to the Colored People of the United States," issued by one such convention in 1848, he predicted, "We shall undoubtedly for many years be compelled to have institutions of a complexional character." At another in 1883, he issued a "special rebuke" to those "traitors" among African Americans who objected to the formation of race-specific associations.[92] In 1871 (during a brief period of available voting rights), he blamed excessive ambition in black office-seekers for producing divisions among black voters and diminishing the number of blacks holding elective positions. Armed with the vote and properly unified, he insisted, "the power is with us to compel respect."[93] He congratulated Tennessee's black mechanics and farmers in 1873 for organizing their trade association.[94] He affirmed the special contribution of an able black press to the cause of racial justice and the special claim of such a press upon black readers.[95] More ambivalent with respect to all-black schools, he supported academies and industrial schools for blacks (even lending his name to one) where no opportunities in integrated institutions existed.[96]

His recurrent expressions of racial partiality confirm that Douglass was indeed, as Moses has observed, a "race man" as well as an individualist and a humanitarian.[97] That does not mean, however, that his thinking on this fundamental issue was incoherent. Douglass firmly denied that he contradicted himself in denouncing racial pride even as he displayed and endorsed a form of it.[98] In 1865, speaking at the inauguration of the Douglass Institute (devoted specially to the education of blacks), he explained, "The latent contempt and prejudice towards our race . . . and also the apparent determination of a portion of the people to hold and treat us in a degraded relation, not only justify for the present such associate effort on our part, but make it eminently necessary."[99] What would be vicious when chosen could be virtuous when necessary. Against a racially targeted attack one was compelled to mount a race-specific defense. Yet the justification by necessity significantly limited Douglass's endorsement of race pride. Race pride was justified, according to this argument, only so far as it was needed for overcoming a regime of racial insult. In the final version of his autobiography, against charges that public office had muted his critical voice, he reaffirmed the constancy of his racial advocacy but in carefully humanitarian terms: "My cause first, midst, last, and always . . . was and is that of the black man—not because he is black, but because he is a man, and a man subjected in the country to peculiar wrongs and hardships."[100] For Douglass, proper race pride signified a negation of racial shame and inferiority, not an affirmation of the right kind of racial superiority.

It is important to make clear that in Douglass's argument, the moderate racial partiality that prevailing circumstances justified was a duty as well as a right. In fact, it was an imperative on patriotic as well as humanitarian grounds. The so-called Negro problem was more than *an* American national problem; it was *the* national problem, upon which the nation's relations and reputation abroad, its domestic security and prosperity, and its moral and civilizational destiny centrally depended.[101] Just as any enlightened American patriot had to desire a lasting, equitable remedy for the debilitating malady of racial injustice, so any such patriot had to partake in (if black) or approve of (if white) those expressions of African American race pride that sustained resistance to it. On the humanitarian ground, the "solitary" character of slavery's oppression and the uniqueness of the disadvantages that the newly freed people faced rendered attention to their condition an imperative of natural justice. At the most general level of this argument, blacks were obligated to make assistance to their fellow blacks a moral priority for the same reason that all were obligated to make assistance to blacks a priority, namely, the general human duty to assist those most in need.

Douglass was not satisfied, however, to leave his argument at that high level of abstraction. His principled humanitarianism notwithstanding, he maintained that the general duty to assist those most in need did not fall equally upon all. Bearers of particular identities held a special, intensified duty to assist their *own.* Douglass assigned to African Americans special, intensified duties to devote themselves to the antislavery and equal rights campaigns, calling more strongly for their participation than for that of whites and condemning black individuals and institutions more strongly than their white counterparts for inaction. It would be "*treason* most scandalous and shocking," he said in his famous Fourth of July oration, for him to forget the cause of the slaves, with whom he peculiarly identified.[102] He made this point even as he praised those who transcended their partial identities in the service of others. In his estimation, John Brown was nobler than he himself was, in that Brown was a white man who sacrificed himself for blacks in the war against slavery. Likewise, Douglass was nobler as a male advocate for woman suffrage than he was in the service of his own people's cause.[103] The nobler actions, in these cases, were those more freely elected—less self-interested and also less morally compulsory. But with this point, the question of self-contradiction arises again, as Douglass's humanitarianism seems beset by a paradox: it assigned to African Americans moral duties of both renouncing and affirming the principle of racial partiality.[104]

To understand Douglass's complicated humanitarianism, one might first acknowledge a measure of realism in his affirmation of racial partiality. It would seem a pallid, bloodless sort of moral reasoning to argue that a person held no stronger obligation to defend against injustice his or her own—family members, neighbors, extended kin, fellow citizens, or the like—than to defend an anonymous, unrelated person simply in view of the latter's personhood. Here again, Douglass's affirmation of the home-feeling implies the moral legitimacy of natural human partiality and the practical limits of moral humanitarianism. Because a human life normally comprises various concentric circles of affection and identification, it seems natural for the intensity of our moral obligations to others to vary accordingly. Yet to infer moral obligation from natural sentiment alone would be an obvious error. It remains necessary to explain how differential degrees of moral obligation can attach to differential degrees of racial identification.

The key to understanding how Douglass's humanitarianism and his racial partiality cohere lies in his conception of the basis of natural human rights. We are natural rights-bearers because we are naturally self-owning persons, properly claiming our actions and character as products of our own moral agency. From this premise, Douglass inferred that all persons bear a primary responsibility to assert and defend their own rights against aggressors. Above all others, "the man deprived of rights is the man to contend for them."[105] As we have seen, his rights doctrine was not an apology for mere egoism; he held that the right and duty of self-defense are to be exercised broadly, in defense of one's extended self or of like others. In its ultimate reach, one's extended self comprehends the entire class of beings who share in one's nature as a rights-bearer, so that all rights-bearers hold some duty to assist other rights-bearers against aggression. But the duty to defend like others is a contingent duty, necessarily weaker than the primary and absolute duty to defend one's own, individual self. The duty to defend like others is contingent upon a satisfactory showing that they *are* like oneself in the decisive respect, that they share in one's nature as a moral person. In Douglass's morally demanding conception of the law of nature, the fact of one's human nature is, at one level, virtually self-evident. But at another level, a demonstrative love of liberty, including a determination to defend it against assault, belongs to the nature of a rightfully free, self-owning being. Because everyone possesses the exclusive power to vindicate, by demonstrating, his or her nature as a rights-bearer, the primary duty to resist assaults on that nature necessarily resides in each individual person.[106] The performance of that primary duty of self-defense constitutes the activating condition for others' secondary, contingent duty to aid in one's defense.

To demonstrate a stronger obligation to defend one's individual self than to defend others against injustice is not yet to demonstrate a similarly stronger obligation to defend members of one's own racial group than to defend any other person. At this point, the fact of natural human pluralism becomes relevant, involving a natural tension between particular and universal identifications. In principle, according to Douglass's argument, we must regard any attack on any innocent person's rights as a potential attack on our own rights. A criminal's failure in one case to distinguish rights-bearers from non-rights-bearers portends a like failure in any case. Yet this general duty allows for variations in degree. Human beings have a moral duty to defend others, *to the extent* that they properly identify with them. Criminals whose aggressions are not simply random pose different degrees of danger to different classes of potential victims and justify different degrees of identification among potential victims. Criminals who specifically target African Americans because of their race obviously pose greater, nearer dangers to members of that racial group than to others and therefore justify intensified senses of identification and mutual obligation among African Americans. In such circumstances, the duty to defend one's racial compatriots against injustice bears a particularly close relation to the primary duty to defend oneself.[107] We can therefore amend Douglass's statement in *Life and Times* to accord more fully with his actions and argument. Douglass did indeed take up the cause of the black man because the latter was generically a man subjected to peculiar wrongs and hardships. But he did so also, with properly intensified interest, because the man subjected was a *black* man—a man with whom the peculiar circumstances of American life compelled him especially to identify. Douglass's long career as a "race man" was a corollary, not a contradiction, of his understanding of the universal law of nature.

Douglass never lost sight of the limited, grudging character of the mandate that his natural-law universalism afforded to racial partiality. So far as he justified such partiality as a dictate of circumstantial necessity, his position was akin to Lincoln's position on slavery: race pride for Douglass, like slavery for Lincoln, was to be regarded as odious in itself, tolerable only so far as circumstances made it necessary to tolerate it and tolerable only in a manner that kept or placed it in the course of its ultimate extinction. In his 1894 speech dedicating the African American industrial school in Manassas, he contended that talk by some black leaders commending "race pride, race love, race effort, race superiority . . . and the like" represented "an effort to cast out Satan by Beelzebub."[108] That did not mean that it was never necessary to use Beelzebub to cast out Satan. But the occasional need to enlist racial partiality in the service of moral humanitarianism made it all the more imperative to issue strong warnings about the dangers inherent in race pride. It was perhaps for this reason that Douglass tended to exaggerate his assimilationism and the degree to which it stood him in opposition to race pride. He conceived of the race pride that he promoted as a homeopathic remedy, for which the proper formula and dosage were all-important: an error in either could infect patients with a crippling disease rather than bolster their defenses against it.

Having established Douglass's affirmation of a circumstantial duty to promote defensive and remedial forms of racial partiality, what remains for us to
consider are his estimations of the specific modes in which such partiality was
necessary. In fact, he interpreted his duty to promote certain forms of it in an
interestingly expansive manner. Here, we come to the limits of the analogy with
Lincoln's position. Lincoln had been willing (to Douglass's great dismay) to
make substantial concessions to slavery, as Douglass would make substantial
concessions to race pride. But for Lincoln, slavery was altogether repugnant, so
that concessions to it were justified only by pure, harsh necessity; there was no
moderately proslavery position capable of contributing anything of positive
value to American republicanism or to humanity. For Douglass, moderate, constructive forms of race pride were both possible and necessary. Race pride could
not be a virtue in itself, but properly conceived, it could be a necessary incident—a stimulus as well as a badge—of genuine virtue. The duty to adopt a
moderate form of race pride in defense against racial supremacy moved him to
take a position that complicated and refined, though it did not contradict, his
principled assimilationism.

Race Pride and Pride in America

As noted earlier, in virtually the same breath as he denounced race pride, Douglass insisted that no one was prouder than he of the virtuous achievements of
persons of color. Moderate and progressive race pride signified achievement-
based race pride. To combat racial supremacy effectively and in keeping with his
fundamental moral principles, Douglass advanced achievement-based arguments for equal citizenship and rights, and he credited virtuous achievements
both to their individual owners and to the capacities of their disrespected racial
group. But the significance of these arguments is two-dimensional. By grounding African Americans' claims to rights and recognition in their virtuous
achievements, Douglass meant, as always, to exert a moral compulsion upon
white Americans to recognize the legitimacy of their claims. He also meant, albeit less obviously, to combat the danger of African American alienation. In the
prevailing circumstances, progressive race pride and rational patriotism were
symbiotically related.

Helpful in clarifying this point are certain resemblances between Douglass's
argument and arguments developed by Aristotle and Locke. The resemblance to
Aristotle pertains to the notion of distributive justice in the allocation of civil

rights and prerogatives: one properly claims a share in a political community's governance by one's active contribution to the community's well-being.[109] Douglass made extensive use of this Aristotelian mode of argument as he insisted on the performance of duties and the cultivation of virtues as necessary conditions for the securing of full rights for African Americans. The resemblance to Locke is equally illuminating. Douglass's Lockean conception of all personal rights as property rights, deriving from the fundamental property in oneself, carries a specific implication concerning the basis of the claim to share in civil government. According to Locke, one possesses a perfected property right in the product of one's labor so far as labor *produces,* not merely gathers, value. Locke accordingly held that whereas government's authority to rule individuals derives from the consent of the governed, the people's claims to representation in government are justified "in proportion to the assistance, which [they afford] to the publick."[110] In Douglass's adaptation of this reasoning, African Americans' rightful claim to U.S. citizenship represented a particularly important element of their general claim to a share in the country's ownership. Both claims were grounded in the fact that they had made it their own, in Lockean terms, by "mixing" their labor with it and thereby improving it in manifold ways.[111]

Still more important is the significance of this argument for the problem of African American alienation. The idea of ownership comprehends not only a rightful claim to property in some objective being but also more subjective senses of identification and belonging. By pressing the claim of blacks that a share in their country was theirs by right, Douglass meant both to convince the white majority and to strengthen blacks' sense of identification with their country. For America to belong effectively to them, in their proper share, African Americans also had to belong to America. They had to love it and thus affirm its claims upon them, as its sons and daughters and also as its parents.

To be a fully developed human being, Douglass maintained, one must have a home, and to have a home, one must have a country. To have a country in turn requires that one harbor a spirit of patriotism, a peculiar identification with one's country. A virtuous patriotism must be creedal and rational in nature, as American patriotism was at its best. But a fully developed patriotism depends for its vitality on sentiment even more than on rational assent. Douglass believed patriotism to be a natural human sentiment, proceeding from gratitude, from affectionate associations, and from pride, reflexively identifying one's own with the good. Such natural sentiments remained alive among African Americans, as illustrated by Douglass's fond recollections of his native Maryland.[112]

But as the stridency of his antiemigrationist rhetoric indicates, Douglass judged black alienation to be a potentially grave danger. Even if it were easier for the sufferers than the perpetrators of great injustice to forgive, as Douglass suggested, it could not be easy for either. African Americans could hardly regard with sentiments of grateful inheritance and purely fond association a country that had enslaved their ancestors and disowned them as a class. In a country in which the majority have always regarded themselves proudly as a nation of enterprising immigrants, the awareness that one's own forebears arrived instead as captive victims of the grandest larceny must be chronically damaging to one's sense of national affiliation. However much they agreed that their highest interests and ideals were best achieved in America, African Americans' simple human pride must naturally pose a powerful obstruction to their patriotism.

In Douglass's Lockean logic, to address this difficulty required a special appeal to pride as a constituent of patriotism. Here is the fuller significance of his achievement-based, property-based conception of blacks' citizenship and civil rights. As rational pride is achievement-based, rational patriotism requires a recognition of the country's virtuous achievements and a claim that they are truly, not merely vicariously, one's own. This sense of ownership is the proper antidote for the revulsion engendered by one's subjection to alien powers. By reminding African Americans of their contributions as a class, Douglass reminded them of more than their capacity for virtue and more than the injustice they suffered as they were denied recognition for it. He reminded them that the greatness that belonged to America also belonged, in substantial part, to them. In this way, he appealed to a peculiar collaboration of sentiments—of negation and affirmation, of hatred and love—to energize their struggles. Amid their pain and outrage at the many injuries that many other Americans inflicted upon them, African Americans could love America as their own. They could love not only the abstract America that the Declaration and the Constitution promised but also the concrete America, visible all around them, that they had labored mightily to build. Even more important, they could love not only the America that they had made but also the America that they would *re*make, including the majority of their fellow Americans, in their own image.

To see this more clearly, it is necessary to turn to Douglass's Aristotelian mode and thereby to consider the various kinds and effects of African American contributions to American national life to which Douglass called his fellow citizens' attention. At the broadest level, those contributions came in the form of the most important instrumental goods, without which no independent, civilized society can exist. Primary among these is national security, both military and economic. Douglass was well aware of the implication for distributive justice as he called African Americans to arms in the Civil War: "He who fights the battles of America may claim America as his country."[113] For black Americans, that claim was not merely hypothetical or prospective, as he made clear in an 1875 Independence Day address. "Colored people have had something to do with almost everything of vital importance in the life and progress of this great country. We have never forsaken the white man in any great emergency, and never expect to forsake him."[114] Scarcely less important as a condition of national well-being is economic security. The contributions of African Americans to this vital good were so obvious as to require mention only in the atmosphere of hostility that surrounded them, as much of America's enormous national wealth—and therewith much of the country's claim to national greatness—derived from their productive labor.[115] By virtue of this material contribution, too, America "belonged to them." They had "cultivated it with their toil and watered it with their tears; their labor had earned it."[116]

These were surely compelling arguments for a share in the American government for African Americans. But they were not necessarily compelling arguments for *equal* shares, relative to those held by whites, and Douglass regarded them as not quite sufficient for the practical purpose that he meant to achieve. Equal shares required equal, actual contributions; agitation grounded only in a principle of theoretical or potential equality would not suffice.[117] Douglass saw indispensable virtue in honest, productive industry at various skill levels; he praised America, with the exception of its southern region, for its distinctively democratic respect for labor.[118] But his respect for more common as well as more distinctive forms of labor did not extend simply to all forms of lawful occupation, nor was it distributed equally even among all respectable forms of employment. He condemned blacks' confinement to "menial" employments as degrading, often to individuals and generally to the race. Such occupations as those of "waiters, porters, and barbers" or of "the boot-black, the cook, or the wood-sawyer" were to be avoided due to their intrinsically stultifying, vice-breeding qualities.[119] They were especially to be avoided in a climate of opinion in which African Americans' relative confinement to such occupations perpetuated the prejudice that as a class, they were naturally capable of no more demanding or elevating work. In an 1854 editorial defending a proposal for an industrial school for colored youth, Douglass argued that although domestic and menial laborers were needed, "no one class or variety of people can furnish them exclusively without degradation." To be properly respected, he reiterated forty years later, the "colored people must furnish their due proportion to each class"—to those who command as well as those who serve.[120]

To break free of their stigmatizing confinement to menial or servile employments, Douglass advised, African Americans first needed to secure for themselves a useful, industrial education.[121] In this aspect, his program resembled the educational program that Booker T. Washington would advocate. The learning of trades was for Douglass what it was for Washington—an imperative of self-defense and a broadly accessible means of cultivating some essential liberal virtues, such as industry and self-reliance. In his broader argument, however, African Americans' industrial labor contribution would be one important element, not the whole or the centerpiece of their claims to equal rights and recognition in America. Addressing Cincinnati's people of color in 1854, he congratulated them on their "variety of employments"; they included numerous "mechanics, traders, and merchants of color, who are doing a good business, getting an honest living."[122] Such variety demonstrated the race's capacities for a range of virtues broader and higher than those needed for menial labors, and it pointed by implication to the need to show the capacity for virtues extending still further. Douglass maintained in his most ambitious, demanding formulations that a fully effective claim to equality required African Americans to demonstrate the entire range of virtues displayed by the ablest representatives of white humanity, not only of white America. He scolded those given to premature assertions of practical equality:

> If we had built great ships, sailed around the world, taught the science of navigation, discovered far-off islands, capes, and continents, enlarged the boundaries of human knowledge, improved the conditions of man's existence, brought valuable contributions of art, science, and literature, revealed great truths, organized great states, administered great governments, defined the laws of the universe, formulated systems of mental and moral philosophy, invented railroads, steam engines, mowing machines, sewing machines, taught the sun to take pictures, the lightning to carry messages, we then might claim, not only potential and theoretical equality, but actual and practical equality.[123]

Obviously, the achievements that so impressed Douglass belonged strictly not to whites as a class but to eminent individuals among them, generally in association with or building upon the achievements of other eminent individuals. Yet he credited them to whites in general, so that the eminent achievements of some could be taken as plausible grounds for whites' claims of practical superiority.[124] To moderate those claims, blacks needed to equal whites in practical achievement at both mass and elite levels. They needed to achieve more than material independence and moderate prosperity among their common folk; they needed also to represent, by demonstrations of individual greatness, the race's endowment with its proper share of the elite virtues. "Woe to us, woe to any people," Douglass declared in his 1875 Independence Day speech, "who has no great men among its own people and of its own people."[125] Conceiving of individuals such as Benjamin Banneker as exemplary, representative figures, he called for African Americans to achieve leadership ranks in the modern army of Baconian scientists.[126] But as the soul holds greater dignity than the body, the highest human achievements serve moral or spiritual rather than merely material ends. The greatest exemplars of the highest virtue were thus the greatest revolutionaries, moral reformers, and statesmen—among white Americans, the likes of Washington, Lincoln, Charles Sumner, and even John Brown.

Against a prediction then prevalent in certain quarters that African Americans would die off in a condition of freedom,[127] it was polemically useful to represent black assimilation to white civilization as a successful survival mechanism. As other black leaders did, Douglass explained the divergent fates of African Americans and American Indians by reference to blacks' superior adaptive qualities. "You see the Indian . . . refusing to imitate, refusing to follow the fashion . . . and the consequence is, that he dies or retreats before the onward march of your civilization," whereas the black man "becomes just what other people become, and herein is the security for his continued life."[128] In Darwinian terms, the power of adaptability provided a decisive advantage in the struggle for natural selection.

In less reductive terms, however, Douglass viewed adaptation as a moral virtue, a condition of civilizational progress rather than of mere survival, as it enabled the overcoming of an excessively proud, self-limiting fealty to one's own tradition. Untroubled by any question of anthropological relativism, he was a civilizationist, firmly convinced that some civilizations were superior to others in animating principles and in achievement. Assimilation represented most importantly not a concession of the weaker to the stronger but an enlightened appreciation of the more civilized by the less civilized. In the 1869 speech just cited, Douglass commented critically on a theory proposed by the woman suffragist and minister Antoinette Brown Blackwell to the effect that the various races could all make distinctive contributions to human civilization, on the condition that they did not imitate one another. He did not reject the racial contributions element of that theory, but he did reject its condemnation of imitation. "I believe in imitation. I think the disposition to imitate what is a little in advance of what we before knew is one of the most civilizing qualities of the human mind."[129] He saw no shame in claiming for African Americans their proper share in America based, in part, on the fact that "[we] have readily adapted ourselves to your civilization, have carefully copied your manners and customs."[130] Affirming, against colonization advocates, that contact with whites promoted civilizational elevation among blacks, Douglass occasionally affirmed even that "the condition of our race has been improved by their situation as slaves."[131]

Douglass's defense of imitation and adaptation, as explained so far, suggests that the need for race pride among African Americans would terminate with the achievement of parity with whites—or, more precisely, with their recognized achievement of the full range of virtues that whites displayed. The objection then arises that Douglass's idea of assimilation suffered from partiality, betraying an Anglophilia or Eurocentrism that verged on racial self-despite.[132] To uphold whites as models for imitation would seem dubious in view of the glaring deficiencies in whites' virtues. Further, it would seem unrealistic if not unjust to expect any group of normally proud human beings to accept as models for emulation another group that had subjected them to grievous injustice. Rather than assimilation through racial self-assertion, as Du Bois claimed, Douglass would seem, on this objection, to commend to African Americans a vision of assimilation through racial self-effacement.[133]

Douglass apparently regarded the objection as substantial. To a significant extent, he agreed that what his critics objected to was indeed objectionable. But what they objected to was an oversimplification of what he believed to be the soundest understanding of assimilation, in form and substance.

Reciprocal Assimilation

In Douglass's argument, what was objectionable was not assimilation itself but the notion of unidirectional or nonreciprocal assimilation—the idea that in the United States, the duty to adapt to the standards of another's civilization fell exclusively upon blacks or people of color.[134] We recall Douglass's argument that in the context of civil society, independence reasonably conceived could only mean interdependence. In like manner, assimilation reasonably conceived meant reciprocal assimilation. The "blended race" that he envisioned in 1866 would bear the markings (physical and cultural) of all its ancestral lineages, not only of one or a few. Douglass did readily affirm blacks' civilizational inferiority to whites, at times in disarmingly blunt terms.[135] But the principle that the less advanced should imitate the more advanced applied in a more complicated manner than might be immediately apparent. First, Douglass conceded whites' civilizational superiority only in some respects. He urged African Americans to imitate whites' virtues judiciously, endeavoring also to correct their vices. Moreover, to imitate a people whose civilizational achievements attested the virtues of discovery and invention among their eminent representatives would mean to cultivate such virtues in one's own group and thus to transcend the virtue of imitation, at least narrowly conceived.

"It is not enough," Douglass said, defending his latest newspaper enterprise in 1871, that blacks "can read books which white men have written, or solve problems by rules which white men have laid down—we must not only be receivers of light, but givers as well." If African Americans "will continue to strut about in the mental 'old clothes' of the white race and refuse to think for themselves they will be a disgraced race. They should not only sing the White Man's Hymns, but be able to make Hymns of their own."[136] In emphasizing the assertive aspect of Douglass's assimilationism, Du Bois was closer to the truth than Douglass's harsher racial-nationalist critics. But Du Bois exaggerated, too, in suggesting an ideal of assimilation as pure self-assertion, "on no other terms." Douglass's idea of assimilation involved a complex interplay of imitation and assertion, to the end of constructing a "composite" America in which blacks and whites and other groups would share in the process of forming and reforming each other as constituents of a progressive civilization.

Douglass's suggestion that African Americans "make Hymns of their own," in accordance with his idea of reciprocal assimilation, received further theoretical elaboration in his important 1869 speech, "Our Composite Nationality." Addressing the then-controversial issue of Chinese immigration, the speech provided his response to nativist despair at the impending decline of a racially and ethnically mixed America. Against such dire prophesies, Douglass endorsed a version of the racial contributions theory mentioned earlier. The composite nation that nativist and racial supremacist critics feared would be a stronger, not a weaker, America. For nations as well as for individuals, "it is not good . . . to be alone." For either to exist in isolation from others is to nurture an illusion of self-sufficiency or to lose sight of essential truths concerning natural human partiality, imperfection, and improvability. "The whole of humanity . . . is ever greater than a part. Men only know themselves by knowing others, and contact is essential to this knowledge." Different varieties of human beings manifest different degrees and kinds of human perfections, and "all are needed to temper, modify, round, and complete the whole man and the whole nation." Based on this reasoning, Douglass affirmed as "broad and beneficent" the "theory that each race of men has some special faculty, some peculiar gift or quality of mind or heart, needed to the perfection and happiness of the whole."[137]

The theory of racial virtues that Douglass sketched in "Our Composite Nationality" represents his adaptation of the romantic racialism present in some antislavery as well as some proslavery arguments in the mid-nineteenth century. To later readers, it also appears surprisingly similar to the arguments propounded by the young Du Bois in his 1897 essay "The Conservation of Races" and in *The Souls of Black Folk*. No less than that of Du Bois, therefore, Douglass's argument would seem exposed to a challenging question: How could the theory of distinctive racial gifts cohere with the ideas of assimilation and human unity? Although Douglass failed to provide a full elaboration of his composite-nationality theory, it is possible to construct a defensible conjecture by a careful consideration of what he said and did not say in this speech and elsewhere.

A crucial difference between Douglass and Du Bois concerns the general significance of the idea of race. An interesting detail of Douglass's speech is his extravagant praise of the German nation and its contributions to America.[138] Nonetheless, he remained solidly anchored in the natural rights philosophy originated in Britain and generally resistant to the ultimately illiberal currents of late-eighteenth-century and nineteenth-century continental, mainly German, philosophy—the racialism and the evolutionary historicism characteristic of Johann Gottfried von Herder, G. W. F. Hegel, and others—that informed Du Bois's early thinking. There was no room in Douglass's thought for Du Bois's estimation of race as "the central thought of all history"; for the latter's characterization of "the race idea, the race spirit, the race ideal . . . as the vastest and most ingenious invention for human progress"; or for his consequent rejection of the "individualistic philosophy of the Declaration of Independence."[139]

In affirming the naturalness of human partiality and endorsing a moderated version of the racial-virtues, racial-gifts argument common among romantic abolitionists and black nationalists, Douglass did not retract or contradict his humanitarian, assimilationist position but instead only displayed its complexity. We have seen how Douglass, optimistic by nature, was moved to interpret the Civil War in apocalyptic terms in its early aftermath. The "Composite Nationality"

speech belongs to the same period and bears the stamp of that millennialist idealism, alongside its realism. As quoted earlier, Douglass declared in that speech that
America's national mission was to provide history's most perfect national illustration of the unity and dignity of humankind.[140] But if America were to succeed in
becoming the world's representative, cosmopolitan nation, it would have to do so
in a spirit of reciprocity, molding descendants of the most extremely divergent
ethnic and racial heritages into Americans, "*each after his kind.*"[141] In Douglass's
vision of assimilation, America would be a blended nationality, with all its constituent elements perpetually melding into a dynamic unity rather than a single
dominant element absorbing all the rest.

The key principle in Douglass's racial contributions theory was his application of the ancient biblical wisdom that "it is not good for man to be alone." To
recognize their own natural partiality was the indispensable, difficult insight
that Douglass urged, finally upon all human beings and foremost upon both
major classes of racial antagonists in America. To recognize one's own partiality
meant, most simply, to acknowledge a tension between what is one's own and
what is wholly right or good. In Douglass's "Composite Nationality" speech, it
meant to address the difficulties between one's own group and other groups in a
spirit of modesty, self-criticism, and openness to the likelihood that different
peoples, with their differing cultural heritages, could contribute to the elevation
of civilization in one's own society. Noting the debts that Anglo-Americans already owed to those of African, Irish, and German descent, Douglass did not
doubt that immigrants from China "might well teach us valuable lessons. . . . I
think a few honest believers in the teachings of Confucius would be well employed in expounding his doctrines among us."[142] As other groups' cultural contributions would raise the level of civilization in one's own society, so one's own
group's contributions would effect improvement in others.

This focus on partiality helps to elucidate Douglass's call for distinctive contributions by African Americans to American national life. To be properly distinctive (hence, fully dignifying), such contributions needed to do more than
augment by degrees goods already sufficiently present in American life. Yet for
Douglass, in contrast to more single-minded black nationalists, they did not
have to be somehow purely African or authentically black. Their worth was to be
judged by universal, not racially exclusive, measures. They needed to be *corrective;* they needed to supply important deficiencies, reflective of the partiality of
the dominant groups, in American life. In Douglass's complex assimilationism,
racial modesty and racial pride collaborated, by turns moderating and leavening

one another. African Americans derived large civilizational benefits from their contact with Anglo- and Euro-Americans; and they would do so all the more industriously, energized by their racial pride in conferring vital civilizational benefits of their own. The idea was not that blacks would submit themselves passively to be changed by whites, nor would they only change themselves; it was also that they would *change whites,* moving them to become less partial specifically by moving them more closely to resemble blacks. By this means, each would come more easily to recognize and sympathize with the other. Blacks in particular would find it easier to regard their white fellow citizens and America at large as their own, having improved them in material and moral respects by the application of their own labor.

A further important difference between Douglass and Du Bois concerned the role of racial institutions in the development and propagation of the race's cultural gifts. Whereas Du Bois declared emphatically that "we need race organizations,"[143] Douglass defended such institutions only as circumstantial necessities. It is significant that his speech's immediate practical purpose was to advocate an openness to racially and ethnically diverse immigration. The remedy for racial partiality was interracial mixing, not racial isolation for the self-conscious cultivation of peculiar racial gifts. Douglass's long-standing objection was that racially exclusive organizations tended to generate "the spirit of proscription," as he editorialized in 1855. But the further implication of his composite-nationality argument was that a policy of racial insularity would represent a moral and cultural deprivation for both black and white Americans.[144] He was neither anti-institutional nor opposed, in the circumstances, to the formation of race-specific institutions in the interests of enlightenment and self-defense. But he seems to have been confident that his people's distinctive cultural gifts would be produced by individuals of genius, naturally and perhaps dutifully moved to represent their racial identity by their own lived experience of it, absent any institutional efforts to shape and sustain that identity. In this way, the production of distinctive racial gifts could best consist with the fluidity of racial identity that, in Douglass's view, was essential to human freedom.[145]

The Gift of Black Americans

Finally, we come to Douglass's ideas concerning the specific contributions whereby African Americans would perfect their claims to full, equal shares of ownership in the American polity. Here again, his suggestions were fragmentary, but a reasonable conjecture begins with his premise that the most important distinctive contributions of African Americans would be corrective of whites' most important partialities. In Douglass's understanding, the "soul" of a nation consisted in its morally formative principles; it is "the soul that makes a nation great or small, noble or ignoble, weak or strong." The formation or reformation of a nation's soul represented the highest contribution to national well-being.[146] The underside of white America's impressive virtues revealed an excessive love of power, an arrogant want of sympathy for less advanced or powerful peoples, and a selfish partiality in its application of the rights doctrine.[147] African Americans were peculiarly suited and called to assist in correcting those vices. Concluding an 1862 address, Douglass suggested that such assistance would stand as their most important contribution to their country's well-being:

> The allotments of Providence seem to make the black man of America the open book out of which the American people are to learn lessons of wisdom, power, and goodness—more sublime and glorious than any yet attained by the nations of the old or the new world. Over the bleeding back of the American bondman we shall learn mercy. In the very extreme difference of color and features of the Negro and the Anglo-Saxon, shall be learned the highest ideas of the sacredness of man and the fullness and perfection of human brotherhood.[148]

The reformation of the American soul that Douglass had in mind involved the completion of Americans' understanding of the first principles of the American Republic and of free government in general. The new nation that the revolutionary fathers had brought forth was still newer, in its prospective significance, than they had clearly understood. The Republic began in a universal declaration of the equal natural rights of human persons, but that declaration had not been clearly understood to imply the possibility or desirability of a republic that was cosmopolitan in its composition and governance. In 1790, the first Congress granted the opportunity for naturalized U.S. citizenship only to "free white person[s]." Only a few years after the Declaration itself was issued, its principal author defended a proposal to colonize all emancipated blacks, removing them "beyond the reach of mixture."[149] When he claimed that Jefferson was the author of the Fourteenth Amendment, Douglass knew he was stating only a partial truth. "We have undertaken . . . a new experiment," he told a gathering of District of Columbia Republicans in 1871. That new experiment concerned "the possibility or impossibility of all nations, kindreds, tongues, and

peoples, living harmoniously . . . under one government."[150] America represented the decisive experiment in such a society, by virtue of the presence of
classes of citizens marked by the most "extreme difference in color and features." In its full development, the idea of a composite nationality was itself
African Americans' most significant gift to America.

Douglass's hoped-for refounding of America as the world's first truly cosmopolitan republic required persistent moral argument from African Americans,
but it required further distinctive contributions from them as well. To develop
feelings of mercy and sympathy toward African Americans, white Americans had
to come to regard them with respect, born of an appreciation of their common
capacity for virtue. In time, Douglass expected, softened by blacks' demonstrated
loyalty and linkage of their own aspirations with America's, white bigotry would
give way to the sheer mass of evidence attesting blacks' competencies and
achievements. But he knew that for the time being, the significance of African
Americans' displays of virtue would hardly be self-evident to most white Americans. Here again, the reformation of the nation's soul could be effected not by
reason alone; rather, it had to be prepared by appeals to sentiment and imagination. To gain recognition as equals, blacks needed to make themselves familiars.
In the realm of politics, this could be achieved via the shared pathos of patriotism. But it also could be and had to be achieved by creative participation in the
nation's cultural life. African Americans needed to tell their story to whites, in
one medium or another, in a powerfully affecting manner.

In his understanding of the importance of pathos, Douglass agreed with the
romantic-racialist argument. Wary of appealing to pathos to the point of ob-
scuring the demand for respect, he presented a more balanced view of racial virtues than those of romantic racialists such as Harriet Beecher Stowe and James
Russell Lowell. He emphasized such heroic virtues as courage, resilience, and
martial prowess, as well as mental virtues such as prudence and inventiveness,
perhaps partly in reaction to the romantics' distorting characterization of blacks
by their softer virtues.[151] More important for our present purposes is his observation of a peculiar, assertive expressiveness—"the natural disposition of the
Negro to make a noise in the world"—manifested especially in an uncommon
musicality in addressing the duties of daily life. The significance of that observation appears more clearly in relation to his more general observation, in his ambitious 1861 speech "Pictures and Progress," that our "natural and primary in-
structors, both as nations and individuals are symbols and songs."[152] By virtue
of their gifts of expression, refined by reflection, African Americans were well

suited to make a distinctive, elevating contribution to their country's moral and political life. Douglass's thoughts on the substance of that contribution appear especially in his discussions of African Americans' actual and prospective achievements in music and literature.

At least in principle, Douglass regarded the development of a representative African American literature as the preferred means of impressing upon America the lessons that blacks had to teach it. Deeply impressed by music's emotional power, he judged the written or spoken word ultimately superior—more elevating, if not more affecting—as a pedagogical instrument and an indicator of high civilization and mental refinement.[153] Throughout his career, Douglass held speech to be central to civilized, political life; there was no higher vocation than "to speak the word" because truth was "the saving power of the world."[154] In contrast to his assessments of their music, however, Douglass viewed African Americans' literary contribution to America as largely prospective. Oddly and unjustly, as late as 1871, he dismissed their actual literary output as a virtual nullity. Presumably excepting his own work, he asserted that they had produced "no literature rising above the dead level of simple narrative."[155] Yet he held high expectations: African American literature was "destined to grow . . . to far greater strength and volume than any enemy has ever feared, or any friend has ever hoped of the colored man."[156] Not only Providence but African Americans themselves would "make the black man of America the open book" from which Americans would learn urgently needed moral lessons. In his calls for a representative African American literature, Douglass summoned new generations of authors to enlarge upon his own achievement—to make characters and books of themselves and their people, inspiring admiration, affection, and sympathetic identification in the hearts and minds of their black and white readers.

Beyond the example he provided in his autobiographies, Douglass supplied no elaborate discussion of what he envisioned in such a literature. He adumbrated its general spirit and major themes in scattered suggestions, and we will turn to the most significant of these shortly. But it was in his analysis of the moral spirit of African American music that he provided his most revealing discussion of the mix of pathos and assertive, respect-commanding virtue that the literature he envisioned would bring to life.

Douglass's most developed analysis of the moral significance of the folk songs produced by African American slaves appears in his autobiographies and comprises several interrelated themes. In accordance with obvious polemical imperatives, the most prominent of those themes is that from which Du Bois drew the title of his own famous discussion.[157] Against claims by slavery's apologists that slaves' habitual singing attested their contentment, Douglass explained that their songs represented the heart's "sorrows, rather than [its] joys." Their "wailing notes" expressed the slaves' "bitterest anguish" and did so with great beauty, power, and subtlety. In the *Narrative*, he interestingly acknowledged that when enslaved, he, too, did not understand the "deep meaning of those rude and apparently incoherent songs." They spoke "to the heart and to the soul of the thoughtful." They awakened sympathy for the slave, as he told a Rochester audience in 1855. As he wrote of slaves' songs, he confessed to the audience of the *Narrative*, "an expression of feeling has already found its way down my cheek." Such was their sentimental, rhetorical power that he "sometimes thought, that the mere hearing of those songs would do more to impress truly spiritual-minded men and women with the soul-crushing and death-dealing character of slavery, than the reading of whole volumes of its physical cruelties."[158]

But the slave songs conveyed much more than their plaintive appeal to the sympathy of sensitive listeners. Along with their affecting display of suffering, they demonstrated various active virtues on the part of their aggrieved composers and performers. Especially in his first two autobiographies, Douglass suggested that slaves' singing was, in significant part, compulsory: they were "generally expected to sing," and to sing happily, as they worked. Their singing aided overseers in monitoring their work, and it also fed slaveowners' pride as evidence, in the latter's perception, of their laborers' contentment. In this regard, one must recall Douglass's report of the penalties slaves could suffer if they disclosed to the wrong ears their real opinions about their condition.[159] Mindful of the pertinent expectations and penalties, slaves did not simply repress their feelings of misery; they expressed them *esoterically*, in "sorrow" songs veiled in seeming expressions of happiness. So the slave's song was no act of submission and no mere expression of passion. It contained at once an act of protest—"a testimony against slavery and a prayer to God for deliverance"[160]—and a demonstration of the justice of that protest. Communicating their misery, slaves also communicated their longing and demand for liberty; further, in communicating those sentiments so as to display their capacities for multileveled speech and for the prudent governance of their own passions, they demonstrated their natural fitness for the liberty they demanded.

Two further aspects of the slave songs' significance are no less crucial to Douglass's subtle, concentrated analysis. The observation with which he concluded his discussion in *Bondage and Freedom,* "Slaves sing more to *make* themselves happy, than to express their happiness," is full of understated significance.[161] In this remark, Douglass did more than repeat his denial of slaves' present happiness; he indicated an additional dimension of the agency that the songs displayed. In their significance as protests, the songs represented appeals to others (divine, if not human) for assistance. So far as they were appeals to others, they were appeals from a position of weakness. But slaves sang not only to act on others, by conveying misery or by feigning happiness; they sang also to act on themselves, to assert real power in one of the few realms subject to their control. And in singing to make their own happiness, they sang to make themselves happy not *in* slavery but *despite* it. Their singing then represented not only a protest and a revelation of slavery's injustice but also a peculiar mode of resistance to its effects. In this respect, their action of resistance represented an oddly musical expression of the seemingly unmusical doctrine of stoicism. Slave singing was an act of self-transcendence, in which slaves summoned the strength to affirm a real, if largely inward, happiness and thereby to ward off the worst of slavery's immiserating effects.

Alternatively, so far as irony involves the concealment of a thing by its opposite, Douglass perceived at the heart of African American slave songs a profound, complex irony. Commenting on the seeming exuberance with which slaves often responded to their misery, he observed, "Such is the constitution of the human mind, that, when pressed to extremes, it often avails itself of the most opposite methods." As a human quality, irony involves a spiritually hardened, even philosophic capacity to see and, where necessary, to *be* beneath the surface of things. It involves the capacities to find happiness or nobility amid apparent misery or baseness (and vice versa) and to dissimulate one's superiority. Attended on its "lower frequencies,"[162] slaves' singing was an ironic assertion of superiority to their oppressive surroundings. In their musical feigning of happiness, slaves to some degree indulged slaveholders in their prejudice regarding slaves' inferiority and fitness for slavery. Yet beneath the slaves' feigning of the happiness proper to the inferior lay a claim to some portion of the real happiness proper to the superior, or to those sufficiently "elastic" or resilient to be indomitable by the worst worldly oppressions.[163] Slaves' songs spoke "to the heart and soul of the thoughtful" by arousing a sympathy more elevated than that accorded any merely sentient suffering creature—one based on a genuine sense of identification, comprising respect and admiration along with compassion.

Douglass's analysis of the genius of the slaves' songs was full of admiration and racial pride as well as hopeful expectation. Without them, he told the Rochester Ladies' Anti-Slavery Society in 1855, "we [would] have no national music." They already constituted a massive contribution to American culture, and he considered a significant part of that contribution to be moral in nature. In context, his mention of music came amid a survey of the antislavery movement's prominent "auxiliaries," in which he included its "allies in the Ethiopian songs."[164] A measure of caution is warranted here, given that Douglass presented his analysis directly against the proslavery claim that slaves' singing attested their contentment, and he supplied no further discussion of music to illustrate his later discussions of the racial contributions theory. Yet, in view of the usefulness that he found in the slaves' songs for the antislavery cause, it is difficult to believe that he could have denied their like potential for assisting in the larger campaign against racial supremacy. Abbreviated as they were, his discussions of slaves' songs suggests a strategic expectation that over time, African Americans' music would succeed in insinuating itself into and vivifying whites' emotional lives. By doing so, it would powerfully enhance the sympathetic identification of members of the two groups with one another.

A final suggestion concerning the spirit of the moral contribution to America that Douglass envisioned appears in his characterization of the black American as "the Jean Valjean of American society," whose story began with his emergence from prison, only to find all legal and societal presumptions against him.[165] In the analogy with the hero of *Les Miserables*, one sees, in part, Douglass's further use of the "self-made men" image in representing the African American story. The virtues of self-reliance and resilience were essential to human dignity and were necessary conditions for winning others' respectful sympathy. For African Americans as for Valjean, the experience and the memory of oppression were inescapable constituents of identity, but they could not be its sum or essence. The experience of oppression needed to function in the African American story as it did in Valjean's, as prologue to a grand triumph. As Douglass summarized in *Life and Times* and elsewhere, the unfolding story of blacks' triumph epitomized the resilient, regenerative, self-making, and self-remaking powers inherent in human nature. Voicing a refrain common among black nationalists, he proudly proclaimed to a Baltimore audience in 1879, "We negroes are an irrepressible people, and there is no keeping us back."[166]

Yet one would hardly characterize the author of *Les Miserables* as a French Horatio Alger. To read Victor Hugo's epic tale mainly as an iteration of the doctrine of self-made men would be to diminish seriously its moral significance, and something similar is true of Douglass's conception of the African American story. From Valjean's story of resilience and overcoming adversity shines forth the grander possibility of human redemption, individual and national. The African American story was not needed to teach other Americans self-reliance, which they knew uncommonly well. Stories of great, arduous ascents humanize us as they epitomize the human story. To be properly inspired by examples of progress from low to high is to be moved also to see the high in the low—to feel a sympathetic identification with those in an unjustly degraded condition. Douglass hoped that all Americans would learn such lessons at the hands of able African American storytellers. He hoped that African Americans would teach their fellow Americans this lesson also by a different sort of example: not only by examples of their own ascents from low to high but also by examples of their own capacity to see the high amid the low in others. A model for both sorts of stories was again Douglass's own, in which he exemplified the latter capacity above all by his steadfast love for his country, keeping faithfully and resolutely in view what was high in America amid so much that was so unconscionably low in American practice.

Finally, to pursue the theme of redemption to its end requires some reflection on Douglass's reference to human *sacredness* as a lesson of the African American story. His understated suggestion was to receive that story as a kind of social gospel or as a moderated expression of racialist theology. Transfiguring and overcoming their own suffering, black Americans in this representation act as redeemers of themselves and others, reminding all of their familiar relation as creatures made in the image of their Creator. In a sense, in his appropriation of the biblical story to illuminate the African American story, Douglass only expressed the common sense of the African American mind. But his racialist theology contained little of the chauvinism evident in some leading black nationalists' representations of blacks as God's singularly chosen people, providentially prepared by their sufferings to assume their rightful supremacy among the nations of the world.[167] In Douglass's inclusive vision, blacks would redeem others and their country as they redeemed themselves, urging America on to its refounding and completion as the world's representative, cosmopolitan nation.

In the wholehearted universalism and Americanism of the civil religion that he meant to propagate, Douglass was more closely akin to Martin Luther King, Jr., than to any of the rival African American leaders of his day. Perhaps a still deeper, more revealing kinship appears between Douglass's African American story and the broader American story fashioned by his greatest counterpart among nineteenth-century Americans. In the poetry of Lincoln's Gettysburg Address and his second inaugural address (a "sacred effort," in Douglass's impromptu review[168]), America appeared as both the Moses and the Jesus of nations: having delivered at its founding a new moral law to humankind, America suffered its national death in the Civil War only to rise again in a new birth of freedom, bearing the promise of eternal life for the republican form of government. In the end, as the great president himself came to realize, Lincoln's story of the whole of America magnified—and required for its completion—Douglass's story of a part. Having suffered the moral death of slavery and gained rebirth in emancipation, thenceforth to bear the promise of redemption for themselves, their fellow citizens, and their nation, Douglass's African Americans were, after all, in the morally crucial respects, the representative Americans.

Conclusion

Righteousness exalteth a nation.
Proverbs 14:34

A S HE NEARED THE CLOSE OF THE 1881 EDITION of his *Life and Times,* Douglass reflected on the sources of his happiness in life. "I have always felt . . . that I had on my side all the invisible forces of the moral government of the universe. Happily for me, I have had the wit to distinguish between what is merely artificial and transient and what is fundamental and permanent, and resting on the latter, I could cheerfully encounter the former."[1] Having considered at length the fundamentals of Douglass's thought, we will conclude with a consideration of its permanence or of its enduring vitality in the continuing striving for justice and progress in U.S. race relations.

In his generally admiring biography of Douglass, published a few years after the turning of a new century, Booker T. Washington (through his ghostwriter) gently expressed a doubt as to his subject's continuing relevance. A new day demanded a new principle of racial leadership; Douglass's predominant virtues, Washington wrote, were those proper to the work of "destruction and liberation, rather than construction and reconciliation." Without naming Douglass, Washington had made the point more bluntly in his landmark "Atlanta Exposition Address," delivered a few months after Douglass's death in 1895: "The wisest among my race understand that the agitation of questions of social equality is the extremest folly." Douglass was a moral lion during the abolitionist period, but he was to be admired mainly as a revolutionary, not as a founder. His political thought was less well suited to the postemancipation period, due to its persisting emphasis on righteous opposition and agitation for civil and political rights.[2]

In the immediate aftermath of *Brown v. Board of Education,* five decades after Washington had written, Philip S. Foner concluded his own Douglass biography with a sharp retort. The great agitator's time had not passed. His valedictory exhortation lived on in the courageous protests of a new generation of African Americans and their white sympathizers against segregation and for the full protection of equal rights. "Frederick Douglass still points the way," Foner concluded. "He takes his deserved place with Jefferson and Lincoln in the democratic tradition of our country."[3]

As a consensus judgment, Foner's opinion proved short-lived. As the civil rights era drew to a close, critics again suggested that Douglass was passé, based on a contention that was the inverted image of Washington's: Douglass's thought lacked vitality in the postabolition era because it was insufficiently oppositional, not excessively so. Pointing the way was Malcolm X, who declared, despite his respect for Douglass, that he "would rather have been taught about Toussaint L'Ouverture." The main failings of Douglass's thinking, continued radical historian Vincent Harding, derived from his tendency "dangerously to dissociate the institution of slavery from its roots in the racist, exploitative American society." In general, Waldo E. Martin, Jr., summarized, Douglass's radical critics in the first generation of the post–civil rights era "chided him for his interracialism, integrationism, and Americanism."[4] As noted in this book's introduction, this view persists in varying degrees among Douglass's critics in our own day. To Charles W. Mills, author of perhaps the sharpest of those critiques, "Douglass was obviously mistaken about his own time," and his principles fare no better today. In a period in which formal equality under the law serves mainly, critics believe, to conceal or to confer legitimacy upon structurally embedded racial inequalities and intransigent de facto segregation, Douglass's and the mainstream protest tradition's prescriptions are too liberal, too bourgeois, too middle class, too integrationist, and too generically American to be of much further use.[5]

The thrust of the present study, however, is that Foner was more right than he knew: in the principled natural rights liberalism of its approach to race relations in America, Douglass's argument lives on. As it withstood Washington's more prudential criticism a century ago, it stands firm against radical objections today.

Critics of various stripes in the nineteenth century were mistaken, Douglass maintained, in losing faith in liberal natural rights principles or in America's ultimate commitment to them. In the face of powerful objections, he argued that the doctrine of inalienable rights summarized in the Declaration of Independence was true as moral prescription and sanctioned as moral law. These convictions stand foremost among the elements that he regarded as fundamental and permanent in his thought. As a moral truth, the doctrine of human equality in natural, inalienable rights provides the strongest possible foundation for free government and for opposition to slavery and racial supremacy. Contrary to radicals' objections, Douglass's argument shows how that doctrine rightly understood supplies no apology for antisocial individualism or oligarchic oppression. It both permitted and required his protests against privately organized obstructions of blacks' efforts to acquire property and against other forms of ostensibly private racial discrimination. Further, it entails a broad societal obligation to remedy as well as to prevent injustice, and it is therefore perfectly compatible with public measures to expand opportunities and to facilitate the fruitful exercise of such formal rights as the rights to vote, to seek gainful employment, and to accumulate property. Further still, Douglass's natural rights liberalism requires no demeaning, one-sided surrender of racial heritage or identity. It implies a long-term need for reciprocal racial assimilation, on terms consistent with African Americans' dignity, and it is hospitable to moderate affirmations of racial identity.

Arguing that the natural rights doctrine was sanctioned as law, Douglass argued persuasively that over time, persistent agitation would succeed in securing the protection of fundamental civil and political rights. To secure the conditions of substantive equality on terms consistent with African Americans' dignity, no more radical program than the full enforcement of those rights was needed—no emigration, no curtailment of the right of private property, no allocation of political sovereignty or civil entitlement by race. The prudent exercise of rights, especially voting rights, in conjunction with efforts to cultivate the virtues that support self-elevation, would effectively expand the economic opportunities available to African Americans and the powers whereby they could take advantage of them. Moreover, the strong public recognition and enforcement of those rights, along with the steadfast displays of virtue and the outsized contributions to national culture that Douglass expected African Americans to make, would decisively diminish antiblack prejudice and advance the emergence of an America blacks could finally claim as their genuine home.

Douglass did not argue that justice would come immediately, inevitably, or by the power of purely moral motives. It is a fact of human nature, in his moral-realist understanding, that human beings are creatures of selfish or partial interest. But the notion that the advancement of justice depends on its convergence with powerful interests, though true enough, constitutes no decisive objection to Douglass's way of thinking. It warrants no inference that justice is merely illusory or evanescent. Human beings are not always receptive to moral reformation, but it is meaningful that we are intermittently so. Though our interests often overpower the imperatives of justice, we do have natural interests in doing

justice, according to Douglass's understanding of natural law. The more fundamental point, however, is that we are not only creatures of interest but also
speaking, reasoning moral animals. The convergence of interests in the promotion of justice serves as the natural starting point for the development of more
solid and permanent moral sympathies. This effect is especially powerful at
times of crisis. Great events, especially great wars, are powerful teachers,[6] arousing passions and interests so as to prepare the deeper impression of moral argument. All told, reformers may be understandably frustrated but should not despair at a pattern in which reform proceeds by advancing three steps, retreating
two steps, and preparing for the next opportunity.

Douglass's natural-law argument implied that the natural sanctions against
injustice would be naturally intensified in a country such as the United States,
explicitly dedicated to the true principles of justice. The ferocity with which the
master class defended slavery and the extended difficulty of achieving racial justice in America do not discredit this part of Douglass's argument. The nation's
two centuries of slavery could only have had staggeringly corrupting and divisive effects, bound to endure long beyond formal emancipation. Nonetheless,
Douglass's natural-law principles yield an overarching view of U.S. history that
is powerfully at odds with that of today's radical critics. America's struggles toward moral reform must be considered in their larger context, as follows. First,
in the wake of its Revolution, America along with Great Britain produced an abolition movement that was unprecedented in human history, within a single
century bringing an end throughout the Western world to the ancient practice
of slavery. Second, the victorious forces of justice in the Civil War laid the constitutional foundation, in the war's aftermath, for their permanent victory by
adopting the Reconstruction Amendments, which provided indispensable tools
for the later dismantling of the regime of racial supremacy that the war failed to
eradicate. Third, having vanquished an even more virulent form of racism in
World War II, America responded to renewed demands for justice in the civil
rights era with dramatic changes in its laws and societal practices with respect to
race relations.

From Douglass's perspective, what is most significant in this history is not
that America had to be pressured to change. Most significant are the facts that
unrelenting moral pressure came; that it came substantially by the efforts of
African Americans in their own cause; that it drew its main moral inspiration
from the nation's founding principles; and that the nation subjected to that
pressure proved, in progressively deepening ways, receptive to change. These

facts show that slavery or white supremacy was not, contrary to the claims of prominent southerners in Douglass's day and to radical critics in ours, the "corner-stone" or the integral, stabilizing condition of the nominally liberal Republic. Whatever solidarity they may have engendered among different classes of whites, America's racial injustices were also seriously destabilizing.

The lesson of history, Douglass argued in response to the *Dred Scott* ruling, is that all measures devised to calm the antislavery agitation "only served to increase, embolden, and intensify that agitation." The same lesson applied to the successor regime of racial supremacy. After the abandonment of Reconstruction, Douglass naturally grew increasingly frustrated at the near-term failure of his demands for the nation to complete the revolution begun (or reborn) in the Civil War. Yet he persisted in his strategy of agitating for justice, convinced that the near-term failings of this program by no means discredited its longer-term promise. The postwar experience had shown that the nation's white majority longed for peace and was prepared to betray its promises to its black minority to achieve it. But the nation's history as a whole had shown, in keeping with Douglass's understanding of the law of nature, that no peace-through-betrayal policy could long succeed. It was an "eternal order of human relation," Douglass observed in 1883, that "purity must go before tranquillity." The agitation for justice "may be arrested and imprisoned for a while, but no power can permanently restrain it."[7] Decades of agitation had been required to bring an end to formal slavery, and decades more might be required to bring an end to the more deeply entrenched regime of white supremacy. But so long as that regime existed, agitation would bedevil it, and the nation would be moved in the end to see that justice and its permanent interest were inseparable. There can be little doubt, therefore, that Douglass would have seen his self-enforcing natural law at work also in the race-related turbulence of the 1950s and 1960s. Viewed in the light of his natural-law principles, that turbulence appears as a natural sanction against racial injustice, whereas the enactment of effective protections of civil and political rights represents a natural reward for the virtue of persistent righteous opposition.

The post–civil rights era is no less amenable to interpretation along lines suggested by Douglass's argument. It is idle to speculate on the precise positions he would take with respect to the income and wealth disparities, the crime statistics, the criminal justice policies, the incidence of single parenthood, the racial preference policies, and the other major topics of race-related controversy in today's America. But it is far from idle—it is, instead, urgently necessary—for us to reflect on the present vitality of Douglass's core conviction that faith in America's promise of justice for all rests on solid rational grounds. Laboring tirelessly on amid the grievous disappointments of the later decades of the slavery era and then of the post-Reconstruction era, Douglass took a larger historical and philosophical view and thereby found solid grounds for hope. Sustaining his hopes, most generally, were the youth of the new nation; its public dedication at its founding, unprecedented in human history, to the natural, universal principles of justice; the progressive spirit of the modern age; and the essential humanity of black and white Americans. Taking a similarly enlarged view of our own circumstances, we might not find in the reforms initiated in the second half of the twentieth century the advent of the millennium in American race relations. But there is solid reason to believe that in the civil rights era and its aftermath, something new, real, and lasting has occurred.

It is readily understandable that many African Americans and well-meaning whites regard the progress of the past few decades with skepticism. Yet to dismiss that progress as a mere illusion, as though it signified no more than the latest rehearsal of a sordid American story of promise and betrayal, is to miss something profoundly important. Douglass was confident that racial justice would grow firm roots in America, first and foremost when African Americans gained the political and economic power to defend their rights and advance their interests. His confidence in the rationality of hopefulness would seem to be powerfully vindicated, therefore, by the evidence of recent decades, including dramatic increases in African Americans' political participation and representation; advances in their educational attainment; elevation of solid majorities of African Americans into the middle and upper socioeconomic classes; and, accompanying all these developments, the remarkable liberalizing of public opinion among whites with respect to racial equality and racial integration. Impressive testimony to the enduring vitality of Douglass's rational hopefulness appears in the observation of eminent sociologist Orlando Patterson, no apologist of the racial status quo, writing in the late 1990s: "The achievements of the American people over the past half century in reducing racial prejudice and discrimination and in improving the socioeconomic and political condition of Afro-Americans are nothing short of astonishing. . . . It can be said, unconditionally, that the changes that have taken place in the United States over the past fifty years are unparalleled in the history of minority-majority relations."[8]

Finally, it is crucial to emphasize that Douglass's rational hopefulness owes its enduring vitality to more than the evident power of persistent moral agitation. In his understanding of the naturally sanctioned moral law, meaningful progress toward racial equality would come as the fruit of constructive virtues no less than of the virtues related to righteous opposition. Hence, he insisted on calling simultaneously for African Americans to "Agitate!" and to "Work!" Critics have a point in noting the ineffectiveness, in the near term, of Douglass's postwar and especially post-Reconstruction calls for the virtues of industry and thrift among people systematically confined to peonage.[9] But there can be no doubt that over the long term, genuine liberation and elevation were inconceivable without those virtues, and it was both a prudential and a moral imperative for him to emphasize all along the need to cultivate them, in conjunction with his emphasis on agitation. Though he maintained that the morality of free society did not properly apply to those enslaved, he refused to extend this principle to the demeaning and self-defeating conclusion that no virtue can be expected of the victims of injustice, prior to their full liberation.

Among the data supporting the optimists' perspective on post–civil rights America, perhaps the most impressive concern the real, elevating power of the virtues that Douglass exhorted audiences to cultivate. As Patterson has documented, between those blacks and whites who display in equal measures what Douglass called the "staying qualities" related to education, steady employment, and family stability, the income disparity narrows to the point of insignificance.[10] Present-day racial pessimists, however, focus primarily on the deteriorating condition of many African Americans remaining in poverty, now increasingly bifurcated from the black middle and upper classes. But the fact of these intensifying miseries in no way sustains the contention that Douglass's or the mainstream tradition's racial liberalism is suitable, at best, only for an African American elite. Douglass's argument is of limited use, of course, for an inquiry into the causes and the proper remedies of these present ills. As to their remedy, his strong convictions concerning the efficacy of virtue and the transforming power of education are unquestionably germane, and those convictions are not reducible to the "pull-up-your-socks sermon" that William S. McFeely has decried. But the strongest suggestion Douglass's core argument yields is a stern rejection of the culture of nihilistic alienation that has lately enveloped the urban poor.

Here, it is necessary to revisit Booker T. Washington's criticism. Foner's protest notwithstanding, the differences between Douglass and Washington, though real and important, are narrower than is apparent in that criticism. What Washington objected to in Douglass's posture of opposition was actually only *public* agitation, which he believed unlikely to achieve its object. As is now well known, Washington privately supported (he financed and lobbied for) various efforts to secure the same legal protection of formal rights that Douglass demanded publicly.[11] And despite his general conviction of the dignifying power of righteous opposition, Douglass held some of the same reservations Washington would hold concerning the dangers of the spirit of opposition taken to an extreme. His feeling of sadness in 1865 at the seeming completion of his abolitionist labors attests to the thrill of righteous opposition and the power of the desire, in those habituated to it, to persist in it even after its external cause has been overcome. Although Douglass never saw a day in the United States when conditions no longer warranted opposition, his late observations concerning the terrible destructiveness of the revolutionary spirit in Haiti, perpetuated and turned inward, vividly illustrate his concern. The same concern inspired his calming words at the outset of his *Civil Rights Cases* speech in 1883. When he exclaimed later in that speech, "Fellow citizens! We want no black Ireland in America," he was first warning white authorities against fostering such alienation. But he was also imploring black Americans not to succumb to it.

Understood in the fullness of his argument, what Frederick Douglass stands for is the spirit of righteous opposition, *wisely governed* to be consistent with the requirements of more constructive virtues. As Washington feared the demoralizing effects of chronically ineffective opposition, so Douglass feared the demoralizing effects of opposition carried beyond its proper objects. A consciousness of deep grievance may be justified by external conditions and yet be harmful to the character and cause of the aggrieved. In his penetrating analysis of slavery and particularly in the story of his encounter with Edward Covey, Douglass taught that the greatest misery for a human being is radical hopelessness. Throughout his career, he stood against the purveyors of hopelessness in all their various incarnations, from unabashed white supremacists to Garrisonian disunionists, Non-Resistant anarchists, socialists, black emigrationists—all whose ideas tended ultimately to propagate a spirit of alienation and disempowerment among African Americans.

Today, a far deeper alienation demoralizes a sizable minority of the urban poor, now resembling the black Ireland Douglass invoked. And this unprecedentedly self-destructive alienation has found its own elite purveyors among academics, politicians, media, and corporate interests who variously excuse it as the inevitable effect of injustice and powerlessness, glorify it as heroic protest, or market it as exotic racial authenticity. Here, too, the argument of Douglass lives

on, in the indignant response to this culture of alienation now rising across partisan divisions to remind the post–civil rights generation, top and bottom, of
African Americans' resilience in generations past and of the tested wisdom of
their great tradition's understanding of the principles of justice and the conditions of progress.[12]

I end with a Lincolnesque reflection that is also in the spirit of Douglass. For
Lincoln, the beginning of political wisdom lay in a recurrence to the "old and
tried" wisdom of the fathers.[13] In our day, a salutary recurrence to the wisdom
of our forebears comprehends those of the civil rights tradition along with those
of the republic that it reformed. And in his own understanding, recurrence to
the wisdom of Douglass would mean recurrence to a much older wisdom yet. "I
have one great political idea," he said in 1852 and could have said at any moment
in his long career. "RIGHTEOUSNESS EXALTETH A NATION."[14] For nations and for
individuals, justice and virtue lift us both morally and materially. At the heart of
the wisdom that Frederick Douglass commended to us are sentiments at once
universally human, profoundly American, and authentically black. Alienation is
needless and pointless; freedom is arduous but ennobling; human nature is progressive; hopefulness is rational.

Notes

Abbreviations

BF   *My Bondage and My Freedom*. Edited by William L. Andrews. Urbana: University of Illinois Press, 1987 (originally published 1855).

DM   *Douglass's Monthly*, 1859–1863.

FDP   *Frederick Douglass's Paper*, 1851–1859.

LT   *Life and Times of Frederick Douglass*. Introduction by Rayford W. Logan. New York: Macmillan, 1962 (originally published 1892).

LW   *The Life and Writings of Frederick Douglass*. 5 vols. Edited by Philip S. Foner. New York: International Publishers, 1950–1975.

N   *Narrative of the Life of Frederick Douglass*. Edited by David W. Blight. Boston: St. Martin's Press, 1993 (originally published 1845).

NS   *North Star*, 1847–1851.

TFDP   *The Frederick Douglass Papers*. Series 1, 5 vols. Edited by John W. Blassingame and John R. McKivigan. New Haven, CT: Yale University Press, 1979–1992.

Preface and Acknowledgments

1. David W. Blight, *Frederick Douglass's Civil War: Keeping Faith in Jubilee* (Baton Rouge: Louisiana State University Press, 1989), 58; Wilson J. Moses, *Creative Conflict in African-American Thought* (Cambridge: Cambridge University Press, 2004), 60.

Introduction

1. Martin Luther King, Jr., *Why We Can't Wait* (1963; repr., New York: Signet Books, 1964), 15, also 22–25, 114; King, *Where Do We Go from Here: Chaos or Community?* (Boston: Beacon Press, 1967), 190. King quoted Isaiah 40:4.

2. On the "Great Tradition," see Vincent Harding, *There Is a River: The Black Struggle for Freedom in America* (New York: Harcourt Brace, 1981). For samples of the colonial era petitions, see Herbert Aptheker, *A Documentary History of the Negro People in the United States* (1951; repr., New York: Citadel Press, 1979), 1:1–9.

3. Martin Luther King, Jr., "I Have A Dream," 8/28/1963, in James M. Washington, ed., *A Testament of Hope: The Essential Writings and Speeches of Martin Luther King, Jr.* (New York: HarperCollins, 1986), 217–19.

4. Martin Luther King, Jr., "A Christmas Sermon on Peace," 12/24/1967, in his *The Trumpet of Conscience* (New York: Harper & Row, 1967), 75.

5. David Howard-Pitney, *The Afro-American Jeremiad: Appeals for Justice in America* (Philadelphia: Temple University Press, 1990).

6. Harding, *There Is a River*, xii.

206

Notes to Pages 2–5

7. For the evidence of racial progress since the 1950s, see Abigail and Stephan Thernstrom, *America in Black and White* (New York: Simon & Schuster, 1997); Orlando Patterson, *The Ordeal of Integration* (New York: Basic Civitas Books, 1997). A vigorous statement of the case for racial optimism is John McWhorter, *Winning the Race* (New York: Gotham Books, 2005).

8. King, "Christmas Sermon on Peace," 75–76; King, "A Time to Break Silence," 4/4/1967, in James M. Washington, *A Testament of Hope: The Essential Writings and Speeches of Martin Luther King, Jr.* (New York: HarperCollins, 1986), 240. See also King, *Where Do We Go from Here?* 132–33, 186–90.

9. Michael Dawson, *Black Visions: The Roots of Contemporary African-American Political Ideologies* (Chicago: University of Chicago Press, 2001), 304.

10. The classic of post–civil rights era racial pessimism is Andrew Hacker, *Two Nations: Black and White—Separate, Hostile, Unequal* (New York: Charles Scribner's Sons, 1992). An update on Hacker is Michael K. Brown, Martin Carnoy, Elliott Currie, Troy Duster, David B. Oppenheimer, Marjorie M. Schultz, and David Wellman, *Whitewashing Race: The Myth of a Color-Blind Society* (Berkeley: University of California Press, 2003). See also Douglass S. Massey and Nancy A. Denton, *American Apartheid: Segregation and the Making of the Underclass* (Cambridge, MA: Harvard University Press, 1993); Melvin L. Oliver and Thomas M. Shapiro, *Black Wealth/White Wealth: A New Perspective on Racial Inequality* (New York: Routledge, 1997).

11. Cornel West, *Race Matters* (Boston: Beacon Press, 1993), 14–15.

12. Manning Marable, *Beyond Black and White: Transforming American Politics* (New York: Verso Press, 1995), 19; Marable, *Living Black History: How Reimagining the African-American Past Can Remake America's Racial Future* (New York: Basic Civitas Books, 2006), 215.

13. Abraham Lincoln, "The Dred Scott Decision: Speech at Springfield, Illinois, June 26, 1857," in Roy P. Basler, ed., *Abraham Lincoln: His Speeches and Writings* (1946; repr., Cambridge, MA: Da Capo Press, 2001), 361.

14. Martin Luther King, Jr., "Letter from a Birmingham Jail," in his *Why We Can't Wait* (1963; repr., New York: Signet Books, 1964), 94.

15. Derrick Bell, "*Brown v. Board of Education* and the Interest-Convergence Dilemma," *Harvard Law Review* 93, no. 3 (January 1980): 518–33. See also Philip A. Klinkner and Rogers M. Smith, *The Unsteady March: The Rise and Decline of Racial Equality in America* (Chicago: University of Chicago Press, 1999).

16. Charles W. Mills, *The Racial Contract* (Ithaca, NY: Cornell University Press, 1997), especially 16, 28, and 56. Cf. Lucius T. Outlaw, *On Race and Philosophy* (New York: Routledge, 1996), 162–65. For Mills's agreement with the *Dred Scott* ruling, see Mills, "Whose Fourth of July? Frederick Douglass and 'Original Intent,'" in Bill E. Lawson and Frank M. Kirkland, eds., *Frederick Douglass: A Critical Reader* (Malden, MA: Blackwell Publishers, 1999), 118–21.

17. John Hope Franklin, "The Moral Legacy of the Founding Fathers," *University of Chicago Magazine* 67 (Summer 1975): 13. Other prominent African American historians agree. See, e.g., August Meier and Elliot M. Rudwick, *From Plantation to Ghetto* (New York: Hill and Wang, 1966), 46–47; Harding, *There Is a River*, 46–48; Nathan I. Huggins, *Black Odyssey* (New York: Pantheon Books, 1977), 91–95.

18. Thurgood Marshall, "Reflections on the Bicentennial of the U.S. Constitution," reprinted in *Harvard Law Review* 101, no. 1 (November 1987): 3. Legal historians supporting this view include Paul Finkelman, *Slavery and the Founders: Race and Liberty in the Age of Jefferson* (New York: M. E. Sharpe, 2001); William M. Wiecek, *The Sources of Antislavery Constitutionalism in America, 1760–1848* (Ithaca, NY: Cornell University Press, 1977).

19. W. E. B. Du Bois, "The Conservation of Races" (1897), in David Levering Lewis, ed., *W. E. B. Du Bois: A Reader* (New York: Henry Holt, 1995), 21.

20. Harding, *There Is a River,* 186; Lani Guinier and Gerald Torres, *The Miner's Canary* (Cambridge, MA: Harvard University Press, 2002), especially 32–66.

21. Du Bois, "Conservation of Races," 25.

22. See Jennifer Hochschild, *The New American Dilemma* (New Haven, CT: Yale University Press, 1984); Derrick Bell, *Faces at the Bottom of the Well: The Permanence of Racism* (New York: Basic Books, 1992), 9–12, 151–55; Mills, *Racial Contract;* Joel Olson, *The Abolition of White Democracy* (Minneapolis: University of Minnesota Press, 2004). On slavery or white supremacy as the "corner-stone," see James Henry Hammond, "Letter to an English Abolitionist" (1845), in Drew Gilpin Faust, ed., *The Ideology of Slavery* (Baton Rouge: Louisiana State University Press, 1981), 176–77; Alexander H. Stephens, "Cornerstone Speech," 3/21/1861, accessed 2/17/2007 at http://teachingamericanhistory.org/library/index.asp?documentprint=76. Cf. Thomas R. Dew, "Abolition of Negro Slavery" (1832), in Drew Gilpin Faust, ed., *The Ideology of Slavery* (Baton Rouge: Louisiana State University Press, 1981), 66.

23. Morrison quoted in the *New York Times,* January 15, 1986, and in Hacker, *Two Nations,* 34.

24. "Speech before the American Anti-Slavery Society," 5/11/1847, *LW* 1.236. (Note: To avoid tedious repetition, I refrain from including Douglass's name when citing his speeches; in citations of all other speeches, however, names are provided.)

25. The reader interested in a fuller account of Douglass's life may consult, in addition to his three autobiographies, several fine scholarly biographies: Benjamin Quarles, *Frederick Douglass* (Washington, DC: Associated Publishers, 1948); Philip S. Foner, *Frederick Douglass* (New York: International Publishers, 1950–1955); Nathan I. Huggins, *Slave and Citizen: The Life of Frederick Douglass* (Boston: Little, Brown, 1980); Dickson Preston, *Young Frederick Douglass* (Baltimore, MD: Johns Hopkins University Press, 1980); William S. McFeely, *Frederick Douglass* (New York: W. W. Norton, 1991).

26. *BF* 43.

27. Kelly Miller, "Douglass and Washington" (1903), in Benjamin Quarles, ed., *Frederick Douglass* (Englewood Cliffs, NJ: Prentice-Hall, 1968), 135.

28. James McCune Smith, "Introduction," in Frederick Douglass, *My Bondage and My Freedom,* edited by William L. Andrews (Urbana: University of Illinois Press, 1987), 17.

29. See Helen Pitts Douglass, ed., *In Memoriam: Frederick Douglass* (1897; repr., Freeport, NY: Books for Libraries Press, 1971), 71 (Lincoln), 216–19 (Crummell), 244 (Harlan), 263 (Hart). Hart's judgment in particular may seem hyperbolic, but it should be considered in light of the pervasiveness of slavery in world history and the historical uniqueness of the modern Western abolitionist movement. See especially Thomas Sowell, *Race and Culture: A World View* (New York: Basic Books, 1994), 186–223.

30. E.g., James A. Colaiaco, *Frederick Douglass and the Fourth of July* (New York: Palgrave Macmillan, 2006). Cf. Leslie Friedman Goldstein, "The Political Thought of Frederick Douglass" (PhD diss., Cornell University, 1975), 1; Waldo E. Martin, Jr., *The Mind of Frederick Douglass* (Chapel Hill: University of North Carolina Press, 1984), ix; David W. Blight, *Frederick Douglass's Civil War: Keeping Faith in Jubilee* (Baton Rouge: Louisiana State University Press, 1989), xi.

31. In addition to the biographies mentioned in Note 25, outstanding studies by historians include several works of intellectual history: Martin, *Mind of Frederick Douglass;* Blight, *Frederick Douglass's Civil War;* Wilson Jeremiah Moses, *Creative Conflict in African American Thought* (Cambridge: Cambridge University Press, 2004). Outstanding studies of

Douglass by literature scholars include Robert B. Stepto, *From behind the Veil: A Study of African-American Narrative* (Urbana: University of Illinois Press, 1979); William L. Andrews, *To Tell a Free Story: The First Century of African-American Autobiography* (Urbana: University of Illinois Press, 1986); Eric J. Sundquist, *To Wake the Nations: Race in the Making of American Literature* (Cambridge, MA: Belknap Press, 1993); Robert S. Levine, *Martin Delany, Frederick Douglass, and the Politics of Representative Identity* (Chapel Hill: University of North Carolina Press, 1997); John Stauffer, *The Black Hearts of Men* (Cambridge, MA: Harvard University Press, 2002). In the fields of moral and political philosophy, especially helpful are the unpublished dissertation of Goldstein, "Political Thought of Frederick Douglass," and numerous articles and essays by Bernard R. Boxill.

32. Moses, *Creative Conflict*, 21–23, 46–50. See also Benjamin Quarles, *Black Abolitionists* (New York: Oxford University Press, 1969); Levine, *Martin Delany*. The first scholarly attack on the lionizing of Douglass was Peter F. Walker, *Moral Choices: Memory, Desire, and Imagination in Nineteenth-Century American Abolition* (Baton Rouge: Louisiana State University Press, 1978), 209–61.

33. Blight, *Frederick Douglass's Civil War*, 58. Cf. Moses, *Creative Conflict*, 2–6, 26–27, 45, 58.

34. Moses, *Creative Conflict*, 3–4, 41–45, 108–9; Martin, *Mind of Frederick Douglass*, 132, 167, also 170, 221, 283–84; Harding, *There Is a River*, 242–45.

35. Walker, *Moral Choices*, 247; Martin, *Mind of Frederick Douglass*, 134, also 115, 199, 208–17; Howard-Pitney, *Afro-American Jeremiad*, 30–31; Moses, *Creative Conflict*, 49. Douglass is also often charged with masculinist bias; see especially Deborah McDowell, "In the First Place: Making Frederick Douglass and the Afro-American Narrative Tradition," in William L. Andrews, ed., *Critical Essays on Frederick Douglass* (Boston: G. K. Hall, 1991), 192–214.

36. Martin, *Mind of Frederick Douglass*, 125–32, also 67, 73–83, 87, 92, 115, 141–44, 167, 192, 199, 213–17, 221–24, 242–43, 261–62. See also Foner, *Frederick Douglass* (*LW* 4.96–105); Walker, *Moral Choices*, 216–19, 276–77; McFeely, *Frederick Douglass*, 293–303. Charging Douglass with personal opportunism are Walker, *Moral Choices*, 273, and Moses, *Creative Conflict*, 48–49.

37. Mills, "Whose Fourth of July?" 134–35.

38. See especially Blight's excellent study, *Frederick Douglass's Civil War*; Howard-Pitney, *Afro-American Jeremiad*, 17–52.

39. "The Decision of the Hour," 6/16/1861, *LW* 3.118 (also *TFDP* 3.436).

40. *BF* 243; also *LT* 260–61; *LW* 2.153, 155–56; *LW* 5.463.

41. W. E. B. Du Bois, *The Souls of Black Folk*, edited by Candace Ward (New York: Dover Publications, 1994), 67.

42. Herbert J. Storing commented insightfully on Du Bois's statement, noting that the thoughtful African American "shares the perspective of the serious revolutionary. He appeals, at least in thought, from the imperfect world of convention and tradition . . . to the world of nature and truth"; see his "Introduction," in Storing, ed., *What Country Have I? Political Writings by Black Americans* (New York: St. Martin's Press, 1970), 2. Also see Goldstein, "Political Thought of Frederick Douglass," 2; David W. Blight, *Beyond the Battlefield: Race, Memory, and the American Civil War* (Amherst: University of Massachusetts Press, 2002), 15–16.

43. *LT* 240. Douglass likely encountered the idea of a self-executing law of nature in the work of another of his great contemporaries, the Transcendentalist philosopher Ralph Waldo Emerson. See especially Emerson's "Compensation," in *The Works of Ralph Waldo Emerson in One Volume* (New York: Black's Readers' Service, n.d.), 114–27; also his "Spiritual Laws," 129.

44. "The Nation's Problem," 4/16/1889, *TFDP* 5.423.
45. "Freedom Has Brought Duties," 1/1/1883, *TFDP* 5.58; *TFDP* 5.403–26, especially 411, 420–21, 423–26.
46. *BF* 60, 85; *LT* 50, 72–73.
47. The phrase belongs to Blight, describing Douglass's propagandist effort in the early years of the Civil War, in *Frederick Douglass's Civil War*, 80–100.
48. Cf. Sundquist, for whom Douglass and Herman Melville were the foremost analysts of slavery in the nineteenth century (*To Wake the Nations*, 22).
49. "Our Composite Nationality," 12/7/1869, *TFDP* 4.240–59.

Chapter 1. "Killed All the Day Long": The True Philosophy of Slavery

1. *BF* 92–93; *LT* 78–80; *N* 58.
2. *BF* 93, also 61, 85; *LT* 50–51, 72–73.
3. *BF* 3–4, 60 (emphasis added).
4. *BF* 219. The Garrisonians' suggestion proceeded first from their concern to preserve his credibility against rising doubts that his remarkable speaking and reasoning powers could be the properties of anyone raised in slavery. That had been a reasonable concern prior to 1845, before Douglass put all such doubts to their final rest with the publication of his *Narrative*. On the suggestion that Douglass's place was as an orator, see Robert B. Stepto, "Storytelling in Early African-American Fiction: Frederick Douglass's 'The Heroic Slave,'" in William L. Andrews, ed., *Critical Essays on Frederick Douglass* (Boston: G. K. Hall, 1991), 110. On Douglass's resistance to the Garrisonian advice, see John Blassingame, "Introduction to Series One," *TFDP* 1.xlviii–lii; Gregory Lampe, *Frederick Douglass, Freedom's Voice: 1818–1845* (East Lansing: Michigan State University Press, 1998), x, 57–96.
5. *BF* 220–21, 243, 69, also 119.
6. "Fremont and Dayton," 8/15/1856, *LW* 2.398; "Shameful Abandonment of Principle," 5/30/1850, *LW* 2.124. See also *TFDP* 3.459–60. Caleb Bingham, who as compiler of the best-selling reader *The Columbian Orator* (originally published in 1797) served as Douglass's first instructor in oratory, advised in his "Introduction" to that work that "the orator's province is not barely to apply to the mind, but likewise to the passions" (Bicentennial Edition, edited by David W. Blight [New York: New York University Press, 1998], 12).
7. The "real difference of interests" at the 1787 Constitutional Convention, James Madison observed, "lay . . . between the Northern and Southern states. The institution of slavery and its consequences formed the line of discrimination"; see Madison, "Speech of July 14, 1787," in Max Farrand, ed., *The Records of the Federal Convention of 1787* (1911), 2:9–10, accessed 8/30/2006 at http://memory.loc.gov/ammem/amlaw/lwfr.html. See Donald L. Robinson, *Slavery in the Structure of American Politics, 1765–1820* (New York: Harcourt Brace Jovanovich, 1971); Don E. Fehrenbacher, *The Slaveholding Republic: An Account of the United States Government's Relations to Slavery*, completed and edited by Ward M. McAfee (New York: Oxford University Press, 2001), 28–47; Paul Finkelman, *Slavery and the Founders: Race and Liberty in the Age of Jefferson* (New York: M. E. Sharpe, 2001), 3–36.
8. John C. Calhoun, "Speech on the Reception of Abolition Petitions," February 6, 1837, in Ross M. Lence, ed., *Union and Liberty: The Political Philosophy of John C. Calhoun* (Indianapolis, IN: Liberty Fund, 1992), 474.
9. James Henry Hammond, "Letter to an English Abolitionist" (1845), in Drew Gilpin Faust, ed., *The Ideology of Slavery: Proslavery Thought in the Antebellum South, 1830–1860*

(Baton Rouge: Louisiana State University Press, 1981), 176. Hammond misquoted the Declaration in a potentially significant way by substituting the phrase *born equal* for the original *created equal.*

10. James Henry Hammond, "Speech on the Admission of Kansas, under the Lecompton Constitution," March 4, 1858, in Paul Finkelman, ed., *Defending Slavery: Proslavery Thought in the Old South* (Boston: Bedford/St. Martin's, 2003), 86; William Harper, "Memoir on Slavery" (1838), in Drew Gilpin Faust, ed., *The Ideology of Slavery* (Baton Rouge: Louisiana State University Press, 1981), 81 (emphasis added).

11. Thomas R. Dew, "Abolition of Negro Slavery" (1832), in Drew Gilpin Faust, ed., *Ideology of Slavery* (Baton Rouge: Louisiana State University Press, 1981), 66. Cf., in the same work, Harper, "Memoir on Slavery," 82; Hammond, "Letter to an English Abolitionist," 192; Thornton Stringfellow, "A Brief Examination of Scripture Testimony on the Institution of Slavery," 166. See also E. N. Elliott, "Introduction," in Elliot, ed., *Cotton Is King, and Proslavery Arguments* (1860; repr., New York: Negro Universities Press, 1969), ix.

12. Harper, "Memoir on Slavery," 99; Hammond, "Letter to an English Abolitionist," 184–86; Henry Hughes, "Treatise on Sociology" (1854), in Drew Gilpin Faust, ed., *Ideology of Slavery* (Baton Rouge: Louisiana State University Press, 1981), 253–54.

13. Hughes, "Treatise on Sociology," 241, 252, and, on the material rights of slaves, 242, 252–56, 270. Cf. Elliott, "Introduction," v–vii, xiii–xiv.

14. Harper, "Memoir on Slavery," 94, 113; Hughes, "Treatise on Sociology," 269–70; Hammond, "Letter to an English Abolitionist," 193–96; George Fitzhugh, "Sociology for the South" (1854) and "Cannibals All!" (1857) in Harvey Wish, ed., *Ante-bellum: Writings of George Fitzhugh and Hinton Rowan Helper* (New York: Capricorn Books, 1960), 41–95, 97–156.

15. *BF* 66; *TFDP* 1.100; *LW* 2.137, 144–45.

16. "Lecture on Slavery No. 1," 12/1/1850, *LW* 2.135 (*TFDP* 2.253–54). Cf. "Speech Delivered in the Courthouse at Chatham, Canada," 8/3/1854, *LW* 5.332.

17. "Aggressions of the Slave Power," 5/22/1856, *TFDP* 3.127; "John Brown and the Slaveholders' Insurrection," 1/30/1860, *TFDP* 3.317. See also *TFDP* 2.327; *LW* 5.166. Cf. John Locke, *Second Treatise of Government*, secs. 17, 23, 24, and *First Treatise of Government*, sec. 1 (both originally published in 1690), in *Locke: Two Treatises of Government,* edited by Peter Laslett (Cambridge: Cambridge University Press, 1988).

18. See "Property in Soil and Property in Man," 11/24/1848, *LW* 5.105; also *TFDP* 3.376, *LT* 228.

19. "A Few Facts and Personal Observations of Slavery," 3/24/1846, *TFDP* 1.204; "The Mission of the War," 1/13/1864, *TFDP* 4.5; "Slavery and the Limits of Nonintervention," 12/7/1859, *TFDP* 3.278. See also *TFDP* 1.39; *LW* 2.138–39, 5.250, 332. On the uniqueness of American slavery, Douglass joined a diverse cast of notable Americans. No less a national eminence than James Madison, at the Constitutional Convention in 1787, had called slavery "the most oppressive dominion ever exercised by man over man"; see Madison, "Speech of June 6, 1787," in Max Farrand, ed., *The Records of the Federal Convention of 1787* (1911), 1:135, accessed 8/30/2006 at http://memory.loc.gov/ammem/amlaw/lwfr.html. Cf. David Walker, "Appeal to the Colored Citizens of the World," in Herbert Aptheker, ed., *One Continual Cry: David Walker's Appeal to the Colored Citizens of the World* (1830; repr., New York: Humanities Press, 1965), 62–81.

20. Abraham Lincoln to Albert Hodges, 4/4/1864, in Richard N. Current, ed., *The Political Thought of Abraham Lincoln* (Indianapolis, IN: Bobbs-Merrill, 1967), 297–98.

21. "The Free Church Connection with the Slave Church," 2/12/1846, *TFDP* 1.160. See also *TFDP* 2.262; *LW* 3.64.

22. *BF* 92, 29 (emphasis added). See also *BF* 194; *N* 57–58; *TFDP* 1.94, 166, 183, 346, 3.441; *LW* 3.121, 5.130, 307–8.

23. "The Meaning of July Fourth for the Negro," 7/5/1852, *LW* 2.190–91.

24. "Decision of the Hour," 6/16/1861, *LW* 3.120–22. See also "Lecture on Slavery No. 2," 12/8/1850, *LW* 2.145 (*TFDP* 2.267); "John Brown and the Slaveholders' Insurrection," *TFDP* 3.317. Cf. Locke, *Second Treatise of Government*, secs. 226–28.

25. "Lecture on Slavery No. 2," *LW* 2.141 (*TFDP* 2.262). See William L. Andrews, *To Tell a Free Story: The First Century of African-American Autobiography* (Urbana: University of Illinois Press, 1986), 105; Donald Gibson, "Reconciling Public and Private in Frederick Douglass's Narrative," *American Literature* 57, no. 4 (December 1985): 557–59; and, alternatively, Houston Baker, *Blues, Ideology, and African-American Literature* (Chicago: University of Chicago Press, 1984), 42–50.

26. *BF* 102; *LT* 87 (emphasis original). Cf. *TFDP* 2.469–70.

27. *BF* 165.

28. See Locke, *Second Treatise of Government*, secs. 16–17, 220, and the Declaration's reference to "a design to reduce them under absolute Despotism."

29. "Speech Delivered in the Courthouse at Chatham, Canada," 8/3/1854, *LW* 5.333. Dickson Preston reported that with the decline of tobacco production in the nineteenth century, Maryland slaves' fear of being sold to the South greatly increased; see Preston, *Young Frederick Douglass: The Maryland Years* (Baltimore, MD: Johns Hopkins University Press, 1980), 75.

30. *BF* 109–10; *LT* 95–97.

31. James Henry Hammond unintentionally corroborated Douglass's argument, as he conceived of slaves' condition as "Eden" and abolitionists' agitation as the work of tempting Satans. By employing this analogy, slaveholders implicitly assimilated themselves to the abundantly provident God of Genesis. See Hammond, "Letter to an English Abolitionist," 192.

32. "A Friendly Word to Maryland," 11/17/1864, *TFDP* 4.46; "Lecture on Slavery No. 1," *LW* 2.135 (*TFDP* 2.254).

33. *BF* 54, and see also 142, 188.

34. Ibid., 54–59. Cf. *TFDP* 1.31. Also cf. Montesquieu, *The Spirit of the Laws* (originally published in 1748), translated and edited by Anne M. Cohler, Basia Carolyn Miller, and Harold Samuel Stone (Cambridge: Cambridge University Press, 1989), bk. 2, chap. 5, and bk. 3, chaps. 8–10.

35. "The Constitution of the United States: Is It Pro-slavery or Anti-slavery?" 3/26/1860, *LW* 2.478. See also *LW* 3.266.

36. "The American Apocalypse," 6/16/1861, *TFDP* 3.441.

37. See Andrews, *To Tell a Free Story*, 214–39; also see William L. Andrews, "Introduction," in Frederick Douglass, *My Bondage and My Freedom*, edited by Andrews (Urbana: University of Illinois Press, 1987), xviii–xxiii.

38. "I Have Come to Tell You Something about Slavery," 10/1841, *TFDP* 1.4–5.

39. *BF* 29, 38 (emphasis original).

40. Ibid., 30, 28. See also *LW* 4.230–31.

41. *BF* 38; *LT* 29.

42. *LT* 28.

43. *BF* 36–37. See also *LW* 1.342.

44. *BF* 43.

45. *LT* 42. See also *BF* 49.

46. "Slavery as It Now Exists in the United States," 8/25/1846, *TFDP* 1.345. Cf. *TFDP* 4.255; *LW* 4.181.

47. *BF* 73–74; *LT* 62. Elsewhere in *Bondage and Freedom*, Douglass cited a strict respect for elders to support his observation that "there is no better material in the world for making a gentleman, than is furnished in the African" (48–49). Viewed in the light of the Barney anecdote, this observation suggests an ironic contrast between the civilized African slaves and their barbarous Anglo-American masters. See also the reading of John David Smith, "Introduction," in Frederick Douglass, *My Bondage and My Freedom*, edited by Smith (New York: Penguin Books, 2003), xxxi.

48. *BF* 167; *LT* 156. See also *TFDP* 4.404, 4.491, 5.45, 5.56–57, 5.201.

49. When Douglass later complained of freedpeople's excessive restiveness after emancipation (see, e.g., *TFDP* 4.372), he was complaining in part about a trait that he believed slavery fostered.

50. Cf. Alexis de Tocqueville, *Democracy in America*, edited by Harvey C. Mansfield and Delba Winthrop (Chicago: University of Chicago Press, 2000), vol. 2, pt. 2, chap. 4, pp. 485–86.

51. Contrast Peter F. Walker, *Moral Choices: Memory, Desire, and Imagination in Nineteenth-Century American Abolition* (Baton Rouge: Louisiana State University Press, 1978), 217. Cf. Eric J. Sundquist, *To Wake the Nations: Race in the Making of American Literature* (Cambridge, MA: Belknap Press, 1993), 91–92.

52. Wilson Jeremiah Moses, *Creative Conflict in African American Thought* (Cambridge: Cambridge University Press, 2004), 66–70.

53. Ibid., 58, 40.

54. "The Free Church of Scotland and American Slavery," 1/30/1846, *TFDP* 1.147; "Emancipation Is an Individual, a National, and an International Responsibility," 5/18/1846, *TFDP* 1.254; *BF* 42. See also *TFDP* 1.376; *LW* 1.271, 2.141–42.

55. *BF* 38.

56. "Our National Capital," 5/8/1877, *TFDP* 4.469.

57. *LW* 1.341; also in *BF* 269, 268 (emphasis added).

58. *BF* 41; *LT* 36 (emphasis original).

59. *BF* 92, 34; *LT* 79.

60. *BF* 202. Also *LT* 193; *N* 98. To some degree, this acknowledgment calls into question Douglass's suggestions of slaveholders' design to dissolve the slaves' familial relations. As Barbara Fields has reported, however, the fact that most Maryland slaveholdings were quite small meant that most slaveholders there could not afford to keep slave families together, even if they had wanted to do so. Under such circumstances, slaveholders did consider familial ties among slaves a danger, as the desire to meet with family members employed elsewhere supplied a strong incentive to escape. See Fields, *Slavery and Freedom on the Middle Ground* (New Haven, CT: Yale University Press, 1985), 24–28.

61. *BF* 124–25, 163–64, 95. Cf. *LW* 5.304; *TFDP* 4.130. On mediating powers as structural barriers against despotism, cf. Montesquieu, *Spirit of the Laws*, bk. 2, chap. 4, pp. 17–18; Tocqueville, *Democracy in America*, vol. 2, pt. 4, chap. 2, pp. 640–43.

62. *BF* 104 (emphasis added), 150–51; *LT* 89, 141–42, 198–201.

63. *BF* 92–93, 99, 194. Cf. *BF* 60; *TFDP* 1.415, 2.255, 3.8–9; *LW* 5.39.

64. "Lecture on Slavery No. 1," *LW* 2.138–39. See also *BF* 55; *LT* 64.

65. *BF* 69, 109–10, 134; *LT* 95–97; *LW* 5.333. On fear as the ruling passion under despotism, see Montesquieu, *Spirit of the Laws*, bk. 3, chap. 9, p. 28.

66. *N* 80; *BF* 155–57.

67. *BF* 119 (emphasis original).

68. *BF* 155.

69. *BF* 57–58, 73–74, 154–57, 90–93, 99–101; *LT* 47–48, 62, 145–48, 78–80, 85–86.

70. W. G. Kendall to FD, 3/26/1850, *LW* 5.157–58 (emphasis original). On "voluntary slavery," cf. Stringfellow, "A Brief Examination," 145, who distinguished voluntary from involuntary servitude, with the former referring to the condition of "hirelings" bound to labor for wages and for a specified time period.

71. Hammond, "Letter to an English Abolitionist," 187. Cf. Dew, "Abolition of Negro Slavery," 64–65; Harper, "Memoir on Slavery," 98–99.

72. Harper, "Memoir on Slavery," 134; Elliot, "Introduction," ix.

73. Hughes, "Treatise on Sociology," 257. Cf. Harper, "Memoir on Slavery," 131–32; Stringfellow, "A Brief Examination," 167; Hammond, "Letter to an English Abolitionist," 187–88.

74. Peter Kolchin, *American Slavery: 1619–1877* (New York: Hill and Wang, 2003), 62. The argument in brief is that the natural population increase among slaves, unique to North America, made the vast majority of nineteenth-century U.S. slaves African *Americans* and that this mixed identity naturally inclined slaveholders to treat them somewhat more humanely than they treated native Africans, whom slaveholders throughout the Americas regarded as alien and savage (37–62, 93–132). In Douglass's telling, prejudices against Africans were harbored by black Americans as well as by whites; see *BF* 52–53, 83.

75. Kolchin, *American Slavery,* 235, 127, 94.

76. "Letter from a Slaveholder: Remarks," 4/12/1850, *LW* 5.160. Cf. *LW* 2.144–45.

77. FD to William Lloyd Garrison, 10/15/1860, *LW* 5.469. But see Douglass's "Eulogy on the Late Honorable William Jay," 5/12/1859, *LW* 5.448.

78. *N* 65–66; FD to Thomas Auld, 9/3/1848, *LW* 1.342 (*BF* 269).

79. Notwithstanding his general condemnation of slavery, Thomas Jefferson had favorably contrasted American slavery with its ancient Roman counterpart. In America, "the exposing them is a crime of which no instance has existed with us; and were it to be followed by death, it would be punished capitally"; see Jefferson, *Notes on the State of Virginia,* Query XIV, in Adrienne Koch and William Peden, eds., *The Life and Selected Writings of Thomas Jefferson* (New York: Random House, 1944) 260.

80. FD to Thomas Auld, 9/3/1849, *LW* 1.403; *BF* 112–14; *LT* 99–100.

81. *BF* 119; cf. *N* 67–68. Douglass's attitude toward Auld was softened in *Life and Times* (1881), which contains an affecting account of their reunion, at Auld's deathbed, in 1879. In this later work, his summary of Auld upon becoming the latter's slave reads: "When I lived with Capt. Auld I *thought* him incapable of a noble action"; see *LT* 106 (emphasis added).

82. Booker T. Washington, *Frederick Douglass* (1906; repr., New York: Greenwood Press, 1969), 17, 49–50; Walker, *Moral Choices,* 233n7; Preston, *Young Frederick Douglass,* xv, 2, 55–56, 129, 140, 167–69; William S. McFeely, *Frederick Douglass* (New York: W. W. Norton, 1991), 23–24, 29, 39, 41, 158–60. See also Eric J. Sundquist, "Introduction," and Wilson Jeremiah Moses, "Writing Freely? Frederick Douglass and the Constraints of Racialized Writing," both in Sundquist, ed., *Frederick Douglass: New Literary and Historical Essays* (Cambridge: Cambridge University Press, 1990), 5–7, 74–75.

83. *LT* 441. See also *BF* 184, 186.

84. *BF* 270–71 (emphasis added).

85. Preston, *Young Frederick Douglass,* 225–26n15. See also McFeely, *Frederick Douglass,* 158–60. Sundquist asserts that Douglass's "charges of brutality against Thomas Auld were deliberately inaccurate"; see Sundquist, "Introduction," 6.

86. Cf. *BF* 90–93, 96–98, 101–2, 111–12, 115, with Douglass's speech in Cork, Ireland ("I Am Here to Spread Light on American Slavery," 10/14/1845, *TFDP* 1.41), in which he implausibly claimed that in the Hugh and Sophia Auld household, "whenever the little boy [young Tommy Auld] got cross, his mother used to say, 'Go and whip Freddy.'"

87. *BF* 84.

88. In *Bondage and Freedom,* besides those of Lucretia, Sophia, and Thomas Auld, instances of humanity amid slavery include Hugh Auld's genuine outrage after Frederick was severely beaten by white apprentices at a shipyard in Baltimore and was then unable to secure judicial redress (187–92); the relative justice of William Freeland's character (161, 164); the glimmers of kindness in the morally disfigured Aaron Anthony, whose cruelty toward other slaves contrasted starkly with occasional expressions of "almost fatherly" affection toward young Frederick, his "little Indian boy" and putative biological son (54–59); and the favored treatment Colonel Edward Lloyd accorded his slave William Wilks, by all appearances the offspring of the wealthy planter himself (74–75).

89. *N* 41.

90. *BF* 54. See also *BF* 56, 91–92; *TFDP* 1.311, 4.519.

91. *BF* 161–62 (emphasis original).

92. Matthew 12:25; Abraham Lincoln, "Speech at Springfield," 6/16/1858, in Roy P. Basler, ed., *Abraham Lincoln: His Speeches and Writings* (1946; repr., Cambridge, MA: Da Capo Press, 2001), 372.

93. *BF* 96; also *LT* 81.

94. "Slavery the Live Issue," 4/11/1854, *TFDP* 2.465. Cf. *TFDP* 1.184, 187, 192.

95. Cf. Machiavelli, *The Prince,* edited by Harvey C. Mansfield, Jr. (Chicago: University of Chicago Press, 1985), 29–30.

96. *N* 41, 45; *BF* 55, 62–63, 134, 139, 140, 150. On Gore, see Preston, *Young Frederick Douglass,* 72–74. Cf. the language of Locke in describing the jural status of tyrants, in *Second Treatise of Government,* secs. 11, 93, 172, 181. See also Leslie Friedman Goldstein, "The Political Thought of Frederick Douglass" (PhD diss., Cornell University, 1975), 36.

97. *BF* 181–82; *LT* 172–73.

98. *BF* 57.

99. Even pursuant to a just war, to enslave in perpetuity one's captives and their offspring was altogether contrary to Locke's principles; see his *Second Treatise of Government,* chap. 4, p. 16. David Brion Davis, in *The Problem of Slavery in Western Culture* (Ithaca, NY: Cornell University Press, 1966), 118–21, and also in *The Problem of Slavery in the Age of Revolution* (Ithaca, NY: Cornell University Press, 1975), 45, misreads Locke on this crucial point. A judicious discussion of Locke on slavery is William Uzgalis, "'... The Same Tyrannical Principle': Locke's Legacy on Slavery," in Tommy L. Lott, ed., *Subjugation and Bondage: Critical Essays on Slavery and Social Philosophy* (Lanham, MD: Rowman & Littlefield, 1998), 49–77.

100. Cf. George M. Fredrickson, *Racism: A Short History* (Princeton, NJ: Princeton University Press, 2002), 11–12, 47, 68, 94–95.

101. "Decision of the Hour," *LW* 3.124; "A Letter to the American Slaves from Those Who Have Fled American Slavery," 9/5/1850, *LW* 5.164; also "The Anti-slavery Movement," 1/1855, *LW* 2.358.

102. *BF* 97.

103. "Decision of the Hour," *LW* 3.124.

104. "Slavery's Northern Bulwarks," 1/12/1851, *TFDP* 2.285; "What to the Slave Is the Fourth of July?" 7/5/1852, *TFDP* 2.378 (*LW* 2.197). See also *TFDP* 2.92; *LW* 2.347.

105. "The American Colonization Society," 5/31/1849, *LW* 1.397; "Brethren, Rouse the Church," 8/6/1847, *TFDP* 2.91.

106. *BF* 60, 145 (emphasis original).

107. *N* 69–71; *BF* 120–22.

108. *BF* 158; also *N* 82. Cf. *N* 92; *BF* 191.

109. *BF* 138–51; *N* 69; also "Baptists, Congregationalists, the Free Church, and Slavery," 12/23/1845, *TFDP* 1.109.

110. See Orlando Patterson's profoundly troubling account of the role of religious zeal in antiblack violence in the post-Reconstruction South, in *Rituals of Blood: Consequences of Slavery in Two American Centuries* (New York: Basic Civitas Books, 1998), 169–232.

111. "The Reproach and Shame of the American Government," 8/3/1858, *LW* 5.401.

112. Hughes, "Treatise on Sociology," 244, 256–59, 262, 268.

113. "The Slaveholders' Rebellion," 7/4/1862, *LW* 3.248; "We Are in the Midst of a Moral Revolution," 5/10/1854, *TFDP* 2.487–88; "Slavery, Freedom, and the Kansas-Nebraska Act," 10/30/1854, *TFDP* 2.545–46 (*LW* 2.321).

114. *LW* 5.178. See also *LW* 2.133–34, 145–47.

115. "Speech Delivered at Convention of Colored Citizens of the State of New York," 9/4/1855, *LW* 5.358.

116. "The Lessons of the Hour," 6/30/1861, *LW* 3.136. On the powerful concern for reputation, see *TFDP* 1.378; also *TFDP* 1.192, 238; *LW* 2.241. This understanding of the power of the concern for reputation also governed Douglass's strategy of appealing to opinion abroad to strengthen antislavery opinion among northerners. See *LW* 1.147; *TFDP* 1.35, 96, 292–93; *BF* 231–32.

117. *BF* 44–45 (emphasis original), 93–94; *LT* 37.

118. "The Kansas-Nebraska Bill," 10/30/1854, *LW* 2.323; "Speech Delivered at the Mass Free Democratic Convention," 10/14/1852, *LW* 5.257. See also *LW* 5.426, 2.195; *TFDP* 3.101–2, 129–32, 422.

119. "The Final Struggle," 11/16/1855, *LW* 2.377. See also *LW* 3.143; *DM* 2/1859.

120. "Speech Delivered at Convention of Colored Citizens," 9/4/1855, *LW* 5.360–61. See also *LW* 2.105, 323, 358, 3.100, 5.177–79, 334; *LT* 292.

121. *LW* 5.164–65.

122. "American Slavery Lecture No. 7," 1/12/1851, *LW* 5.178 (emphasis original). See also FD to William Lloyd Garrison, 5/23/1846, *LW* 1.168, 5.251, 283, 334.

123. "Speech Delivered at the Mass Free Democratic Convention," 10/14/1852, *LW* 5.260. On the Fugitive Slave Law and northern complicity, see *LT* 278–79. On the federal government's support of slavery, see Fehrenbacher, *Slaveholding Republic.*

124. "The Dred Scott Decision," 5/11/1857, *TFDP* 3.165 (*LW* 2.408).

Chapter 2. The Moral Government of the Universe: Natural Rights, Natural Law, and the Natural Demise of Slavery

1. Leon F. Litwack, *North of Slavery: The Negro in the Free States, 1790–1860* (Chicago: University of Chicago Press, 1961), 249. On the emigration of other black leaders, see "The Colored People and Our Paper," *FDP* 11/27/1851, *LW* 5.216–17.

2. Martin R. Delany, *The Condition, Elevation, Emigration and Destiny of the Colored People of the United States, Politically Considered* (1852; repr., New York: Arno Press, 1968), 160.

3. "The Prospect in the Future," *DM* 8/1860, *LW* 2.494–95. See also "The Abolition Movement Re-organized," *DM* 10/1860, *LW* 2.522.

4. "Emigration to Hayti," *DM* 1/1861.

5. David W. Blight, *Frederick Douglass's Civil War: Keeping Faith in Jubilee* (Baton Rouge: Louisiana State University Press, 1989), provides an excellent chronicling and analysis of Douglass's optimism.

6. "Lecture on Slavery No. 2," 12/8/1850, *LW* 2.148.

7. "The End of All Compromises with Slavery—Now and Forever," *FDP* 5/26/1854, *LW* 2.283. The Missouri Compromise of 1820 allowed the admission of Missouri into the Union as a slave state, with the proviso that slavery would be prohibited everywhere else in the Louisiana Territory above Missouri's southern border, or 36°30′ north latitude. Douglass viewed the law as an obstruction to the advance of freedom rather than as a containment of slavery's expansion, as Lincoln saw it. He believed that in its practical effect, the measure had lent authority to the opinion that the southwestern region of the United States was conceded to slavery. Slavery's opponents in the Southwest, he reported, "perceive that the repeal of the Missouri Compromise opens the door for the introduction of freedom into Missouri, Texas, and indeed, all the southwestern States"; see "Policy of Restoring the Missouri Compromise," *FDP* 8/3/1855.

8. "The Dred Scott Decision," 5/11/1857, *LW* 2.411, 414.

9. "To My American Readers and Friends," *DM* 11/1859, *LW* 2.464.

10. This is not to deny the rhetorical dimension of the great orator's speech during this and other grim periods. We *need* a faith that "the divine powers of the Universe are on the side of freedom and progress," he wrote at the outset of the Civil War, "the better to enable us to work"; see "Danger to the Abolition Cause," *DM* 6/1861, *LW* 3.112; cf. *LW* 2.243–44. But his acknowledgment of its usefulness was not a detraction from its truth.

11. "The Doom of the Black Power," *FDP* 7/27/1855, *LW* 2.363 (emphasis added).

12. Blight, *Frederick Douglass's Civil War*, 120.

13. *N* 56, 65; *BF* 89, 112, 178.

14. Blight, *Frederick Douglass's Civil War*, especially 101–21. See also Blight's criticism of Douglass biographer William S. McFeely on this point, in "The Private Worlds of Frederick Douglass," *Transition* 61 (1993): 166.

15. "Lecture on Slavery No. 2," *LW* 2.148 (emphasis added). See also *LW* 2.111, 359, 3.197; *TFDP* 1.219, 3.171, 4.504, 5.11.

16. "Dred Scott Decision," *LW* 2.411; "American Slavery Lecture No. 7," 1/12/1851, *LW* 5.174 (emphasis original).

17. "We Are Here and Want the Ballot Box," 9/4/1866, *TFDP* 4.126; "Remarks at Soiree, Paisely, Scotland," 3/1846, *LW* 5.36; "A Friendly Word to Maryland," 11/17/1864, *TFDP* 4.46; "The Kansas-Nebraska Bill," 10/30/1854, *LW* 2.331; "The Slaveholders' Rebellion," 7/4/1862, *LW* 3.248; "The Reasons for Our Troubles," 1/14/1862, *LW* 3.197.

18. See, e.g., "Lecture on Slavery No. 2," *LW* 2.140; "Freedom, the Eternal Truth," 5/2/1852, *TFDP* 2.352–53; "The Anti-slavery Movement," 1/1855, *LW* 2.342, 355.

19. See, e.g., "International Moral Force Can Destroy Slavery," 3/17/1846, *TFDP* 1.184; also *TFDP* 1.192; "Lecture on Slavery No. 2," *LW* 2.145. Cf. John Locke, *Second Treatise of Government*, sec. 11 (originally published in 1690), in *Locke: Two Treatises of Government*, edited by Peter Laslett (Cambridge: Cambridge University Press, 1988).

20. "The Meaning of July Fourth for the Negro," 7/5/1852, *LW* 2.191–92 (emphasis original). See also "Lecture on Slavery No. 2," *LW* 2.141; "Dred Scott Decision," *LW* 2.411.

21. "The Claims of the Negro Ethnologically Considered," 7/12/1854, *LW* 2.295 (emphasis original). On the American School, see Samuel G. Morton, *Crania Americana* (Philadelphia: J. Dobson, 1839); Josiah Nott and George Glidden, *Types of Mankind* (Philadelphia: J. B. Lippincott, 1854); William Stanton, *The Leopard's Spots: Scientific Attitudes toward Race in America, 1815–1859* (Chicago: University of Chicago Press, 1960); George Fredrickson, *The Black Image in the White Mind: The Debate on African-American Character and Destiny, 1817–1914* (New York: Harper & Row, 1971), 71–96.

22. "Claims of the Negro," *LW* 2.290, 291.

23. Nott and Glidden, *Types of Mankind,* 457; on civilizational inferiority, see 50–52, 260, 306–7, 456–62.

24. "Claims of the Negro," 295.

25. Wilson Jeremiah Moses, *The Golden Age of Black Nationalism: 1850–1925* (Hamden, CT: Archon Books, 1978), 11.

26. Wilson Jeremiah Moses has noted the irony of African Americans identifying themselves both with the enslaved nation of Israel and the enslaving nation of Egypt, in *Creative Conflict in African American Thought* (Cambridge: Cambridge University Press, 2004), xiii.

27. "Claims of the Negro," 296, 301–4.

28. Ibid., 291, 294 (emphasis original).

29. See his later remarks on Egypt, in "My Foreign Travels," 12/15/1887, *TFDP* 5.306; *LT* 579–80.

30. "Claims of the Negro," *LW* 2.291, 308, 304–6, 295.

31. Cf. John Locke, *An Essay Concerning Human Understanding,* edited by Peter Nidditch (Oxford: Clarendon Press, 1975), bk. 3, chap. 11, sec. 16. See also Bernard R. Boxill, "Radical Implications of Locke's Moral Theory: The Views of Frederick Douglass," in Tommy L. Lott, ed., *Subjugation and Bondage: Critical Essays on Slavery and Social Philosophy* (Lanham, MD: Rowman & Littlefield, 1998), 37–38.

32. "Claims of the Negro," 291.

33. Ibid., 307.

34. "Friendly Word to Maryland," 11/17/1864, *TFDP* 4.42 (emphasis original); "I Am a Radical Woman Suffrage Man," 5/28/1888, *TFDP* 5.386. Douglass approvingly paraphrased fellow abolitionist Theodore Weld: "The right of the individual to himself, is the post in the centre of all rights—strike that down, and down go all rights"; see "Slavery the Live Issue," 4/11/1854, *TFDP* 2.462. See also *TFDP* 1.191–92, 1.379–80, 2.118, 2.392, 2.454–55, 4.316, 5.255; *LW* 2.208, 3.105, 5.78, 223.

35. "The Horrors of Slavery and England's Duty to Free the Bondsman," 9/1/1846, *TFDP* 1.379.

36. "Woman Suffrage Movement," 10/20/1870, *LW* 4.232. See also *LW* 2.140.

37. *BF* 194; "The Present and Future of the Colored Race in America," 5/1863, *LW* 3.353.

38. "Lecture on Slavery No. 2," *LW* 2.140.

39. "Slavery and the Slave Power (Lecture on Slavery No. 1)," 12/1/1850, *TFDP* 2.255. The same quality supplied the foundation of Douglass's argument for woman suffrage; see "Woman Suffrage Movement," *LW* 4.232. See also *LW* 1.321, 2.491.

40. See Locke, *Essay Concerning Human Understanding,* bk. 2, chap. 27, secs. 17–18, 26; also Locke, *Second Treatise of Government,* secs. 27, 44, 123.

41. *BF* 166–67; *TFDP* 4.266, 404, 491; *LT* 156; *TFDP* 5.45, 56, 201.

42. *LT* 472–73 (emphasis added).

43. *N* 68; *BF* 118–19 (emphasis original).

44. *N* 78; *BF* 148–51. On Douglass's moral reasoning in the battle with Covey, see the excellent account by Bernard Boxill, "The Fight with Covey," in Lewis Gordon, ed., *Existence in Black: An Anthology of Black Existential Philosophy* (New York: Routledge, 1997), 273–90. On his exemplary self-control, see Donald Gibson, "Reconciling Public and Private in Frederick Douglass's Narrative," *American Literature* 57, no. 4 (December 1985): 561–64. Cynthia Willett has helpfully drawn attention to Douglass's use of the "fighting madness" or the animal spirit as an element of the human, but in her enthusiasm for a postmodern Douglass who rejected European-American standards of rational liberty, she has misconceived the grounds of Douglass's moral thought; see Willett, *Maternal Ethics and Other Slave Moralities* (New York: Routledge, 1995), 102–4; Willett, *The Soul of Justice: Social Bonds and Racial Hubris* (Ithaca, NY: Cornell University Press, 2001), 192–201.

45. *LW* 2.140. Cf. "Slavery and the Slave Power," *TFDP* 2.259–60; "Dred Scott Decision," 5/11/1857, *LW* 2.408–21.

46. *BF* 61 (emphasis added), 64–66, 156; *N* 80; "Slavery, the Free Church, and British Agitation against Bondage," 8/3/1846, *TFDP* 1.319. For the suggestion that the love of liberty is innate, see also "Lecture on Slavery No. 2," *LW* 2.145; "John Brown and the Slaveholders' Insurrection," 1/30/1860, *TFDP* 3.313.

47. "The American Temperance Movement, Slavery, and Prejudice," *TFDP* 1.345; *BF* 167. Cf. George Combe, *The Constitution of Man Considered in Relation to External Objects* (1834; repr., Delmar, NY: Scholars' Facsimiles and Reprints, 1974), 45, 52–56.

48. "Meaning of July Fourth for the Negro," 7/5/1852, *LW* 2.191 (emphasis original); "Slavery, the Free Church, and British Agitation against Bondage," 8/3/1846, *TFDP* 1.327. Cf. *LW* 1.109. Cf. Lincoln's famous epitome of antislavery reasoning: "As I would not be a *slave*, so I would not be a *master*," in Lincoln, "Fragment: On Slavery," 8/1/1858? in Roy P. Basler, ed., *Abraham Lincoln: His Speeches and Writings* (1946; repr., Cambridge MA: Da Capo Press, 2001), 427 (emphasis original).

49. "Slavery the Live Issue," *TFDP* 2.462 (emphasis original); "Dred Scott Decision," *TFDP* 3.176, also *LW* 2.418. Cf. *TFDP* 2.392, *LW* 5.327.

50. "Is It Right and Wise to Kill a Kidnapper?" *LW* 2.286.

51. "Shooting a Negro," *FDP* 2/24/1854, *LW* 5.318. Cf. "Meaning of July Fourth," *LW* 2.200. Disappointed with the inaction of the Virginia legislature on slavery, Jefferson had written to a French correspondent in 1786: "What a stupendous, what an incomprehensible machine is man! Who can endure toil, famine, stripes, imprisonment, and death itself in vindication of his own liberty, and the next moment . . . inflict on his fellow men a bondage, one hour of which is fraught with more misery than ages of that which he rose in rebellion to oppose"; see Jefferson to J. N. Demeunier, 1/24/1786, accessed 10/30/2006 at http://memory .loc.gov/ammem/collections/jefferson_papers/.

52. "Peaceful Annihilation of Slavery Is Hopeless," *LW* 2.406.

53. "Duty Has Been the Moving Power in My Life," 7/12/1891, *TFDP* 5.458.

54. "Northern Whigs and Democrats," 7/7/1848, *LW* 1.310. Cf. *LW* 1.283, 2.133, 2.176, 2.372; *LT* 256.

55. "Is It Right and Wise to Kill a Kidnapper? (II)," 6/9/1854, *LW* 5.328. Cf. *LW* 1.400, 2.311.

56. *BF* 176; *LT* 166; also *N* 85.

57. "West India Emancipation," 8/4/1857, *LW* 2.435, 437.

58. "The Lessons of the Hour," 1/9/1894, *TFDP* 5.581; "Address to the People of the United States," 9/24/1883, *LW* 4.388.

59. Waldo E. Martin, Jr., *The Mind of Frederick Douglass* (Chapel Hill: University of North Carolina Press, 1984), 69, 249.

60. *BF* 176; *LW* 2.434–35.

61. "Is It Right and Wise to Kill a Kidnapper?" *LW* 2.287.

62. *BF* 69; "'It Moves,' or the Philosophy of Reform," *TFDP* 5.137–40. See also *LW* 2.285–86, 390; *FDP* 8/3/1855; *LW* 3.200–201; *TFDP* 5.11; *LT* 480, 506.

63. Combe, *Constitution of Man*, 8, 9. Combe's argument was a version of what present-day philosophers call "ethical explanation," whose central claim is that moral principles can act as efficient causes of events in the world. See Joshua Cohen, "The Arc of the Moral Universe," in Tommy L. Lott, ed., *Subjugation and Bondage: Critical Essays on Slavery and Social Philosophy* (Lanham, MD: Rowman & Littlefield, 1998), 281–327.

64. "Did John Brown Fail?" 5/30/1881, *TFDP* 5.11.

65. Combe, *Constitution of Man*, 8–9, 180, 73–78, 171 (emphasis original).

66. *BF* 69.

67. *BF* 54–56. Less dramatic instances of slaveholders' psychological dividedness and unhappiness appear in Douglass's analyses of the Auld brothers. His second master, Thomas Auld, "was not a *born* slaveholder," Douglass noted, suggesting that Auld's cruelties represented compensatory attempts to reassure himself of his personal fitness for slaveholding; see *BF* 119 (emphasis original); also *N* 68, *LT* 106. Douglass also blamed slavery for the corruption of Sophia Auld's character and the disappearance of domestic happiness from the home she made with Hugh; see *BF* 115, 97.

68. *BF* 70, 72 (emphasis original); Combe, *Constitution of Man*, 9: "Those who disobey [the moral] law, are tormented with insatiable desires, which, from the nature of things, cannot be gratified."

69. *BF* 54.

70. This is the meaning of Montesquieu's epitome of despotism, in *The Spirit of the Laws* (originally published in 1748), translated and edited by Anne M. Cohler, Basia Carolyn Miller, and Harold Samuel Stone (Cambridge: Cambridge University Press, 1989), bk. 5, chap. 13; cf. bk. 3, chap. 10. I suppose that Douglass would have readily identified the real "savages of Louisiana" to whom Montesquieu referred. Cf. John David Smith, "Introduction," in *Frederick Douglass, My Bondage and My Freedom,* edited by Smith (New York: Penguin Books, 2003), xxxvi; Aristotle, *Politics,* edited by Carnes Lord (Chicago: University of Chicago Press, 1984), 5.11, 1313a17–1315b10; 5.12, 1315b11.

71. Combe, *Constitution of Man*, 9.

72. "Woman and the Ballot," 10/27/1870, *LW* 4.237.

73. "Learn Trades or Starve!" 3/4/1853, *LW* 2.224 (emphasis original). Cf. "Colored Newspapers," 1/8/1848, *LW* 1.291.

74. "What Are the Colored People Doing for Themselves?" *LW* 1.316; cf. *LW* 3.342.

75. "Freedom in the West Indies," 8/2/1858, *TFDP* 3.219; "What Shall Be Done with the Slaves If Emancipated?" *LW* 3.188. Cf. Locke, *Second Treatise of Government,* secs. 59–61.

76. *BF* 114, 151; *TFDP* 1.60; *LW* 3.356; *TFDP* 5.562. See also Boxill, "Radical Implications," 45; Sharon Krause, *Liberalism with Honor* (Cambridge, MA: Harvard University Press, 2002), 237–38n93.

77. *BF* 148, 150, 152 (emphasis original). See also *N* 78–79; *LT* 139–43.

78. *BF* 150–51, 178; *LT* 142, 168–69. Contrast *N* 78–79, 88–89.

79. *BF* 61–63; *LT* 51–52. Also deserving of notice are those who assisted Douglass's ultimate escape at great risk to their own lives and who could be freely credited only in *Life and Times*

(*LT* 197–201). Douglass unaccountably neglected to mention the assistance of Anna Murray, then his betrothed, who provided crucial monetary aid, helped fashion his sailor's disguise, and must have been intimately involved in the planning of his escape. See Rosetta Douglass Sprague, "Anna Murray Douglass—My Mother as I Recall Her," *Journal of Negro History* 8, no. 1 (January 1923): 94; William McFeely, *Frederick Douglass* (New York: W. W. Norton, 1991), 70.

80. "Why Should a Colored Man Enlist?" *LW* 3.343.

81. "The Douglass Institute," 9/29/1865, *TFDP* 4.95 (also *LW* 4.181) (emphasis added). See also "Pictures and Progress,"12/3/1861, *TFDP* 3.472.

82. "The Danger of the Republican Movement," 5/28/1856, *LW* 5.388.

83. "The True Remedy for the Fugitive Slave Bill," 6/9/1854, *LW* 5.326. Cf. Aristotle, *Nicomachean Ethics*, edited by Martin Ostwald (Indianapolis, IN: Bobbs-Merrill, 1962), bk. 3, chap. 6, 1115a24–33.

84. "Is It Right and Wise to Kill a Kidnapper?" 6/2/1854, *LW* 2.284–85.

85. "The Significance of Emancipation in the West Indies," 8/3/1857, *TFDP* 3.189.

86. *BF* 138.

87. Margaret Kohn, "Frederick Douglass's Master-Slave Dialectic," *Journal of Politics* 67, no. 2 (May 2005): 509–13; Boxill, "Fight with Covey," 273–90.

88. *BF* 139–42.

89. See also *BF* 63, 183, and Douglass's 1850 "Letter to the American Slaves," in which, exhorting them to escape, he referred to the prospect of death upon recapture as "but a welcome release to men, who had, all their lifetime, been killed every day, and 'killed all the day long'"; see *LW* 5.169. Some scholars read the Covey episode in the light of G. W. F. Hegel's classic master-slave dialectic, in which the archetypal master and slave engage in a primordial struggle for recognition by each other. See Hegel, *Phenomenology of Spirit* (originally published in 1807), translated by A. V. Miller (New York: Oxford University Press, 1977), chap. 4, secs. 189–96; Paul Gilroy, *The Black Atlantic: Modernity and Double-Consciousness* (Cambridge, MA: Harvard University Press, 1993), 60–64; Willett, *Maternal Ethics*, chaps. 5–6; Kohn, "Frederick Douglass's Master-Slave Dialectic." Without dismissing those insightful readings, I think of the Covey battle primarily as a crucial Lockean moment in Douglass's development, teaching the lesson about the nature of the summum malum whereby Locke had corrected Thomas Hobbes.

90. *BF* 142–44 (emphasis original). See also Blight, *Frederick Douglass's Civil War*, especially 1–58; Blight, "Up from 'Twoness': Frederick Douglass and the Meaning of W. E. B. Du Bois's Concept of Double Consciousness," *Canadian Review of American Studies* 21, no. 3 (Winter 1990): 301–19; Eric J. Sundquist, *To Wake the Nations: Race in the Making of American Literature* (Cambridge, MA: Belknap Press, 1993), 125.

91. *BF* 144–45.

92. Ibid., 149, 4.

93. Cf. Montesquieu, *Spirit of the Laws*, bk. 3, chap. 8, p. 27: "How could honor be endured by the despot? It glories in scorning life, and the despot is strong only because he can take life away."

94. *BF* 151–52. See also *LW* 4.237.

95. Leslie Friedman Goldstein, "Violence as an Instrument for Social Change: The Views of Frederick Douglass (1817–1895)," *Journal of Negro History* 61, no. 1 (January 1976): 61–66.

96. *LT* 226, 275. See also *LW* 1.114–15, 164–65, 227; William Lloyd Garrison, "Declaration of Sentiments Adopted by the Peace Convention," in William E. Cain, ed., *William Lloyd Garrison and the Fight against Slavery* (Boston: Bedford Books, 1995), 104.

97. Douglass revisited the controversy in a 7/27/1849 editorial, "Rev. Henry Highland Garnet," *LW* 5.143–44. Garnet's 1843 speech entitled "An Address to the Slaves of the United States of America" is printed in Sterling Stuckey, ed., *The Ideological Origins of Black Nationalism* (Boston: Beacon Press, 1972), 165–73.

98. "Dred Scott Decision," *LW* 2.408; *TFDP* 3.164.

99. James Henry Hammond, "Letter to an English Abolitionist," in Drew Gilpin Faust, ed., *The Ideology of Slavery* (Baton Rouge: Louisiana State University Press, 1981), 198.

100. "Captain John Brown Not Insane," 11/1859, *LW* 2.460. See also *LW* 5.221–22, 328, 2.487.

101. "An Antislavery Tocsin (Lecture on Slavery No. 2)," *TFDP* 2.271–72 (*LW* 2.149). For Jefferson's fear, see his *Notes on the State of Virginia*, Query XVIII, in Adrienne Koch and William Peden, eds., *The Life and Selected Writings of Thomas Jefferson* (New York: Random House, 1944), 278–79.

102. For Douglass on Uncle Tom, see *BF* 115, 106; also "Colored Men's Rights in This Republic," 5/14/1857, *TFDP* 3.148, a speech in which he objected to a characterization of African Americans as "a nation of Uncle Toms, who could shout 'glory' and sing hymns" but who were "not a fighting people." On his similar intention in *The Heroic Slave*, see Robert Stepto, "Sharing the Thunder: The Literary Exchanges of Harriet Beecher Stowe, Henry Bibb, and Frederick Douglass," in Eric J. Sundquist, ed., *New Essays on Uncle Tom's Cabin* (New York: Cambridge University Press, 1986), 136–37, 143–52.

103. *BF* 104; *LT* 89. See also "The Revolution of 1848," 8/1/1848, *LW* 1.328, in which Douglass called Turner "a man of noble courage."

104. "The Fall of Sumter," 5/1861, *LW* 3.89; also "The American Apocalypse," 6/16/1861, *TFDP* 3.437. At the same time, Douglass expressed compassion for those who would bear most directly the sorrows of the war; see "Revolutions Never Go Backward," 5/5/1861, *TFDP* 3.429.

105. "Editorial Correspondence," 9/23/1853, *LW* 2.271. See also *LW* 5.169–70.

106. "An Appeal to the British People," 5/2/1846, *LW* 1.159. In all three autobiographies, without commenting on the rightness or wrongness of such a course, Douglass disclosed that as an adolescent boy, he, too, was tempted by the thought of suicide; see *N* 62; *BF* 103; *LT* 88.

107. *LW* 2.437, 568n30.

108. "It was not my enslavement, at the then-present time, that most affected me," Douglass explained as he described his increasingly troubled mind in his early teen years; "the being a slave *for life*, was the saddest thought"; see *BF* 107 (emphasis original); see also *BF* 167. As R. M. Hare has perceptively observed, the human power of foresight (the fact that we "can look a long way ahead") is "the most fundamental point about . . . human nature" that makes ownership by another uniquely intolerable; see Hare, "What Is Wrong with Slavery," in Tommy L. Lott, ed., *Subjugation and Bondage: Critical Essays on Slavery and Social Philosophy* (Lanham, MD: Rowman & Littlefield, 1998), 225.

109. *BF* 182–84. Douglass's closing advice to American slaves in his 1850 open letter to them is characteristic of his hopefulness: "Brethren, our last word to you is to bid you be of good cheer, and not to despair of your deliverance. Do not abandon yourselves, as have many thousands of American slaves, to the crime of suicide. Live! live to escape from slavery, live to serve God!"; see "A Letter to the American Slaves from Those Who Have Fled from American Slavery," 9/5/1850, *LW* 5.169.

110. Despite his reading of Douglass's ambivalence with respect to violence, Ronald Takaki chose as epigraphs for his chapter on Douglass passages from Jean-Paul Sartre's preface to Frantz Fanon's *Wretched of the Earth* and from Richard Wright's *Native Son,* both of which affirm the relation between violence and manhood. See Takaki, *Violence in the Black*

Imagination: Essays and Documents (New York: G. P. Putnam's Sons, 1972), 17–18. See also John Stauffer, *The Black Hearts of Men* (Cambridge, MA: Harvard University Press, 2002).

111. FD to Francis Jackson, 1/29/1846, *LW* 1.135–37.

112. *BF* 151–53.

113. "Freedom in the West Indies," 8/2/1858, *TFDP* 3.215.

114. "American Civilization," 10/1859, *LW* 5.456. See also *BF* 173 (*LT* 163).

115. "Is It Right and Wise to Kill a Kidnapper?" *LW* 2.287.

116. *BF* 161–62.

117. *N* 74; *BF* 136. See also David Van Leer, "Reading Slavery: The Anxiety of Ethnicity in Douglass's *Narrative*," in Eric Sundquist, ed., *Frederick Douglass: New Literary and Historical Essays* (Cambridge: Cambridge University Press, 1990), 120–23.

118. *BF* 130–33; *N* 71–72.

119. This phrase translates as "nevertheless it always returns." See *Horace: Satires, Epistles, and Ars Poetica,* translated by H. Rushton Fairclough (Cambridge, MA: Harvard University Press, 1926), "Epistles," bk. 1, epistle 10,1. 24, p. 316.

120. Machiavelli, *The Prince,* edited by Harvey C. Mansfield, Jr. (Chicago: University of Chicago Press, 1985), chap. 3, p. 10.

121. Shakespeare, *Macbeth* II.2.47; "Vote the Regular Republican Ticket," 7/25/1872, *TFDP* 4.317–18. See also *LW* 5.362–63; *TFDP* 4.366.

122. *LW* 2.149 (emphasis original); cf. *LW* 2.406.

123. An example was Henry Clay, the prominent senator from Kentucky, who observed that the slaves "are rational beings like ourselves, capable of feeling and reflection and of judging what belongs to them as a portion of the human race" and so would be rationally motivated to mount insurrections wherever success seemed possible to them. Quoted in Fredrickson, *The Black Image in the White Mind,* 11.

124. "Letter to the American Slaves from Those Who Have Fled from American Slavery," *LW* 5.165–66. See also "Agriculture and Black Progress," 9/18/1873, *TFDP* 4.387.

125. *BF* 269.

126. *BF* 55–59 (quotation at 57); *N* 41–43.

127. For development of this theme, see especially Harriet Jacobs, "Incidents in the Life of a Slave Girl: Written by Herself" (1861), in Henry Louis Gates, ed., *Classic Slave Narratives* (New York: Mentor Books, 1987), 333–513. Consider also Howard McGary's understated comment, "The experiences of female slaves cast serious doubt on paternalistic explanations of slavery," in "Paternalism and Slavery," in Tommy L. Lott, ed., *Subjugation and Bondage: Critical Essays on Slavery and Social Philosophy* (Lanham, MD: Rowman & Littlefield, 1998), 204.

128. *N* 43; *BF* 59.

129. See especially Moses, *Creative Conflict,* 66–70.

130. *N* 42; *BF* 57–58.

131. *N* 42; *BF* 61.

132. Jenny Franchot refers to Esther as a "surrogate" for Frederick's mother, Harriet·Bailey; see Franchot, "The Punishment of Esther: Frederick Douglass and the Construction of the Feminine," in Eric Sundquist, ed., *Frederick Douglass: New Literary and Historical Essays* (Cambridge: Cambridge University Press, 1990), 141. Harriet Jacobs supplied a likely reason for Harriet Bailey's silence in this matter, explaining that slave mothers often remained silent about the white fathers of their children to shield themselves from the wrath of both the master-fathers and the slave masters' wives; see Jacobs, *Incidents,* 348–49.

133. Compare and contrast *N* 40; *BF* 38, 42; *LT* 29.

134. For the charge of abolitionist pornography, see McFeely, *Frederick Douglass,* 124; Van Leer, "Reading Slavery," 132; Franchot, "The Punishment of Esther," 144; Deborah McDowell, "In the First Place: Making Frederick Douglass and the African-American Narrative Tradition," in William L. Andrews, ed., *Critical Essays on Frederick Douglass* (Boston: G. K. Hall, 1991), 201–6; Willett, *Maternal Ethics,* 146. In his review of McFeely, James McPherson called the charge "arrant nonsense. . . . The post-Freudian biographer here projects what few nineteenth-century reformers intended or saw"; see McPherson, "The Agitator," *New Republic,* March 11, 1991, 38. See also David W. Blight, "Review of Eric J. Sundquist, ed., *Frederick Douglass: New Literary and Historical Essays,*" *Journal of American History* 78, no. 3 (December 1991): 1080–81.

135. See "The Progress of the African Slave Trade" and "Higher Law," *DM* 8/1859; "Dissolution of the American Union," 1/1861, *LW* 3.60–61.

136. "Anti-slavery Movement," *LW* 2.350–51. See also "Dissolution of the Union," 8/31/1855, *LW* 5.354–56; "Dred Scott Decision," *LW* 2.415–17.

137. "Selections," 1/29/1852, *LW* 5.221.

138. "John Brown's Contributions to the Abolition Movement," 12/3/1860, *TFDP* 3.415–16. See also "Is Civil Government Right?" 10/23/1851, *LW* 5.213: "Men need to be taught . . . the dreadful consequences which result from injustice; their fears, therefore, may be as legitimately appealed to as their hopes, and he who repudiates such appeals, throws away an important instrumentality for establishing justice among men."

139. Bernard R. Boxill, "Fear and Shame as Forms of Moral Suasion in the Thought of Frederick Douglass," *Transactions of the Charles S. Pierce Society* 31, no. 4 (1993): 713–44.

140. "John Brown's Contributions to the Abolition Movement," *TFDP* 3.416–17; "West India Emancipation," *LW* 2.439.

141. *BF* 150, 151, 152 (emphasis original); *LT* 142–43.

142. *BF* 61–63; *LT* 51–52.

143. *N* 79–80; *BF* 152; *LT* 143–44.

144. Dickson Preston, *Young Frederick Douglass* (Baltimore, MD: Johns Hopkins University Press, 1980), 129; Moses, *Creative Conflict,* 72. It is possible that Douglass only feigned puzzlement at Covey's forbearance, suspecting all along a benefaction by Auld and refusing to allow any such suspicion to complicate his polemical use of Auld as archetypal slaveholder; consider Douglass's account of masters' general treatment of slaves' complaints of brutality by overseers, in *BF* 56–57. His unsatisfying conjecture in the specific story was that Covey's forbearance was necessitated by his pride and his material interest as a slave breaker, which would have suffered intolerable damage by any publicity of the incident. Margaret Kohn suggests that more immediate material interests dictated Covey's inaction. Having learned from the battle what Douglass himself maintained, that whoever would succeed in whipping Frederick had to succeed in killing him, Covey concluded that the costs were too high: to kill Frederick would have deprived him of Frederick's labor for the year and indebted him to Thomas Auld, along with damaging his valuable reputation as a slave breaker. See Kohn, "Frederick Douglass's Master-Slave Dialectic," 504–5.

The difficulties with both explanations are as follows. It is doubtful that Covey was a paid slave breaker; Thomas Auld told Frederick that Covey had paid him for Frederick's service; see Preston, *Young Frederick Douglass,* 226n22. Covey's restraint was an unlikely means of protecting his reputation, as Douglass reported that "the report got abroad" of his resistance; see *BF* 154. It would seem that a more likely means for Covey to protect his investment in Frederick's labor and his reputation for severity would have been to acknowledge the incident and subject Frederick to a truly terrible chastisement that stopped short of killing him.

145. E.g., see *NS* 2/11/1848, 8/24/1849, 10/19/1849, 9/5/1850; *FDP* 9/10/1852, 7/15/1853, 11/9/ 1855.

146. "Pierce M. Butler's Slave Auction," 4/1859, *LW* 5.426.

147. *BF* 151 (emphasis original).

148. "Anti-slavery Movement," 1/1855, *LW* 2.358. See also *LW* 2.186, 3.342–43, 4.237.

149. "Prospect in the Future," *DM* 8/1860, *LW* 2.496–97.

150. *The Heroic Slave, LW* 5.504, 473–74; "Meaning of July Fourth for the Negro," *LW* 2.186. See also *LW* 2.288, 411, 414–15, 5.318, 3.243, 246; *TFDP* 4.25, 307.

151. "Meaning of July Fourth," *LW* 2.188 (emphasis original).

152. "Capt. John Brown Not Insane," 11/1859, *LW* 2.458–59. See also "Lessons of the Hour," 6/30/1861, *LW* 3.137–41.

153. *BF* 119–20; "The Rebels, the Government, and the Difference between Them," 8/1861, *LW* 3.131. A nice illustration of the general point appears in a contrast between Douglass's literary-cultural judgment and that of a renowned contemporary. In *Life on the Mississippi*, Mark Twain charged that Douglass's much-admired Sir Walter Scott had "run the people mad, a couple of generations ago, with his medieval romances. The South has not yet recovered from the debilitating influence of his books. . . . He did measureless harm; more real and lasting harm, perhaps, than any other individual that ever wrote"; see *The Writings of Mark Twain*, vol. 9 (New York: Harper and Brothers, 1917), 332–33, also 374–76. For the antislavery Twain as for proslavery celebrants of southern chivalry, the heroic spirit was incompatible with liberal, democratic-republican society. But for Douglass, the spirit of Sir Walter Scott, from whom he drew the very emblem of his public identity, should be not exorcised but repatriated, restored to its proper service to the principles of freedom and justice in a liberal, republican America.

154. "Revolutions Never Go Backward," 5/5/1861, *TFDP* 3.433–34.

155. "Anti-slavery Movement," 1/1855, *LW* 2.355–56. See also "Equal Rights for All," 5/14/ 1868, *TFDP* 4.173.

156. "Doom of the Black Power," *LW* 2.364.

157. "Dred Scott Decision," *LW* 2.412–13.

158. "Speech Delivered at the Mass Free Democratic Convention at Ithaca, New York," 10/ 14/1852, *LW* 5.260. Cf. Aileen Kraditor, *Means and Ends in American Abolitionism* (New York: Pantheon Books, 1967), 107–8.

159. *LW* 2.323. See also *LW* 2.358–59, 364, 386, 5.360. Reflecting in 1871 on slavery's demise, Douglass opined, "Nothing on the part of the South . . . did half so much to arouse the hatred of the North against the infernal institution . . . as their absolute denial of the freedom of speech in their midst upon everything touching that question"; see "Liberty of Speech South," 5/4/1871, *LW* 4.245.

160. "Doom of the Black Power," *LW* 2.366.

161. Ibid., 365. In moments of pessimism regarding northern opinion, Douglass also speculated on the possibility of an alliance with southern nonslaveholding whites, disgruntled with the slaveholding class's oligarchic arrogance. Though he did not pursue this theme in his war commentary, this would become an important source of support for the Union in the war. See "Impending Crisis of the South," *DM* 2/1859.

162. "We Are Not Yet Quite Free," *TFDP* 4.230.

163. Jefferson to John Holmes, 4/22/1820, in Adrienne Koch and William Peden, eds., *The Life and Selected Writings of Thomas Jefferson* (New York: Random House, 1944), 698.

164. "Dred Scott Decision," *LW* 2.417; "Meaning of July Fourth for the Negro," *LW* 2.202 and, on the greatness of the Founders, 186–87.

Chapter 3. "The Pound of Flesh, but Not One Drop of Blood": The Constitution against Slavery

1. "The Danger of the Republican Movement," 6/1856, *LW* 5.389. Cf. "Fremont and Dayton," 8/15/1856, *LW* 2.397.

2. See Leslie Friedman Goldstein, "The Political Thought of Frederick Douglass" (PhD diss., Cornell University, 1975), 15, 175–91, and Goldstein, "Morality and Prudence in the Statesmanship of Frederick Douglass: Radical as Reformer," *Polity* 16, no. 4 (Summer 1984): 610; also Robert S. Levine, *Martin Delany, Frederick Douglass, and the Politics of Representative Identity* (Chapel Hill: University of North Carolina Press, 1997), 99–143. Contrast John Stauffer, *The Black Hearts of Men* (Cambridge, MA: Harvard University Press, 2002).

3. In Wendell Phillips, *The Constitution: A Pro-Slavery Compact* (1844; repr., New York: Negro Universities Press, 1969), 108.

4. William Lloyd Garrison, "Declaration of Sentiments of the American Anti-slavery Convention," in *Selections from the Writings and Speeches of William Lloyd Garrison* (1852; repr., New York: Negro Universities Press, 1968), 66.

5. See the New England Non-Resistance Society's 1838 "Declaration of Sentiments," composed by Garrison himself: "As every human government is upheld by physical strength . . . we therefore voluntarily exclude ourselves from every legislative and judicial body, and repudiate all human politics"; see *Liberator*, 9/28/1838. See also Garrison's "The Practical Working of Non-Resistance," "War Essentially Wrong," and "'The Powers That Be Are Ordained of God,'" in *Selections from the Writings and Speeches of William Lloyd Garrison* (1852; repr., New York: Negro Universities Press, 1968), 86–97; letter of Henry C. Wright to Gerrit Smith, 8/26/1851, in *FDP* 10/23/1851.

6. *Liberator*, 3/23/42, cited in Lewis Perry, *Radical Abolitionism* (Ithaca, NY: Cornell University Press, 1973), 89. Douglass referred to this remark in his speech "The Anti-slavery Movement," 1/1855, *LW* 2.351–52.

7. *Liberator*, 12/29/1832, in William E. Cain, ed., *William Lloyd Garrison and the Fight against Slavery* (Boston: Bedford Books, 1995), 87. William M. Wiecek was incorrect in his claims that Garrisonian constitutional ideas were dependent on their embrace of Non-Resistance and perfectionism and that they were little more than rebuttals of Liberty Party arguments; see Wiecek, *The Sources of Antislavery Constitutionalism in America, 1760–1848* (Ithaca, NY: Cornell University Press, 1977), 228.

8. "The American Union," 1/10/1845, in William E. Cain, ed., *William Lloyd Garrison and the Fight against Slavery* (Boston: Bedford Books, 1995), 115.

9. Although Douglass certainly had little desire for personal martyrdom, his main objection to Brown's revised plan was that it "would be an attack on the federal government, and would array the whole country against us"; see *LT* 319. Cf. FD to the *Rochester (NY) Democrat and American*, 10/31/1859, *LW* 2.461–62. This criticism of Brown did not come easily to Douglass, who voiced it despite believing from the beginning that "the old man" was a hero and martyr and despite his strong aversion to conceding any moral

ground to his adversaries. After the outbreak of war, his public judgment of Brown became wholly enthusiastic, facilitated by the fact that northern opinion could then regard Brown not as a treasonous enemy of the United States but rather as something akin to the captain of a vanguard anti-Confederate force. See "The Reasons for Our Troubles," 1/14/1862, *LW* 3.208.

10. "Anti-slavery Movement," 1/1855, *LW* 2.350–52; "Is the United States Constitution for or against Slavery?" *FDP* 7/24/1851, *LW* 5.193; "The Dred Scott Decision," *LW* 2.415–17; "The Dissolution of the Union," *LW* 5.354–56. See also "American Slavery," 1/24/1854, *LW* 5.310.

11. "Is Civil Government Right?" *LW* 5.209–14.

12. "Is the United States Constitution for or against Slavery?" *LW* 5.192.

13. See especially Wiecek, *Sources of Antislavery Constitutionalism,* chaps. 9, 11.

14. Phillips, *The Constitution,* 4–7.

15. Ibid., 5–6, also 96.

16. Ibid., 101, 98, 104, 107.

17. Ibid., 6, 7, also 98–100. See also Garrison, "The United States Constitution," in *Selections from the Writings and Speeches of William Lloyd Garrison* (1852; repr., New York: Negro Universities Press, 1968), 302–15; William I. Bowditch, *Slavery and the Constitution* (Boston: R. F. Walcut, 1849).

18. *BF* 243.

19. See "Change of Opinion Announced," *Liberator,* 5/23/1851, *LW* 2.155–56. On the charge that Douglass had bartered his opinion for Smith's financial support, see FD to Gerrit Smith, 5/21/1851, *LW* 2.156–57. Two years earlier, Douglass had hinted at his impending change of mind; see "The Constitution and Slavery," *NS* 3/16/1849.

20. E.g., Charles Chesnutt, *Frederick Douglass* (1899; repr., Mineola, NY: Dover Publications, 2002), 17; Philip S. Foner, *Frederick Douglass, LW* 2.53; Thomas E. Schneider, *Lincoln's Defense of Politics* (Columbia: University of Missouri Press, 2006), 125–44; James Oakes, *The Radical and the Republican: Frederick Douglass, Abraham Lincoln, and the Triumph of Antislavery Politics* (New York: W. W. Norton, 2007), 14–19. A harsher judgment is that by Charles W. Mills, "Whose Fourth of July? Frederick Douglass and 'Original Intent,'" in Bill E. Lawson and Frank M. Kirkland, eds., *Frederick Douglass: A Critical Reader* (Malden, MA: Blackwell Publishers, 1999), 118–21. More sympathetic are Herbert Storing, "Frederick Douglass," in Morton Frisch and Richard Stevens, eds., *American Political Thought* (Itasca, IL: F. E. Peacock, 1983), 215–36; Goldstein, "Political Thought of Frederick Douglass," 82–150; Diana J. Schaub, "Frederick Douglass's Constitution," in Peter Augustine Lawler and Robert Martin Schaefer, eds., *The American Experiment: Essays on the Theory and Practice of Liberty* (Lanham, MD: Rowman & Littlefield, 1994), 459–77; David E. Schrader, "Natural Law in the Constitutional Thought of Frederick Douglass," in Bill E. Lawson and Frank M. Kirkland, eds., *Frederick Douglass: A Critical Reader* (Malden, MA: Blackwell Publishers, 1999), 85–99.

21. "Slavery Unconstitutional," *FDP* 2/1/1856, *LW* 5.373; "The Final Struggle," 11/16/1855, *LW* 2.378.

22. *BF* 243; also *LT* 260–61; *LW* 2.153, 155–56, 5.463.

23. On this point, I am indebted to Carl Dibble, who generously shared with me a draft chapter, focusing on Douglass, of a larger work on constitutional interpretation.

24. "Change of Opinion Announced," *LW* 2.155; also *LW* 2.420, 5.285. Douglass declared Spooner's work the ablest argument ever written for the antislavery Constitution (*DM* 11/1860), and his argument shows a closer indebtedness to Spooner's than to that of any other

political abolitionist. See Lysander Spooner, *Unconstitutionality of Slavery* (Boston: Bela Marsh, 1845); also Randy Barnett, "Was Slavery Unconstitutional before the Thirteenth Amendment? Lysander Spooner's Theory of Interpretation," *Pacific Law Journal* 28 (Summer 1997): 977–1014. Wilson Jeremiah Moses has also plausibly suggested that Samuel Ringgold Ward, whom Douglass had debated in 1849, probably exercised some influence in persuading Douglass away from the Garrisonian position; see Moses, *Creative Conflict in African American Thought* (Cambridge: Cambridge University Press, 2004), 53–54. See *TFDP* 2.193–97.

25. "Slavery Unconstitutional," *LW* 5.373; "Dred Scott Decision," *LW* 2.418.

26. "The Constitution of the United States: Is It Pro-slavery or Anti-slavery?" 3/26/1860, *LW* 2.476; also *LW* 2.418.

27. "Slavery the Live Issue," 4/11/1854, *TFDP* 2.462. Douglass misquoted slightly. See William Blackstone, "Introduction," sec. 2, *Commentaries on the Laws of England* (Oxford: Clarendon Press, 1765–1769), 53. Some political abolitionists criticized Blackstone for ambiguity with respect to natural-law jurisprudence; see, e.g., William Goodell, *Views of American Constitutional Law, in Its Bearing upon American Slavery* (1845; repr., Freeport, NY: Books for Libraries Press, 1971), 4. See also Robert M. Cover, *Justice Accused: Antislavery and the Judicial Process* (New Haven, CT: Yale University Press, 1975), 25. For the Garrisonian reading of Blackstone, see Wendell Phillips, *Review of Lysander Spooner's Essay on the Unconstitutionality of Slavery* (1847; repr., New York: Arno Press, 1967), 8, 19.

28. "Is It Right and Wise to Kill a Kidnapper?" 6/9/1854, *LW* 5.327, 2.208, 476.

29. "When human government destroys human rights, it ceases to be a government . . . *and is entitled to no respect whatever*"; see "The Fugitive Slave Law," 8/1852, *LW* 2.208 (emphasis added); cf. *LW* 5.327–28.

30. "Constitution of the United States: Is It Pro-slavery or Anti-slavery?" *LW* 2.476 (emphasis added). See also *LW* 5.199.

31. *LW* 2.475–76; "Slavery the Live Issue," *TFDP* 2.465.

32. "Slavery Unconstitutional," *LW* 5.373 (emphasis original); also *LW* 5.198, 2.476. Spooner, *Unconstitutionality of Slavery*, 192, see also 18–19, 164, 189–93, 200–204.

33. "Constitution of the United States: Is It Pro-slavery or Anti-slavery?" *LW* 2.467–68.

34. Ibid., 469; also *LW* 2.157, 418, 5.196, 373. In support of his textualism, Douglass could appeal to the authority of James Madison himself: "The legitimate meaning of the Instrument must be derived from the text itself; or if a key is to be sought elsewhere, it must not be in the opinions or intentions of the Body which planned & proposed the Constitution, but in the sense attached to it by the people in their respective State Conventions"; see James Madison to Thomas Ritchie, 9/15/1821, in Philip B. Kurland and Ralph Lerner, eds., *The Founders' Constitution* (Chicago: University of Chicago Press, 1987), 1:74. Cf. Spooner, *Unconstitutionality of Slavery*, 57–58, 114–23, 171–79; William Goodell, *Slavery and Anti-slavery: A History of the Great Struggle in Both Hemispheres; with a View of the Slavery Question in the United States* (New York: William Harned Publisher, 1852), 574.

35. Joseph Story, *A Familiar Exposition of the Constitution of the United States* (1840; repr., Lake Bluff, IL: Regnery Gateway, 1986), 56: "This Preamble is very important, not only as explanatory of the motives and objects of framing the Constitution; but, as affording the best key to the true interpretation thereof."

36. "Dred Scott Decision," 5/11/1857, *LW* 2.418; "Slavery Unconstitutional," *LW* 5.375–76; Spooner, *Unconstitutionality of Slavery*, 94, 180–81, 198–99.

37. "Slavery Unconstitutional," *LW* 5.374 (emphasis original); Spooner, *Unconstitutionality of Slavery*, 196–97.

38. *Dred Scott v. Sandford*, 60 U.S. 393 (1857), at 451.

39. *BF* 243; "We Are in the Midst of a Moral Revolution," 5/10/1854, *TFDP* 2.481; "Colored Men's Rights in This Republic," 5/14/1857, *TFDP* 3.147. Cf. *TFDP* 3.178–79; *LW* 2.420–21; Phillips, *The Constitution*, 5–6, 96.

40. Phillips, *The Constitution*, 100–101.

41. "What to the Slave Is the Fourth of July?" *LW* 2.202 (*TFDP* 2.386).

42. "Constitution of the United States," *LW* 2.475, 477; "Dred Scott Decision," *LW* 2.418–19, 424. For Madison on the exclusion of the word *slavery* from the Constitution, see James Madison, *Notes of Debates in the Federal Convention of 1787*, edited by Adrienne Koch (1840; repr., Athens: Ohio University Press, 1966), 532.

43. "Constitution of the United States: Is It Pro-slavery or Anti-slavery?" *LW* 2.471–76; Spooner, *Unconstitutionality of Slavery*, 67–72, 277–87; Goodell, *Views of American Constitutional Law*, 21–27.

44. "Dred Scott Decision," *LW* 2.419. Spooner presented a still more emphatic statement of the constitutional importance of the Declaration, in *Unconstitutionality of Slavery*, 36–39.

45. Phillips, *The Constitution*, 97; "Strong to Suffer, and Yet Strong to Strive," 4/16/1886, *TFDP* 5.217–18; "Slavery Unconstitutional," *LW* 5.375.

46. Douglass seems to have been guilty of an excessively enthusiastic nationalism in his reading of the habeas corpus guarantee and the Fifth Amendment here. Article I, section 9, containing the habeas corpus guarantee, seems clearly marked as a set of denials of power to the Congress or the U.S. government, in contrast to Article I, section 10, which denies powers specifically to the states (and makes no mention of the habeas corpus right). Cf. Spooner, *Unconstitutionality of Slavery*, 102–4. Douglass's reading of the Fifth Amendment may reflect the influence of Goodell (see his *Views of American Constitutional Law*, 58–67), although Douglass went beyond Goodell in his nationalistic reading of the amendment. Wiecek has pointed out that the Supreme Court's ruling in *Barron v. Baltimore* (1833), holding that the Bill of Rights, in particular the Fifth Amendment, restrained exclusively the national government and not the states, remained a matter of legal controversy even in state and federal courts at least through the 1840s; see Wiecek, *Sources of Antislavery Constitutionalism*, 265–67.

47. "The Republican Party—Our Position," 12/7/1855, *LW* 2.379–82. See also *LW* 2.109, 473, 477–78, 3.137, 5.197–98; *TFDP* 3.177.

48. "Republican Party," *LW* 2.381; *BF* 242.

49. "Constitution of the United States: Is It Pro-slavery or Anti-slavery?" *LW* 2.480. See also *LW* 5.197.

50. "Constitution of the United States: Is It Pro-slavery or Anti-slavery?" 469. See Spooner, *Unconstitutionality of Slavery*, 119, 122.

51. Phillips, *The Constitution*, 3–6, 94, 96, 98, 104; also Phillips, *Review of Lysander Spooner*, 27–34.

52. Phillips, *The Constitution*, 96 (emphasis original). Justice Joseph Story accepted this claim with particular reference to the fugitive slave clause (Article IV, section 2.3), writing for the Supreme Court majority in *Prigg v. Pennsylvania*, 41 U.S. 539 (1842), at 564–65, 611–12.

53. FD to Gerrit Smith, 1/21/1851, *LW* 2.149–50.

54. Gouverneur Morris summarized the dissenting Founders' view: "The admission of slaves into the Representation when fairly explained comes to this: that the inhabitant of

Georgia and South Carolina who goes to the coast of Africa, and in defiance of the most sacred laws of humanity tears away his fellow creatures from their dearest connections and damns them to the most cruel bondages, shall have more votes in a Government instituted for protection of the rights of mankind, than the Citizen of Pennsylvania or New Jersey who views with such a laudable horror, so nefarious a practice"; quoted in Madison, *Notes of Debates in the Federal Convention of 1787,* 411.

55. "Constitution of the United States: Is It Pro-slavery or Anti-slavery?" *LW* 2.472. Some support for Douglass's position appears in *Federalist* no. 54, where Publius defends Article I, section 2 as a concession made by slaveholding states, who "waived" application of the principle "that the slaves, as inhabitants, should have been admitted into the census according to their full number." Cf. Don E. Fehrenbacher's remark: "[The] characterization of the three-fifths clause as a *bonus* for slaveholders . . . is not intrinsically sounder than the view (held by Frederick Douglass, for instance) that it was a *penalty* on slaveholding"; see Fehrenbacher, *The Slaveholding Republic: An Account of the United States Government's Relations to Slavery,* completed and edited by Ward M. McAfee (New York: Oxford University Press, 2001), 40 (emphasis original). For a rejoinder, see Akhil Reed Amar, *America's Constitution: A Biography* (New York: Random House, 2005), 87–98. See also Paul Finkelman, *Slavery and the Founders: Race and Liberty in the Age of Jefferson* (New York: M. E. Sharpe, 2001), 3–36, 109–11.

56. Declaring that part of the price of union to slaveholders was that "the slave trade shall be put an end to in twenty years," Douglass seemed to confuse the delegation of a *power* to abolish the slave trade, which Congress could choose or decline to exercise, with a *mandate* to abolish the slave trade at a date certain. This was either a simple error or a polemical exaggeration, confirmed by events, of the confidence of many framers that this clause would ensure the abolition of the slave trade in twenty years. Cf. Goodell, *Views of American Constitutional Law,* 29, 110.

57. "Constitution of the United States," *LW* 2.473; "Is the United States Constitution for or against Slavery?" 7/24/1851, *LW* 5.197–98.

58. "Constitution of the United States: Is It Pro-slavery or Anti-slavery?" *LW* 2.474–75. See also *LW* 5.310, 328. Cf. Phillips, *The Constitution,* 31–33, 105–6; Madison, *Notes of Debates in the Federal Convention,* 532, 545–46, 552, 648.

59. See 60 U.S. 393 (1857), at 534–64, 624–26.

60. *LT* 265–67; Benjamin Quarles, *Frederick Douglass* (1948; repr., New York: Atheneum, 1969), 116–19.

61. "Is It Right and Wise to Kill a Kidnapper?" *FDP* 6/9/1854, *LW* 5.327–28.

62. FD to Gerrit Smith, 1/21/1851, *LW* 2.149; "Is the U.S. Constitution for or against Slavery?" *FDP* 7/24/1851, *LW* 5.196.

63. "Constitution of the United States," *LW* 2.474; "Eulogy on the Late Honorable William Jay," *LW* 5.449.

64. "Progress of Slavery," 8/1859, *LW* 2.454; "Constitution of the United States: Is It Pro-slavery or Anti-slavery?" *LW* 2.473. Cf. "Dred Scott Decision," *LW* 2.422–23; "The Reproach and Shame of the American Government," 8/2/1858, *LW* 5.401–2. For elaborations of this argument, see Thomas G. West, *Vindicating the Founders* (Lanham, MD: Rowman & Littlefield, 1997), 1–36; Harry V. Jaffa, *A New Birth of Freedom* (Lanham, MD: Rowman & Littlefield, 2000), 216–22, 285–98.

65. "Reproach and Shame of the American Government," *LW* 5.402; "Is the Plan of the American Union under the Constitution, Anti-slavery or Not?" 5/20/1857, *TFDP* 3.153. See also *LW* 2.473; *TFDP* 3.180.

66. "The American statesmen, in providing for the abolition of the slave trade, thought they were providing for the abolition of slavery"; see "Constitution of the United States," *LW* 2.473. At the Pennsylvania ratifying convention, James Wilson remarked on this clause in Article I, section 9: "I consider this as laying the foundation for banishing slavery out of this country"; quoted in Jonathan Elliot, ed., *The Debates in the Several State Conventions on the Adoption of the Federal Constitution* (Washington, DC: Printed for the editor, 1836), 2:452, accessed 11/30/2006 at http://memory.loc.gov/ammem/amlaw/lwed.html. Cf. David Brion Davis, *The Problem of Slavery in the Age of Revolution* (Ithaca, NY: Cornell University Press, 1975), 129, 311–13, 404–19.

67. "The Cause of the Negro People," 10/4/1864, *LW* 3.417.

68. "The Slaveholders' Rebellion," *DM* 8/1862, *LW* 3.247.

69. "Address for the Promotion of Colored Enlistments," 8/1863, *LW* 3.365.

70. Herbert Storing, "Slavery and the Moral Foundations of the American Republic," in Robert H. Horwitz, ed., *The Moral Foundations of the American Republic* (Charlottesville: University Press of Virginia, 1979), 221; Goldstein, "Political Thought of Frederick Douglass," 115–17; Schaub, "Frederick Douglass's Constitution," 473–74.

71. *LW* 3.249.

72. E.g., "The Fugitive Slave Law (Address to the National Free-Soil Convention)," 8/11/1852, *LW* 2.206–7; "Anti-slavery Movement," *LW* 2.353; "Republican Party—Our Position," *LW* 2.379–83; "What Is My Duty as an Anti-slavery Voter?" *FDP* 4/25/1856, *LW* 2.391–93; "Danger of the Republican Movement," 5/28/1856, *LW* 5.386–87; "Fremont and Dayton," *FDP* 8/25/1856, *LW* 2.396–401.

73. Spooner, *Unconstitutionality of Slavery,* 126 (emphasis added).

74. "Dred Scott Decision," *LW* 2.422; *TFDP* 3.180 (emphasis added). See also "Is the U.S. Constitution for or against Slavery?" *LW* 5.196.

75. Cf. Don Fehrenbacher's incisive comment: "It is as though the framers were half-consciously trying to frame two constitutions, one for their own time and the other for the ages, with slavery viewed bifocally—that is, plainly visible at their feet, but disappearing when they lifted their eyes"; see Fehrenbacher, *The Dred Scott Case: Its Significance in American Law and Politics* (Oxford: Oxford University Press, 1978), 27.

76. I take the term from Wiecek, *Sources of Antislavery Constitutionalism,* e.g., at 16.

77. "Report of Speech at Anti-slavery Meeting," 1/15/1860, *LW* 5.464; "Slaveholders' Rebellion," 7/4/1862, *LW* 3.249. At times, Douglass doubted that a specific consensus concerning slavery existed even among the framers; see "Is the United States Constitution for or against Slavery?" *LW* 5.198. See also Fehrenbacher, *Dred Scott Case,* 11–27.

78. Phillips, *The Constitution,* 96.

79. See "Dred Scott Decision," *LW* 2.410; "Slaveholders' Rebellion," *LW* 3.246–50.

80. The language belongs to Lincoln, for whom the wisdom of the Founders and subsequent compromisers such as Kentucky senator Henry Clay (a main architect of the Compromise of 1850) consisted in settling the American public mind in the conviction that slavery was unjust and fated to ultimate extinction. See Lincoln, "'A House Divided': Speech before the Republican State Convention," 6/16/1858, and "First Debate, at Ottawa, Illinois," 8/21/1858, both in Roy P. Basler, ed., *Abraham Lincoln: His Speeches and Writings* (Cambridge, MA: Da Capo Press, 2001), 372–73, 446–47.

81. "The True Ground Upon Which to Meet Slavery," 8/24/1855, *LW* 2.369; also *LW* 2.382.

82. Foner, *Frederick Douglass,* in *LW* 2.12, 3.9–10, 11–29. See also James A. Colaiaco, *Frederick Douglass and the Fourth of July* (New York: Palgrave Macmillan, 2006), 192–98. Contrast

Allison Davis, *Leadership, Love, and Aggression* (New York: Harcourt Brace Jovanovich, 1983), 77–81; Schneider, *Lincoln's Defense of Politics;* Oakes, *The Radical and the Republican,* especially 149–52, 217–19, 266–75.

83. Cover, *Justice Accused,* 154–58; Wiecek, *Sources of Antislavery Constitutionalism,* 249; Mills, "Whose Fourth of July?" 115–16.

84. See Oakes, *The Radical and the Republican,* 82–85, 171.

85. William H. Seward, U.S. senator from New York and leading Republican candidate for the presidency in the 1860 election, made famous the phrase *irrepressible conflict* in a campaign speech on October 25, 1858; it is excerpted in William H. Pease and Jane H. Pease, eds., *The Antislavery Argument* (Indianapolis, IN: Bobbs-Merrill, 1965), 177–81. See *LW* 2.483; *TFDP* 3.376.

86. From the onset of war until Lincoln's Preliminary Emancipation Proclamation in September 1862, this insistence on an abolitionist (not merely restorationist) war sharply divided Douglass from Lincoln. See "The Inaugural Address," *DM* 4/1861, *LW* 3.71–80; "General Fremont's Proclamation to the Rebels of Missouri," *DM* 10/1861, *LW* 3.159–62; "The Slave Power Still Omnipotent at Washington," *DM* 1/1862, *LW* 3.185–87; "The President and His Speeches," *DM* 9/1862, *LW* 3.266–70. Evidence unknown to Douglass shows, however, that Lincoln affirmed from the early months the ultimate need for an abolition war. See Allen C. Guelzo, *Lincoln's Emancipation Proclamation* (New York: Simon & Schuster, 2004). Lincoln's refusal to order emancipation earlier stemmed largely from his concern to avoid alienating the loyal slave states, whose continued loyalty to the Union he regarded as crucial to the Union cause. On this vital point of military strategy, Douglass simply disagreed; see *LW* 3.123, 155, 186. But if Douglass was wrong on this point, then his policy of immediate federally imposed abolition would have proved a calamitous error. Years later, he seemed to concede that Lincoln had been right after all, as he praised the martyred president's comprehensive statesmanship in his oration at the unveiling of the Freedmen's Monument in 1876; see "The Freedmen's Monument to Abraham Lincoln," *TFDP* 4.436–37. See Oakes, *The Radical and the Republican,* 133–202, especially 149–52.

87. "Hope and Despair in These Cowardly Times," 4/28/1861, *TFDP* 3.427–28.

Chapter 4. "Let Us Alone": Race and the Constitution of Liberty

1. *LT* 373.

2. "In What New Skin Will the Old Snake Come Forth?" 5/10/1865, *TFDP* 4.79–85; William Lloyd Garrison, "Valedictory: The Last Number of *The Liberator*" (12/29/1865), in William E. Cain, ed., *William Lloyd Garrison and the Fight against Slavery* (Boston: Bedford Books, 1995), 179–83.

3. "What the Black Man Wants," 1/26/1865, *TFDP* 4.68 (*LW* 4.164). See also "What Shall Be Done with the Slaves If Emancipated?" *DM* 1/1862, *LW* 3.188–91; "The Future of the Negro People of the Slave States," *DM* 3/1862, *LW* 3.217–18; "The Present and Future of the Colored Race in America," *DM* 6/1863, *LW* 3.347.

4. "Present and Future of the Colored Race in America," *LW* 3.347.

5. E.g., Thomas R. Dew, "Abolition of Slavery," in Drew Gilpin Faust, ed., *The Ideology of Slavery* (Baton Rouge: Louisiana State University Press, 1981), 56–57; E. N. Elliot, "Introduction," in Elliot, ed., *Cotton Is King, and Pro-slavery Arguments* (1860; repr., New York: Negro Universities Press, 1969), ix; Thomas R. R. Cobb, "What Is Slavery, and Its Foundation in

the Natural Law," in Paul Finkelman, ed., *Defending Slavery: Proslavery Thought in the Old South* (Boston: Bedford/St. Martin's, 2003), 155–56.

6. "What Shall Be Done with the Slaves If Emancipated?" *LW* 3.188.

7. *Federalist* no. 14, in Clinton Rossiter, ed., *The Federalist Papers* (New York: Mentor Books, 1961), 104.

8. "The Work of the Future," *DM* 11/1862, *LW* 3.290.

9. "What the Black Man Wants," *TFDP* 4.68; also *LW* 3.188–89, 218, 4.272.

10. William S. McFeely, *Frederick Douglass* (New York: W. W. Norton, 1991), 242, 293, 303. Cf. Peter F. Walker, *Moral Choices: Memory, Desire, and Imagination in Nineteenth-Century American Abolition* (Baton Rouge: Louisiana State University Press, 1978), 216–17, 276–77; Waldo E. Martin, Jr., *The Mind of Frederick Douglass* (Chapel Hill: University of North Carolina Press, 1984), 67–69, 132.

11. Wilson Jeremiah Moses, *Creative Conflict in African American Thought* (Cambridge: Cambridge University Press, 2004), 5–7, 43–45, 107–8. Cf. David W. Blight, *Frederick Douglass's Civil War: Keeping Faith in Jubilee* (Baton Rouge: Louisiana State University Press, 1989), 178, 194.

12. "Let the Negro Alone," 5/11/1869, *TFDP* 4.202–3.

13. Ibid. (emphasis added).

14. "Future of the Negro People of the Slave States," *LW* 3.218 (emphasis added). See also "What Shall Be Done with the Slaves If Emancipated?" *LW* 3.190.

15. "Self-Made Men," 3/1893, *TFDP* 5.557.

16. Allison Davis, *Leadership, Love, and Aggression* (New York: Harcourt Brace Jovanovich, 1983), 17–98; Eric J. Sundquist, *To Wake the Nations: Race in the Making of American Literature* (Cambridge, MA: Belknap Press, 1993), 93–106.

17. *LT* 480.

18. Douglass's exhortations to self-reliance in one form or another are too numerous for particular citation. For a representative sampling, see *LW* 1.281, 314–16, 334, 2.119, 150, 360, 403, 435–36, 497, 518, 4.224, 449, 5.238, 305; *TFDP* 2.453, 3.611–23, 5.545–75.

19. On the Emersonian influence or relation, see Martin, *Mind of Frederick Douglass,* 255, 262–63; McFeely, *Frederick Douglass,* 115; John Stauffer, *The Black Hearts of Men* (Cambridge, MA: Harvard University Press, 2002), 35–37. For the comparison of Douglass to Franklin, see especially Rafia Zafar, "Franklinian Douglass: The African-American as Representative Man," in Eric J. Sundquist, ed., *Frederick Douglass: New Literary and Historical Essays* (Cambridge: Cambridge University Press, 1990), 99–117; also Martin, *Mind of Frederick Douglass,* 254; William L. Andrews, *To Tell a Free Story: The First Century of African-American Autobiography* (Urbana: University of Illinois Press, 1986), 118; Moses, *Creative Conflict,* 153.

20. See John Locke, *Second Treatise of Government* (originally published in 1690), in *Locke: Two Treatises of Government,* edited by Peter Laslett (Cambridge: Cambridge University Press, 1988), secs. 27, 44, 123 (on self-ownership, also on rights as properties), and 27–30, 36–46 (on productive labor as the basis of property rights), and also Locke, *An Essay Concerning Human Understanding,* edited by Peter Nidditch (Oxford: Clarendon Press, 1975), secs. 2.27.17–18, 26 (on the nature of the human self or person).

21. "Great Britain's Example Is High, Noble, and Grand," 8/6/1885, *TFDP* 5.206.

22. "Introduction to the Reason Why the Colored American Is Not in the World's Columbian Exposition," *LW* 4.476–77. On the success of other peoples in rising despite adversity, see *LW* 3.327, 5.190; *TFDP* 3.146; *LT* 503–5.

23. "The Blessings of Liberty and Education," 9/3/1894, *TFDP* 5.622. See also *TFDP* 5.128–37.

24. See "Black Freedom Is the Prerequisite of Victory," 1/13/1865, *TFDP* 4.57; George Fredrickson, *The Black Image in the White Mind: The Debate on African-American Character and Destiny, 1817–1914* (New York: Harper & Row, 1971), chap. 8.

25. "Agriculture and Black Progress," 9/18/1873, *TFDP* 4.393. See also *LT* 283 (recalling an 1853 conversation with Harriet Beecher Stowe); "Remarks at the Odd Fellows Festival," 1/1854, *LW* 5.305; "The Lessons of Emancipation to the New Generation," 8/3/1880, *TFDP* 4.565; "Coming Home," 6/17/1877, *TFDP* 4.480.

26. "Lessons of Emancipation to the New Generation," *TFDP* 4.566. See also FD to Harriet Beecher Stowe, 3/8/1853, *LW* 2.235 (also *LT* 289); "Measuring the Progress of the Colored Race," 5/22/1886, *TFDP* 5.241; "Boyhood in Baltimore," 9/6/1891, *TFDP* 5.484.

27. "Agriculture and Black Progress," *TFDP* 4.393–94.

28. Ibid., 394; *BF* 160 (*LT* 149).

29. "A Friendly Word to Maryland," 11/17/1864, *TFDP* 4.50. See also *TFDP* 4.479–80, 5.206–7.

30. Leon F. Litwack, *Been in the Storm So Long: The Aftermath of Slavery* (New York: Random House, 1979), 340–41.

31. *BF* 143, 155; *LT* 133, 147; "The Negro Exodus from the Gulf States," 9/12/1879, *LW* 4.340 (also *LT* 438). On masters' aversion to labor, see also *LW* 5.333, 3.222, 3.332; *TFDP* 2.404, 4.465–66, 4.514, 5.568–70. Cf. Thomas Jefferson, *Notes on the State of Virginia*, Query XVIII: "Of the proprietors of slaves a very small proportion indeed are ever seen to labour," in Adrienne Koch and William Peden, eds., *The Life and Selected Writings of Thomas Jefferson* (New York: Random House, 1944), 278.

32. *BF* 393 (emphasis added).

33. *BF* 148; *LT* 139. Cf. *TFDP* 4.188. Douglass was aware, however, that the religious beliefs of slaves could hardly be characterized as exclusively nonresistant, as the example of Nat Turner, above all, made clear. See Lawrence W. Levine, *Black Culture and Black Consciousness: African-American Folk Thought from Slavery to Freedom* (New York: Oxford University Press, 1977), 43–50, 76–77; Albert Raboteau, *Slave Religion: The "Invisible Institution" in the Antebellum South* (New York: Oxford University Press, 1978), 290–318.

34. "Great Britain's Example Is High, Noble, and Grand," 8/6/1885, *TFDP* 5.207–8.

35. "West India Emancipation," *LW* 2.436. See also *LW* 3.112. On Douglass and the "gospel of wealth," see Benjamin Quarles, *Frederick Douglass* (1948; repr., New York: Atheneum, 1969), 335; Walker, *Moral Choices*, 216.

36. *TFDP* 5.514–18.

37. "Agriculture and Black Progress," *TFDP* 4.391–92.

38. *TFDP* 5.556, 558. See also *LT* 505–6; "Measuring the Progress of the Colored Race," 5/22/1886, *TFDP* 5.241.

39. "Present and Future of the Colored Race in America," *LW* 3.350–51.

40. It was also an issue on which he remained in complete agreement with Garrison, who had published his anticolonization views in *Thoughts on African Colonization* (1832; repr., New York: Arno Press, 1968). An excerpt appeared as "Exposure of the American Colonization Society," in *Selections from the Writings and Speeches of William Lloyd Garrison* (1852; repr., New York: Negro Universities Press, 1968), 13–44.

41. Benjamin Quarles, *Black Abolitionists* (New York: Oxford University Press, 1969), chap. 1.

42. "American Colonization Society," 6/8/1849, *LW* 1.390.

43. See Jefferson, *Notes on the State of Virginia*, Query XIV, in Adrienne Koch and William Peden, eds., *The Life and Selected Writings of Thomas Jefferson* (New York: Random House, 1944), 255–62; James Madison, "Memorandum on an African Colony for Freed Slaves," in Philip Kurland and Ralph Lerner, eds., *The Founders' Constitution* (Indianapolis, IN: Liberty Fund Press, 1987), 1:552.

44. See Thomas G. West, *Vindicating the Founders* (Lanham, MD: Rowman & Littlefield, 1997), 25–30.

45. "The Destiny of Colored Americans," 11/16/1849, *LW* 1.417 (emphasis original); "Why Is the Negro Lynched?" 1/1894, *LW* 4.515.

46. "Destiny of Colored Americans," *LW* 1.417; "Colonization," *NS* 1/26/1849, *LW* 1.351 (emphasis original). See also "Present and Future of the Colored Race in America," *LW* 3.350.

47. "Why Should a Colored Man Enlist?" 4/1863, *LW* 3.343; "American Colonization Society," *LW* 1.394; "Future of the Negro People of the Slave States," 3/1862, *LW* 3.223; "Work and Self-Elevation," *TFDP* 2.478. See also *TFDP* 3.311; *LW* 3.197, 5.456; *TFDP* 4.415.

48. "Present and Future of the Colored Race in America," *LW* 3.351.

49. E.g., *BF* 214–15, 244–45; *LT* 223–25, 268–69; *LW* 1.301–3, 371–74, 2.121–30, 449–50, 5.72–74, 167–68, 231–33.

50. "Our Recent Western Tour," *DM* 4/1859, *LW* 2.450; "Colored Churches—No. III," *NS* 3/10/1848, *LW* 5.72.

51. *LT* 462–63; cf. "The Would-Be Democrats at Syracuse," *DM* 12/1861, *LW* 3.182. Booker T. Washington, "On Making Our Race Life Count in the Life of the Nation" (1906), in Howard Brotz, ed., *African-American Social and Political Thought: 1850–1920* (New Brunswick, NJ: Transaction Publishers, 1991), 382.

52. *LT* 474; cf. *LW* 2.123, 448, 3.351; *TFDP* 4.63; *LW* 4.288, 5.72–73. Contrast Herbert Storing, "Frederick Douglass," in Morton Frisch and Richard Stevens, eds., *American Political Thought* (Itasca, IL: F. E. Peacock, 1983), 231.

53. "Present and Future of the Colored Race in America," *LW* 3.351.

54. "A Day for Poetry and Song," *DM* 1/1863, *LW* 3.311–12; "Emancipation, Racism, and the Work before Us," 12/4/1863, *TFDP* 3.599–600.

55. "Let the Negro Alone," 5/11/1869, *TFDP* 4.200–201.

56. "The Color Line," 6/1881, *LW* 4.347.

57. Orlando Patterson, *Rituals of Blood: Consequences of Slavery in Two American Centuries* (New York: Basic Civitas Books, 1998), 169–232; Fredrickson, *Black Image*, 171–76, 255.

58. Du Bois, *Black Reconstruction in America, 1860–1880* (1935; repr., New York: Atheneum, 1969), 167, 166–81. My brief summary of the Black Codes draws also on Theodore Brantner Wilson, *The Black Codes of the South* (Tuscaloosa: University of Alabama Press, 1965), who takes a more even-handed view of the codes than did Du Bois; Litwack, *Been in the Storm So Long*, 366–71; Eric Foner, *Reconstruction: America's Unfinished Revolution, 1863–1877* (New York: Harper & Row, 1988), 199–210.

59. "We Are Not Yet Quite Free," 8/3/1869, *TFDP* 4.235–36. See also "Let the Negro Alone," 5/11/1869, *TFDP* 4.202; "In Law Free; In Fact, a Slave," 4/16/1888, *TFDP* 5.362–70.

60. "Give Us the Freedom Intended for Us," 12/5/1872, *LW* 4.298; "At Last, at Last, the Black Man Has a Future," 4/22/1870, *TFDP* 4.271–72.

61. "This Democratic Conversion Should Not Be Trusted," 9/25/1872, *TFDP* 4.341. See also *TFDP* 4.83, 299, 328–29.

62. "What Shall Be Done with the Slaves If Emancipated?" 1/1862, *LW* 3.189.

63. "Politics an Evil to the Negro?" 8/24/1871, *LW* 4.272. See also "Comments on Gerrit Smith's Address," 3/30/1849, *LW* 1.374–75; "In Law Free; In Fact, a Slave," 4/16/1888, *TFDP* 5.369.

64. "Is Civil Government Right?" *FDP* 10/23/1851, *LW* 5.209–10. See also FD to Gerrit Smith, 8/4/1851, *LW* 5.200, and "Neutrality," *DM* 4/1860; Leslie Friedman Goldstein, "The Political Thought of Frederick Douglass" (PhD diss., Cornell University, 1975), 66–81.

65. "What the Black Man Wants," 1/26/1865, *TFDP* 4.62; "In What New Skin Will the Old Snake Come Forth?" 5/10/1865, *TFDP* 4.83.

66. "Equal Rights for All," 5/14/1868, *TFDP* 4.175; "At Last, at Last, the Black Man Has a Future," 4/22/1870, *TFDP* 4.266–67.

67. "What the Black Man Wants," *TFDP* 4.63 (emphasis original); "Women's Rights Are Not Inconsistent with Negro Rights," 11/19/1868, *TFDP* 4.183; "Black Freedom Is the Prerequisite of Victory," 1/13/1865, *TFDP* 4.59.

68. "Who and What Is Woman?" 5/24/1886, *TFDP* 5.255.

69. "The Cause of the Negro People," 10/4–7/1864, *LW* 3.420; "Reply of the Colored Delegation to the President," 2/7/1866, *LW* 4.192–93; "Give Us the Freedom Intended for Us," 12/5/1872, *LW* 4.298, *LT* 379–81, 396; "Women's Rights Are Not Inconsistent with Negro Rights," 11/19/1868, *TFDP* 4.183.

70. "What the Black Man Wants," *TFDP* 4.63 (emphasis added). See also "Politics an Evil to the Negro?" *LW* 4.273.

71. "Representatives of the Future South," 4/12/1864, *TFDP* 4.29; "What the Black Man Wants," *TFDP* 4.63–64. On friendship and republicanism, see also *LW* 3.291.

72. "Reconstruction," 12/1866, *LW* 4.199.

73. *LT* 379–80.

74. "The Issues of the Day," 3/10/1866, *TFDP* 4.120–21; "Reconstruction," *LW* 4.199–200.

75. "The Material and Moral Requirements of Antislavery Work," 8/5/1847, *TFDP* 2.89; *LW* 4.381; *BF* 152 (emphasis original). Douglass referred to Gore as Austin Gore (*BF* 77); the evidence of his real name was unearthed by Dickson Preston, *Young Frederick Douglass* (Baltimore, MD: Johns Hopkins University Press, 1980), 222n8.

76. "Is Civil Government Right?" *LW* 5.211.

77. *BF* 223; "Abolition in Russia," 1/7/1853, *LW* 5.263; "The Meaning of July Fourth for the Negro," 7/5/1852, *LW* 2.201; "Politics an Evil to the Negro?" *LW* 4.271; "Women's Rights Are Not Inconsistent with Negro Rights," 11/19/1868, *TFDP* 4.182.

78. "Sources of Danger to the Republic," 2/7/1867, *TFDP* 4.152, 162–70.

79. Summarized in "Appendix A: Précis of Alternate Texts," *TFDP* 4.594.

80. Quarles, *Frederick Douglass*, 235.

81. In addition to "Is Civil Government Right?" (1851), see Douglass's scathing denunciation of spurious American republicanism as represented by the James Buchanan administration, in "Slavery and the Irrepressible Conflict," 8/1/1860, *TFDP* 3.373.

82. "Sources of Danger," *TFDP* 4.158 (emphasis added).

83. In at least one version of the "Sources of Danger" speech, Douglass counseled against attacking the Supreme Court. Summarized in Appendix A, *TFDP* 4.593.

84. "This Decision Has Humbled the Nation," 10/22/1883, *TFDP* 5.111–23.

85. *TFDP* 4.157.

86. For an extended discussion of this theme, see Harry V. Jaffa, *A New Birth of Freedom* (Lanham, MD: Rowman & Littlefield, 2000), 1–72.

87. "Sources of Danger to the Republic," *TFDP* 4.157–58; also *TFDP* 4.182, 472. Contrast *Federalist* no. 39.

88. "Sources of Danger," *TFDP* 4.164. On legislative primacy, see also "Our National Capital," 5/8/1877, *TFDP* 4.470. On "auxiliary precautions," see *Federalist* no. 51.

89. *TFDP* 5.114.

90. "Is Civil Government Right?" *LW* 5.211–12; "Women's Rights Are Not Inconsistent with Negro Rights," *TFDP* 4.184.

91. "Sources of Danger to the Republic," *TFDP* 4.164–65, 154–56.

92. "Cause of the Negro People," 10/4–7/1864, *LW* 3.420.

93. For Calhoun on the "numerical majority" and on southern unity, see, respectively, "A Disquisition on Government," and "Speech at the Meeting of the Citizens of Charleston," 3/9/1847, both in Ross M. Lence, ed., *Union and Liberty: The Political Philosophy of John C. Calhoun* (Indianapolis, IN: Liberty Fund, 1992), 23–24, 525–37.

94. According to David W. Blight, in advocating federal coercion of the formerly rebellious states, "Douglass had abandoned one of his own first principles," namely, the Declaration's principle of consent; Blight, *Frederick Douglass's Civil War,* 71. But the suspension of consent that Douglass contemplated was consistent with the argument of the Declaration. The right of consent presupposes moral rationality and thus a commitment to law-abidingness. Union forces therefore had a right to rule ex-Confederates without their consent until the latter showed themselves to be free of further criminal intention against the rights of their fellow citizens and the security of the Union. See Locke, *Second Treatise of Government,* secs. 7–11, 16–20, 23–24, 172.

95. *Federalist* no. 10, in Clinton Rossiter, ed., *The Federalist Papers* (New York: Mentor Books, 1961), 81; also *Federalist* no. 9.

96. "Let the Negro Alone," *TFDP* 4.205.

97. "In Law Free; In Fact, a Slave," *TFDP* 5.369; "Comments on Gerrit Smith's Address," 3/30/1849, *LW* 1.374–75.

98. "We Are Not Yet Quite Free," *TFDP* 4.235–36; "In Law Free; In Fact, a Slave," *TFDP* 5.363–70; "The Nation's Problem," 4/16/1889, *TFDP* 5.419–20. In "What the Black Man Wants," Douglass asked, "What is freedom?" and answered simply, "It is the right to choose one's own employment"; *TFDP* 4.61.

99. "What the Black Man Wants," *TFDP* 4.62; "In What New Skin Will the Old Snake Come Forth?" *TFDP* 4.81–82.

100. McFeely, *Frederick Douglass,* 289–95, is unjustly harsh in his judgment of Douglass's position relative to the compromise and to the Hayes administration. He charges Douglass with complicity in the betrayal of the freedpeople, purchased by his lucrative and prestigious appointment as marshal of the District of Columbia, and he fails to mention Douglass's denunciations of the policy when still in that position. Foner, *Frederick Douglass,* in *LW* 4.100–103, and Martin, *Mind of Frederick Douglass,* 83–85, present more balanced assessments. For Douglass's statements of his own position, see "There Was a Right Side in the Late War," 5/30/1878, *TFDP* 4.485–86; "The President's Southern Policy," *TFDP* 4.493–95; "Alonzo B. Cornell and the Republican Party," 10/30/1879, *TFDP* 4.539–41; "In Law Free; In Fact, a Slave," *TFDP* 5.371–72; *LT* 536.

101. FD to Gerrit Smith, 7/3/1874, *LW* 4.306. See also *TFDP* 4.280, 5.403; *LW* 5.418.

102. On unity or homogeneity, see "I Am a Republican," 11/4/1870, *TFDP* 4.280; also "Emancipation Proclaimed," *DM* 10/1862, *LW* 3.274; "Future of the Negro," 7/1884, *LW* 4.412; "Nation's Problem," *TFDP* 5.413, 415. Against sectionalism, see *LT* 434; "One Country, One Law, One Liberty for All Citizens," 1/1889, *TFDP* 5.399–401.

103. *Cruikshank,* 92 U.S. 542 (1875), concerned an indictment brought in the wake of the Colfax Massacre of 1873, the single bloodiest incident of racial violence in the Reconstruction period. Amid an election dispute in Colfax, Louisiana, local African Americans congregated in the Colfax courthouse, whereupon a large group of whites, including members of the Ku Klux Klan, placed them under siege and ultimately killed nearly 300 of them. Charges were brought under the federal Civil Rights Enforcement Act of 1870. In *Harris,* 106 U.S. 629 (1883), twenty whites in Tennessee were charged under the federal Force Act of 1871 with kidnapping and lynching four African Americans.

104. *LT* 539–40; "This Decision Has Humbled the Nation," 10/22/1883, *TFDP* 5.112–13.

105. *TFDP* 5.118. See also *TFDP* 5.244–45; *LW* 4.423–24; *LT* 539–40.

106. "This Decision Has Humbled the Nation," *TFDP* 5.119, 115–16.

107. Ibid., 111–12. Evidently, Douglass read the full text of Justice Harlan's dissent shortly after delivering this speech. In a fragment of a letter to Justice Harlan, dated 11/22/1883, he praised the dissent as follows: "I have read every word of that luminous paper and . . . to my mind, yours is the grandest word that has [illegible] the Bench of the Supreme Court since the dissenting opinion of Justice Curtis in the Dred Scott case"; see Frederick Douglass Papers at the Library of Congress (Correspondence, year 1883, image 36), accessed at http://memory.loc.gov/mss/mfd/05/05011/0036d.gif. See also "In Law Free; In Fact, a Slave," *TFDP* 5.372–73.

108. "This Decision Has Humbled the Nation," *TFDP* 5.119; "We Are Confronted by a New Administration," 4/16/1885, *TFDP* 5.189. In Harlan's words, "The substance and spirit of the recent amendments of the constitution have been sacrificed by a subtle and ingenious verbal criticism. . . . 'The letter of the law is the body; the sense and reason of the law is the soul'" (109 U.S. 3 [1883], at 26).

109. Harlan, J., dissent, 109 U.S. 3 (1883), at 52–53.

110. "This Decision Has Humbled the Nation," *TFDP* 5.121.

111. 109 U.S. 3 (1883), at 44, 46–57.

112. Even the operators of places of public amusement had to operate under state license and so had to be considered, to some degree, state agents; see ibid., at 37–43, 57–59. Support for the grounding of this argument in common law was provided by Blackstone: "If an innkeeper, or other victualler, hangs out a sign and opens his house for travellers, it is an implied engagement to entertain all persons who travel that way; and upon this universal assumpsit an action will lie against him for damages, if he without good reason refuses to admit a traveller"; see Blackstone, *Commentaries on the Laws of England* (Oxford: Clarendon Press, 1765–1769), bk. 3, chap. 9, p. 164, accessed at http://www.yale.edu/lawweb/avalon/blackstone/blacksto.htm. This passage in Blackstone came to my attention via John C. Eastman and Harry V. Jaffa, "Review of Hadley Arkes, *Understanding Justice Sutherland as He Understood Himself,*" *University of Chicago Law Review* 63 (Summer 1996): 1357–64.

113. "Our Recent Western Tour," 4/1859, *LW* 2.450; see also *LW* 2.126, 4.301.

114. See Michael P. Zuckert, "Congressional Power under the Fourteenth Amendment—The Original Understanding of Section Five," *Constitutional Commentary* 3, no. 1 (Winter 1986): 123–56; Zuckert, "Completing the Constitution: The Fourteenth Amendment and Constitutional Rights," *Publius: The Journal of Federalism* 22 (Spring 1992): 69–91.

115. Contrast Moses, who emphasizes Hamilton's influence on Douglass rival Alexander Crummell and Crummell's successor W. E. B. Du Bois, presenting their Hamiltonianism in sharp opposition to Douglass's "Jeffersonian individualism"; Moses, *Creative Conflict,* 7, 9,

116–18, 199–201, 205. Douglass was certainly a Jeffersonian individualist and democrat in important respects, but he was not a laissez-faire liberal. Defending the Republicans as the "national party," he went so far as to remark that "it was from the National Government that the colored men had received all they have"; see "Republican Party Must Be Maintained in Power," 4/13/1872, *TFDP* 4.299.

116. In this respect, Douglass's objection to the *Civil Rights Cases* would extend also to *Plessy v. Ferguson,* the still more infamous, "equal-but-separate" ruling that provoked Justice Harlan's most famous utterance in dissent: "Our Constitution is color-blind, and neither knows nor tolerates classes among citizens"; 163 U.S. 537 (1896), at 559.

117. "In Law Free; In Fact, a Slave," *TFDP* 5.369.

118. Foner, *Frederick Douglass,* in *LW* 4.149.

119. "Celebrating the Past, Anticipating the Future," 4/14/1875, *TFDP* 4.413. See also "Looking the Republican Party Squarely in the Face," 6/14/1876, *TFDP* 4.441–42; *LT* 377–78.

120. "In Law, Free; In Fact, a Slave," *TFDP* 5.369.

121. "Our Martyred President," 4/15/1865, *TFDP* 4.77; also *TFDP* 4.297, *TFDP* 5.343, 543.

122. "Blessings of Liberty and Education," 9/3/1894, *TFDP* 5.624. Cf. "Salutatory" (to readers of the *New National Era*), 9/8/1870, *LW* 4.225: "The white people of this country can never do too much for us"; also *TFDP* 5.557.

123. "Let the Negro Alone," *TFDP* 4.202; "We Are Not Yet Quite Free," *TFDP* 4.235–36; "Address to the People of the United States," 9/24/1883, *LW* 4.386; "In Law Free; In Fact, a Slave," *TFDP* 5.360–69.

124. "Let the Negro Alone," *TFDP* 4.202; Foner, *Frederick Douglass, LW* 4.31–32; Blight, *Frederick Douglass's Civil War,* 198–203.

125. "Address to the People of the United States," *LW* 4.387; "To the Editor of the *National Republican," LW* 4.459. Foner notes that the Blair bill (named for its sponsor, New Hampshire senator Henry Blair) "provided for federal aid and supervision of education to do away with illiteracy in the South"; *LW* 4.555n48. Targeting illiteracy among all children, especially in the South, it also would have served a political purpose of facilitating African Americans' voting by enabling them to pass literacy tests imposed by southern state governments. Beyond education and land reform, Douglass also, after rethinking his objections to the exodus, advocated federal assistance for blacks' voluntary relocation out of the South. See "Strong to Suffer, and Yet Strong to Strive," 4/16/1886, *TFDP* 5.233 (*LW* 4.438).

126. "In Law Free; In Fact, a Slave," *TFDP* 5.369.

127. "To the Editor of the *National Republican,*" 1890, *LW* 4.458–59; also *LW* 4.225, 438; *FDP* 5.543, 557, 624. Earlier, he implied that public education promoted a fourth object of the Preamble, the formation of a more perfect union; see "Schools Are a Common Platform of Nationality," 5/9/1872, *TFDP* 4.302.

128. For Stevens's proposed bill, see *Congressional Globe,* March 19, 1867, 203, reprinted in Walter L. Fleming, ed., *A Documentary History of Reconstruction* (New York: Peter Smith, 1950), 1:151–53. On Radical Republicans and confiscation, see also E. Foner, *Reconstruction,* 235–37, 308–11. Douglass's untitled and undated land reform manuscript is dated 1869 by Blight, *Frederick Douglass's Civil War,* 202; Philip S. Foner named it "Plan to Buy Land to Be Sold to Freedmen," *LW* 4.527n44. The manuscript itself is available in the Frederick Douglass Papers at the Library of Congress (Speech, Article, and Book File; Miscellany, Folder 7 of 20); I thank librarian Jeffrey M. Flannery for his diligent assistance in locating this manuscript at the library's Douglass Papers website, accessed 4/20/2007 at http://memory.loc.gov/ammem/doughtml/doughome.html.

129. See "West Indies Emancipation," 8/1/1880, *LT* 502–3, in which Douglass commented that had the counsels of "Thaddeus Stevens, Charles Sumner, and leading stalwart Republicans" prevailed, "the terrible evils from which we now suffer would have been averted" and "the Negro today" would be "tilling his soil in comparative independence."

130. Martin, *Mind of Frederick Douglass*, 71–72; Blight, *Frederick Douglass's Civil War*, 201–2. On the rights of just conquerors to confiscate property, see Locke, *Second Treatise*, secs. 180–84.

131. "What Shall Be Done with the Slaves If Emancipated?" *LW* 3.190.

132. *LT* 377.

133. Jefferson, *Notes on the State of Virginia* [1782], Query XIX, in Adrienne Koch and William Peden, eds., *The Life and Selected Writings of Thomas Jefferson* (New York: Random House, 1944), 280.

134. "The Color Question," 7/5/1875, *TFDP* 4.420–21; Litwack, *Been in the Storm So Long*, 493–501.

135. "Self-Made Men," *TFDP* 5.549–50 (emphasis added).

136. Ibid., 549. See also "Address to the Colored People of the United States," 9/29/1848, *LW* 1.334.

137. "The United States Cannot Remain Half-Slave and Half-Free," 4/1883, *LW* 4.356, 355; "Lessons of the Hour," 1/9/1894, *TFDP* 5.575–607. As C. Vann Woodward pointed out, however, southern blacks voted in large numbers even into the 1890s. Their mass disfranchisement took place around 1900; see Woodward, *The Strange Career of Jim Crow*, 3rd ed. (New York: Oxford University Press, 1974), 105–6.

138. "Freedom Has Brought Duties," 1/1/1883, *TFDP* 5.58; "Blessings of Liberty and Education," *TFDP* 5.627.

139. "United States Cannot Remain Half-Slave and Half-Free," *LW* 4.369–70.

140. "Blessings of Liberty and Education," *TFDP* 5.628–29; "Freedom Has Brought Duties," *TFDP* 5.58–59; "United States Cannot Remain Half-Slave and Half-Free," *LW* 4.358–60, 370.

141. "Did John Brown Fail?" 5/30/1881, *TFDP* 5.11.

142. "We Are Not Yet Quite Free," *TFDP* 4.221; "Our Work Is Not Done," 12/3–4/1863, *LW* 3.379; *LT* 503.

143. "Great Bodies Move Slowly," 10/25/1880, *TFDP* 4.584.

Chapter 5. The Waves and the Sea: Race, America, and Humanity

1. "Why Is the Negro Lynched?" 1/1894, *LW* 4.512–15.

2. W. E. B. Du Bois, *The Souls of Black Folk*, edited by Candace Ward (New York: Dover Publications, 1994), chap. 1, pp. 2–3.

3. For a history of this movement, see Floyd J. Miller, *The Search for a Black Nationality: Black Emigration and Colonization, 1787–1863* (Urbana: University of Illinois Press, 1975).

4. Garnet, "Henry Highland Garnet's Speech at an Enthusiastic Meeting of the Colored Citizens of Boston," 8/29/1859, in Sterling Stuckey, ed., *The Ideological Origins of Black Nationalism* (Boston: Beacon Press, 1972), 181 (emphasis original). See also Garnet, "H. H. Garnet's Reply to S. R. Ward," *North Star*, 3/2/1849.

5. Martin R. Delany, *The Condition, Elevation, Emigration, and Destiny of the Colored People of the United States* (1852; repr., New York: Arno Press, 1968), 31, 35.

6. "Persecution on Account of Faith, Persecution on Account of Color," *TFDP* 2.300; "The Letter of J. M. Whitfield," 12/2/1853, *LW* 5.300. For Douglass's views on the ACS in particular, see also *LW* 1.350–52, 1.394, 4.301–2, 5.168, 5.201, 5.280, 5.446; *TFDP* 2.149–53, 2.318.

7. See Delany, *Condition,* chaps. 1, 2, 16–17, 24; Bernard R. Boxill, "Douglass against the Emigrationists," in Bill E. Lawson and Frank M. Kirkland, eds., *Frederick Douglass: A Critical Reader* (Malden, MA: Blackwell Publishers, 1999), 21–49.

8. Delany, *Condition,* 215; Alexander Crummell, "The Relations and Duties of Free Colored Men in American to Africa" (1860), in Howard Brotz, ed., *African-American Social and Political Thought: 1850–1920* (New Brunswick, NJ: Transaction Publishers, 1991), 179.

9. To some emigrationists, Douglass seemed guilty of opportunist hypocrisy in reproving a course of action similar to the one he himself had taken as a fugitive slave. "I think you would hardly like to be judged by your own principles," objected Benjamin Coates, a leader in the African Civilization movement; see Coates to FD, 6/17/1850, in *NS* 6/27/1850. See also *LW* 5.300–301; *LT* 428. In a letter printed in *NS* 3/2/49, Garnet referred to his own flight from Maryland slavery as an act of laudable emigration.

10. J. M. Whitfield to FD, 9/25/1853, *LW* 5.292 (emphasis original). Cf. Delany, *Condition,* "Appendix," 210, 214; also Edward W. Blyden, "The Call of Providence to the Descendants of Africa in America" (1862), in Howard Brotz, ed., *African-American Social and Political Thought: 1850–1920* (New Brunswick, NJ: Transaction Publishers, 1991), 116. On mass emigration, see Whitfield to FD, 9/25/1853, *LW* 5.294.

11. "The Letter of Benjamin Coates," 9/17/1858, *LW* 5.414.

12. FD to Montgomery Blair, *LW* 3.284. See also *LW* 2.446, 5.416.

13. "Our Plan for Making Kansas a Free State," 9/15/1854, *LW* 2.311.

14. "Letter of Benjamin Coates," *LW* 5.415, 414, 417 (emphasis original).

15. "African Civilization Society," *LW* 2.444.

16. "Colored Americans, Come Home!" 7/31/1851, *LW* 5.199; "The Colored People and Our Paper," 11/27/1851, *LW* 5.216–17. In issuing such appeals, Douglass also proclaimed, in tacit contrast, his own dutiful constancy in maintaining his station in the United States; see also *LW* 1.394–95, 2.443, 498; *TFDP* 4.87.

17. "African Civilization Society," 2/1859, *LW* 2.444; "Letter of J. M. Whitfield," 12/2/1853, *LW* 5.295. In his initial response, Douglass held a similar view of the black exodus from the post-Reconstruction South, which meant "an abandonment of the great and paramount principle of protection to person and property in every State of the Union.... It is a surrender, a premature, disheartening surrender"; see "The Negro Exodus from the Gulf States," 9/12/1879, *LW* 4.336.

18. "Arguments on the Call for a National Emigrationist Convention," 7/25/1853, *LW* 5.289; "Letter of Benjamin Coates," 9/17/1858, *LW* 5.417.

19. Some responded more or less in kind, although Garnet's imputations of vicious ambition in Douglass predated their disagreement on emigration. See Garnet's letters to Douglass, printed in *NS* 9/7/1849 (*LW* 5.151) and *NS* 6/22/1849.

20. *LT* 436 (emphasis added); cf. *TFDP* 4.527, *LW* 4.337.

21. See Delany, *Condition,* 202, 214; Delany, "The Political Destiny of the Colored Race on the American Continent" (1854), in Robert Levine, ed., *Martin Delany: A Documentary Reader* (Chapel Hill: University of North Carolina Press, 2003), 262.

22. "Letter of J. M. Whitfield," *LW* 5.299.

23. "Boyhood in Baltimore," 9/6/1891, *TFDP* 5.484; "African Civilization Society," *DM* 2/1859, *LW* 2.446. See also *LW* 3.289; *TFDP* 4.372, 394; *LT* 439.

24. Viewed in this light, the seminal achievement of Dickson Preston's biography, *Young Frederick Douglass,* was to show with special clarity how Douglass's formative experience was not simple homelessness but instead a peculiar interplay of home and homelessness,

advantage and deprivation. See also David W. Blight, "Up from 'Twoness': Frederick Douglass and the Meaning of W. E. B. Du Bois's Concept of Double Consciousness," *Canadian Review of American Studies* 21, no. 3 (Winter 1990): 301–19.

25. "Why Is the Negro Lynched?" *LW* 4.514.

26. Crummell, "Relations and Duties," 177.

27. See "Negro Exodus from the Gulf States," 5/1880, *LW* 4.329, and *BF* 110–11.

28. *TFDP* 5.572. On Tocqueville, see "The Case of Rev. Dr. Pennington," 6/8/1855, *LW* 5.354.

29. Crummell, "Relations and Duties," 176–77.

30. "Recollections of the Anti-slavery Conflict," 4/21/1873, *TFDP* 4.372.

31. See Leon F. Litwack, *Been in the Storm So Long: The Aftermath of Slavery* (New York: Random House, 1979), 292–335.

32. "The South Knows Us," 5/4/1879, *TFDP* 4.501. Douglass's remark was likely drawn from a similar remark by Emerson: "They who made England, Italy, or Greece venerable in the imagination did so by sticking fast where they were, like an axis of the earth"; see Emerson, "Self-Reliance," in *The Works of Ralph Waldo Emerson in One Volume* (New York: Black's Readers' Service, n.d.), 111.

33. "Why Is the Negro Lynched?" *LW* 4.514.

34. See Boxill, "Douglass against the Emigrationists," 33.

35. *BF* 152 (emphasis original).

36. "Why Is the Negro Lynched?" *LW* 4.513. See also *LW* 5.280, 2.443.

37. "Persecution on Account of Faith, Persecution on Account of Color," 1/26/1851, *TFDP* 2.294; "Slavery and the Irrepressible Conflict," 8/1/1860, *TFDP* 3.369; "This Decision Has Humbled the Nation," 10/22/1883, *TFDP* 5.118. See also *LW* 3.106.

38. Declaring his opposition to the proposed National Emigration Convention to be held in 1854, Douglass concluded, "We hope no colored man will omit . . . any opportunity which may offer to buy a piece of property, a house, a lot, a farm, or anything else in the United States, which looks to permanent residence here. On account of any prospective Canaan which may be spread out in the lofty imaginations of the projectors of this Cleveland Convention [*sic*]"; see *LW* 5.290.

39. "Letter of Benjamin Coates," *LW* 5.412.

40. "Why Is the Negro Lynched?" *LW* 4.514.

41. Thomas Jefferson, *Notes on the State of Virginia*, Query XIX, in Adrienne Koch and William Peden, eds., *The Life and Selected Writings of Thomas Jefferson* (New York: Random House, 1944), 280. For Rousseau, "all wickedness comes from weakness"; Jean-Jacques Rousseau, *Emile*, edited by Allan Bloom (New York: Basic Books, 1979), 67, and see also 84–85, 213–14.

42. "The Present and Future of the Colored Race in America," 5/1863, *LW* 3.347, 351. See also *LW* 2.308–9.

43. "This Decision Has Humbled the Nation," *TFDP* 5.117–18; "Parties Were Made for Men, Not Men for Parties," 9/25/1883, *TFDP* 5.101. On a "black Ireland," see also *TFDP* 5.68 (*LW* 4.361).

44. E.g., *LW* 2.426, 488.

45. "Prejudice against Color," 6/13/1850, *LW* 2.127. See also *BF* 237; "Seeming and Real," 10/6/1870, *LW* 4.227–28.

46. "The Color Line," 6/1881, *LW* 4.345–46; "Colored Churches—No. III," 3/10/1848, *LW* 5.73; "Prejudice against Color," 5/5/1848, *LW* 5.75–78. See the evidence of initial white-black encounters in Winthrop Jordan, *White over Black: American Attitudes toward the Negro,*

1550–1812 (1968; repr., Baltimore, MD: Penguin Books, 1969), pt. 1. On occasion, Douglass maintained the unnaturalness of color prejudice in greatly exaggerated terms, as in his assertions that such prejudice existed only in the United States. See "Black Teachers for Black Pupils," 12/4/1879, *TFDP* 4.546; also *LW* 1.387, 4.346–47, 4.379.

47. "The President and His Speeches," 9/1862, *LW* 3.268. See also "Color Line," 6/1881, *LW* 4.348.

48. The "malignant spirit of caste . . . is at the foundation, and is the cause, as well as the ef-fect of our American slave system"; see "Citizenship and the Spirit of Caste," 5/11/1858, *TFDP* 3.209.

49. "Lecture on Slavery No. 2," 12/8/1850, *LW* 2.146. Douglass suggested variously that racism among northern whites arose also as a defense against their consciences, guilt-ridden by their complicity in slavery's crimes (*LW* 2.350, 479); as an unreflective inference from their experiences with a slavery-degraded people (*TFDP* 5.196); and also in consequence of their devotion to political union with the powerful slaveholding interest (*LW* 3.139–41, *TFDP* 4.19–23, 417).

50. "Communipaw and the American A. S. Society," *LW* 5.350–51. See also *LW* 5.88; *BF* 219–20, 243–44.

51. "Our Composite Nationality," 12/7/1869, *TFDP* 4.250; "The Negro Problem," 10/21/1890, *TFDP* 5.455. See also *LW* 2.343.

52. "Our National Capital," 5/8/1877, *TFDP* 4.460; "Our Composite Nationality," *TFDP* 4.251. See also *LW* 4.351.

53. FD to Garrison, 1/1/1846, *LW* 1.129; "The Prospect in the Future," 8/1860, *LW* 2.497. See also *TFDP* 3.545, 3.600–605, 4.519; *LW* 3.379.

54. "Color Line," *LW* 4.345–52.

55. "Our Composite Nationality," *TFDP* 4.251.

56. *LT* 226; "Proscriptive Schools Abolished," 9/7/1855, *LW* 5.357; "Great Is the Miracle of Human Speech," 8/31/1891, *TFDP* 5.477.

57. "Great Britain's Example Is High, Noble, and Grand," *TFDP* 5.193; "The United States Cannot Remain Half-Slave and Half-Free," 4/1883, *LW* 4.361. Cf. "The Revolution of 1848," 8/1/1848, *LW* 1.323; also *TFDP* 2.136, 2.307, 3.382, 5.267–68.

58. "The Woman Suffrage Movement," 4/1888, *LW* 4.454.

59. *TFDP* 2.387, 3.472; *LW* 4.422.

60. "Revolution of 1848," *LW* 1.323; "The Do-Nothing Policy," 9/12/1856, *LW* 2.404. See also *TFDP* 3.544.

61. E.g., "Great Britain's Example Is High, Noble, and Grand," *TFDP* 5.196.

62. "Our Composite Nationality," *TFDP* 4.253; Abraham Lincoln, "Gettysburg Address," in Roy P. Basler, ed., *Abraham Lincoln: His Speeches and Writings* (1946; repr., Cambridge, MA: Da Capo Press, 2001), 734.

63. Consider, in this light, Douglass's postwar reversal of his antebellum disapproval of U.S. imperialism, on the grounds that postemancipation America promised to act as a progressive, liberating influence abroad; see *TFDP* 2.333; *LT* 4.408–9, 602–3.

64. "Great Britain's Example Is High, Noble, and Grand," *TFDP* 5.192–200. On the Civil War as revolution, see *TFDP* 4.42, 260, 267, 274, 295, 361, 446. On the triumph of enlightenment, see *TFDP* 4.280, 524; *LW* 3.274, 280, 4.306.

65. "Pictures and Progress," *TFDP* 3.472; also *LW* 4.487, *TFDP* 4.380, 5.139–42.

66. "Our Composite Nationality," *TFDP* 4.251.

67. Contrast Wilson Jeremiah Moses, *Creative Conflict in African American Thought* (Cambridge: Cambridge University Press, 2004), 4.

68. *BF* 246–47. See also *LT* 427–28.

69. It has become common among scholars to see in Douglass an illustration of Du Bois's conception of the divided self. See especially Blight, "Up from 'Twoness'"; also Peter F. Walker, *Moral Choices: Memory, Desire, and Imagination in Nineteenth-Century American Abolition* (Baton Rouge: Louisiana State University Press, 1978), 236, 254, 261; Waldo E. Martin, Jr., *The Mind of Frederick Douglass* (Chapel Hill: University of North Carolina Press, 1984), ix, 106; David W. Blight, *Frederick Douglass's Civil War: Keeping Faith in Jubilee* (Baton Rouge: Louisiana State University Press, 1989), 2–3; Eric J. Sundquist, "Introduction," in Sundquist, ed., *Frederick Douglas: New Literary and Historical Essays* (Cambridge: Cambridge University Press, 1990), 1; Rafia Zafar, "Franklinian Douglass: The African-American as Representative Man," in Eric J. Sundquist, ed., *Frederick Douglass: New Literary and Historical Essays* (Cambridge: Cambridge University Press, 1990), 114; Maria Diedrich, *Love across Color Lines* (New York: Hill and Wang, 1999), 174; James McCune Smith, "Introduction," in Frederick Douglass, *My Bondage and My Freedom,* edited by William L. Andrews (Urbana: University of Illinois Press, 1987), xlvii–xlviii.

70. Du Bois, *Souls of Black Folk,* chap. 3, pp. 29–30 (emphasis original). See also Cynthia Willett, *Maternal Ethics and Other Slave Moralities* (New York: Routledge, 1995), 131–32; Robert S. Levine, *Martin Delany, Frederick Douglass, and the Politics of Representative Identity* (Chapel Hill: University of North Carolina Press, 1997), 225, comments that Du Bois's formulation "could be termed a contradiction (or oxymoron)."

71. "The Condition of the Freedmen," 12/8/1883, *LW* 4.404.

72. "The Spirit of Colonization," 9/1862, *LW* 3.264–65. See also *TFDP* 5.451–52.

73. "A Sentimental Visit to England," 9/22/1887, *TFDP* 5.267.

74. "The Future of the Colored Race," 5/1866, *LW* 4.196, 195. See also *LW* 4.370.

75. "Our Composite Nationality," 12/7/1869, *TFDP* 4.245; FD to Montgomery Blair, 9/16/1862, *LW* 3.286–87.

76. "Future of the Colored Race," *LW* 4.195; "The Future of the Negro," 7/1884, *LW* 4.412. See also *TFDP* 5.147, 240.

77. "We Need a True, Strong, and Principled Party," 3/29/1871, *TFDP* 4.283, 5.147. See Acts 17:25–26.

78. "The Nation's Problem," 4/16/1889, *TFDP* 5.411. See also *TFDP* 5.625–26.

79. "Negro Problem," 10/21/1890, *TFDP* 5.450. In an 1884 letter to his longtime friend Amy Post, Douglass complained accordingly of the controversy over his second marriage: "I have had very little sympathy with the curiosity of the world about my domestic relations. What business has the world with the color of my wife?"; see FD to Amy Post, 8/27/1884, in James O. Horton, "'What Business has the World With the Color of My Wife? A Letter From Frederick Douglass," *OAH Magazine of History* (January 2005): 53. I thank Fred Woodward for drawing my attention to this letter.

80. "Our Composite Nationality," 12/7/1869, *TFDP* 4.252–53.

81. "Future of the Colored Race," *LW* 4.195. See also *LW* 4.343.

82. "Our Composite Nationality," *TFDP* 4.253.

83. "Vote the Regular Republican Ticket," 7/25/1872, *TFDP* 4.314. See also *TFDP* 5.146–47, 240.

84. Chesnutt, "The Future American," in *Charles W. Chesnutt: Stories, Novels, and Essays,* edited by Werner Sollors (New York: Library of America, 2002), 849.

85. Josiah Nott and George Glidden, *Types of Mankind* (Philadelphia: J. B. Lippincott, 1854), 50, 271.

86. "Lecture on Haiti," 1/2/1893, *LW* 4.479.

87. "Nation's Problem," *TFDP* 5.412–13.

88. *BF* 42 (emphasis original); also *LT* 36.

89. *TFDP* 1.69; *LT* 277; *TFDP* 5.567–68.

90. On Egypt, see *TFDP* 2.507–20 (*LW* 2.296–304), 5.305–6, 329–30. On Haiti, see especially *LW* 4.478–86, *TFDP* 5.506–9, 510.

91. *LW* 1.399–400, 408, 5.279, 4.248–49; *TFDP* 2.368, 4.418; *BF* 154.

92. *LW* 1.333; "Address to the People of the United States," 9/24/1883, *LW* 4.375–76.

93. "A Word on Mr. Downing's Letter," 6/8/1871, *LW* 4.248–49.

94. "Agriculture and Black Progress," *TFDP* 4.379.

95. See, e.g., "Colored Newspapers," 1/8/1848, *LW* 1.291; "Color Question," 7/5/1875, *TFDP* 4.419; "Nation's Problem," *TFDP* 5.416; "The Negro Press," 1891 interview, *LW* 4.469.

96. See *TFDP* 2.449; *LW* 1.371–74, 4.172–73, 289–90, 5.275–76, 347–48; *LT* 268–69. For a more detailed chronicling of Douglass's positions on racial unity and race-specific associations, see especially Martin, *Mind of Frederick Douglass*, 92–106.

97. Moses, *Creative Conflict*, 5, 77–79. Cf. Leslie Friedman Goldstein, "Racial Loyalty in America: The Example of Frederick Douglass," *Western Political Quarterly* 28, no. 3 (September 1975): 463–76; Martin, *Mind of Frederick Douglass*, 92.

98. "Nation's Problem," *TFDP* 5.413.

99. "The Douglass Institute," 10/1865, *LW* 4.179. See also *LW* 4.304, 377, 5.321–22, 347; *TFDP* 2.449, 4.91, 334, 5.415.

100. *LT* 527; also *TFDP* 5.413.

101. See *LW* 2.289, 448, 3.347, 4.491, 5.422; *TFDP* 4.318, 5.399, 437–38.

102. "The Meaning of July Fourth for the Negro," *LW* 2.189–90 (emphasis added). Likewise in 1848, he called out several black churches in Philadelphia for closing their doors to abolitionist meetings; see "Visit to Philadelphia," *NS* 10/13/1848, *LW* 5.98. He denounced "the Black Swan," singer Elizabeth Greenfield, for performing a concert in New York's Metropolitan Hall to which African Americans were refused admission; see *FDP* 4/8/1853, *LW* 2.239–40. He also privately denounced the great French novelist Alexandre Dumas on the report of a prominent French abolitionist that Dumas "never said one word for his race"; see "To Friends Hayden and Watson," 11/19/1886, *LW* 4.446. Evidently, the report was false; see Moses, *Creative Conflict*, 56–57.

103. On Brown, see *LW* 2.458; *TFDP* 5.11, 22; on Douglass, see *LW* 4.452, but contrast *LT* 469–72.

104. Goldstein, "Racial Loyalty," 470; Martin, *Mind of Frederick Douglass*, 92.

105. "Do-Nothing Policy," 9/12/1856, *LW* 2.403. See also *LW* 2.360, 370; *TFDP* 2.427–28, 3.88.

106. Cf. Goldstein, "Racial Loyalty," 466.

107. See "Do-Nothing Policy," *LW* 2.403: "Who of all the people in this country have the deepest stake in the contest for supremacy between slavery and freedom? . . . Who ought then to be the most active, the most vigilant and self sacrificing? The colored people." See also "A Nation in the Midst of a Nation," 5/11/1853, *TFDP* 2.427.

108. "The Blessings of Liberty and Education," 9/3/1894, *TFDP* 5.625.

109. See Aristotle, *The Politics*, edited by Carnes Lord (Chicago: University of Chicago Press, 1984), 1282b14–1284b34; also 1280a24–31, 1280b40–1281a10.

110. John Locke, *Second Treatise of Government* (originally published in 1690), in *Locke: Two Treatises of Government*, edited by Peter Laslett (Cambridge: Cambridge University Press, 1988), especially secs. 37, 40–48, 158.

111. See "Work and Self-Elevation," 4/14/1854, *TFDP* 2.478. See also *TFDP* 3.93, 4.542. Cf. Locke, *Second Treatise of Government*, secs. 27, 37–48.

112. On the naturalness of patriotism, see *TFDP* 2.270, *BF* 224–25, *TFDP* 4.449–50; on patriotism and sentimental association, see *TFDP* 4.39–44, 478–79.

113. Cf. Aristotle, *Politics*, 1279a37–1279b4, 1283a15–22.

114. "Why Should a Colored Man Enlist?" 4/1863, *LW* 3.343; "Color Question," 7/5/1875, *TFDP* 4.415.

115. See *TFDP* 3.311; *LW* 3.197, 5.456.

116. "Work and Self-Elevation," *TFDP* 2.478. The argument applied throughout America, in Douglass's understanding, but with particular force in the South; see "The Future of the Negro People of the Slave States," 3/1862, *LW* 3.223.

117. See "Nation's Problem," *TFDP* 5.413.

118. "Self-Made Men," *TFDP* 5.568.

119. "Make Your Sons Mechanics and Farmers," 4/1/1853, *LW* 5.271–72; "Speech at Chatham, Canada," 8/18/1854, *LW* 5.338; "Blessings of Liberty and Education," *TFDP* 5.620–21; FD to Mrs. Tappan, 3/21/1856, *LW* 2.383.

120. "The Plan for the Industrial School," 3/24/1854, *LW* 5.321; "Blessings of Liberty and Education," *TFDP* 5.620.

121. See, in addition to texts previously cited, *LW* 2.223–25, 229–37, 272–75.

122. "The Colored People of Cincinnati," 4/28/1854, *LW* 5.323.

123. "Nation's Problem," *TFDP* 5.413. See also *LT* 288; *TFDP* 4.372; *LW* 5.338.

124. A central expression of bigotry against blacks, therefore, was the tendency to accept only their vices as representative while explaining away the virtues of eminent individuals as merely individual or anomalous. See "Douglass Institute," 10/1865, *LW* 4.179.

125. "Color Question," 7/5/1875, *TFDP* 4.418–19.

126. See "Self-Made Men," *TFDP* 5.566–68.

127. Shortly after the war, Douglass assailed "certain ethnological statesmen who are predicting [the Negro's] disappearance from the republic; that he will die out like the Indian"; see "We Are Here and Want the Ballot Box," 9/4/1866, *TFDP* 4.129. See also George Fredrickson, *The Black Image in the White Mind: The Debate on African-American Character and Destiny, 1817–1914* (New York: Harper & Row, 1971), 228–55; William Stanton, *The Leopard's Spots: Scientific Attitudes toward Race in America, 1815–1859* (Chicago: University of Chicago Press, 1960), 195.

128. "Let the Negro Alone," 5/11/1869, *TFDP* 4.207–8. See also Delany, *Condition*, 62–64; Alexander Crummell, "The Destined Superiority of the Negro," in *Alexander Crummell, Destiny and Race: Selected Writings, 1840–1898*, edited by Wilson Jeremiah Moses (Amherst: University of Massachusetts Press, 1992), 200–202.

129. "Let the Negro Alone," 5/11/1869, *TFDP* 4.205–6.

130. FD to Montgomery Blair, 9/16/1862, *LW* 3.286. See also *LW* 3.224, 2.291; *TFDP* 5.279.

131. "Horace Greeley and Colonization," 2/26/1852, *LW* 2.173. Douglass's concessions concerning the inadvertent benefits of enslavement in America may have been polemically driven by his anticolonization position; see his public letter to Henry Clay, *NS* 12/3/1847, *LW* 1.288–89. They may also be traceable to the more strongly pro-American position that he held after his break from the Garrisonian camp in 1851.

132. For Douglass's contemporaries' charges that he was deficient in race pride, see Martin, *Mind of Frederick Douglass*, 95–96. For like charges by later commentators, see Walker, *Moral Choices*, 244–47; Diedrich, *Love across Color Lines*, 174; Martin, *Mind of Frederick Douglass*, 115, 199, 208–217; and (more moderately) Moses, *Creative Conflict*, 34–36, 58–59.

133. Martin, *Mind of Frederick Douglass*, 224.

134. Cf. John P. Pittman, "Douglass's Assimilationism and Antislavery," in Bill E. Lawson and Frank M. Kirkland, eds., *Frederick Douglass: A Critical Reader* (Malden, MA: Blackwell Publishers, 1999), 74–79.

135. See especially "What the Black Man Wants," *TFDP* 4.65; also *TFDP* 4.50, 392; *LT* 288–89.

136. "A Year at the *Era*," 8/24/1871, *LW* 4.275; FD to Rev. C. S. Smith, M.D., 10/13/1882, *LW* 4.354. See also *TFDP* 2.535, 3.88, 4.50, 392; *LW* 4.304.

137. "Our Composite Nationality," 12/7/1869, *TFDP* 4.254–55.

138. Ibid., 256: "To no class of our population are we more indebted for valuable qualities of head, heart, and hand, than to the German." By the time of this speech, Douglass had shared a long, close relationship with a radical German émigré journalist, Ottilie Assing, and had even taken it upon himself to learn the German language. See Diedrich, *Love across Color Lines*.

139. W. E. B. Du Bois, "The Conservation of Races," in *W. E. B. Du Bois: A Reader,* edited by David Levering Lewis (New York: Henry Holt, 1995), 21.

140. See also "We Need a True, Strong, and Principled Party," 3/29/1871, *TFDP* 4.283.

141. "Our Composite Nationality," *TFDP* 4.253, 259 (emphasis added).

142. Ibid., 256, 254, 258; Genesis 2:18. Douglass's implication was that America should open itself to Chinese immigration because the duration and accomplishments of Chinese culture made a prima facie case for the worth of its potential contribution to this country. On this point, his argument resembles that of Charles Taylor, "The Politics of Recognition," in Taylor, *Multiculturalism and the Politics of Recognition,* edited by Amy Gutmann (Princeton, NJ: Princeton University Press, 1992), 70–73.

143. Du Bois, "Conservation of Races," 25.

144. "Equal School Rights," 4/20/1855, *LW* 5.347; "Nation's Problem," 4/16/1889, *TFDP* 5.415. This fear of racial insularity should also be considered in the light of Douglass's tacit rejection of minoritarian politics, discussed in the preceding chapter.

145. Douglass's understanding, in contrast to that of Du Bois, of the mode of production of the African American cultural gifts that he envisioned is powerfully represented by the lecture of Professor Woodridge in Ralph Ellison's *Invisible Man* (1947; repr., New York: Vintage International, 1995), 354: "Stephan's problem, like ours, was not actually one of creating the uncreated conscience of his race, but of creating the *uncreated features of his face.* Our task is that of making ourselves individuals. The conscience of a race is the gift of its individuals who see, evaluate, record. . . . We create the race by creating ourselves and then to our great astonishment we will have created something far more important: We will have created a culture" (emphasis original).

146. "The Return of the Democratic Party to Power," 4/16/1885, *TFDP* 5.191 (*LW* 4.425). Cf. FD to Gerrit Smith, 8/4/1851, *LW* 5.200; Aristotle, *Politics,* 1280b40–1281a8.

147. On excessive Anglo-Saxon love of power, see *TFDP* 5.360, also *LW* 5.351; on white Americans' arrogance, *LW* 4.477; on selfishness, *LW* 2.355–56, 415–16, *TFDP* 4.173.

148. "Future of the Negro People of the Slave States," 3/1862, *LW* 3.225.

149. "An Act to Establish a Uniform Rule of Naturalization," 3/26/1790, accessed 2/12/2007 at http://rs6.10c.gov/cgi-bin/ampage?collId=llsl&fileName=001/llsl001.db&recNum=226; Jefferson, *Notes on the State of Virginia,* Query XIV, in Adrienne Koch and William Peden, eds., *The Life and Selected Writings of Thomas Jefferson* (New York: Random House, 1944), 262. Cf. Charles W. Mills, "Whose Fourth of July? Frederick Douglass and 'Original Intent,'" in Bill E. Lawson and Frank M. Kirkland, eds., *Frederick Douglass: A Critical Reader* (Malden, MA: Blackwell Publishers, 1999), 115.

150. "We Need a True, Strong, and Principled Party," 3/29/1871, *TFDP* 4.282–83. Cf. *LW* 4.352.

151. The most influential example appears in *Uncle Tom's Cabin,* in which blacks, in contrast to both whites and mulattoes, are represented as naturally home-loving, affectionate, patient, timid, unenterprising people; see Harriet Beecher Stowe, *Uncle Tom's Cabin* (New York: Signet Classics, 1966), chap. 10, p. 109, also pp. 289–90. The suggestion, in part, was that blacks were natural Christians; Douglass once referred derisively to the opinion that "the negro" was "so well born that he needed not to be born again"; see "We Are Here and Want the Ballot-Box," 9/4/1866, *TFDP* 4.129. The romantic-racialist argument also ascribed to blacks qualities associated with femininity; for a recent variant, see Cynthia Willett's *Maternal Ethics* and also her *Soul of Justice: Social Bonds and Racial Hubris* (Ithaca, NY: Cornell University Press, 2001), 188–202. More generally, see the very helpful discussion in Fredrickson, *Black Image,* 97–129; also Moses, *Golden Age of Black Nationalism,* 25, 46–49. Some of Douglass's observations concerning the African or African American character were congruent with those of the romantic racialists, e.g., on the home-feeling (*LW* 4.329) and on elder respect, suggestive of a deeper ancestral piety (*BF* 48–49).

152. *LT* 54; *TFDP* 3.459. See also *LT* 580; *TFDP* 5.331.

153. In his references to slave songs' "wildness," Douglass perhaps underestimated the formative influence of African cultural traditions; his language suggests the relative naturalness of their music or of music in general, implying its lesser dependence than literary speech on the perfection of the arts of civilized society. See *N* 47; *BF* 65–66.

154. "Great Is the Miracle of Human Speech," *TFDP* 5.476–77, cf. 5.562; Aristotle, *Politics,* 1253a5–19.

155. "Year with the *Era,*" *LW* 4.276. Douglass reaffirmed by implication Thomas Jefferson's contemptuous review of the works of the famous poet Phyllis Wheatley and her older contemporary the Anglo-African Ignatius Sancho; see Jefferson, *Notes on the State of Virginia,* Query XIV, in Adrienne Koch and William Peden, eds., *The Life and Selected Writings of Thomas Jefferson* (New York: Random House, 1944), 259. He also failed to acknowledge the wealth of African American autobiography that preceded his own; see William L. Andrews, *To Tell a Free Story: The First Century of African-American Autobiography* (Urbana: University of Illinois Press, 1985), chaps. 1–3; he more directly insulted William Wells Brown, author of *Clotel* (which Douglass had noticed in a favorable 1863 review of Brown's *The Black Man, LW* 3.312–13), and Delany, whose ambitious, black nationalist novel *Blake* was published in 1859. It seems unlikely, too, that Douglass was then unaware of Harriet Jacobs's *Incidents in the Life of a Slave Girl* (1861), given Jacobs's close association with Lydia Marie Child, an old abolitionist acquaintance of Douglass's, and the notice of Jacobs's book in an 1861 edition of the *Anti-slavery Standard.* For a discussion of Douglass's displacement of Wheatley as the literary world's representative African American, see Henry Louis Gates, "From Wheatley to Douglass: The Politics of Displacement," in Eric J. Sundquist, ed., *Frederick Douglass: New Literary and Historical Essays* (Cambridge: Cambridge University Press, 1990), 47–65.

156. "Review of *The Black Man,*" 1/1863, *LW* 3.313.

157. See Du Bois, *Souls of Black Folk,* chap. 14, entitled "The Sorrow Songs." My discussion of Douglass on the slave songs is indebted to Sterling Stuckey, "'Ironic Tenacity': Frederick Douglass's Seizure of the Dialectic," in Eric J. Sundquist, ed., *Frederick Douglass: New Literary and Historical Essays* (Cambridge: Cambridge University Press, 1990), 32–36.

158. *BF* 65–66; *N* 47; "Anti-slavery Movement," *LW* 2.357. See also *LT* 54–55.

159. *BF* 75–76; *LT* 63–64.

160. *N* 47.

161. *BF* 66 (emphasis original); also *LW* 2.137.

162. Ellison, *Invisible Man,* 581.

163. Stuckey's invocation of James Baldwin is apt: as Baldwin would, Douglass found in the slave songs an expression of "ironic tenacity." See James Baldwin, *The Fire Next Time* (1962; repr., New York: Vintage International, 1993), 42.

164. "Anti-slavery Movement," 1/1855, *LW* 2.357.

165. "Color Line," 6/1881, *LW* 4.343–45. On Victor Hugo, see *TFDP* 5.298–99.

166. "Black Teachers for Black Pupils," 12/4/1879, *TFDP* 4.544. At times, Douglass verged on the racial chauvinism more characteristic of Delany and other black nationalists; see, e.g., *LW* 4.365–66, *LT* 504. Cf. Delany, "Political Destiny of the Colored Race," 262–63; also Crummell, "Destined Superiority of the Negro," 200–201, 204.

167. Crummell, "Destined Superiority of the Negro," 194–204; Moses, *Golden Age,* 24–25, 156–69.

168. "Abraham Lincoln, the Great Man of Our Century," 2/13/1893, *TFDP* 5.545.

Conclusion

1. *LT* 462.

2. Booker T. Washington, *Frederick Douglass* (1907; repr., New York: Greenwood Press, 1969), 349, also 5; Washington, "Atlanta Exposition Address," in Howard Brotz, ed., *African-American Social and Political Thought: 1850–1920* (New Brunswick, NJ: Transaction Publishers, 1991), 359. See also Alexander Crummell, "The Social Principle among a People" (1875), in *Alexander Crummell, Destiny and Race: Selected Writings, 1840–1898,* edited by Wilson Jeremiah Moses (Amherst: University of Massachusetts Press, 1992), 267; Wilson Jeremiah Moses, *Creative Conflict in African American Thought* (Cambridge: Cambridge University Press, 2004), 42, 108–113.

3. Philip S. Foner, *Frederick Douglass, LW* 4.149–54; Waldo E. Martin, Jr., "Images of Frederick Douglass in the Afro-American Mind: The Recent Black Freedom Struggle," in Eric J. Sundquist, ed., *Frederick Douglass: New Literary and Historical Essays* (Cambridge: Cambridge University Press, 1990), 271–85.

4. Malcolm X, "At a Meeting in Paris," 11/23/1964, in George Breitman, ed., *By Any Means Necessary: Speeches, Interviews, and a Letter by Malcolm X* (New York: Pathfinder Press, 1970), 124; Vincent Harding, *There Is a River: The Black Struggle for Freedom in America* (New York: Harcourt Brace, 1981), 167; Martin, "Images of Frederick Douglass," 280–82.

5. Charles W. Mills, "Whose Fourth of July? Frederick Douglass and 'Original Intent,'" in Bill E. Lawson and Frank M. Kirkland, eds. *Frederick Douglass: A Critical Reader* (Malden, MA: Blackwell Publishers, 1999), 134. Further statements of these post–civil rights era criticisms of Douglass appear in Peter F. Walker, *Moral Choices: Memory, Desire, and Imagination in Nineteenth-Century American Abolition* (Baton Rouge: Louisiana State University Press, 1978), 209–61; Waldo E. Martin, Jr., *The Mind of Frederick Douglass* (Chapel Hill: University of North Carolina Press, 1984), 115, 132–34, 167–70, 199, 208–17, 221, 283–84; William S. McFeely, *Frederick Douglass* (New York: W. W. Norton, 1991), 293–303; Moses, *Creative Conflict,* 3–4, 41–45, 48–49, 108–9.

6. *TFDP* 4.187; *LW* 3.110, 332, 402.

7. *LW* 2.412; "The United States Cannot Remain Half-Slave and Half-Free," *LW* 4.359.

8. Orlando Patterson, *The Ordeal of Integration* (New York: Basic Civitas Books, 1997), 15–16.

9. David W. Blight, *Frederick Douglass's Civil War: Keeping Faith in Jubilee* (Baton Rouge: Louisiana State University Press, 1989), 203–7; McFeely, *Frederick Douglass,* 293–304.

10. Patterson, *Ordeal,* 21–27.

11. August Meier, "Toward a Reinterpretation of Booker T. Washington," *Journal of Southern History* 23 (May 1957): 220–27; Louis R. Harlan, "The Secret Life of Booker T. Washington," *Journal of Southern History* 37, no. 3 (August 1971): 393–416; Harlan, *Booker T. Washington: The Wizard of Tuskegee, 1901–1915* (New York: Oxford University Press, 1983), 244–51.

12. This response is powerfully articulated by the likes of Orlando Patterson and Juan Williams to the left of center and by Thomas Sowell, Shelby Steele, and John McWhorter to the right. See especially Patterson, *Rituals of Blood: Consequences of Slavery in Two American Centuries* (New York: Basic Civitas Books, 1998), pt. 1, and his *Ordeal;* Williams, *Enough: The Phony Leaders, Dead-End Movements, and Culture of Failure That Are Undermining Black America—and What We Can Do About It* (New York: Crown Publishers, 2006); Sowell, *Race and Culture: A World View* (New York: Basic Books, 1994), and also (most recently) his *Black Rednecks and White Liberals* (San Francisco: Encounter Books, 2005); Steele, *White Guilt: How Blacks and Whites Together Destroyed the Promise of the Civil Rights Era* (New York: HarperCollins, 2006); McWhorter, *Winning the Race* (New York: Gotham Books, 2005), as well as his *Losing the Race: Self-Sabotage in Black America* (New York: Free Press, 2000), and *Authentically Black: Essays for the Black Silent Majority* (New York: Gotham Books, 2003).

13. Abraham Lincoln, "Speech at Cooper Institute," 2/27/1860, in Roy P. Basler, ed., *Abraham Lincoln: His Speeches and Writings* (1946; repr., Cambridge, MA: Da Capo Press, 2001), 528.

14. "Northern Ballots and the Election of 1852," 10/14/1852, *TFDP* 2.397.

Index

abolition. *See* emancipation
abolitionists
  African American, 173
  factions, 84, 85–86, 120
  militant, 23
  moderate, 85–86, 101, 105
  political, 86, 88, 89, 109
  in postwar period, 124
  publications, 44
  slave resistance and, 81–82
abolitionists, Garrisonian
  American Anti-Slavery Society, 83, 86,
    110, 124, 136, 161
  disunion strategy, 75, 84–85, 86, 109
  Douglass's agreements with, 50, 68
  Douglass's disagreements with, 75, 84–
    85, 88–89, 96–97, 108–109
  Douglass's work with, 8, 21–22, 209n4
  Massachusetts Anti-Slavery Society, 8, 21,
    84, 112, 127
  Non-Resistance doctrine, 68, 75, 83–84, 85
  predictions of civil war, 105
  proslavery reading of Constitution, 84,
    86–88, 91, 94, 96, 98, 100
  racism, 161
  revolutionary zeal, 83–85
ACS. *See* African Civilization Society
Adams, John Quincy, 85, 108
adaptation, 156, 181, 182
"An Address to the Colored People of the
  United States" (Douglass), 171
Africa
  black civilizations, 52, 171
  colonization proposals, 120, 152, 153, 154
  Du Bois in, 3
  missionaries, 152
  slavery, 52
African Americans
  achievements, 171, 176–177, 180–181
  alienation, 6–7, 176, 177–178, 202

  citizenship claims, 121, 142, 177, 178
  divisions among, 171
  educational attainment, 2, 3, 149
  emigration supporters, 48, 151, 152, 153,
    158
  hopelessness, 3
  identities, 166–167, 171–172
  mainstream protest tradition, 1–2, 5, 7
  middle and upper classes, 201
  newspapers, 171–172
  occupations, 179–180
  organizations, 171
  poverty, 3, 116, 119, 143, 145, 146, 148, 201,
    202–203
  progress toward equality, 2, 198, 200
  racial partiality, 171–176
  romantic racialist views of, 188, 247n151
  seen as inferior, 24, 40, 51–52, 115, 123, 125,
    128, 179
  soldiers, 9, 64, 122, 179
  See also freedpeople; slaves
African Civilization Society (ACS), 152, 154,
  155–156
agency
  destroyed by alienation, 159
  displayed in slave songs, 191
  of self-made man, 147
agitation for justice, 19, 197, 199, 201–202
alienation
  of African Americans, 6–7, 176, 177–178,
    202
  effects on personality, 157–158
  from home, 157–159
  rejection of, 109
  of urban poor, 201, 202–203
amalgamation, 18, 136, 167. *See also*
  assimilation
American Anti-Slavery Society, 83, 86, 110,
  124, 136, 161. *See also* abolitionists,
  Garrisonian

Index

American Colonization Society, 120, 152, 153. *See also* emigration
American identity
of African Americans, 160, 166–167, 177, 178–179
composite nationality, 183–185, 186, 188
Du Bois on, 151, 166
immigration and, 169, 186
restless activity, 156
See also assimilation
American Indians, 181
American Revolution, principles of, 22, 78, 82, 111
American School of ethnology, 50–52
anger, 74–75, 159
Anthony, Aaron
character, 214n88
daughter, 37
death, 27
moral disfigurement, 60–61, 62
overseer, 39
possible paternity of Douglass, 7–8, 74, 214n88
treatment of Douglass, 36
treatment of slaves, 73–74
Aristotle, 17, 61, 176–177, 178
arts, African American contributions, 188–189
assimilation
adaptation and, 181, 182
advocacy of, 167–170, 175, 181–186
critiques of Douglass's support, 11
reciprocal, 18–19, 182–186, 197
self-assertion and, 167, 182, 183
unidirectional, 182
association, right of, 142, 169
Auld, Hugh, 8, 9, 20, 31, 32, 36, 62, 214n88
Auld, Lucretia, 37
Auld, Sophia, 8, 20, 36, 219n67
Auld, Thomas, 8, 62
Douglass's view of, 213n81
employment of Covey, 40, 65–66, 76, 223n144
"Letter to My Old Master, Thomas Auld," 30–31, 35–36
religious conversion, 41, 42
treatment of slaves, 35–36, 55, 219n67

autobiographies, 21–22, 58. See also *Life and Times; My Bondage and My Freedom; The Narrative of the Life of Frederick Douglass*

Bailey, Betsey, 35–36
Bailey, Harriet (mother), 7, 28, 31, 74, 171, 222n132
Banks, Nathaniel, 127
Banneker, Benjamin, 171, 181
Bell, Derrick, 4–5
Beloved (Morrison), 70
Bible, seen as antislavery, 49
Bill of Rights
applied only to federal government, 139, 228n46
Fifth Amendment, 95, 228n46
Birney, James, 85
Black Codes, 125–126
black nationalism, 2–3, 152, 184, 185, 193
blacks. *See* African Americans; freedpeople; slaves
Blackstone, William, 57, 89, 90, 237n112
Blackwell, Antoinette Brown, 181
Blair education bill, 144–145, 238n125
Blight, David W., 10, 49, 145
Boxill, Bernard R., 75
Britain
abolitionists, 198
Douglass's visit, 9
rule of Ireland, 159–160
See also Scotland
British West Indies. *See* West Indies, emancipation of slaves
Brown, John
arrest, 48
Douglass and, 68, 225–226n9
Harper's Ferry raid, 47, 68–69, 75, 78, 84
self-sacrifice, 173, 225–226n9
Butler, Pierce, 98, 99

Calhoun, John C., 23, 43, 135, 139
Canada, black emigration to, 47–48
caste system. *See* racial caste system
Chase, Salmon, 85
checks and balances, 132–133, 134, 135–136
Chesnutt, Charles, 170

children
of Douglass, 31
fathered by slaveholders, 30, 74, 222n132
slaves, 30–31, 73, 74
of slaves killed to avoid recapture, 70
slaves seen as, 24, 29
Chinese immigration, 162, 169, 183, 185,
246n142
Christianity
black churches, 244n102
churches supporting slavery, 41
Douglass's faith, 49, 117
justification of white supremacy, 125
missionaries, 152
self-making, 117
of slaveholders, 41–42, 159
social gospel, 193
of southern whites, 125
view of racial differences, 168
citizenship
claims of African Americans, 121, 142, 177,
178
national and state, 139, 141
naturalized, 187
protection of individual rights, 137
See also civil rights; Fourteenth
Amendment
civilization
adaptation of blacks, 181, 182
in Africa, 52, 171
conflict with barbarism, 164
distinction from barbarism, 52
progressive view of, 181
slavery as antithesis, 27–28, 33
white, 181, 183
civil religion, 194
civil rights
claims of African Americans, 178
of freed slaves, 128
jury service and trials, 128
just allocation, 176–177
Reconstruction Amendments and, 137–
142
state protection, 139–140
Supreme Court rulings, 138–142
See also Fourteenth Amendment; Thirteenth Amendment

Civil Rights Act of 1866, 126
Civil Rights Act of 1875, 131, 140–142
Civil Rights Cases, 131–132, 140–142, 158, 159,
202, 237n107
civil rights movement, 1, 4, 5, 10–11,
195–196, 198, 199
Civil War
abolition as goal, 9, 231n86
African American soldiers, 9, 64, 122, 179
aftermath, 110–112
beginning, 69
constitutional implications, 133
end, 110, 118
predictions, 105
significance, 164, 170, 184
"The Claims of the Negro Ethnologically
Considered" (Douglass), 51, 53–54
Clarkson, Thomas, 23
class bias, 6, 11
Clay, Henry, 120, 222n123, 230n80
Collins, John, 21
colonization, distinction from emigration,
152
See also American Colonization Society;
emigration
Colored Industrial School, Manassas, 115,
149, 175
Colored National Convention (1864), 135
"The Color Line" (Douglass), 162
Combe, George, The Constitution of Man,
15, 59–60, 62
composite nationality, 18, 183–185, 186, 188
Compromise of 1877, 138, 236n100
Confucianism, 185
Congress
abolition of slave trade, 95
abuses, 133, 134
debates on slavery, 23, 87
enforcement of Fourteenth Amendment,
139, 140
powers, 132, 141, 142, 144
radical Republicans, 126, 130–131, 145
Constitution
ambiguous provisions, 92, 94, 98–99, 138
antislavery reading, 69, 85–86, 88, 91, 93–
96, 97–106, 108–109, 126
checks and balances, 132–133, 134, 135–136

Constitution *(continued)*
    clauses related to slavery, 86, 100–105, 108
    as contingently antislavery, 103–104, 105, 108
    criticism of antislavery reading, 106–107
    defects, 132–133
    federal role in public education, 144–145
    fugitive slave clause, 86, 87, 98–100
    guarantees to states, 86, 87
    habeas corpus, 95, 228n46
    insurrections clause, 86, 87, 95, 98
    as "living" document, 103
    nonrepublican elements, 132
    objects cited in Preamble, 92, 94–95, 102, 109, 144–145
    omission of slavery references, 94
    original intentions reading, 87, 107, 141
    proslavery reading, 5, 84, 86–88, 91, 96, 101
    restoration of original, 133
    rules of legal interpretation, 89–93, 109, 141
    slavery as scaffolding to government, 101–104
    slave trade clause, 86, 87, 88, 94, 98, 100, 229n56
    state ratifying conventions, 87, 98, 227n34, 230n66
    supremacy clause, 96
    three-fifths clause, 86, 87, 94, 97–98, 229n55
The Constitution, a Pro-slavery Compact (Phillips), 86–88, 96
Constitutional amendments. *See* Bill of Rights; Fifteenth Amendment; Fourteenth Amendment; Thirteenth Amendment
Constitutional Convention
    debates on slavery, 5, 94, 100, 209n7, 210n19
    intentions, 87, 91, 97, 98, 99, 100–105, 141
    northern delegates, 88, 103
    See also founders
Convention of Colored Citizens of the State of New York (1855), speech to, 43, 44–45
Cover, Robert M., 106
Covey, Edward
    abuse of Douglass, 8, 42, 72

church attendance, 42
    description of, 39–40
    Douglass's fight with, 8, 55–56, 63–64, 65–67, 71, 76, 223–224n144
Critical Race Theory, 4–5
Cruikshank, U.S. v., 139, 237n103
Crummell, Alexander, 10, 152, 153, 154–155, 156
Curtis, Benjamin R., 99

Darwinism, 58, 181
Dawson, Michael, 3
death
    fear of, 65
    as preferable to slavery, 70
    suicides, 69–70
Declaration of Independence
    application to post-Civil War situation, 148
    consistency with Reconstruction Amendments, 126
    draft, 26
    function of government, 85
    individualism, 5–6
    natural laws as basis, 49, 57
    natural rights principles, 2, 4, 6
    obligations to freed slaves based on, 120
    popular consent to government, 130
    radical critiques, 5–6
    resistance to tyranny, 57, 58
Declaration of Independence, equality principle as basis for equal rights claims of African Americans, 1–2
    exclusion of blacks, 5, 42–43
    full implementation, 187–188
    importance, 49–50, 196–197
    link to Preamble of Constitution, 95
    reconciliation with proslavery views, 42–43
    rejection by slavery's defenders, 23, 43
Delany, Martin
    followers, 3
    novel, 247n155
    support of emigration, 48, 152, 153, 155
democracy
    Douglass's radical conception, 130–137

majority-rule, 130–137
See also voting rights
"The Destiny of Colored Americans"
  (Douglass), 121
Dew, Thomas Roderick, 24
Dietz, William, 171
dignity, 129, 170
discrimination, 3. *See also* racial prejudice;
  segregation
"Do nothing" doctrine, 112–113, 115–116, 126,
  147
"The Doom of Black Power" (Douglass),
  79–80
Douglass, Frederick
  attempted escapes, 8, 36, 40, 64
  children, 31
  death, 10
  education, 8, 20, 32
  escape from slavery, 8, 31, 32, 219–220n79
  experiences in slavery, 7–8, 26–27, 36–37,
    38, 55, 70, 214n88
  family, 28–29, 36
  federal government jobs, 9, 138, 168,
    236n100
  fight with Covey, 8, 55–56, 63–64, 65–67,
    71, 76, 223–224n144
  as lecturer, 8, 21–22, 209n4
  legal freedom, 9
  life story, 7–10
  literacy, 8, 20
  marriages, 8, 168, 243n79
  mother, 7, 28, 31, 74, 171, 222n132
  oratorical skills, 8
  paternity, 7–8, 28, 74, 170, 171, 214n88,
    222n132
  reputation, 8–9, 10
  scholarly criticism of, 10–11
  See also political thought of Douglass
Douglass Institute, 64, 172
Dred Scott case
  Douglass's response, 48, 49, 68, 80, 93,
    103, 158, 199
  effects, 45, 47
  Lincoln's response, 4
  Taney opinion, 5, 42–43, 93
Du Bois, W. E. B.
  on assimilation, 167, 182, 183

*Black Reconstruction in America,
  1860–1880,* 125
"The Conservation of Races," 184
critiques of founding principles, 5–6
differences from Douglass, 184, 186
on education, 14
on racial and American identities, 151, 166
radicalism, 3, 5–6
The Souls of Black Folk, 151, 184
Dumas, Alexandre, 244n102
duties
  moral, 173–174
  natural, 57–58, 174–175
  resistance as, 58–59, 62–63, 64, 82
  self-defense, 174
  self-making, 114–115

education
  achievements of African Americans, 2, 3,
    149
  compulsory, 144
  of Douglass, 8, 20, 32
  Douglass Institute, 64, 172
  for freed slaves, 144–145, 146, 238n125
  importance, 180, 201
  industrial schools, 172, 179, 180
  public, 144–145
  segregated schools, 172, 179
Egypt, ancient, 52, 171
Ellison, Ralph, *Invisible Man,* 246n145
emancipation
  anticipation of, 48
  deferred and gradual, 34, 100–105, 121,
    230n66
  effects, 110
  emigration proposals linked to, 120–121,
    158
  fears of, 111
  as goal of Civil War, 9, 231n86
  in Haiti and West Indies, 34, 63, 111
  immediate, 102–103, 105, 231n86
  possible outcomes, 119
  significance, 164
  slave rebellions prevented by, 95, 98
  timing, 103–105
  in Western world, 164
  See also freedpeople

emigration
  after passage of Fugitive Slave Law, 47–48,
    121, 152
  arguments against, 121–122, 151
  to Canada, 47–48
  Douglass's position, 48, 119–122, 151, 152–159
  Garrison's opposition, 233n40
  linkage to emancipation, 120–121, 158
  progressive or regressive, 153–154
  supporters, 48, 120–121, 151, 152, 153,
    155–156, 158, 187
enervation, 159
Enforcement Act of 1870, 139
enlightenment rationalism, 164–165
equality
  claims of African Americans, 176–177,
    179–181, 186
  fears of, 125
  for freed slaves, 119
  moral, 53
  moral pressure, 197–199
  predictions of future, 197–198
  progress made, 2, 198, 200
  See also Declaration of Independence,
    equality principle
Esther (slave), 33, 73–74
ethnology, 50–53, 167
exceptionalism, black, 126, 128

fair play
  for freed slaves, 113, 119, 126–127, 128, 137,
    143, 147
  in land acquisition, 144
  meanings, 119
  reparations and, 143
families, destroyed by slavery, 28–29, 30–31,
  212n60. See also marriages
Fanon, Frantz, 71
farmers, African American, 116
fathers
  responsibilities, 30
  slaveholders, 30, 74, 222n132
  in slavery, 30
Federalist, 132
  no. 10, 134–135
  no. 51, 132–133, 135
  no. 54, 229n55

Fifteenth Amendment, 127, 139–140
  See also voting rights
Fifth Amendment, 95, 228n46
Fisher, U.S. v., 90–91
Foner, Philip S., 106, 107, 195–196
Force Act of 1871, 139, 237n103
founders
  critiques of principles, 5–6
  goals, 82
  legacy, 82
  praise of, 78
  racial views, 5
  slaveholders, 100
  slavery opponents, 5, 22, 100, 103, 107
  slavery supporters, 100
  support for colonization proposals, 120
  support of gradual emancipation, 100–
    105, 230n66
  See also Constitutional Convention
Fourteenth Amendment
  adoption, 126
  Douglass's support, 126
  enforcement, 126, 139, 140
  importance, 127, 138
  interpretation, 126, 138–139, 142
  rights of citizenship, 138, 141
Fourth of July speech (1852), 26, 50, 78, 173
Fourth of July speech (1875), 146, 179, 181
Franklin, Benjamin, 114
Franklin, John Hope, 5
freedom. See liberty
freedpeople
  advice to, 116–117, 119
  competition for jobs, 111
  dependence, 146
  "do nothing" doctrine, 112–113, 115–116,
    126, 147
  education, 144–145, 146, 238n125
  effects of slavery, 116–119
  fair treatment, 113, 119, 126–127, 128, 143, 147
  improved conditions after Civil War, 16,
    149
  land acquisition, 144, 145–146
  occupations, 116
  political power in Reconstruction, 129
  potential reenslavement, 123–124
  poverty, 116, 119, 143, 145, 146, 148

protection of rights, 112–113, 126–127
public responsibilities toward, 112
question of what to do with, 110–111, 112, 119
religious beliefs, 117
rights violations, 125
violence against, 148
voting rights, 127–129, 136, 239n137
work ethic, 116–117
See also emigration
Freeland, William, 26, 36, 38, 64, 214n88
Free Soil party, 101
fugitive slave clause, Constitution, 86, 87, 98–100
Fugitive Slave Law (1850)
Douglass's response, 57, 65, 99, 158
effects, 45, 47–48, 121, 152
obligations of northerners, 80
passage, 24
resistance to, 69, 99
significance, 47

Garner, Margaret, 70
Garnet, Henry Highland, 68, 152, 154–156, 171
Garrison, William Lloyd, 83, 88
Liberator, 8, 23, 35, 110
opposition to colonization, 233n40
proslavery reading of Constitution, 84
relationship with Douglass, 8, 9
Garrisonian abolitionists. *See* abolitionists, Garrisonian
Garvey, Marcus, 3
Germany
nation, 184, 246n138
philosophers, 184
Giddings, Joshua, 85
Glidden, George, 50, 51–52, 170
globalization, 163–164
Goldstein, Leslie Friedman, 68
Goodell, William, 85, 89
Gore, Orson, 39
governmental functions
coercion, 85
preserving gains from Civil War, 129
protection of rights, 126–127, 128, 137, 147
public education, 144–145, 238n125
repairing past injustices, 143–146

Grant, Ulysses S., 131
Greenfield, Elizabeth, 244n102

habeas corpus, 95, 228n46
Haiti
black rule, 154, 159, 171
elites, 118
emancipation of slaves, 34, 111
revolution, 118, 171
women, 118
Hamilton, Alexander, 142, 163
Hammond, James Henry, 23, 34, 68, 211n31
happiness, 195
Harding, Vincent, 2, 11, 196
Harlan, John Marshall, 10, 141–142, 237nn107–8, 238n116
Harper, William, 23
Harris, Henry, 64, 71
Harris, U.S. v., 139
Hart, W. H. H., 10
Hayes administration, 9, 138, 236n100
Hegel, G. W. F., 184, 220n89
The Heroic Slave (Douglass), 69, 77
home
meanings, 157
patriotism and, 177
home-feeling, 155–157, 160, 165, 173
homelessness, 157–159
hopefulness
of Douglass, 7, 9, 48, 106, 200, 202
in postwar period, 116, 148–150, 160
rational, 14–16, 81, 82, 109, 149, 200–201, 203
Hopkins, Rigby, 64, 76
Horace, 72
Hughes, Henry, 24, 42
Hugo, Victor, *Les Miserables,* 192–193
humanitarianism, 172–174
human nature
affirmation, 114–115
desire and capacity for liberty, 56–57
dynamism, 14, 156
goodness, 130
malign forces, 124
negation by slavery, 28–32, 57, 114–115
human rights. *See* natural rights principles

Index

idealism, 4, 11, 184–185
identities, of slaves, 29–30, 55, 114. *See also* American identity; racial identity
immigration
  Chinese, 162, 169, 183, 185, 246n142
  naturalized citizens, 187
  opponents, 183
  policies, 169–170
  racial and ethnic diversity, 186
indentured servants, 86, 87, 98
Independence Day. *See* Fourth of July speech
individualism
  critiques of, 5–6
  in Declaration of Independence, 5–6
  of Douglass, 12, 30
  self-reliant, 147
  See also self-making
integration, racial, 12, 167. *See also* assimilation; segregation
interdependence, 147
intermarriage. *See* marriages
Ireland, 159–160
"Is Civil Government Right?" (Douglass), 85

Jackson, Francis, 71
Jay, William, 85
Jean Valjean (*Les Miserables*), 192–193
Jefferson, Thomas, 126, 159
  on dependence, 146
  drafting of Declaration of Independence, 26
  Notes on the State of Virginia, 120, 247n155
  opposition to emancipation, 111
  on rebellious slave, 57
  as slaveholder, 100
  on slavery, 69, 81, 100, 213n79, 218n51
  support for colonization proposals, 120, 187
  view of black authors, 247n155
Jeremiah, 2
Johnson, Andrew, 130–131, 132
jury service and trials, 128
justice
  agitation for, 197, 199, 201–202

arguments against colonization based on, 121–122
Darwinian understanding, 58
distributive, 121–122, 176–177
importance of Declaration of Independence, 49–50
natural, 59, 93–96

Kansas-Nebraska Act of 1854, 47, 48, 80, 153
Kendall, W. G., 33–35, 37
King, Martin Luther, Jr., 1, 2, 3, 4, 6, 193
Kolchin, Peter, 35
Ku Klux Klan, 237n103

labor
  aversion to, 117, 118, 119
  productive, 117
  property rights in products, 177
  respect for, 179
  virtue of industry, 201
land reform proposals, 144, 145–146
law. *See* natural law
legal interpretation, rules of, 89–93, 109, 141
"Letter to My Old Master, Thomas Auld" (Douglass), 30–31, 35–36
"Letter to the American Slaves" (Douglass), 73
liberalism
  disillusioned, 3–4
  of Douglass, 7, 114
  influence on black protest tradition, 2, 4
  principles, 2
  See also natural rights principles
Liberator, 8, 23, 35, 110
Liberia, 152. *See also* emigration
liberty
  choice of employment, 236n98
  human passion for, 67, 72
  presumption for in reading Constitution, 93–96, 109, 138
  right to, 63
Liberty Party, 86
life, right to, 65
Life and Times of Frederick Douglass (Douglass), 28, 31, 110, 114, 123, 146, 175, 192, 195
Lincoln, Abraham
  on Declaration of Independence, 4

on Douglass, 10
Emancipation Proclamation, 231n86
Gettysburg Address, 194
idealism, 4
moderate position on abolition, 101, 105, 107–108, 176
on political wisdom, 203
response to *Dred Scott* case, 4
second inaugural address, 124, 143, 194
slave power's reaction to election, 107–108
support for colonization proposals, 120, 161
view of slavery, 25, 44, 218n48, 230n80
literature
    African American contributions, 189, 247n155
    The Heroic Slave (Douglass), 69, 77
Litwack, Leon F., 117
Lloyd, Edward, V, 8, 29, 64, 76, 214n88
Lloyd family, 60–61, 62
Lloyd plantation, 29, 31, 36, 39, 44
Locke, John
    natural rights principles, 15, 54, 114, 177
    popular consent to government, 130
    on summum malum, 220n89
locomotion, right of, 142, 153, 157
Louisiana, Reconstruction in, 127, 237n103
Louisiana Purchase, 22, 45
lynchings, 58, 237n103

Madison, James
    on American Revolution, 111
    on Constitutional Convention, 209n7
    on constitutional interpretation, 227n34
    on factions, 134
    Federalist no. 10, 134–135, 136
    Notes of Debates in the Federal Conventions of 1787, 87, 91, 94
    on slavery, 210n19
    support for colonization proposals, 120
    at Virginia ratifying convention, 98
Malcolm X, 3, 196
Marable, Manning, 4
marriages
    choice of partner, 169
    of Douglass, 8, 168, 243n79
    interracial, 2, 168, 169–170, 243n79
    laws prohibiting interracial, 170

prohibited among slaves, 30
    Victorian mores, 30
Marshall, Thurgood, 5
Martin, Waldo E., Jr., 11, 145, 196
Massachusetts Anti-Slavery Society, 8, 21, 84, 112, 127. *See also* abolitionists, Garrisonian
master class
    formation of, 39–45, 80
    in postwar South, 138
master-slave relation, 24–25, 28. *See also* slaveholders
materialism, 163
McFeely, William S., 36, 112, 201
McLean, John, 99
middle class, 201
migration
    positive view of, 156
    right of, 153, 169
    from Southern states, 16, 112, 240n17
    See also emigration; immigration
Mills, Charles W., 5, 11, 107, 196
miscegenation, 125, 167, 168, 170
Les Miserables (Hugo), 192–193
Missouri Compromise, 48, 101, 104, 216n7
Missouri statehood, 23, 101
mixed-race population, 168, 170
modernity, 163–164
monogenesis theory, 53, 167
Montesquieu, Charles de Secondat, baron de, 17, 61
moral equality, 53
morality
    duties of African Americans, 173–174
    human capacity for choice, 55
    natural law, 15, 39, 49, 60–63
    rationality and, 54–56
    sanctions for slavery, 60–63
    of slaves, 55–56
Morrison, Toni, 7, 70
Morton, Samuel, 50
Moses, Wilson Jeremiah, 10, 11, 52, 76, 112, 172
Murray, Anna, 8, 219–220n79
music
    African American, 247n153
    power, 189
    slave songs, 189–192

Index

My Bondage and My Freedom (Douglass), 9, 16, 21–22, 25, 28, 31, 32, 36, 55–56, 57, 63, 73–74, 76, 88, 117, 171, 191

The Narrative of the Life of Frederick Douglass, 8–9, 21, 35–36, 55, 73, 74, 190
nationalism
  black, 2–3, 152, 184, 185, 193
  radical, 142
  See also American identity
National Negro Convention (1843), 68
"The Nation's Problem" (Douglass), 16
Native Americans, 181
nativism, 183
naturalized citizens, 187
natural law
  as basis of Douglass's thinking, 49, 198
  demise of slavery and, 81–82
  Douglass's understanding, 59–60
  moral, 15, 39, 49, 60–63
  relationship to positive law, 85, 90–91, 95
  right of resistance, 57
  sanctions for slavery, 60–63, 72–75
  sanctions for violations, 59–60
  self-executing, 15
  self-making as duty, 114–115
natural-law jurisprudence, 89–93, 109
natural rights principles
  in Declaration of Independence, 2, 4, 6
  defending rights of others, 174–175
  of Douglass, 7, 12–13, 15, 53–57, 63, 196–197
  faculties and powers argument, 54, 62
  Lockean, 15, 54, 114, 177
  natural duties and, 57–58, 174–175
  radical critiques of, 4, 6, 11
  right to life, 65
negro convention movement, 135, 171
Nelly (slave), 64, 76
newspapers, 171–172
Non-Resistance doctrine, 68, 75, 83–84, 85
Northern states
  allies of African Americans, 77–80, 81
  black migration to, 16, 112, 240n17
  Constitutional Convention delegates, 88, 103
  dangers of slave power, 79–80
  opposition to abolition, 79

racial prejudice, 161, 242n49
reactions to Harper's Ferry raid, 78
reducing racial prejudice, 165–166
North Star, 9, 14, 33–35, 88
Nott, Josiah, 50, 51–52, 170

Old Barney (slave), 29, 33
optimism, 11, 15, 48. *See also* hopefulness
"Our Composite Nationality" (Douglass), 169, 183–185, 186
overseers, 30, 39–40, 43, 73, 190

Paine, Thomas, 133
parents, roles, 30, 31. *See also* families
paternalism, of slaveholders, 24, 29, 31, 35, 37–38
pathos, 188
patriotism
  natural, 177
  pride and, 178
  rational, 176, 177, 178
  shared pathos, 188
  as virtue, 166
Patterson, Orlando, 200, 201
Phillips, Wendell, *The Constitution, a Proslavery Compact*, 86–88, 96
Philosophers, German, 184
"Pictures and Progress" (Douglass), 188
Pinckney, Charles, 98, 99
Pinckney, Charles Cotesworth, 98, 99
Pitts, Helen, marriage to Douglass, 168, 243n79
Plessy v. Ferguson, 238n116
Plummer (overseer), 39, 73
political abolitionists, 86, 88, 89, 109. *See also* abolitionists
political rights. *See* voting rights
political thought of Douglass
  agitation for justice, 197, 199, 201–202
  continuing relevance, 195–203
  core principles, 12–13, 14
  "do nothing" doctrine, 112–113, 115–116, 126, 147
  equality principle of Declaration of Independence, 49–50, 196–197
  misjudgments, 11–12
  moderation, 12

natural rights principles, 7, 12–13, 15, 53–57, 63, 196–197
  radical critiques of, 196
  readings of Constitution, 88–89
  realism, 12
  See also specific topics
politicians, African American, 171
polygenesis theory, 50–52
popular consent to government, 130–137, 177
positive law, relationship to natural law, 85, 90–91, 95
poverty
  African Americans in, 3, 116, 119, 143, 145, 146, 148, 201
  alienation and, 201, 202–203
powers, 54, 62
prejudice. *See* racial prejudice
presidents
  critique of constitutional powers, 131
  powers, 131
Preston, Dickson, 36, 76, 240n24
pride. *See* racial pride
progressive modernity, 163–164
property rights
  of African Americans, 143, 145
  Douglass's support, 12
  of laborers, 177
  personal rights as, 114, 177
  radical critiques of, 6
  See also self-ownership

Quarles, Benjamin, 131

race pride, 171–172, 175, 176, 182
racial caste system, 119–120, 122–126, 139
racial identity, 171–172
racial partiality, 171–176, 185
racial prejudice
  African Americans seen as inferior, 24, 40, 51–52, 115, 123, 125, 128, 179
  development, 40
  Douglass's experiences, 123, 165
  duties to fight, 244n102
  hopes for future reduction, 160, 162–166, 188, 197
  influence of authority figures in reducing, 165–166

link to slavery, 160–162
  in northern states, 161, 242n49
  as obstacle, 160
  persistence, 3, 120, 124–126, 149, 161, 162
  in Reconstruction South, 4, 124–126, 148, 149
  reduction of public, 2, 200
  sources, 160–162, 165, 242n49
  toward Chinese immigrants, 162
  universality, 161–162
racial pride, 169, 172, 184, 185–186, 192
racial supremacy. *See* white supremacy
racial theories
  hierarchies, 125
  monogenesis, 52–53, 167
  polygenesis, 50–52
radical critiques, 2–3, 4–6, 11, 196, 198
Radical Republicans, 125, 126, 130–131, 145
rationality
  Enlightenment thought, 164–165
  faith and, 49
  human faculty, 54–56, 61
  of slaveholders, 61
  as source of moral responsibility, 54–56
rebellions. *See* slave rebellions
Reconstruction
  apprentice system proposal, 127
  Douglass's vision, 112, 128
  end of, 138, 199
  land acquisition, 144
  political conflicts, 130–131, 136
  purpose, 141
  racial prejudice in period, 4, 124–126, 148, 149
  Union forces in South, 138, 236n94
  violence, 139, 148, 237n103
  See also freedpeople
"Reconstruction" (Douglass), 128–129
Reconstruction Amendments, 126, 137–142, 198. *See also* Fifteenth Amendment; Fourteenth Amendment; Thirteenth Amendment
Reese, U.S. v. , 139–140
religion. *See* Christianity
reparations for slavery, 143–146
Republican form of government, 128, 130, 134–135

Index

Republican Party
  Compromise of 1877, 138
  Douglass's support, 9, 101
  moderate position on abolition, 101, 105, 107
  presidential election (1860), 96
  radical Republicans, 125, 126, 130–131, 145
resistance
  collective, 32
  by Douglass, 8, 63–64, 76, 223–224n144
  duty of, 58–59, 62–63, 64, 82
  effective, 67–68, 71, 76
  expressed in Declaration of Independence, 57, 58
  pacifist, 68
  right of, 57–59
  of slaves, 56, 57, 64, 68, 76–77, 81–82
  slave songs as, 191
  suicide as, 70
  violent, 68–71
  virtuous, 63–68, 70
  See also slave rebellions
Richmond Examiner, 51
rights
  of freedpeople, 112–113, 126–127
  governmental protection of, 126–127, 128, 137, 147
  of locomotion, 142, 153, 157
  of slaves, 24, 42, 55–56
  See also civil rights; natural rights principles; property rights; voting rights
Roberts, Edward (Ned), 74
romantic racialists, 188, 247n151
Rousseau, Jean-Jacques, 159

sacredness, human, 193–194
scaffolding metaphor, 101–104
science. See ethnology
Scotland, 71, 91, 97. See also Britain
Scott, Sir Walter, 224n153
Scott v. Sandford. See Dred Scott case
segregation
  Black Codes, 125–126
  laws prohibiting, 131, 140–142
  occupational, 179–180
  opposition to, 122–123
  persistence, 3, 131

Plessy v. Ferguson, 238n116
  in public accommodations, 125, 131, 140–142, 237n112
  racial institutions, 172, 179, 186
self-assertion, assimilation and, 167, 182, 183
self-defense, 174
self-help, 115–119
self-made men, 112, 113–119, 192–193
"Self-Made Men" (Douglass), 113–114, 119, 146–147, 156, 166
self-making, 113–115, 145, 146–147, 192
self-ownership, 54–55, 114, 127, 174, 177
self-reliance, 112, 113–119, 145, 146–147, 192
Senate. See Congress
Sevier (overseer), 39, 76
Shakespeare, William
  Douglass and, 14
  Macbeth, 72
Slaughterhouse Cases, 138–139
slaveholders
  abolition consciences, 39, 41
  arguments in defense of slavery, 23–24, 33–35, 40–41, 50–51, 211n31
  children fathered by, 30, 74, 222n132
  Christianity, 41–42, 159
  concerns for reputations, 43–44
  dread of work, 117
  humane treatment of slaves, 36, 37
  as master class, 39–45, 80
  mendacity, 40–41
  moderate, 33–35
  paternalism, 24, 29, 31, 35, 37–38
  political power, 43, 44, 45, 47, 68, 97, 104–106, 135
  reactions to Lincoln's election, 107–108
  responses to slave resistance, 77
  sanctions for slavery, 60–62, 72–73
  sexual relations with female slaves, 30, 73–74
  unhappiness, 60
  See also master-slave relation
"Slaveholders Rebellion" (Douglass), 101
slave rebellions
  Brown's attempt to incite, 47
  calls for, 68
  fiction describing, 69
  motives, 222n123

of Nat Turner, 69, 75
potential success, 75–77
prevention, 56, 95, 98
responses, 77
slavery
brutality, 27, 32, 45, 72
complexity, 34, 37
defenders' arguments, 23–24, 33–35, 40–41, 50–51, 211n31
despotism, 24–25, 28, 29–30, 31, 37, 38, 45
destruction of families, 28–29, 30–31, 212n60
Douglass's analysis of, 21, 24–33
Douglass's opposition to, 20–21, 25–27
Douglass's response to defenders, 24–27, 35–38, 50–53
evil effects, 26
as evil in itself, 25–26
expansion into territories, 22–23, 44–45, 121
flaws, 80–82
master class formed by, 39–45, 80
moral effects, 32–33, 39, 219n67
nationalization, 44–45, 81, 87
natural sanctions, 60–63, 72–75
nature of, 24–27
negation of human nature, 28–32, 57, 114–115
predicted demise, 60, 61, 62, 80–82, 102–103
primary effects, 27–33
public opinion as restraint on, 43–44
reinstatement, 123–124
reparations, 143–146
as scaffolding to government, 101–104
See also master-slave relation
slaves
brutalization, 39, 72, 73–74
children, 30–31, 70, 73, 74
degraded moral character, 32–33
dehumanization, 25–26, 28, 42
desires for freedom, 56
failure to resist, 58–59, 63
holidays, 32, 33, 56
ignorance, 20–21, 31, 32, 114
isolation of individuals, 28–30, 31–32
mistrust of authority, 118

motivations, 32
names, 29–30
physical seclusion, 43–44
punishable offenses, 64
rationality destroyed, 54
resilience, 72
resistance acts, 56, 57, 64, 68, 76–77, 81–82
rights, 24, 42, 55–56
seen as children, 24, 29
social ties among, 31
suicides, 69–70
temporal identities, 29–30, 55, 114
See also freedpeople
slave songs, 189–192
slave trade
abolition, 95
constitutional clause on abolition, 86, 87, 88, 94, 98, 100, 229n56
slave traders, 40
Smith, Gerrit, 85, 88, 89, 97, 139
Smith, James McCune, 10
social beings, assault on slaves as, 28–32
Social Darwinism, 59
songs, slave, 189–192
souls, of nations, 187, 188
"Sources of Danger to the Republic" (Douglass), 130–131, 132, 134
southern states
African American voters, 128–129
Black Codes, 125–126
black emigration from, 16, 112, 240n17
control of abolitionist discussion, 44
effects of defeat, 124–125, 149
land redistribution proposals, 145–146
nonslaveholding whites, 77, 224n161
political power, 135
postwar labor relations, 125, 138, 148
racial prejudice in postwar period, 4, 124–126, 148, 149
rejoining Union, 128–129
state governments controlled by slaveholders, 43
white supremacist ideology, 124–125, 136, 149
See also Reconstruction; segregation; slaveholders
speech, importance, 189

Spooner, Lysander
  antislavery reading of Constitution, 85–86, 95, 96, 98, 102
  influence on Douglass, 97
  legal interpretation rules, 89, 90, 91
  on unjust laws, 91
state governments
  civil rights protection responsibilities, 139–140
  during Reconstruction, 129
  slaveholder control, 43
State ratifying conventions, 87, 98, 227n34, 230n66
states' rights, 128–129, 139
Stephens, Alexander, 6, 100
Stevens, Thaddeus, 145, 146
Stewart, Alvin, 85
Story, Joseph, 86, 92, 142, 228n52
Stowe, Harriet Beecher, *Uncle Tom's Cabin,* 69, 247n151
suffrage. *See* voting rights; woman suffrage
suicides, of slaves, 69–70
Sumner, Charles, 85
Supreme Court
  application of Bill of Rights, 228n46
  Civil Rights Cases, 131–132, 140–142, 158, 159, 202, 237n107
  civil rights rulings, 138–142
  interpretation of Fourteenth Amendment, 138–139
  Slaughterhouse Cases, 138–139
  U.S. v. Cruikshank, 139, 237n103
  U.S. v. Fisher, 90–91
  U.S. v. Harris, 139
  U.S. v. Reese, 139–140
  See also *Dred Scott* case

Taney, Roger, 5, 42–43, 93, 100
technological advances, 163, 180
territories, slavery in
  debates on, 22–23, 121
  goals of slave power, 44–45
  Kansas-Nebraska Act, 47, 48, 80, 153
  Missouri Compromise, 101, 104, 216n7
  See also *Dred Scott* case
theology, racialist, 193. *See also* Christianity
Thirteenth Amendment, 110, 127, 138

Thompson, George, 91
three-fifths clause, Constitution, 86, 87, 94, 97–98, 229n55
Tocqueville, Alexis de, *Democracy in America,* 156
Toussaint L'Ouverture, 171, 196
Turner, Nat, 69, 71, 75
Twain, Mark, *Life on the Mississippi,* 224n153

Uncle Tom's Cabin (Stowe), 69, 247n151
Underground Railroad, 8, 99
Union army
  African American soldiers, 9, 64, 122, 179
  forces in South, 138, 236n94
United States
  contributions of African Americans, 178–179, 180–181, 185–194, 197
  as great power, 164
  history, 198–199
  mission, 170, 185
  unity, 139
  See also American identity
U.S. v. Cruikshank, 139, 237n103
U.S. v. Fisher, 90–91
U.S. v. Harris, 139
U.S. v. Reese, 139–140

Valjean, Jean (*Les Miserables*), 192–193
violence
  against African Americans in Reconstruction South, 139, 148, 237n103
  lynchings, 58, 237n103
  treatment of slaves, 73–74
violent resistance
  advocacy of, 68–71
  innocent victims, 69–71
  limits, 71
  motives, 73
  opponents, 68, 75
Virginia ratifying convention, 98
virtues
  adaptation, 181
  cultivating, 201
  of discovery, 164–165
  of industry and thrift, 201
  patriotism, 166

racial, 188
racial pride, 184
self-reliance, 113–119, 192
virtuous resistance, 63–68, 70. *See also*
  resistance
voting rights
  for African Americans, 127–129, 136
  arguments for, 127–129
  disfranchisement of southern blacks,
    239n137
  Fifteenth Amendment, 127, 139–140
  literacy tests, 238n125
  universal suffrage, 128, 133, 134–135, 136–137
  See also woman suffrage

Walker, David, *Appeal to the Coloured Citi-*
  zens of the World, 23, 120
Walker, Peter F., 11
Ward, Samuel R., 171
war of extermination, 119, 123–124
Washington, Booker T., 123, 180, 195, 201–202
Washington, George, 78, 83, 100
wealth, accumulating, 117
Webster, Daniel, 120
Wesley, John, 25
West, Cornel, 3
"West India Emancipation" (Douglass), 58–
  59, 70, 75
West Indies, emancipation of slaves, 34, 63,
  111
"What the Black Man Wants" (Douglass),
  127
whites
  achievements, 180

allies of African Americans, 77–80
civilizations, 181, 183
competition with freed slaves for employment, 111
current racial attitudes, 2, 200
dynamism, 156
imitating, 182, 183
nonslaveholders, 77–80, 161, 224n161
racial pride, 169
reciprocal assimilation, 182–186, 197
southern, in postwar period, 124–126,
  148, 149
vices, 187, 188
See also racial prejudice; slaveholders
White supremacy
  achievement-based claims, 181
  alleged in founders' thought, 5, 6
  claims based on ethnology, 50–53
  opposition to multiracial society, 183
  in postwar South, 124–125, 136, 149
  predicted demise, 149, 199
  radical critiques, 6
  religious justification, 125
  strength, 15, 149
Wiecek, William, 106–107
woman suffrage
  arguments for, 131, 133
  Douglass's support, 9–10, 127, 128, 130,
  173
women
  Haitian, 118
  slaves, 30, 33, 73–74
work. *See* labor
Wright, Henry C., 84, 85